Autowork

Gift of the Estate of
Robert (1938-2013)
and Gay Zieger (1938-2013)
October 2013

SUNY Series in American Labor History
Robert Asher and Amy Kesselman, editors

Autowork

Edited by
Robert Asher and Ronald Edsforth
with the assistance of Stephen Merlino

State University of New York Press

Cover photo courtesy of The Archives of Labor and Urban Affairs,
Wayne State University

Published by
State University of New York Press, Albany

Grateful acknowledgment is extended to the Institute of Economics and Statistics,
University of Oxford, for permission to reprint previously published material
(Table 1 and Table 2).

For information, address State University of New York Press,
State University Plaza, Albany, N.Y., 12246

Production by Cynthia Tenace Lassonde
Marketing by Terry Abad Swierzowski

Library of Congress Catalog-in-Publication Data

Autowork / edited by Robert Asher and Ronald Edsforth.
    p. cm.—(SUNY series in American labor history)
    Includes bibliographical references and index.
    ISBN 0-7914-2409-X (HC : acid free).—ISBN 0-7914-2410-3 (pbk. :
acid free)
    1. Automobile industry workers—United States—History.
    2. Automobile industry and trade—United States—History. 3. Trade
-unions—Automobile industry workers—United States— History.
    4. International Union, United Automobile, Aerospace, and
Agricultural Implement Workers of America—History. I. Asher,
    Robert, 1994. II. Edsforth, Ronald, 1948- . III. Series.
HD8039.A82U6253   1995
331.7'6292'0973—dc20.   94-17685
                                                              CIP

Dedications

To the memory of Jim Secundy, whose courage in the fight to maintain respect for human dignity is a model for all who truly care.

R.A.

To the newest members of the UAW, may they find a way to keep their union strong in the twenty-first century.

R.E.

CONTENTS

TABLES

....

1

A HALF CENTURY OF STRUGGLE:
AUTO WORKERS FIGHTING FOR JUSTICE

....

Robert Asher and Ronald Edsforth

The Politics of Autowork

Throughout the first quarter of the twentieth century, American automobile manufacturers developed a new way to organize human labor—the machine-based mass production system. By 1925, auto work was performed by hundreds of thousands of men and women in huge factories built by the Ford Motor Company, General Motors Corporation, the Dodge Corporation, and other producers. These factories housed assembly lines, delivery chutes, and tools that were designed for specific, individualized production and assembly operations. Autowork was an efficiency-driven, continually rationalized process designed by engineers and managers who applied "scientific" methods, including time study, to develop systems that increased output per worker. In the United States, and throughout the world, American automobile factories were hailed by businessmen, politicians, and journalists as the most modern work environments; they were the harbinger of a universal prosperity based on efficient production technology and high wages.

In the 1920s, Americans learned that the economic health of their nation was tied to the health of the automobile industry. Industry publicists, popular writers, editorialists, and social scientists also taught the public to view the work on the automobile assembly lines as the best indication of the condition and mentalité of the industrial worker in the United States. Henry Ford, who had become the country's most famous citizen by offering the general public an affordable car and by paying an unprecedented five dollars a day to workers willing to work at the fast pace he demanded, spoke for the entire auto industry when he claimed,

> I have not been able to discover that repetitive labor injures a man in any
> way . . . Industry need not exact a human toll.[1]

But many other observers challenged this monolithic view. In his *USA*
trilogy John Dos Passos mocked Ford's defense of mass production work:

> At Ford's, production was improving all the time; less waste, more spotters,
> strawbosses, stool-pigeons (fifteen minutes for lunch, three minutes to go to
> the toilet, the Taylorized speedup everywhere, reachunder, adjustwasher,
> screwdown bolt, shove in cotter pin, reachunder, adjust washer, screw down
> bolt, reachunderadjusterscrewdownreachunderadjust, until every ounce of
> life was sucked off into production and at night the workmen went home
> gray hulking husks).[2]

Dos Passos' frightening view of autowork also found expression in the visual arts. Diego Rivera's murals, in the central court of the Detroit Institute of
Arts, depicted the workers in Ford's River Rouge plant as dehumanized by the
exhausting labor they were performing.

Many more Americans were familiar with Charlie Chaplin's satirization
of the effects of unceasing, repetitive assembly line work in *Modern Times*.
The factory depicted in Chaplin's film was not an auto factory; but the way in
which the factory's owner and engineers tried to plan efficiently every minute
of the production day, including lunchtime, when an experimental machine
systematically fed an assembly line worker (Chaplin of course), captured the
essence of the Fordist system's approach to workers. Ford and his engineers
did not see the worker as a human being first and a producer second; rather
they considered the worker to be one of several factors of production, all of
which had to be utilized as efficiently as possible.

The Dos Passos-Rivera-Chaplin images of men and women locked into
the rhythm of rationalized machine production established an important cultural archetype—auto workers "on the line." Archetypal assembly line workers evoked the empathy of many observers because when the worker entered
the workplace, his or her freedom was *severely* circumscribed. The dehumanized assembly line worker has been an enduring symbol. Since the Great
Depression, two generations of Americans have been exposed to literary and
visual presentations of this critical imagery of autowork: Harvey Swados' collection of stories about the reactions of auto workers to assembly line work,
On the Line (1957); E. L. Doctorow's bestselling novel, *Loon Lake* (1980); hit
movie comedies like *Blue Collar* (1978), and *Take this Job and Shove It*
(1981). The experiences of alienated blue collar workers were portrayed in the
songs of Bob Seger ("Feel Like a Number") and Bachman-Turner Overdrive
("Blue Collar"), rock performers who grew up in the midwestern industrial

heartland. As the auto industry as a whole entered into a period of decline, management policies and the quality of the work experiences of auto workers were critiqued in Michael Moore's *Roger and Me* (1989), a scathing film about General Motors' role in the deindustrialization of Flint, Michigan, and Ben Hamper's haunting *Rivethead* (1991), an autobiographical tale which describes how the monotony of disagreeable mass production jobs in a Flint truck plant dominated by insensitive, authoritarian foremen, psychologically damaged the men and women who worked "on the line."

"On the line" imagery has endured because it reveals hidden, contradictory truths about our automobile/truck-centered mass consumer society. The image of automobile assembly line work celebrated the great productivity increases that resulted from the union of human labor and machinery in the Fordist system, productivity growth that lowered the prices of gasoline-powered vehicles, and created the basis for the world's first true mass consumer society. At the same time, images of machine-like auto workers "on the line" also evoke the great physical and psychological costs of sustaining the productivity potential of Fordism, as well as our own complicity in inflicting those costs on fellow human beings when we buy the cars they make. In this way the archetypal image of auto workers presents the worker as both producer and victim, evoking a complex set of emotions—admiration, compassion, outrage, and guilt.

The authors who have contributed essays to this volume have been moved by the contradictions embodied in the "on the line" archetype. Their essays describe the emergence of the mass production system in automobile factories, the way that the auto companies have tried to manage that system, and the ways workers tried to use union organization and group job actions at the point of production to try to make autowork more secure, more remunerative, and less harmful to their physical and mental well-being. These essays focus on the experiences of the men and women who labored on production lines, making components or attaching components to the frame of the automobile. Large numbers of workers in the automobile industry did not work on production lines. However, constraints of time and space, the kinds of archival sources available, and our desire to more fully illuminate the politics of the experiences of the workers behind the "on the line" archetype have determined this volume's emphasis.[3]

As historians who have been influenced by the disciplines of sociology and anthropology, the authors have sought to go beyond the popular images of auto workers to examine the *politics* of the relations of production in the auto industry in the years since auto workers gained the right to bargain collectively with management about working conditions, personnel policies, pay, and fringe benefits. The politics of work in the auto industry were very complex. Management directly interacted with workers on the shopfloor, with local union officers at the factory, and with national union officers at the corporate headquarters of each auto company. Auto workers formed many small, informal work groups that bargained with foremen and other supervisors, and interacted with union officials on the factory floor and at meetings of the union locals to which they belonged. The United Automobile Workers of America (UAW), the union that represented most auto workers after 1937, had its own politics within each district. Its national officers were often at odds with one another and/or with the rank and file.

No simplistic interpretation can explain the intricate relationships that developed between the auto companies, auto workers, and union leaders. The auto companies have always possessed enormous economic and political power. They had their way on most issues central to the control of production technology. Auto workers shifted between militancy and a desire for uninterrupted earnings; between anger at arbitrary management decisions and the knowledge that constant job actions and strikes would lead the auto companies to try to destroy the UAW. Union leaders were caught between the strong anger of frustrated production workers and the intimidating power of the auto companies; between the leaders' desire to preserve their union's organization (retaining the social prestige they garnered as "responsible" labor leaders) and their desire to improve the working and living conditions of auto workers in particular and American wage-earners in general. The UAW's leaders made mistakes. At times they were overly cautious or over-reacted to ideological challenges. But the UAW leaders worked very hard, aggressively, and imaginatively, within the constraints of the system of collective bargaining that was mandated by Congress and dominated by corporate power, to expand the autonomy and dignity of auto workers. The UAW bargained for the highest wages, pensions, health care benefits, and income security enjoyed by any group of mass production workers in the nation. Auto workers also benefitted from the UAW's bargaining for improved working conditions that made the factory floor safer and less detrimental to the physical and mental health of workers. The strong support that virtually all auto workers have given their union, even though many questioned some union policies and condemned the performance of particular officials, indicates that auto workers have understood the value that the UAW has added to their lives.[4]

As the modern American auto industry took shape, numerous auto workers sought to advance their interests, and to enlarge their freedom of action and autonomy, by joining unions. Auto workers expected collective organization to bring them higher financial rewards for their labor, and to provide protection against the unilateral exercise of management power. Until the 1930s, these efforts, which at times involved significant labor-management conflict, were largely unsuccessful. However, by the end of the 1930s, the UAW had become the dominant union in the industry. The UAW was initially organized under the aegis of the American Federation of Labor (AFL). Most of the rank and file and grass roots leaders of the fledgling UAW wanted to organize workers of all crafts into an industrial union. But the national leaders of the AFL opposed chartering any new industrial unions (they would alter their view after 1938) and refused to allow the auto workers to form an autonomous industrial union. Rebelling against this policy, the auto workers took their union out of the AFL and then formally joined the Congress of Industrial Organizations (CIO), which itself had been created by proponents of industrial unionism who had seceded from the AFL.

By April 1941, all the major U.S. auto companies had entered into collective bargaining agreements with the UAW. Within individual locals and at the UAW's national conventions, many debates about production standard policies, strike policies, and strategies to increase and stabilize earnings were complicated by the pragmatic political maneuvering of the union's liberal, socialist, and communist factions, whose main areas of disagreement were in the realm of domestic politics (support the Democrats or a labor/progressive party), and foreign policy. A small minority of auto workers, with a syndicalist orientation, almost always criticized contracts which limited in any way the workers' right to conduct production slow-downs and to call spontaneous strikes. Between 1955 and 1965, auto workers in plants undergoing automation argued that reducing the length of the average work week was more important than bargaining to obtain higher wages and fringe benefits because it would have diminished the threat of technological unemployment. Throughout the post-War era, black auto workers often complained that the UAW, as an institution, did not do enough to combat racial discrimination within the union and in the auto plants. But auto workers were also united by their common perception that the executives of the auto companies were autocratic, overpaid bosses, by shared resentment against arbitrary and self-serving foremen and plant managers, and by their anger at the auto companies' frequent violation of collective bargaining agreements (contracts).

Organizing and Managing Mass Production Technology

The automobile industry grew out of the horse-drawn wagon and carriage industry, an industry that depended on the labor of skilled metal workers and carpenters. Before 1913, most auto workers were also skilled workers: machinists, carpenters, upholsterers, iron molders, and painters. Almost exclusively male, and organized into small production groups, these auto workers performed a variety of operations on the different parts of the automobile, building and assembling the components that went into a gasoline-powered car.

In the decade between 1913 and 1923, the industry was transformed dramatically. Technological innovations made the automobile a more reliable all-weather vehicle than the horse-drawn wagon or carriage. Farmers, doctors, executives, and many professionals provided the first significant market for the automobile industry. By 1920, mass production techniques and a technological breakthrough in the refining of Texas/Oklahoma petroleum had brought the cost of owning and running an automobile (or truck) within the income range of an increasing number of businesses, and allowed skilled workers to purchase the lower-priced models. Installment payment plans introduced by General Motors and Ford, and the rapid growth of the used car business, soon made it possible for most regularly employed wage-earners and farmers to afford some kind of automobile.

Inspired by the "scientific management" theory and methods of Frederick W. Taylor, between 1910 and 1917 Henry Ford and his team of engineers took the lead in reorganizing motor vehicle production, creating a mass production system. The Ford Motor Company simplified the labor of as many workers as possible, assigning each worker a specific, limited number of physical tasks. This simplification of the work process was facilitated by the assembly line and by the introduction of many single-purpose machine tools to produce automobile parts.

By subdividing jobs that had once involved many operations into jobs with many fewer tasks, management expected that *workers would labor at a faster pace*. Because learning a simplified job took less time than mastering a more varied and complex set of tasks, workers could be trained more rapidly. This made it easier to fire and replace workers who could not or would not labor at the increased work pace demanded by the auto companies. Since most auto workers did not need prior auto industry experience, replacement workers could easily be found. Enlarging the pool of potential workers also helped to restrain the rate of increase in industry wages.

By 1923, Ford reported that 43 percent of the jobs in its factories could be learned in one day, 36 percent could be learned within one week, 6 percent in one to two weeks, 14 percent in one month to one year, and 1 percent in up to six years.[5] Of course, all jobs, even the low-skill jobs, had a learning curve. Management expected increased worker speed of operation and fewer mistakes (damaged parts or assembly operations not completed) as a worker became more experienced.[6]

As Lindy Biggs explains in chapter 2, Ford's job simplification was accompanied by the equally important reorganization of the movement of materials and parts within the automobile factory. Delivery chutes and mechanized conveyor belts (assembly lines) were added to an increasing number of production sites. Instead of having groups of workers move from car to car or part to part, which created chaos on the factory floor, the car frames and car parts were moved from worker to worker. Ideally, workers, without moving from their work stations, would be supplied with the parts and/or components needed for the specific task they had to perform. To accomplish these goals, Ford and other producers had to build larger and larger factories, with more and more auto workers employed under the same roof. Auto industry managers also reported that the introduction of mechanized materials handling (i.e., the assembly line), which involved a well-ordered, *linear* layout, made it easier for foremen and managers to identify workers who were not working quickly and steadily. Those workers would be told that if they did not improve their performance they would be fired.

With the assembly line system in place, management now had a new means of trying to make workers intensify their labor effort: foremen could increase the speed of the motors that powered the assembly line. Time-study engineers, who noticed that a worker's job did not have enough tasks to keep him working most of the time, would often redesign the worker's job to add operations. While engineers often used time study as the basis for redesigning jobs to reduce the absolute amount of physical exertion and the duration of exertion necessary for each work task, time-study engineers often offset these savings by increasing the total number of work tasks the worker was expected to perform in each hour. Such restructuring frequently reduced the number of seconds workers had to catch their breath between job operations.

Lindy Biggs argues persuasively that the rationalized, regimented work of the Ford system was a new kind of experience for laboring men and women. Neither household activities nor previously held jobs prepared assembly line workers for their new work environment. As mass production techniques were developed in the automobile industry, worker turnover rates rose, exceeding the rates in most manufacturing industry. In 1913 and 1914, the turnover rate in the auto industry was 156 percent (annually), while a sample of eighty-four other industries had an average turnover rate of 93 percent. When the Ford engineers introduced their assembly line, turnover skyrocketed to nearly 400 percent.[7] It is very likely that the *intensity* of the labor effort demanded by the auto factories explains most of this turnover. The push for faster body movements, combined with the redesign of jobs to reduce the amount of time when a worker did not have to perform work operations, created a particular type of stressful work for assembly line workers and many categories of machine operators. The high turnover at Ford's in Detroit before World War I cannot be attributed solely to the unfamiliarity of many immigrant auto workers with industrial work rhythms. Wherever it was introduced, the Fordist regime was intrinsically alienating. The passage of time did not change Fordism's basic characteristics. In 1962, Ford brought a new factory on line in Liverpool, England, during an era when industrial work rhythms were certainly familiar to English workers. Yet the new factory had worker turnover rates that were as high as 33 percent yearly.[8]

Most jobs in the modern auto factory made workers feel "alienated."[9] Sociological theory suggests that non-line workers, whether they were skilled maintenance men, tool and die makers, machine operators, clerks, inspectors, or warehouse people, were not as likely to be as alienated as production line workers. The latter suffer a) from the monotony of their repetitive jobs, and b) from a sense of powerlessness, since until unionization managers made all the decisions about the organization of work and had unrestricted authority to fire workers on a whim, an authority that foremen often used to terrorize workers. To make matters worse, auto workers often were not allowed to go to the bathroom until lunch or until quitting time. Many humiliating "accidents" occurred. Nor were the auto workers in the early mass production factories given any relief time for relaxing and recuperating. Working without reasonable rest intervals has always created considerable psychological and physical stress for people who perform manual labor.

Despite the alienating character of line work, many workers kept showing up at the gates of the auto factories. Why? Some were desperate for a job. Others were attracted by the relatively high wages paid by the auto manufacturers. Henry Ford introduced his five-dollar-a-day-bonus plan in 1914 to reduce turnover, and to give workers a financial incentive to work fast enough to meet the production standards in his new factories. Ford's male workers received their bonus pay only when they had demonstrated, over the course of a full year, that they were willing and able to meet the intense standards of the Fordist regime. Ford believed that women workers were not heads of families and therefore did not deserve to earn a "family wage." Many workers obviously considered work in the Fordist factory preferable to more hazardous and unpleasant jobs in mines, steel mills, lumbering operations, slaughterhouses, and meat packing plants. The main compensation for unpleasant, alienating work was financial: U.S. auto workers received, and continue to receive, hourly wages close to the top of the scale for the nation's manufacturing workers. High wages led workers to expect that as long as they held onto their jobs, they could buy a home, purchase desired consumer durables, or save to start a small business that offered a way to gain more direct control over their work life.

As the auto industry expanded, it employed increasing numbers of women. By 1920, women constituted 7 percent of the labor force, a figure that was stable during the rest of the decade, but rose throughout the 1930s until it reached 10.5 percent in 1940. Women auto workers were concentrated in four types of jobs: sewing machine operation, materials trimming, small parts assembly, and inspection. Two and one-half percent of the jobs in assembly and body plants were held by women. The patriarchal values embraced by most male auto workers and management led to the exclusion of women from the highest-paying jobs in the industry. All the evidence at our disposal indicates that those women who worked on production lines were subjected to the same kinds of alienating experiences and the same types of adverse working conditions as their male counterparts.[10]

In 1912, American auto factories took an average of 4,666 worker hours to build a car. By 1923, the time required had dropped to 813 hours. This increase in productivity reflected a combination of new labor-saving technology, reorganization of the production process, and the increased ability of auto-industry managers to force workers to speed up production. As chapter 3 demonstrates, auto company managers in the United States also developed a set of regular practices (involving wage manipulation, altering assembly line speeds, and changing the mix of car types on the lines) which institutionalized the speedup during the 1920s. By 1930, as Phil A. Raymond, Treasurer of the tiny Auto Workers Union observed, in "no American industry has rationalization and scientific management proceeded so far and so fast as in the auto industry."[11] Among the manufacturing nations of the world, only in the United States was the productivity potential of mass production fully realized before World War II. Not even England, where British companies and Ford had built the world's second largest automobile industry, could match the efficiency of the American car makers. In fact, Morris Motors, England's largest independent producer, did not even introduce assembly line methods until 1934.[12]

The Depression Nightmare and the Auto Workers' Response

When the full force of the Great Depression hit the automobile industry in 1931, insecurity permeated the world of the auto worker. Auto companies discarded the informal seniority systems that they had established in the 1920s. Older workers were especially vulnerable to layoffs, while younger workers, and friends of foremen and mill managers, were given preference for most of the jobs that remained, and for the jobs that were restored when auto factories rehired in response to upswings in consumer demand. Auto workers were also hit with the worst speedup in the history of American manufacturing, described in great detail in chapter 3. Plant superintendents and foremen drove their workers at an inhumane pace that increased injuries and under-mined the mental and physical health of the men and women who were "lucky" enough to have kept their jobs. It is clear that the significant speedup of auto work that has been implemented in the last twenty years is not even remotely comparable to the grueling intensity of labor that existed in most auto plants in the 1930s.

When, in 1937, auto workers were finally able to force GM and Chrysler to bargain with unions controlled by the workers, as opposed to company-financed unions, the workers used independent union organization and direct action on the shopfloor to fight the hellish speedup. Reductions in the inten-sity of labor were achieved in many factories. Auto workers also pressed for formal, contractually mandated seniority plans similar to the ones that the National Recovery Administration had promulgated in March 1934.[13] Effective seniority plans were expected to promote three types of security. First, seniority would reduce the ability of foremen and managers to play favorites, and extort bribes when hiring, promoting, and laying off workers. Second, seniority would protect older workers against being laid off because management wanted younger workers who would work for lower wages and who could withstand a faster work pace and large amounts of overtime. Third, seniority would allow workers, especially *as they aged*, the option of using their seniority rights to switch to less strenuous jobs. (Such jobs often had lower pay.)[14]

Ten years of worker struggles were necessary before the auto industry was fully unionized in 1941. Numerous strikes, both small and large, were staged by auto workers between 1930 and 1936, but the crucial breakthrough in unionization did not come until after Franklin D. Roosevelt's re-election in November 1936. The recently created militant Congress of Industrial Organizations provided vital support to the auto workers and their struggling union, the UAW. When a few thousand activist workers seized control of two strategic General Motors plants in Flint, Michigan, at the end of 1936, their confrontational tactics succeeded because Frank Murphy, the newly elected governor of Michigan, was a New Deal liberal who backed unionization, and because John L. Lewis, the head of the CIO, who came to Detroit to lead the strike, was a charismatic leader and an intimidating negotiator. Pressured by the Roosevelt Administration, which believed that General Motors was delib-erately violating the National Labor Relations Act, GM finally accorded the UAW limited recognition on February 11, 1937. The following month the UAW obtained a contract that made it the sole bargaining agent at all GM fac-tories. Chrysler Corporation signed a contract with the UAW on April 6, 1937. Briggs, a major independent producer of car bodies, came round by the end of the year, but the adamantly anti-union Henry Ford held out until April 1941.

After the advent of collective bargaining at GM, Chrysler, and Ford many workers felt empowered and took direct action to diminish the work pace by using physical assaults, slowdowns, sit-downs, quickie strikes, and even sabotage. Some workers threatened bodily harm to foremen who enforced production standards. Fellow workers who refused to participate in production slowdowns, or in compacts by piece rate workers to avoid exceeding base rate levels by a large margin, were also harassed. These tactics reflected the historically conditioned, deep-seated fears auto workers had of being overworked or of producing themselves out of a job.

Following its limited recognition of the UAW in 1937, GM was initially reluctant to punish workers for militant shopfloor actions, fearing that retribution would bring additional worker protests. But the national economy began to slump disastrously in the fall of 1937,[15] and the UAW split, with a conservative faction led by its first president seceding and affiliating with the AFL. Capitalizing on the division, GM's management cracked down on shopfloor protest. In September 1937, GM forced the UAW to accept a contract revision that obligated the union to discipline workers engaging in job actions and wildcat strikes. Failure of the UAW to implement this clause would "be deemed a breach of the agreement and a just cause for immediate suspension or cancellation" by GM.[16] This management position was consistent with the National Labor Relations Act, which banned wildcat strikes, although the law did not attach any automatic penalties to unions or workers involved in such strikes. Since the turn of the century, employers who had been willing to bargain with unions had insisted that unions prevent wildcat strikes. Auto manufacturers, whose profits depended on the coordination of the manufacture and assembly of thousands of parts, believed that they could not produce cars efficiently if there were frequent interruptions of production.

This was true, but it was not that simple. Auto workers understood that the extreme variability of conditions of production in auto factories—changes in car design, the various car models assembled by a given group of workers, the quality of the components to be assembled, and the number of cars to be assembled in a given week—would give rise to many shopfloor disputes. Of course, auto workers had every reason to expect that anti-union bias, the quirks of human nature, and the general elitism and insensitivity of managers would lead to continued incidents in which workers believed they were unfairly disciplined. Workers wanted these disputes to be settled on the spot, through negotiation between workers, shop stewards, foremen, and managers. Production workers distrusted any system that postponed a final management decision about a complaint because the passage of time meant that workers could be working under unfair and debilitating conditions. When arbitrators found that workers had been given unfair production standards workers *never received any financial compensation for the time they had worked under those standards.*

The UAW-CIO defeated the AFL faction in a series of National Labor Relations Board elections in 1939–1940. During this period auto workers did not have union contracts, which meant they were not constrained legally from job actions and spontaneous strikes. Chrysler workers were especially militant in taking advantage of this opportunity. In September 1939, at Chrysler's Dodge Main plant, management ordered a significant increase in production standards on the new 1940 models. Chrysler fired workers, and especially shop stewards, who had refused to work at the faster pace demanded by management. In the course of the ensuing forty-five day strike, UAW Local 3, which represented the Dodge Main workers, demanded a joint union-management body that would set production standards.[17] This attempt at bargaining for co-management failed. The Dodge workers were unable to get the new production standards rolled back; however, they negotiated the return of the dismissed workers, super-seniority protection for shop stewards—which protected the most militant leaders of Local 3 from being intimidated by the threat of quick dismissal or punitive reassignment—and the authorization of foremen to adjust production standards. The last part of the settlement allowed workers to pressure foremen to compromise on increases in production standards, although the Local 3 records do not indicate how this power was actually used before the outbreak of World War II.[18]

In an October 30, 1939 interview, Walter Reuther, then head of the UAW's General Motors Department, discussed the dilemma union leaders and workers faced in devising a system of shopfloor bargaining over production standards. Reuther, who would serve as the UAW's president from 1946 to his death in 1970, acknowledged that the UAW leadership had to come up with a strategy to help workers. Otherwise, he said,

> They would turn to measures of resistance such of [sic] slowdowns and kindred weapons. This would result in the *wrecking of the union*." [Emphasis added.][19]

Reuther's last statement is crucial. He understood that in the United States organized workers lacked a strong labor or socialist political party that could secure and defend national labor legislation to protect workers' collective bargaining rights. Union political activists were but a small faction within the national Democratic Party, which itself split into conservative, moderate, and liberal factions.

In 1938, conservative Southern Democrats and Republicans in the House of Representatives began a counter-offensive against the kind of militant trade unionism and social democratic political activism practiced by the CIO. The Dies Committee, with the cooperation of the AFL's leaders, recklessly red-baited the CIO, misrepresenting the significant contributions of CIO radicals to the labor movement. Dies' hearings tarnished the public image of the entire labor movement. After trying to bring the AFL and the CIO together, President Roosevelt took a slap at organized labor, declaring "a plague" on both groups. Worried about the political and economic effects of the militancy of the CIO rank and file, Roosevelt deliberately undercut the liberalism of the National Labor Relations Board. He appointed several new members who shared his concern about reducing the support the NLRB had given to the organization of new unions and to industrial unions when they were involved in conflicts with craft unions.

In this hostile political climate, Walter Reuther and most other leaders of the UAW believed that they had to strike a delicate balance between supporting worker militancy and maintaining the integrity of the UAW as an institution. Auto management and the executive branch of the federal government pressured the UAW's leaders to restrain workers so they did not interrupt production too frequently. In the absence of actual worker control of production or a system of co-management or co-determination, which could only be achieved through national legislation, as in Germany after World War II, the leaders of the UAW believed they had to accede to the management demand that the union leadership discourage and actually discipline illegal shopfloor action.[20] To avoid losing everything the union had gained since 1936, the UAW leaders had to be politically flexible and pragmatic. However, as Robert Asher argues in chapter 5, labor historians have not appreciated the extent to which UAW leaders were willing, at strategic moments, and especially when auto management violated contractual agreements, to stand behind workers who staged illegal wildcats and job actions.

The most important limitation on the right of workers to protest immediately against management decisions with regard to pay classifications, seniority, worker behavior, production rates, and line staffing was the mandatory grievance/arbitration process. Yet even here it is important to note that the UAW secured some "slack" for production workers. In 1940, GM proposed that an arbitrator or umpire, selected by consensus by both company and union, would make binding rulings on all grievances that were not settled by negotiations between union shop stewards and management, or between higher-level union and management officials. Most grievance systems had three steps of negotiations before a grievance was submitted to the umpire. Step one involved shop level discussions between a union steward, the worker who had grieved, and a foreman or manager. Step two involved bargaining at the plant level. Step three saw the relevant UAW national department—Chrysler, Ford,

GM, or Studebaker—negotiate on the grievances that had not been resolved in steps one and two. Many auto workers were uncomfortable with this model. They feared that justice delayed—and the grievance process could take months or even years—was justice denied. (See chapters 3 and 8.) But most national leaders of the UAW understood the real constraints on union power.[21] The UAW accepted binding arbitration of most grievances at GM (1940), Chrysler (1943) and Ford (1943).

However, the UAW's leaders also knew that auto workers believed that disputes over changes in required production standards, and therefore the intensity of labor, should not be treated like all other grievances. (See chapter 3.) The 1940 GM contract stipulated that *production standard disputes would not be decided by the umpires.* The 1943 Chrysler and Ford contracts followed suit. These developments reflected a bargaining impasse: the UAW would not abandon the right to strike over production standards without achieving some restraint on managerial power; and management was loathe to give a neutral umpire *any* authority over production standards. Hence the auto companies agreed to legalize authorized production standard strikes by auto workers. If workers in a particular factory were not pleased with management's final response to a production standard grievance, they could hold a strike vote. A majority vote for a strike did not automatically begin the strike. Next, the International Executive Board would discuss the situation, and after notifying management of the strike vote, the IEB could authorize a legal strike. The 1946 Ford contract gave Ford workers a broader opening: they also could strike on health and safety issues, which were also removed from the purview of the umpire. As Robert Asher argues in chapter 5, Walter Reuther and the Ford Department favored aggressive use of this clause.

Thus, on the kinds of issues that were most likely to anger workers and incline them towards immediate direct action on the factory floor the UAW contracts gave workers latitude—with a strong degree of centralized union control—to strike on important issues during the time when a national contract was in force. Perhaps auto management understood that failure to make concessions in the area of production standard disputes and health and safety disputes would create a large number of *unanticipated* disruptions of production that would be more costly to the companies than authorized strikes, for which management could prepare. Perhaps management understood that if workers were not given some kind of safety valve in this crucial arena of conflict, there would be so much discontent that the UAW leaders would be unable to enforce effectively contractual prohibitions against wildcat strikes on issues that were supposed to be decided only by the arbitrator. Management concessions on production standard and health and safety grievances entailed accepting a lesser form of production disruption to avoid a more dangerous kind of chaos.

Securing authorization to strike after the grieving process was completed could take weeks or months. Authorized production standard strikes could be very effective, but they did not offer workers the emotional satisfaction of immediate protest against perceived injustices. The UAW never had the economic and political clout to improve upon the *quid pro quo* that was negotiated in 1940, 1946, and 1947. It would never be able to secure some form of the social democratic co-management preferred by its non-communist left wing leaders, especially Walter Reuther and Emil Mazey, and by many rank-and-file militants. But within the framework of this accommodation, which the UAW successfully defended for thirty years against subsequent management demands for roll-backs, the UAW sought to give workers maximum protection from excessive management disciplinary action against workers whose protests violated contract rules.

For example, at the February 7, 1941 UAW-GM Department conference, department head Walter Reuther argued for giving the umpire, who issued binding arbitration orders, authority to rule on the justice of the *magnitude* of the penalties that management exacted against workers who violated contract terms:

> A worker might make a mistake...but that certainly might not mean that he ought to have his head chopped off, maybe he ought to have just a kick in the pants.[22]

Such a worker "mistake" might be a deliberate protest against managerial policy or reflect the worker's inability to contain his anger at having to do an unpleasant job in an authoritarian environment.

The existence of a grievance system with a neutral umpire benefitted workers in another way. Knowing that the umpire required strict standards of proof before he would approve severe penalties, especially dismissal or long disciplinary layoffs without pay for workers who did not meet production standards, General Motors often filed lesser charges against these workers. While the standards of proof required to make the lesser charges were looser, so too were the penalties that were assigned.[23] Thus workers who protested management policy by not meeting production standards received some protection. *Even though the UAW often made only small inroads against managerial absolutism, these gains gave working people meaningful recognition of their humanity.* The grievance/arbitration process was not an authoritarian system. Its formal rules gave protesting workers some elbow room and informal processes further mitigated the impact of potentially severe discipline. Auto company labor relations managers did not always discipline workers who staged slowdowns or wildcat strikes. Management concerns about public opinion, especially if wildcatters protested serious health and safety problems, and strategic considerations, especially if national negotiations were pending, often overrode the policy of punishing those who violated the rules of the game.

World War II and the Government's Opposition to Worker Militancy

The United States directly entered World War II only eight months after the UAW's victory at Ford completed unionization of the auto industry's Big Three. During the war, many workers in the auto and electrical industries successfully challenged management over production standards, forcing lower standards or higher piece rates. Flush with enthusiasm after successful unionization drives, and expecting that tight wartime labor markets would give them an edge, workers got their way by threatening wildcat strikes, by intimidating foremen and managers, by conducting unauthorized work stoppages, and by sabotaging production equipment. Management often acceded to the workers' pressure because military contracts guaranteed a target rate of profit, with all the costs of production, including mis-management and worker job-actions, being absorbed by the federal government. Moreover, the rapid conversion to war production, and the construction of new plants, as well as the expansion of existing plants, created a chaotic situation that often overtaxed management capacities, and especially the abilities of the inexperienced managers who had to be hired in large numbers. Under these circumstances, management in many auto plants often acceded to worker challenges to particular production standards. As Kevin Boyle points out in chapter 4, auto workers used job actions, or the threat of such tactics, to obtain favorable shopfloor settlements of work pace disputes. Other issues—seniority, racial discrimination, underpayment when workers were placed in higher job classifications but not given the pay commensurate with these jobs, wages, and safety—were paramount in formal grievance bargaining.

As the war continued, many auto workers were frustrated when management increasingly stalled in processing grievances. Most American unions, including the UAW, had adopted wartime no-strike pledges. Auto workers were torn between their loyalty to the war effort and their inability to legitimately take strike action to protest the denial of hard-won, contractually guaranteed rights. Wildcat strikes were the answer, especially in 1943 as it became clear that the war was being won and that a tight labor market made disciplinary action against strikers relatively ineffective, because dismissed workers could easily find another job. In 1943, fully one-fourth of all auto industry workers staged some kind of wildcat strike or in-plant job action.[24]

But government arbitrators, appointed by the National War Labor Board (NWLB), would not tolerate departures from the grievance process. They believed production should not be interrupted by any type of worker action, and especially not before the arbitrator or umpire had ruled on a grievance. By June 1942, Congress intervened, passing the Smith-Connally Act. This law came down hard on strikes that were not announced thirty days in advance, making unions financially liable for the loss of production. And the President's authority to seize war plants that were being struck was expanded. The NWLB then offered unions a *quid pro quo*: if union leaders would stop rank and file workers from striking, their unions would be granted maintenance of membership rights that preserved the unions' status as legally certified collective bargaining agents. The large number of new wartime workers threatened the UAW's stability because most new auto workers had no knowledge of the working conditions that existed in the 1930s or of the struggles that built the UAW. UAW leaders feared that such workers would not understand the dangers of craft unionism and might be convinced to vote for an AFL union that challenged the UAW for collective bargaining rights. Hence, they genuinely appreciated the carrot offered by the NWLB.[25]

The NWLB's actions in response to a March 1943 wildcat strike, that began at the Dodge Main factory and spread to all Chrysler plants in Detroit, were especially ominous. The strike was in response to Chrysler management's overt assault on union recognition. But the National War Labor Board punished the UAW's Chrysler Department because it had not moved quickly and decisively to quash the production standard dispute at the Detroit Dodge Main plant. The NWLB withdrew UAW-Chrysler's maintenance of membership right.

As the war neared its end, rank and file militancy soared. In March 1945, Dodge Main workers, 19,000 strong, were angered when management unilaterally announced new production standards that required a 23 percent increase in labor intensity on the plant's main assembly line. The workers filed the appropriate grievances. Chrysler management violated the collective bargaining contract by not waiting until the grievance procedure had been exhausted before it sacked seven workers who had not met the new standards. Three days later, all the Dodge Main workers struck. The eleven-day strike was settled by the National War Labor Board, which did not penalize the strikers, reinstated the seven fired workers, and *upheld the new management-set pro-duction standard*, ruling that Chrysler workers had no contractual right to stage wildcat strikes.[26]

The "Golden" Years, 1945–1975: Progress and Conflict

When World War II ended, the UAW, led by Walter Reuther's General Motors Department, launched a critical 114-day strike. Reuther's strategy involved a UAW demand that GM give its workers raises without increasing prices. The UAW proposed that GM open up its account books to allow the UAW and the federal government, which still retained its wartime price control authority, to determine the validity of GM's claim that it needed price increases to compensate for wage increases. Reuther's audacious strategy was aimed at forcing GM to accept some kind of joint management structure, in which decisions about pricing and production would be made by labor, capital, and government.

Historians have only begun to recognize the long term impact of the defeat of this strategy. In chapter 6, Ronald Edsforth suggests that Reuther, who became president of the UAW in 1946, thereafter eschewed radical attempts to challenge management control over decisions about pricing and plant location. Rather, the UAW sought, and won, higher wages, greater income security (productivity increases, cost of living adjustments, supplementary unemployment benefits, and job retraining programs) and greater social security (group life, health, and dental insurance plans), a safe work environment, and management observance of the rights workers were accorded in the contracts signed by the auto companies. The UAW under Reuther also pressured the national government to adopt Keynesian policies that would increase general consumer purchasing power, thereby protecting the jobs of auto workers and advancing the welfare of all wage earners.

It is tempting to draw a parallel between the UAW's approach, which involved strategic decisions to 1) try to equalize pay and working conditions within the auto industry and 2) to protect the U.S. auto industry against foreign competition, and Samuel Gompers' business unionist dictum that labor should not kill the goose that lays the golden egg. The difference is that the UAW advocated means to protect the egg, especially the authority of government to regulate and sustain the economy, that the classic business unionist found anathema. The UAW's national leaders made strategic decisions to protect the earnings of weak companies, especially Chrysler, and to aid the entire industry. These decisions sacrificed the jobs or work standards of particular locals or sub-groups of workers within the industry, especially in the years after 1975. Minority interests were superseded by the interests of the majority. The minority were understandably irate, and charged that they had been ignored or sold out. This kind of internal division was inevitable. It made the jobs of elected local leaders and national leaders all the more difficult.

The UAW's lobbying for government policies and auto contract provisions that increased the stability and overall extent of consumer purchasing power, i.e., Keynesian policies, does not mean that the union's leaders viewed workers solely as consumers. UAW leaders understood the organic character of worker consciousness. Auto workers and other wage earners were *both producers and consumers*. No matter how much they enjoyed the security of home ownership, pensions that would enable them to have consumption security in their old age, and the purchase of consumer durables (autos, washing machines, televisions, etc.), workers were deeply concerned about being treated with dignity at the workplace, and did not want to be so enervated by an inhumane work pace, whether it was enforced in spurts or on a sustained basis, that they lacked the ability to consume and to enjoy their leisure time.

The 1946 strike wave, the most intense since 1919, produced an anti-union political backlash. In November 1946, the Democratic Party, which most unions had strongly backed, lost control of Congress. A coalition of conservative Republican and most Southern Democrats (including New Dealers like Lyndon B. Johnson, whose main financial backers were notoriously anti-union),[27] combined to pass the 1947 Taft Hartley law. Besides making expansion of union organization into the South and Southwest extremely difficult, the Taft Hartley law banned wildcat strikes, and held union treasuries liable for the economic losses that a wildcat strike inflicted upon an employer. In this new legal environment, union officials had to be wary of even appearing to sanction wildcat strike action. At Ford, the UAW traded a union promise to crack down on unauthorized strikes and work stoppages for a management pledge to refrain from suing for financial compensation when workers staged such actions.[28]

In 1948, the Democrats improved their position in Congress, but in 1950 these gains evaporated. The outbreak of the Korean War, accompanied by loose price controls, relatively strict wage controls,[29] and federal suppression of most large-scale strikes, made the UAW's leaders painfully aware of their political vulnerability. They became increasingly stymied when they lobbied for civil rights legislation, more public housing, and a Keynesian policy of government stimulus of the economy and government mandated income-maintenance programs.

Even the most dedicated national union leaders, who had come from the shopfloor and continued to empathize with the day-to-day discomfort and indignity suffered by so many production workers, were constrained by the legal/political environment of the American industrial system. Sociologist Huw Beynon's cogent analysis of the political constraints on militant socialist leaders of national unions in Britain in the early 1970s applies equally well to the situation faced by UAW leaders in the post-War years. "No matter how radical or well intentioned the men who become leaders of the trade unions are," Beynon concluded,

> their position within the union (and hence within capitalist society)[30] . . . creates severe problems for them if they try to put such intentions into practice. Without the backing of a vigorous socialist [political] movement . . . the vigorous trade unionist finds himself in an insoluble dilemma. He fights by the rules of a system that he hardly approves of, within an organization that has proved itself manifestly incapable of changing those [basic] rules.[31]

UAW national leaders, most of them social democrats, understood this dilemma. Within the constraints imposed on them by the Taft-Hartley law, and by the economic power of the auto companies, UAW leaders instituted policies that were much more confrontational than most union critics realize.[32]

In the years after World War II, the UAW tried to negotiate plant-level agreements to keep assembly line speeds constant during the course of a model run, and during the course of the working day. This policy was designed to make work on the production line more predictable for workers. As Robert Howard notes, the UAW, like other newly established CIO industrial unions, "developed a series of practices and protective measures designed to restrain arbitrary management authority by explicitly defining the rights and duties of workers at every step of the production process."[33] This policy represented a fall-back position from the demand to share management power to determine the actual rate of assembly lines, and the mix and spacing of jobs on the line, all of which determined the intensity of the worker's labor on the lines. Once *management* determined labor standards on a particular model run on an assembly line, auto workers wanted these standards to be fixed, not manipulated at the discretion of management. These goals protected workers against speedups that stole from workers the benefits—the ability to relax—that they created for themselves by *developing methods of saving time* on assembly line operations. (See discussion in chapter 5.)

From the end of World War II to the onset of the 1958 recession, auto workers experienced relatively strong demand for their labor (although during the Korean war there were some painful temporary layoffs), consistently obtained higher wages, and acquired new fringe benefits, such as retirement pensions and medical insurance. On the shopfloor they had divergent experiences with management. Speedups were usually sectoral within each company, and the timing and degree of speedup efforts varied considerably from company to company. Overall, it would appear that GM workers enjoyed more stable levels of required labor intensity, Chrysler workers fought repeated management attempts to raise production standards, and Ford workers forced management to accept the GM policy of setting production standards that, once they were set at the beginning of the model year, were not manipulated to increase worker effort.

Between 1947 and 1952, GM held its workers to tight production standards but *rarely made attempts to gain an extra edge by manipulating assembly line speeds to increase output*, a practice that had historically goaded auto workers into shopfloor protests. Once production standards were set on a new model or on a job that had been transformed by a new production technology, and assembly line speeds were balanced, GM usually made no attempt to increase the intensity of worker labor. Since a major cause of shopfloor discontent had been minimized, GM workers staged few wildcat strikes during this period. General Motors' "stable" production standards policy appears to have reflected its ability to hold its existing market shares, and its decision to avoid trying to use price competition to penetrate the markets of its competitors. Thus, GM was not faced with the imperative that intense price competition created to reduce costs by increasing labor intensity.

During this period, Chrysler's management, which was especially hostile to collective bargaining, sporadically tried to arbitrarily increase production standards.[34] Vigorous shopfloor bargaining by union stewards and many bitter, often unauthorized strikes forced Chrysler to roll back, by varying amounts, many intensified production standards.[35] Jack Conway, Walter Reuther's chief troubleshooter, observed in 1949 that

> "the peculiar thing about the Chrysler plants is that if they violate the [local plant] manpower agreements [line staffing], which they have, they have wildcats and they have them every damn time."[36]

The UAW's national leadership appears to have been worried that the extralegal militancy of the Chrysler workers, and especially the workers at the Dodge Main plant, would set a bad example for auto workers throughout the industry and would threaten Chrysler's economic viability, which in turn would undermine the UAW's strategy of pattern bargaining. The International Executive Board forced Local 3 to alter the method of choosing shop stewards, requiring that instead of being directly elected by production workers, the shopfloor stewards, who were production workers themselves, would be appointed by the plant-wide chief stewards. The latter were not actual production workers.[37]

In 1950 Chrysler took on the UAW in a 104-day strike because its management refused to offer its workers an actuarially sound pension plan.[38] In the wake of the 1950 strike, Chrysler's directors had selected a new management, which appears to have concluded that fully recognizing the UAW would be less disruptive than a blatantly hostile, rigidly obstructionist collective bargaining policy. But until October 1954, Chrysler refused to follow GM and Ford in contracting to avoid altering established production standards unless there was a change in manufacturing technology or product. Between 1950 and 1954, Chrysler workers responded with a sharp increase in wildcat strike actions. It appears that the overall militancy of Chrysler workers, combined with inconsistent managerial decisions on both the plant level and the corporate level, allowed Chrysler workers to attain production standards that were often lower than those in force at GM and Ford.[39]

In the 1930s, Henry Ford had turned over management of his company's labor relations to Harry Bennett, a Detroit gangster who hired many managers who were sadistic, authoritarian, and corrupt. As chapter 3 explains, conditions for Ford workers often became a living hell. In 1937, Irene Young, a GM worker, compared Ford with GM: "Before we ever had a Union in General Motors conditions were so far ahead of Ford that you could never even compare them."[40] After Henry Ford II took control of the Ford Motor Company in 1946, he eliminated gangsterism. But Ford and his new labor relations team, headed by John Bugas, a former FBI agent, did not appreciate the GM strategy of production standard stability that reduced worker shopfloor protest.

Concerned about the Ford Company's inefficient organization of production technology, and worried about low profit margins, Ford's new leaders moved to rationalize the management of technology and labor inputs. New production standards were instituted, and efforts were made to increase labor intensity further by compensating for delays in materials delivery and production line breakdowns by arbitrarily increasing the speeds of assembly lines in a way that forced some workers to work at a killing pace. In 1948 Ford management reneged on a written agreement with Local 900 workers to lock assembly line speeds. In 1949 Ford refused to set fixed labor-effort standards on many assembly line jobs at the River Rouge plant (Local 600). With full support from the national officers of the UAW, Local 900 and Local 600 staged the May 1949 massive Speed Up strike, which forced Ford to provide additional workers to reduce the labor effort of any worker who was forced by an increase in assembly line speed to complete work tasks in less time than management's own production standards stipulated. By 1952, Ford's central management was actively implementing this settlement.[41] (See chapter 5.)

Documents from the UAW's Ford Department, and interviews with UAW officials, support James R. Zetka's findings that during the postwar era, the auto companies generally did not pressure parts production workers to increase their labor intensity. Instead, the manufacturers pushed their *assembly line* workers to meet more intense production standards.[42] The auto companies well understood that when they pressured workers in an assembly plant, even if the plant was closed by strikes, production could continue at all other plants. Strikes at parts plants hurt an automaker much more, since many parts plants manufactured components that were needed for many or most car models. Thus, operations at many assembly plants could be stalled by a strike in a strategic parts plant.[43]

During the Korean War, GM tried to take advantage of worker vulnerability by speeding up production. In 1952, as one-seventh of all auto workers were laid off, GM initiated a speedup in some plants, and enforced the action by many disciplinary lay offs and threats of discharge. At Flint, Michigan, GM workers in Local 581 responded with production slowdowns and wildcat strikes.[44] That same year, *some* divisions within GM shifted gears and began to press workers hard to meet higher production standards. The speedups were concentrated in the Buick, Oldsmobile, and Pontiac divisions, often referred to as B.O.P., which had recently been ordered by GM's central management to assemble all their models on the same standardized assembly lines. GM was pressuring each B.O.P. plant manager to increase production. Trying to look good in the eyes of central management, many B.O.P managers pushed their assembly workers harder and harder. Wildcat strikes at GM increased between 1951 and 1955. The UAW authorized production standard strikes at parts plants to force GM to reopen its national contract.

In 1955, workers in the B.O.P. assembly plants reported frequent assembly line speed changes and many alterations in car body styles and options. New technologies, e.g., power steering, power windows, and power brakes, made the assembly process much more complex. Until the bugs in the production and installation of these components were ironed out, in many plants workers were pressured into extra effort to compensate for management's inability to schedule efficiently, and *evenly*, as required by contract, the mix of assembly parts and assembly jobs. Inconsistent managerial policies also encouraged worker militancy. When workers in a particular B.O.P. plant were moving towards an authorized strike over production standards, management would "sometimes grant wholesale concession[s] to avoid a strike in one plant, while 'freezing' in another, even though market and sales conditions appear identical."[45]

In late 1957 and early 1958, a sharp recession hit the auto industry. GM management pressured the workers fortunate enough to have a job to work more intensely. In response, many GM plants were hit by a wave of worker sabotage, the first since World War II. In 1958, a federal grand jury indicted

GM for anti-trust activity. Fearing the political consequences of additional bad publicity from speedup strikes by disgruntled workers, in 1959 GM's central management ordered managers to ease up on assembly workers.[46]

Increasing market competition after the Korean War led the smaller auto manufacturers to pursue more confrontational labor policies. At Studebaker, management drastically altered lax production standard policies. Time study led to the elimination of the rampant featherbedding that existed at Studebaker. The managerial goal was to redesign each job so that the worker worked for 85 percent of the 480 standard minutes of each working day.[47] The militants among the Studebaker workers responded with work stoppages and spurts of sabotage. Nevertheless, labor intensity increased markedly.

In 1954, Chrysler's central management also determined that it would increase production standards,[48] aiming to match the higher general labor effort rates in effect at GM and Ford, its two major competitors. By 1956, Chrysler had beefed-up the company's severely understaffed time-study department. Chrysler's newly hired industrial engineers retimed all jobs and promulgated new production standards. Chrysler workers understood that these new standards would require a significant increase in labor effort.

Between September 1956 and December 19, 1958, Chrysler fought out the work speed issue with its employees, especially those at the pivotal Dodge Main plant. Advice from Chrysler's more capable managers and the onset of adverse economic conditions (the severe 1957–58 recession, the worst since World War II) convinced even some of Local 3's most militant leaders that if concessions were not made, Chrysler would close its Detroit area plants and initiate production at other facilities, thereby eliminating the jobs of thousands of Detroit area workers. In December 1958, workers at the Dodge Main Plant made one last-ditch, unsuccessful effort to stem the tide, staging a seventeen-day *authorized strike* over plant relief standards, production rates, and safety.[49] One year later the threat to close the Dodge Main plant brought further concessions, reducing the number of relief workers in the stamping building, where the work was especially exhausting. [50]

At both Chrysler and Studebaker new, more capable management and the end of the post-war bull market for cars resulted in new, successful managerial offensives against auto workers, whose militancy had previously sustained production standards that were much less intense than the norm at GM and Ford. By 1958 there was a relative uniformity in the labor effort required of workers in all auto plants. Auto workers at GM and Ford did not lose ground. They had successfully fought to gain, and maintain, a more predictable, less enervating work pace.

Job security had been one of the major concerns of auto workers in the 1930s. Seniority protections, achieved with unionization, and a thirty-hour work week, never attained, had been the means auto workers favored to achieve fairer, more secure access to jobs. In the booming post-World War II years, as Ronald Edsforth explains in chapter 6, significant groups of auto workers—generally those in the plants where new labor-displacing machinery was being introduced—were anxious about the prospects of technological unemployment. By 1957, it was clear that highly mechanized and automated production technologies, especially in the boring of engine blocks, had eliminated about 150,000 jobs from the auto industry. A disproportionate number of the jobs eliminated were the lower-paying jobs that were held by black workers, many of whom had been prevented, by the racial prejudice that was endemic among plant managers, foremen, and white workers, from being promoted to more secure, higher paying jobs. From 1949 through the mid-1960s a militant minority of auto workers demanded shorter hours—a thirty hour work week—which would have increased the total number of jobs in the industry.[51]

Although backing the shorter work week in principle, Walter Reuther and his closest advisors did not believe their union, or organized labor in general, had enough economic or political clout to secure shorter hours. Thus they did not develop a long term bargaining strategy, which emphasized economic gains in boom times and worktime reductions when the economy slowed, a bargaining strategy used by Western European unions since the mid-1950s. Instead, the UAW leaders, with a few dissenters, most notably Emil Mazey, focused on bargaining for fringe benefits, including supplemental unemployment benefits, the granting of special seniority rights to workers displaced by technological innovation, and early retirement options for auto workers. But the leaders of the UAW were sensitive to the question of employment levels and the effect on employment of bargaining strategies other than a sizeable reduction of the length of the work day. During the 1949 Ford Speed Up strike, Ken Bannon, the UAW's Ford Director pointed out that reducing the number of overworked assembly line workers would create additional jobs at Ford. (See chapter 5.) In 1964, as auto production levels reached very high levels and management pressure for increased worker effort mounted, the UAW struck GM. The settlement forced the Big Three to accept a 50 percent increase in relief time (an additional twelve minutes a day), which both reduced the speedup pressure on overworked assembly laborers and created ten thousand additional industry jobs.

Walter Reuther, who believed that the first priority of collective bargaining should be income security, understood the labor displacing effects of mechanization and automation. Reuther expected that auto workers whose jobs were eliminated by new production technologies would find jobs in the other sectors of a growing economy. Thus, he advocated Keynesian stimulation of the overall economy, as well as tax reform to redistribute income and enlarge consumer purchasing power.[52] Reuther did not understand that the

American economy was generating fewer and fewer jobs, and especially industrial jobs, relative to the size of the labor force. But few of his contemporaries recognized this tragic, ongoing trend.[53]

From 1963 to 1965, car production surged from 5.5 million units to 9.3 million units. Truck sales also boomed. But there were signs of future trouble for the auto industry. In 1960, imported cars took 7.6 percent of the U.S. market; ten years later the market share of imports had almost doubled to 14.7 percent.[54] The real wages and fringe benefits of auto workers were also rising during this period. At the time, the managements of major U.S. auto companies did not seem worried about these trends. But they were under pressure to meet the tremendous increase in consumer demand for motor vehicles. The auto companies responded with a mix of new, cost-saving, labor-displacing production technologies, *and* direct pressure was placed on production workers to speed up production. GM, Ford, and Chrysler also increasingly centralized the management of their operations, striving to determine production schedules at headquarters and establishing production "efficiency" units that were directly responsible to headquarters.

By the mid-1960s, the Big Three auto companies paid auto workers higher wages and offered them better fringe benefits than any group of industrial workers in the nation. But when it came to controlling workers' output, the auto companies still wanted to call most of the shots. When auto managers felt the need for more output or higher labor efficiency, they broke contractual agreements with workers. Rather than turning the screws on auto workers in a uniform, across the board manner, which would have engendered widespread protest actions, the auto companies shifted the speedup from plant to plant, trying to avoid the factories that had the most militant workers or produced parts that were critical to assembly operations.

Between 1961 and 1968, the UAW leadership concluded that Chrysler and especially Ford were driving their assembly workers harder than GM. It is likely that Ford's plant managers were receiving speedup directives from the corporate finance department, which had emerged as the real power within the company. The finance men sought to please stockholders by increasing output, hence sales, profits, and dividends. But the finance men had another agenda. They wanted to either scare the remaining older, production-oriented factory managers, who were afraid of being displaced by younger men, into driving their workers harder, or to create justifications for dismissing the plant managers who could not meet their assigned production quotas.[55]

Whatever the cause for the new Ford policy, its contours were clear. When consumer demand for a particular Ford car or truck was strong, Ford adhered to the terms of the 1949 Speed Up Strike settlement. When demand dropped, and especially at the end of the model year, Ford made "wholesale reallocation on work loads, thus eliminating manpower and creating abnormal work loads . . ."[56] In many cases, immediately after signing local contracts that included settlements of production standards disputes, local managements violated the agreements by increasing standards. In other instances, management made concessions in production standard disputes and then immediately changed the composition of the job, establishing a production standard that the UAW local officials felt was equally out of line.[57]

In November 1963, Ken Bannon, head of the UAW's Ford Department, claimed that Ford had "tightened standards so much on our guys that a revolution is brewing." Workers who complained about excessive work loads on new jobs were told to be patient, that the standards were only experimental. But then management frequently stalled, waiting weeks and even months to set *permanent* production standards. In the interim, workers believed they were being sweated. Moreover, as UAW negotiators pointed out in 1967, this policy meant that "95 percent of the line foremen don't know what the standards are themselves." Pressured by plant managers to make sure that assembly line workers worked hard, the foremen responded by using "intimidation as a subterfuge to get the work out." Without permanent standards, which workers could grieve, foremen were encouraged to drive workers to meet interim standards, leaving the aggravated assembly workers without any legal way to complain about exhausting jobs. The leaders of the UAW's Ford Council concluded that "no employee should have to work under the fear of any hour or any day throughout a model run, that he will be given an abnormal work load assignment . . .."[58] Starting in 1964, UAW negotiators demanded that Ford fix production standards no later than sixty days after the annual model changeover and to put all standards in writing. Gaining this protection helped, but constant union vigilance was needed to curb management violations of the sixty-day rule.

Throughout the fall of 1963, the UAW International approved speedup strikes at Ford and GM assembly plants. The results were disappointing to the assembly workers. Strikes at the huge, older assembly plants of the pre-World War II era were becoming less and less effective as the auto makers cut back on production at these plants, while transferring their manufacturing to medium sized plants, including many new factories that incorporated the state-of-the-art in production technologies. Recognizing this problem, in 1964 the UAW's Ford Department tried to get national contract language allowing all plants making the same car model to strike at the same time over production standards disputes. Management refused and the Ford Council did not want to risk a costly national strike on this issue.

During the 1960s, as the Chrysler Corporation moved to establish new plants outside of Detroit, it starved its older, inner-city plants for funds. Plant safety, which is costly, became a low priority in Chrysler's Detroit plants. Work conditions at Dodge Main and the Jefferson Avenue plant became particularly onerous, and dangerous. As the economy boomed after 1964, strong demand for autos led to more and more compulsory overtime, which magnified the risks faced by workers in the Chrysler inner-city plants. White foremen were often racists who treated black workers contemptuously. White workers, and some union officials, often resisted efforts by black workers to get promoted to the skilled trades jobs in the plants, jobs which were in the top pay classifications. Large scale migration from the South to Detroit since World War II meant that black workers often were in the majority in many departments of Detroit's auto plants. Many black workers in the Chrysler plants formed radical organizations. Angered by the discrimination they encountered, they were inspired by both the legacy of the civil rights movement and a local revolutionary socialist black power movement that flourished among younger blacks.

These plant-level groups, analyzed by Heather Ann Thompson in chapter 7, agitated against the capitalist system in general and criticized the labor relations system that had emerged in the plants. The militants believed that abandoning the right to stage job actions and wildcats left workers at the mercy of a dilatory grievance system. The black nationalists criticized the UAW as an institution, charging that its leaders, who had vigorously supported the enactment of civil rights legislation in 1964 and 1965, were laggard in combatting racism within the UAW bureaucracy and within the auto plants. From 1968 to 1973, the radical black groups also fought to correct specific problems, like the racism of foremen, discrimination in promoting blacks, and Chrysler's callous indifference to worker safety. As Heather Ann Thompson points out, sit-downs and wildcat strikes over safety issues could unite Detroit's black and white workers.

When auto workers who staged wildcat strikes over safety and production standards had credible complaints about management's contract violations, the UAW's national leaders usually backed them by approving authorized strikes over the same issues. These legal strikes were not ended until management assured the UAW that the workers who had violated the ban against job actions and wildcat strikes would not be fired. However, light disciplinary actions, e.g., disciplinary layoffs for several days, were accepted by the UAW. In the summer of 1973, the UAW leadership twice departed from this pattern.

In the first instance, at the Chrysler Forge plant, the UAW supported wildcat strikers by telling Chrysler the UAW would authorize a strike if safety hazards were not corrected. But the IEB backed the executive board of Local 47 when, by a 4-3 vote, it accepted a settlement that allowed the *dismissal* of three militant wildcat leaders, all men who were ideological radicals. The second instance of a break with its pattern of helping wildcatters with major legitimate complaints against management came a week after the wildcat strike at Chrysler Forge. Workers at the Mack truck plant used force to prevent the police from evicting two workers who had stopped a conveyor belt to protest the speedup and safety hazards. The police evicted the workers. Many Mack workers then organized a picket line around the plant. At Solidarity House, the national headquarters of the UAW, the union's top leaders, including socialists like Emil Mazey, were furious. They believed, erroneously in Heather Thompson's view, that revolutionary black nationalists were behind the Mack strike. UAW officials from the Detroit area mobilized, armed themselves with baseball bats and clubs, and attacked the picketing Mack workers on the second day of their strike. These two incidents indicate the way highly publicized radicalism and racial divisions within American society complicated industrial relations after 1965.

Throughout the 1960s General Motors invested heavily in new labor-saving technology, but did not initiate a company-wide intensification of workers' labor effort until 1968. Sensing that GM was ripe for a rollback of production standards because it was worried about the anti-trust action under consideration by the Kennedy Administration, in 1961 the UAW's GM Department approved 92 of 129 requests by locals to strike over unresolved issues in local contracts, issues that usually involved production standards.[59] Many of these strikes were modestly successful. GM could afford the concessions, since it was earning high profits at this time.

Late in 1967 or early in 1968, perhaps in response to concerns about increasing import penetration of the American auto market and a decline in returns on capital invested, General Motors' management resolved to initiate a drive to raise production standards. In February, March, and April, 1968, GM demanded an increase in labor intensity in several assembly plants. The UAW responded with authorized strikes at GM plants at Lordstown, Atlanta, Framingham, Van Nuys, Flint, and St. Louis. At first, the strikes had no effect. But the UAW International then authorized a strategic strike at a critical stamping plant in Willow Springs, Illinois. The UAW had some very minor production standards grievances at this plant. Deprived of the stampings for all GM cars, management made concessions on production standards in the assembly plants that had walked out. Throughout the next five years, GM workers staged many hard-fought speedup strikes.

In November 1968, the top management at General Motors gave the General Motors Assembly Division (GMAD) a new mandate. It was to increase production efficiency by combining GM's six Chevrolet assembly plants with their six companion Fisher Body plants. Local managers remained, but GMAD effectively operated these plants. GMAD tried to impose uniform job standards[60] at all the GM plants it managed.[61] To implement this policy, GMAD time-study engineers developed computer models that generated production standards for similar jobs in each plant. This attempt to achieve "objective" standards angered many production workers, since each plant varied with respect to equipment quality, prior assembly quality, and the quality of the work environment. GMAD also used the elimination and reassignment of jobs during the Chevrolet-Fisher mergers as a smokescreen for a drastic reduction in the number of workers on assembly lines, usually by one-third, *without lowering the number of operations that had to be performed each hour.*[62]

In 1969, GM workers continued, with the approval of the UAW International, to use authorized strikes to fight GM's speedup policy. After a long, costly two-month national strike against GM in 1970 and the loss of a 174-day strike at the Norwood, Ohio, assembly plant, the UAW decided to put even more emphasis on authorized local strikes, especially short duration, "quickie" strikes, at key GM parts plants.[63] This strategy, developed by Irving Bluestone, Director of the GM Department, was nicknamed "Operation Apache." UAW officials in Detroit often directed plant officials to "develop" strikeable grievances, at carefully selected parts plants, so that the UAW could *legally* stage short strategic strikes to pressure GM to ease up on workers at assembly plants.[64]

In 1972, at Lordstown, Ohio the GMAD strategy was blocked by militant UAW workers, with full support from their International Union. GM was vulnerable at Lordstown because it had to sell large numbers of the newly developed Vega, on which it had spent millions of advertising dollars in an attempt to head off competition from foreign imports. (See chapter 7.) Additional "Operation Apache" strikes led GM to ease off on its speedup.

By the mid-1970s, there was minimal speedup pressure on auto workers. However, to produce enough cars to meet market demand, many auto plants required substantial amounts of overtime from their workers. While auto workers were handsomely paid for the compulsory overtime, many resented their inability to choose to decline occasionally or completely the extra work and extra pay. Among the reasons given by some workers who opposed compulsory overtime was the exhaustion that they experienced from frequent extended work weeks.[65]

From the end of the 1930s to the 1970s, legal and illegal worker/actions had forced the auto makers to abandon the brutal Depression-era labor policies that had dehumanized workers. The agency of the UAW allowed auto workers to achieve a safer, more predictable work environment. After 1937 auto manufacturers and workers were locked in a continuous tug-of-war over the intensity of labor in the auto plants. Unionization gave the auto workers more "pull" against the tendency of managers and engineers to try to use the capabilities of the Fordist system to squeeze more effort out of workers. Without the UAW, auto workers would have been subjected to a much faster work pace, one that would have been debilitating and demoralizing.

Unionization also enhanced the effectiveness of individual workers' acts of protest against managerial autocracy. Craig Zabala's close examination of worker sabotage during the 1970s at the Van Nuys, California Camaro plant (chapter 8), shows how workers used sabotage to resist management breeches of contract agreements. Zabala views sabotage as a supplement to grievance bargaining. Management's difficulty in proving sabotage, which the union contract requires if management seeks to punish workers who practice sabotage, allowed workers at Van Nuys to get away with individual, intermittent acts of resistance. This "freedom" had two functions: it allowed workers an emotional outlet for their frustration with alienating work and unfair managerial actions, and it gave workers, on occasion, an informal bargaining weapon to use to try to fight the speedup and other unwanted management policies.

It is impossible to delineate precisely the overall changes in the intensity of the work effort of auto workers between the mid-1960s and the mid-1980s. Company records are closed to outside researchers. But a set of oral histories with Ford truck workers in Michigan provides some suggestive evidence. One measure of labor intensity is the number of standard minutes that industrial engineers assign to time-studied jobs. An eight-hour day contains 480 standard minutes. Don Mushinsky, an inspector at the Ford Michigan Truck Plant, reports that in 1967 most jobs at his plant contained 400 standard minutes. A generation later, in 1986, most jobs required 440 standard minutes of work, a 10 percent increase.[66] Other workers at the same plant also indicated that there had been a significant increase in the speed of each worker's job movements. Betty Foote, a general assembler, believed that

> The jobs haven't gotten harder over the years [since 1976], but we have more work, and we're working faster.

Raymon Reyes, a spot welder, observed that

> The line has speeded up since EI [employee involvement] was instituted from forty-one units an hour to forty-nine units. And we're doing the same amount of work on each unit as we did then.[67]

More efficient production technologies can allow output to be increased without requiring an intensification of the labor effort by workers. But it appears that many auto workers had to confront new production technologies that also called for increased worker effort. Al Commons, one of the most senior employees in the Ford Michigan Truck plant, complained that

> . . . we keep losing more people each year as management streamlines the work force and increases production. Retooling does not compensate for all the work added onto the remaining people when people are cut.[68]

Future studies may provide hard statistics on the changes in job content and job effort that have been produced by the adoption of increasingly sophisticated production technologies since the mid-1970s. But clearly since 1979, the labor intensity demanded of auto workers in the United States has increased.

World Competition and
the End of the Dream

1979 was a watershed year for auto workers and the U.S. auto industry. The Iranian oil embargo that followed the overthrow of the Shah produced an oil price surge that generated a consumer switch to smaller cars, many of them imports. A new era of international competition and technological unemployment eliminated auto production jobs and seriously undermined the power of the UAW. The closing of obsolete plants, and the elimination of excess capacity, had begun in the mid-1970s. But it intensified with a vengeance in the early 1980s. By 1985, the U.S. automobile industry had eliminated half its jobs.

The brave new world[69] of auto work is one in which most auto workers have lost the high degree of union protection they had enjoyed in the preceding thirty-five years. Auto workers could no longer expect to spend their adult working careers in a high-wage industry where seniority systems allowed laboring men and women, as they aged, to obtain some relief from the stress of tedious, debilitating manual labor.

Just-in-time production, the reduction of parts inventories, and the tight scheduling of parts deliveries has had a generally unappreciated effect on assembly workers. Traditionally, assembly line workers obtained breaks from the monotony of line work when parts shortages forced the line to shut down for periods ranging from a few minutes to several hours. With more efficient scheduling of parts deliveries, this kind of respite, which is very important to the psychological well-being of workers engaged in boring, repetitive work, is virtually eliminated.[70]

Another new aspect of the highly rationalized auto factories of the late 1980s and 1990s is the tendency towards increased length of the work day.

Unlike the Western European automobile industry, which has reduced the standard work week significantly since 1982, American producers have insisted on maintaining the forty hour work week standard. Moreover, in many U.S. factories, ten hour work days (with a four day week) have become common, as has compulsory overtime. On the other hand, auto companies have eliminated many jobs that involve heavy lifting and exposure to dangerous paints and metal particles, and have increasingly applied ergonomic principles to designing assembly line work.

When the new production technologies of the 1980s reduced worker effort per job operation but *increased the number of job operations a worker had to perform in an hour*, many workers became afflicted by a type of injury known as repetitive stress injury. Accurate, unbiased statistical studies of the impact of these injuries on employment tenure, and job turnover records, are lacking because auto company archives remain closed to non-company researchers. Workers' compensation data from Michigan, the state with the largest number of auto workers, suggest something of the magnitude of the problem. Today, approximately 40 percent of the compensation claims in Michigan are for repetitive stress injuries.[71]

The auto companies have also insisted on restricted seniority arrangements since 1979. For many workers, and especially for aging workers,[72] the effects of job redesign and diluted seniority protection have been pernicious. In many plants, workers who were trained in multiple tasks were given a pay increase, usually 20-60 cents an hour, and were classified as variable workers. But in GM plants, variable workers discovered that management-imposed rules allowed foremen to ignore their seniority and place them on any job for which they were qualified, even if they complained that the job was particularly unhealthful. For example, in a Wentville, Missouri GM plant a variable worker with significant seniority, who was 6''2" tall, was assigned to a job that hurt his back. It required him to bend very low to install parts under a car fender. When he asked for a change in jobs, he was turned down because a management rule stipulated that for variable workers, seniority had no bearing on requests for job transfers.[73]

The severe recession of the early 1980s, which created the highest automotive unemployment since 1938, left the entire work force fearful of plant closings and permanent layoffs. Many auto workers were afraid to use the kind of resistance tactics they had favored in the past:

> We in the union advocate that if a job is overloaded [i.e., has more than 480 standard minutes], the best way to prove it is to [not do the extra work and] let it go down the line. Now some people have more of a tendency to run and get it [complete the work]. They are afraid to let stuff go because they might get written up and disciplined.[73]

Workers also found that new managerial tactics, and especially the introduction of "Team Concept" management, made it more difficult for them to challenge the speedup.[75]

Starting in the mid-1980s, the Big Three auto makers began introducing
the Team Concept model of industrial management in their plants. By 1990,
most auto plants had implemented some variant of Team Concept, which
ostensibly was a more democratic mode of managing work in auto plants than
the management-led authoritarian system of the past seventy years. All workers were to be part of small production teams of ten to fifteen people that were
to be encouraged to provide input about ways to improve production conditions, the overall plant environment, and production efficiency. Workers were
to be trained for several jobs and to be allowed to combat job monotony by
requesting changes in job assignment. Within each production team, the
members were supposed to make decisions about job allocations. As Steve
Babson demonstrates in chapter 9, the reality of the Team Concept system at
the Ford plant in Dearborn, Michigan, was very different. Plant managers
usurped most of the power promised to the teams.[76]

Babson's findings mirror the conclusions reached by Mike Parker and
Jane Slaughter in their seminal 1988 study, *Team Concept*.[77] Examining the
Team Concept at scores of plants, they found that when workers complained
that some jobs were "overloaded", i.e., involved too many tasks to be done
without significant speeding up, the officers of UAW locals were increasingly unwilling to support workers who wanted to file official grievances.[78] It
seems clear that the threat of losing jobs to foreign competition, or to other
plants within the same company, forced the UAW to tacitly accept almost
total managerial control in an area where workers had formerly exercised
some power. Between 1945 and 1975, the UAW had not faced the threat of
foreign competition. Nor had new production technologies reduced the size of
the work force during this period because the demand for cars and trucks continued to grow. However, after 1975, unprecedented job destruction undermined workers' security and union power. The new technologies available to
management made it increasingly possible to circumvent strikes in parts
plants, since companies with world-wide production facilities could immediately manufacture substitute parts in factories outside the U.S., and then
quickly transport the parts to assembly plants.

Within the UAW, national and local leaders floundered, unable to develop a strategy that would protect seniority rights and the quality of the work
environment. Proposals to fight for a shorter work week as a way to preserve
more jobs had twice been rejected by UAW presidents since 1978. In the late
1980s, as auto employment continued to decline, a significant dissident move-

ment emerged. New Directions formed around Jerry Tucker's challenge to the UAW establishment. Tucker ran for the directorship of District 5 (St. Louis) in 1986 and 1989. In 1992 he campaigned for the UAW's presidency, arguing that incumbent president Owen Bieber had steered the union away from its historic mission. Ironically, Tucker's "new directions" amounted to a call to return to a more confrontational bargaining strategy, and a more independent social democratic political agenda. New Directions' claim to be the "true" representative of the UAW's historic legacy was strengthened by the prominence of Victor Reuther (Walter Reuther's brother) in the movement. The New Directions Movement has pockets of strength, especially in Michigan and the St. Louis area. Thus, a New Directions candidate won the presidency of the 13,000 member Buick Local 599 in 1993. However, within the national union, the New Directions Movement remains very much a minority, with no more than 10,000 members on its mailing list.[79]

Of course, at the plant level auto workers did not always have to retreat. For example, in 1987 and 1988 one militant UAW local, Local 594 at the GM Pontiac Truck and Bus Plant 6, successfully used the strategic strike, timed to interfere with production on new models that GM expected to be best sellers, to challenge management on the speedup and other issues. The plant management had called together production teams to discuss speedup grievances filed by a member of the team, a procedure that was in direct violation of the plant's contract. Management's tactic was designed to use group pressure to intimidate workers who asserted their rights to grieve. In any group, there will often be some people who will try to curry favor with management by taking management's side. Local 594 also prevailed on the other issues it raised: general job classifications that undermined seniority rights, the elimination of customary short work breaks, safety problems, illegal subcontracting, and bans on newspaper reading and fraternizing during assembly line breakdowns.[80] But they did not cut to the core of management power over the pace of production.

In 1991, UAW workers at the Mazda Flat Rock plant near Detroit protested against the lack of democracy in the Team Concept regime that Mazda had unilaterally imposed. Threatening an authorized strike, the workers forced Mazda to permit the election and *recall* of team leaders. More relief workers were to be provided for absentees, thereby preventing intense, short term increases in work effort. A union health and safety representative was added for the second shift, and the new contract doubled the number of empty jobs that had to be filled on the basis of seniority. These changes brought the Mazda workers' working conditions and representational rights closer to the industry standard.[81]

Surviving, But No Exit

Gary Bryner was the president of the UAW local that won the 1972 Lordstown strike. Interviewed in 1991, he remarked that the strike, which had forced GM to honor the contracts it had signed, had given workers "a measure of control."[82] The phrase is apt. It captures the significance of unionization for auto workers and workers in other industries.[83] Clearly unions do not enable workers to control completely their work environment. Above all, in the absence of substantial worker representation on corporate boards of directors, auto workers have had virtually no input into decisions about investment in production technology and plant location, decisions that have led to the export of substantial numbers of auto industry jobs in the last two decades. But, depending on economic and political conditions, the UAW has historically been able to give auto workers the power to obtain "a measure of control." That measure of control may take the form of protection against hazardous working conditions; it may be manifested in a seniority system that offers some degree of protection against inequitable promotion, demotion, and discharge; and it may take the form of guarantees that once a piece rate, line speed, or production standard has been negotiated, the worker can count on some stability and predictability in his or her life.

The structural and technological changes in the auto industry since 1979 have greatly undermined the power of the UAW, reducing the ability of auto workers to use their union to protect their interests against management's power. The understandably lower rate of organized protest against the new regime does not mean that auto workers are content. Many auto workers are ambivalent about the trade-off between having a high-paying job and the new work regime that endangers their health and sanity. Understandably, many such workers are reluctant to talk candidly about their views to outsiders.

Mike Parker, himself a skilled auto plant repairman, has intensively studied recent developments in management practices and worker opinion. Parker concludes that workers are above all troubled by the finality of their position in the modern auto factory. In the past, auto workers had coped with the boredom and powerlessness of their jobs by dreaming about leaving the line and switching to another factory job. Some workers hoped to start their own small businesses. Workers who left the auto plants could usually return if their alternative jobs did not pan out. But after 1990, and perhaps earlier, auto workers realized that this safety valve no longer existed. Employment in the auto industry was shrinking and the overall economy was stagnant. Parker believes that today auto workers are experiencing "incredible insecurity." Their attitude is "You're in a prison for ten hours." This formulation recalls the classic

Depression era "on the line" imagery of Dos Passos, Rivera, and Chaplin. The auto factory still resembles a prison, because workers' actions are so closely controlled, and because workers are not confident about their prospects if they should "escape" to another job.[84]

Most auto workers in the United States are realists. They perceive that only one aspect of the future of auto work can be predicted with confidence: with each passing decade, fewer and fewer men and women will be employed in the production of automobiles. Auto workers also understand that technological displacement has, and will, leave many redundant workers unemployed for long periods of time. They realize that most of the displaced workers who find new jobs will be paid much less than they had earned making motor vehicles. Auto workers in the United States are employed in one of the last of the high-paying blue collar sectors in an economy that offers them no exit to a better world. They know that their union is unable to preserve their jobs, and is increasingly unable to protect them against a regime that makes them work harder and harder and shows them little mercy as they get older.[85]

Acknowledgments

The authors' research was funded by grants from the Henry J. Kaiser Family Foundation. Robert Asher's research was also funded by the Research Foundation of the University of Connecticut. The authors wish to give special thanks to Raymond Boryczka, Chief of Research at the Walter P. Reuther Library, Wayne State University, for his expert assistance in locating materals and for sharing his knowledge of the history of the UAW; Warner Pflug, Associate Director, Walter P. Reuther Library; and Tom C. Featherstone, Audio Visual Archivist, Walter P. Reuther Library. The entire staff of the Reuther Library provided friendly, generous assistance to all the contributors to this volume. It would have been impossible to write a history of autowork without the resources of the Reuther Library. The authors also wish to thank Carol J. Williams, Rebecca Mlynarczyk, Kevin Boyle, Allen Ward and Irving Bluestone for their constructive criticisms of the chapter. The authors alone are responsible for its contents.

2

BUILDING FOR MASS PRODUCTION: FACTORY DESIGN AND WORK PROCESS AT THE FORD MOTOR COMPANY

....

Lindy Biggs

As the pioneers of the American automobile industry sought the best way to produce good cars at affordable prices, they experimented with every piece of the manufacturing operation, from the tools used by workers to the size and shape of the factory building. Henry Ford proved to be one of the most aggressive of the auto manufacturers when it came to experimenting with changes in his factory and in the production process. The story of Ford's success with the Model T entails his shrewd business sense as well as his willingness, even eagerness, to manipulate his workers, and factories, in his quest for a system that would produce cars cheaply.

While best known for his early use of the assembly line, Ford's other innovations proved equally important in creating the rational factory that Ford and other industrialists sought. The changes that Ford and his engineers introduced between 1904 and 1920 completely changed the organization of the automobile factory and the way work was done.

The Early Shops

The early automobile shop looked like any other machine shop of the early twentieth century. In his 1926 reflections on the auto industry, Fred Colvin, a prominent industrial journalist, reminded his readers that the early auto industry "was not particularly important. The average automobile shop . . . was building automobiles in a small way and by ordinary machine shop methods."[1] The first factory of the Ford Motor Company, established in 1903, was such a shop. A small wood-frame building on Mack Avenue in Detroit, it consisted of one room measuring 50 by 250 with a shop inventory of two lathes, two drill presses, one milling machine, one hand saw, one grinding wheel, and one forge. The shop contained no specialized tools and employed "ten or a dozen boys [men] and a foreman."[2]

The first auto companies designed and assembled cars, buying components from small manufacturers. The job of assembling a car in 1903 required the skill of an experienced hand and the use of standard machine tools. Every piece had to be cut, filed, and fitted because the automobile industry had not yet achieved the production of standardized, interchangeable parts. This work was done by small groups of skilled machinists working together to build one car at a time.[3] (See Figure 1.)

Though the early auto workers left little behind to tell us what they thought of their jobs, we can imagine that the work, a respected trade with a small number of fellow workers in a new and exciting industry, was agreeable to a skilled mechanic. The work was anything but routine, presenting challenges and paying good wages to workers with the skill to do the job. The wages paid by the auto industry were among the highest in the country; in 1914 it ranked seventh in average annual wages, by 1919 it was fifth, and by 1925, first.[4]

By 1904, Ford's success with his Models C, F, and B made him think about moving to larger quarters. When the company began construction on a second factory on Piquette Avenue in Detroit, Ford and his associates knew that they

Figure 1. Piquette Plant assembly room, 1906, illustrating static assembly. (FMC Archives, Edison Institue, Neg. 833-7307)

needed a factory significantly different from the Mack Avenue shop. Henry Ford and John Dodge, an early partner, planned and oversaw the building of the new factory.[5] It provided better organization and more space for growing production, but did not offer a new model for production or factory design.

The three-story building measured 402 by 52 feet on a lot about four times as large as the building. The building's long, narrow dimensions were typical of most nineteenth- and early twentieth-century factories that depended on the sun to help light the shopfloor. In a wider building the center of the shopfloor would have received too little light for the machinist's detailed work. The standard mill-type building also proved most efficient for the transmission of power by means of belts attached to shafting that ran the length of the building.[6]

Unlike the Mack Avenue shop, the new building held more than work-shop rooms. A visitor to the Piquette Avenue shop would enter the first floor through a proper lobby with a receptionist and might have been directed to one of the private offices of the company's officers. Such formality was unknown in the Mack Avenue shop's one room. The rest of Piquette's first floor contained the general offices for clerks and stenographers, as well as storage areas and a machine shop with the heaviest machines—the cylinder, crank-case, and crankshaft departments.[7] The factory section of the first floor would have seemed dark due to windows slightly smaller than those on the top two floors, and the quantity of stored supplies stacked the perimeter of the floor. The second floor looked and sounded different from the first. Larger and lighter, it housed a variety of operations from assembly stations and machine shop, to offices, and Henry Ford's private experimental room. The third floor looked much like the second. It held pattern rooms, storage, and the final assembly area where twelve to fifteen groups did the final work of putting the car together. (See Figure 2.)

Even with the company's growth, the Ford Motor Company remained a minor auto maker compared to the large producers like Oldsmobile and Packard. Though Henry Ford employed more workers at Piquette Avenue than he had in the earlier shop, the production process initially remained the same. In the small shop, workers knew what was happening in all facets of the operation, and like the Mack Avenue shop, the workers and managers worked together in a relationship more collegial than hierarchical. In describing their relationship with Henry Ford, early Ford workers remember him as one of the boys. They called him Henry and he was always there on the shopfloor.

Late in 1906, Ford and his managers began to reorganize work in the Piquette Avenue shop and in the company's newly established parts manufacturing operation. The changes began with the introduction of the idea of interchangeable parts. To produce interchangeable parts the machine tools

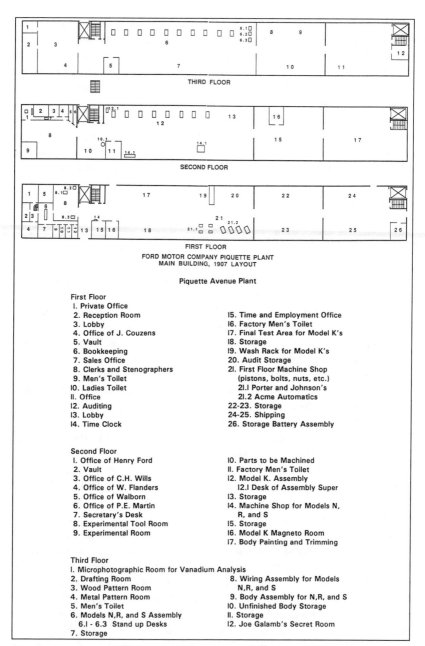

Figure 2. Diagram of Piquette Plant, showing 1907 layout of the pre-assembly-line plant. (Drawn from photos and drawings in FMC Archives, Edison Institute, Blueprints and Drawings-FMC Plants)

were fitted with fixtures, jigs, and gauges that assured precise machining of each piece, and allowed less-skilled workers to do the job. To speed production, machines were arranged sequentially. Rather than placing machine tools in the traditional pattern with groups of like machines together, the new arrangement placed machines in the order in which they were used. In the assembly area, management initiated changes that would lead to assembly-line production in just a few years. No longer would workers work in small groups, each one doing whatever needed to be done. Instead, for final assembly, they would walk along a row of stationary cars performing one operation over and over.[8] The scale of the early experiments in the new production style did not tax the Piquette Avenue building. But that would change within a few years and the company would have to move.

Highland Park

Four years later the company had outgrown the Piquette Avenue shop due to the extraordinary success of the 1908 Ford Model T. The Model T's popularity overwhelmed the company and it could not build enough cars to satisfy the demand. As Henry Ford thought about more space, he envisioned more than a simple expansion of the existing facility; he imagined a different kind of factory.

When the company moved its operations in January 1910, the new Highland Park plant was considered to be one of the most modern of any auto manufacturing operation. Expanding on innovations in building construction at Detroit's Packard plant, the new Ford plant boasted the latest construction technology, reinforced concrete, which allowed important changes in building design, as well as what the company believed would be significant advances in manufacturing efficiency.

Ford and his engineers had decided on an internal factory arrangement quite different from that at Piquette Avenue and hired Albert Kahn to design the building's shell. At his first meeting with Kahn, Ford told him "I want the whole thing under one roof. If you can design it the way I want it, say so and do it."[9] Kahn did it and continued building for Ford. Kahn had already designed the innovative Packard plant in which he used some pioneering reinforced concrete construction. Other auto companies also hired him, making him the country's first industrial architect.

The new plant must have seemed very different to the workers who moved with the company from the Piquette Avenue shop. If they could have anticipated the events of the next few years, they might have reconsidered remaining in the company's employ. But they couldn't know that the new factory represented the beginning of major changes in auto production, that the changes they saw in 1910 only hinted at the production revolution that would, over the next decade, transform everything about work in the auto industry.

In 1910, when the company began production at Highland Park, the plant consisted of three large factory buildings and one very large machine shop, all connected to form a manufacturing complex essentially under one roof.(See Figure 3.) The first four-story building measured 860 by 75 feet (the other two were slightly smaller), the single-story machine shops covered even more ground (176 by 799 feet). These buildings represented some of the largest in the city.

The new plant increased the volume of operations tenfold. The size of the plant significantly changed the experience of the workplace. The worker now entered a large, and to some, disorienting, factory as compared to the small, more personal Piquette Avenue shop. It was undoubtedly the largest building some of the workers had ever been in. The other large auto producers, Packard

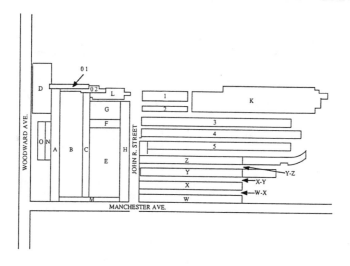

A. 4-story Factory Building	L. Gas Producer and	01. Coal Bunker &
B. 1-story Machine	Refrig Plant	Conveyor
C. 1-story Craneway	M. 4-story Factory Bldg	02. Unloading Dock
D. 5-story Power House	N. Garage	1-2 Heat Treat
E. 1-story Machine Shop	O. 4-story Admin Bldg	Building
F. 1-story Craneway	W,X,Y,Z. 6-story Factory	3-4 Forge
H. 4-story Factory Building	Building	5. Factory and
K. Foundry		Storeroom

Figure 3. Diagram of Highland Park Plant, including New Shop buildings; illustrates the different layout of New Shop and Old Shop. (Drawn from plans in Insurance Appraisal, 1919, FMC Archives, Edison Institute, Acc. 73, Box 1)

and Oldsmobile, also boasted of large factory buildings but most industrial buildings, were comparable to the Piquette Avenue shop rather than a large, newly-designed auto factory.

The most talked-about innovation was the large number of windows in the factory buildings. Those window-walls, as they came to be called, were made possible by the pioneering use of reinforced concrete.[10] Workers and visitors alike could also see what Henry Ford considered his showpiece—the power plant with its giant generators, contained behind a large expanse of glass and surrounded by a striking interior filled with shining brass and tile. Atop the powerhouse, between five smoke stacks, hung the huge FORD sign. William Vernor, the mechanical engineer for the power house, explained years later that only two stacks were needed, but Henry Ford wanted the sign and insisted it be hung from the power house stacks, so five stacks were built.[11] More important for workers, however, was the presence of the administration building, situated at the front of the plant complex, surrounded on three sides by an attractive lawn. The most significant feature of this building was not the elaborately furnished lobby with high carved ceilings, wide curving staircase, and marble floors, or the fact that it housed the only dining facility in the plant, but that it was a free-standing building, separate from the factory buildings. In Ford's first two factories, workers and management had enjoyed close working arrangements. This proximity reinforced the lack of rigid hierarchy. But by 1910, the industry had changed. In the new plant the highest level management was housed in a fancy, segregated building, reflecting a new relationship between management and worker. The new arrangement also reinforced the new relationship by diminishing, and in some cases eliminating, any common experience between the workers and management.

The relationship of the factory to the street would not have seemed unusual to the worker in 1910. Built right up to the sidewalks, the Highland Park plant was not surrounded by high fences and the kind of industrial no-man's land that would characterize later plants. Rather, the Highland Park plant was surrounded by houses and stores. Workers stepped right off the sidewalk through the plant gate. This proximity proved to be convenient for labor organizers. In 1913, when Industrial Workers of the World (IWW) members began efforts to organize the company, Ford workers listened to union speeches outside the main entrance during their lunch break. When police dispersed the crowd at the Ford gates, the unionists merely relocated down the block in an empty lot. This kind of easy access to the workforce would be impossible in later plants that deliberately constructed barriers to public entry.[12]

The dramatically different factory buildings were only the beginning of the changes that Ford workers experienced in the Highland Park plant. During the company's Highland Park years, 1910 to 1919, changes made in production revolutionized the auto industry. Ford engineers realized that to achieve higher production volume they had to change the way workers worked. In the Highland Park plant they began the process of limiting worker's freedom of movement around the factory and their discretion over tasks and timing.[13] The first step was to limit acceptable travel away from work stations. As auto production was increasingly rationalized, management would try to control every moment of the work day.

As production began in the new plant in 1910, engineers focused on division of labor and specialization of work. They began to introduce the changes that would lead directly to the system of assembly-line production known as Fordism. In 1910, the system begun at Piquette Avenue was expanded and workers were assigned to the assembly of a particular section of the car. David Hounshell has described in detail how some of the sub-assembly groups operated. At the engine assembly stations, workers labored at open workbenches with parts bins placed in the middle of the benches, each worker thus assembling one engine. Dashboard assembly stands, placed with just enough room to allow hand trucks to move between them, allowed the dashboard unit to hang in the individual stand while the worker attached the parts held in the bins at the botton of the stand. Similar operations characterized magneto, rear axle, and radiator assembly. Final assembly remained static in 1910. The car frame rested on wooden assembly horses, or stands, while assembly teams moved down the row of chassis, each gang performing a specific task or series of tasks.[14]

In addition to the assembling operations in the four-story buildings, the new plant housed a large and comprehensive machine shop located in the single-story space at the center of the plant. The machine shop was the heart of the factory. A jungle of leather belting and gears, it shaped the essential parts of the Model T. Except for the abundant light admitted through and the saw-tooth roof with its northern facing windows, the closely placed machines and the power belts would have made the machine shop a dark and gloomy part of the factory. An English invention, the saw-tooth roof took its name from the jagged profile which resembled the tooth edge of a saw blade. The special roof style was common on industrial buildings because it provided nonglaring northern light, important for detailed work like machining.

The machine shop contained sophisticated, highly specialized machines that allowed the work of skilled machinists to be done by less-skilled workers. No longer were all of the machine-shop workers necessarily experienced machinists. Ford would later declare that he would rather have operators with no experience at all. He wanted workers who had "nothing to unlearn" who would work just as they were told.[15] The machines were designed to do one operation over and over. The single operation assigned to a worker meant that he repeated one task for the entire day.[16] He had no reason to move around the shopfloor, much less the rest of the factory. Contrasted with the Piquette Avenue days when workers had enjoyed control over how they performed a task, Highland Park workers had little discretion over time and work procedures, and the little bit that remained in 1910 would soon be gone.

In the Piquette Avenue shop, the workers had always been able to vary their routine. They could take an unofficial break from their work by moving from one job to another or going for supplies. In the Highland Park plant, all that changed. The building was too large to have workers stocking their own stations and the new production system would not allow such independent movement.

As the production process changed, workers' movements were restricted within the factory, and as production volume increased dramatically every year, the factory managers had to figure out how to get the necessary parts and components to work stations, and how to get the completed sub-assemblies to the final assembly floor. This movement of parts and assemblies around the factory is called materials handling. From 1910 to 1917, it was one of the major concerns of the Ford Motor Company. In 1910, the materials handling system was relatively simple. Parts and materials delivered to the back of the factory were unloaded onto the docks and moved into the storage area by a crane, which could also move materials into the machine shop. From the storage area, unskilled workers, called pushers and shovers, would move parts and materials in barrels, boxes, and pallets to the appropriate areas of the factory, removing all need for machine operators and assemblers to move from their stations in search of supplies.

In order to understand the significance of materials handling, visualize the beehive of activity in the Ford factory. Production rates were doubling almost every year: 1909—13,840 cars; 1910—20,727; 1911—53,488; 1913—189,088. That is, a factory designed when the company produced roughly 70 cars per day, was turning out 630 cars per day four years later. The number of workers increased with the number of cars. In 1910, the Highland Park workforce numbered about 3,000 workers; by 1913 over 14,000 were on the payroll; in 1917, the number of employees had increased to about 36,000. In 1914, the workforce was divided into three shifts rather than two.[17] Nevertheless, the plant grew more and more crowded as, in addition to more workers, more machines were added, and the number of cars produced increased each year. Increased speed and volume of production, along with crowding on the shopfloor, exacerbated the job of materials transportation.

In 1910, most of the handling in the Highland Park plant was done by unskilled laborers. The original buildings contained only a few mechanical handling devices—two cranes, which moved materials as well as heavy equipment through the single-story machine shop, and a monorail, which moved along tracks placed around the entire first floor to deliver goods to areas beyond the craneways. (See Figure 4.) The machine-shop craneway formed the main distribution artery in the plant. In general, parts purchased from outside, as well as materials to be shaped at the factory, were unloaded from wagons and railroad cars directly into the craneway. Next, they were placed either into bins to be moved to a specific department, or directly onto the craneway floor for temporary storage. Materials and parts destined for longer storage traveled by elevator to the upper floors of the four-story buildings, and then down by elevator to the first-floor assembly area when needed.[18] Materials, parts, and sub-assemblies were constantly on the move in the factory. They traveled from railroad cars to loading dock, to departments, and then to individual work stations. All movement had to be timed and coordinated so that materials reached the appropriate place when needed, but not so early to cause a backup of supplies on the shopfloor. By 1912, Ford engineers had mapped out all movements of parts and sub-assemblies, correlating the movement with plant layout.[19]

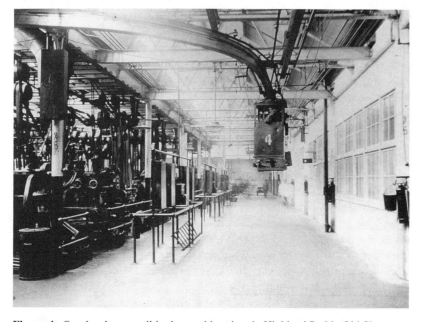

Figure 4. Overhead monorail in the machine shop in Highland Park's Old Shop: one of the few mechancial handling devices in the Old Shop. (FMC Archives, Edison Institute, Neg. 833-809)

Some might call Ford's system of materials handling an early version of the modern "just-in-time" inventory management. Indeed, just-in-time is based on the principle that parts are passed down the line rather than accumulated in large banks between operations.[20] The implementation of the just-in-time type system developed over several years at Ford. In 1912, one of the problems the company struggled with was the clutter and crowding of parts and partially-completed assemblies stacked around the factory floor. O.J. Abell described the condition in one of his *Iron Age* articles, saying that "the handling of materials with sufficient freedom has been possible only because the materials at the machines are limited to a maximum of two days' supply."[21]

At the end of 1913, Oscar Bornholt, one of Ford's engineers, wrote about the sequential arrangement of machines that eliminated trucking of parts after the first operation, "each operator lays the part down in such a place and manner as to allow the next operator to pick it up and perform his operation."[22] This was the beginning of just-in-time inventory control. It was not yet complete however. The company did not yet have a comparable policy for the buying of parts from outside. Rather, supplies were ordered in bulk, which then had to be stored around the factory until needed.

From the craneway, most materials were moved through the factory by the pushers and shovers, but the manual handling was slow and often unreliable because the pushers and shovers could not be supervised the way that stationary workers could. Ford felt that such workers were an unnecessary expense. They frustrated him because they were what he considered "nonproductive labor." Beyond Ford's personal frustration, the pushers and shovers contributed to the materials handling problems in the factory. Managers constantly worried about the timely delivery of parts and materials because of the slowness of the manual handling. If workers on the shopfloors ran out of parts, their idle time added up to a significant loss of money and delayed output. To help keep the system moving, a force of thirty-six clerks, called shortage chasers, "straighten[ed] out tangles of all description in the handling of materials, trac[ed] lost items which range from the smallest part to finished cars, and ferret[ed] out opportunities for improving conditions."[23] By 1914, expert observers of the auto industry concluded that materials handling and the movement of work in process, was "the principle problem of motor car cost reduction."[24] As late as 1934, a National Bureau of Economic Research study found that 40 percent of the auto industry's labor-saving changes came from improving the handling of materials.[25]

The design of the new Highland Park buildings helped to reduce the time it took to move materials around the factory. In 1910, most large factories still consisted of several separate buildings and some type of transportation system to move materials between them. In some, a simple horse-drawn wagon still moved supplies; others used a narrow-gauge rail system. At Highland Park neither was necessary because what would have been distinct buildings at other factories was essentially one large, integrated building. (See Figure 5.) This contiguity meant that, as the Model T was built, parts and sub-assemblies traveled shorter distances resulting in faster movement of materials and savings in time and labor. The cost of handling accounted for a small, but important, portion of the company's costs. In general, labor costs figured as the smallest cost category, with materials, machinery, and buildings demanding the greatest outlays. The pushers and shovers were the lowest paid of all workers, probably around $1.25 per day in 1910. Nevertheless, Henry Ford was known for his efforts to reduce costs anywhere he could, even if the savings amounted to only a few cents, and he was determined to eliminate as many of the unskilled, nonproductive workers as possible.[26]

Ford's new production system exacerbated the problems with handling. With the move away from group assembly, the *completed components* had to somehow travel *between* work stations, and then from the work stations to the final assembly area. With workers confined to their individual stations, the work had to be delivered to them; thus completed components and assemblies-in-process were constantly on the move from one work station to the next. A more logical shopfloor layout, which reduced the amount of necessary travel, and the flexibility of the more open interior spaces of the concrete buildings facilitated materials movement in the factory. By 1913, movement of materials around the factory had been greatly reduced. Arnold and Faurote wrote:

> it is of record that the old Piquette Avenue days, previous to the time when any attempts at Ford shops systemization were made and chaos reigned supreme, the first systematizer found that the Ford [engine] travelled no less than 4,000 feet in course of finishing, a distance now reduced to 334.[27]

To the Ford engineers, progress only served as an incentive to try more changes. In 1913, Ford engineers began experiments with the assembly line in the flywheel magneto department. The first assembly line was not the well-known moving conveyor belt but a simpler arrangement. The magneto assemblies rested on a waist-high steel rack beside which stood a row of workers, each with his simple operation to perform. When finished with his part of the job, each worker would slide the assembly along to the next worker much like one would slide a cafeteria tray. Later, assemblies were placed on moving conveyor belts to create the famous moving assembly line, which provided engineers the means to control production even more.[28]

Housing the Assembly Line: The New Shop

Between 1910 and 1913, monthly production of Model T's increased from 2,000 to over 15,000.[29] In general, the auto industry had more than tripled production during those years, and Ford was growing faster than other companies.[30] In the face of the dramatic rise in production volume and the related increase in numbers of workers, Ford began to think about another building campaign. The decision to expand the plant stemmed from the clear need for additional manufacturing space, but also from the realization that the design of the new buidings could be instrumental in advancing the new assembly-line system. More than just the simple addition of manufacturing space, the engineers intended the new buildings, by virtue of improved design and layout, to aid in the organization and control of production.

General dissatisfaction over the early buildings existed among shop managers. As one related to Arnold and Faurote:

"there was not floor space enough; machine tools and factory departments were not placed as the management knew they should be, and . . . truckers, pushers, and draggers engaged in needless handlings of materials and works in progress."[31]

This, in sum, was the problem with all factory buildings by 1914. Though sufficient space would always be a concern, materials handling emerged as a new priority. Thus smooth movement of workers and materials through the plant became increasingly important to automobile manufacturing, and a major concern in the design of new buildings.

The experiments with the assembly line in 1913 presaged the company's future, for with the moving assembly line came the realization that *almost all movement of parts and materials through the factory could be more efficient.* The 1913 experiments with the sliding assembly line for the magneto coil had inspired Ford and his engineers to push the idea further; if an assembly line worked so well in one department, why not in them all? Within a year all departments had been reorganized according to the assembly line principle; soon they would all be mechanized.[32] Then, with the success of the moving assembly line, Ford engineers reasoned, why not mechanize as much of the production process as possible? The mechanization of materials handling, the logical next step, would prove to be one of the most important innovations of the company's New Shop era, for the moving assembly line and mechanized handling gave management unprecedented control over the work process and work pace. Fordism was emerging.

By 1914, workers were urged to work faster; the company employed supervisors called pushers (not the materials handlers) to "push" the workers to work faster. Most workers did not like the transformation of work in the automobile factory. By 1914, the jobs of most Ford workers bore little resemblance to what they had been just five years earlier. Workers registered their dissatisfaction with the changes by quitting. The Ford Motor Company, like all auto makers in Detroit, suffered a high turnover rate. At Ford, turnover was 370 percent in 1913 as workers left in search of easier, more satisfying, or better paying work. Henry Ford addressed the problem in 1914 when he announced he would pay five dollars a day to qualified workers.[33] Though the turnover was not eliminated, fewer workers had to be hired each subsequent year to fulfill production demands.[34] Nevertheless, workers did not find the new work satisfying and tended to work for the Ford Motor Company for shorter lengths of time. The average work record for workers in the company's employ between 1910 and 1912 was 57 months. That record decreased between 1913 and 1914 to 28 months. Workers employed between 1915 and 1916 stayed with the company for an average of only 6 months.[35]

In the new Ford system, managers sought to make workers machine-like as many operations were routinized and others eliminated. Even as early as 1912, job restructuring sought an "exceptionally specialized division of labor [to bring] the human element into condition of performing automatically with machine-like regularity and speed."[36] A good example of these changes appears in Arnold and Faurote's description of the piston and rod assembly. Under the old method fourteen men worked on one bench, each completing all six of the operations required in about three minutes:

1. drive out pin with special hammer,
2. oil pin by dipping end in box of oil,
3. slip pin in rod-eye,
4. turn pin to take screw,
5. turn in pinch screw,
6. tighten screw.

Under the new regimen, the work was divided and placed on a slide bench with three men on each side of the bench. The first two drove out the pin, oiled pin, and placed in piston; the second two placed the rod in the piston, passed the pin through the rod and piston, and turned the screw; the third pair tightened the screw with a wrench and placed and spread the cotter pin. The new process took thirty seconds. The labor savings was 84 percent.

In the ideal factory, as one consulting engineer explained about efficiency work in general in 1915, "whatever they may be outside the factory, [workers] are while in the factory simply animate machines . . . [trained] to do their work with all the precision of the most marvelous engine."[37] In such a factory, workers had no choice but to perform their jobs with a set of movements prescribed by machines and work conditions; little discretion over time or work process remained.

If the workers were going to work like machines, Ford engineers concluded that the entire factory had to work like a machine, that the success of assembly-line production depended on efficient supply of materials and parts to work stations on the line. The effectiveness of the line would be eroded by the continuation of the old handling methods. Though hardly ignored before that time, materials handling had not received the kind of attention given specialized machines and interchangeability. By 1913, the engineers turned their attention to mechanized handling and it, in turn, provided the final piece of Fordism. The new handling system meant that problems of supplying individual work stations would be significantly reduced. Materials and supplies would reach work stations at regular intervals, eliminating idle time while workers waited for their station to be restocked. The new system would also eliminate the problem of stock piled around work stations, and thereby clear up floor space for additional machines. Finally, the number of pushers and draggers, who so annoyed Ford, would be reduced because they no longer consituted the major materials handling system.[38]

Shortly after the introducton of the assembly line technique in 1913, Ford engineers, along with architect Albert Kahn, began work on plans for a new addition to the plant. The engineers, especially Edward Gray, worked more closely with Kahn than they had in designing the earlier building. To distinguish between the new and old sections, Ford personnel at that time began to call them the New Shop and the Old Shop. The Old Shop referred to buildings built between 1910 and 1914 and the New Shop to buildings built after 1914. In a 1915 report William Knudsen, the head of the assembly department, indicated that the new buildings had been more carefully planned than the ones built in 1910, and that planning for shopfloor layout went along with planning the buildings. The new buildings were planned with the production process and the necessary machines in mind. In the new buildings, "all mechanical equipment was arranged for in the contract," in order to lower the cost of the building, reported Knudsen.[39] In the first buildings, changes in equipment had required the removal of walls, which had significantly added to the building and maintenance costs.

Completed in 1914, the first two six-story buildings of the New Shop resembled the Old Shop buildings in external appearance and construction style—they were long and narrow and made of reinforced concrete faced with brick.[40] However, the new buildings included a giant six-story craneway built between two buildings, running the entire 840 foot length of the buildings.

(See Figure 5.) Craneways had certainly been used by other manufacturing concerns, but the Ford Motor Company used its craneway in a new way—to aid in developing the rational factory. The craneway became the heart of the New Shop and did much to solve Ford's materials handling problems.

Figure 5. Craneway in Building W, Highland Park's New Shop, the craneway was the life line of the assembly-line system in the New Shop. (Courtesy of Kahn Associates, Detroit, Michigan)

Railroad tracks laid in the craneway allowed supply trains to pull right into the factory. Two five-ton cranes moved along the length of the craneway, lifting materials from the railroad cars to any one of almost two hundred cantilevered platforms distributed over the six floors. Workers then transported materials to the appropriate work stations with the old-fashioned pushcarts. But because the platforms were so numerous, no work station was very far from the incoming raw materials. This proximity significantly reduced the amount of transportation around the shopfloor.

To make the best use of the cranes, M. L. Weismyer and other layout engineers, reorganized the sequence of production operations. Heavy materials for foundry and machining were raised to the top floor;[41] work then proceeded to lower floors "in natural course of operations, until it reached final assembly on the ground floor."[42] By reducing movement around the factory, the new design restricted even more workers to their assigned stations.

Fordism in the New Shop

In the New Shop, Ford's system was completed. Ford could claim the highest level of rationalization realized by any manufacturer of heavy metal goods at that time. Fordism consisted of the manufacture of a single, standard model; the division and simplification of work through the use of specialized machines; and a mechanized materials handling system which included the moving assembly line. The first two features of the system had been successfully introduced between 1908 and 1914. In the New Shop, those innovations were integrated with mechanized handling and improved shopfloor layout.

The most dramatic innovation in the rationalization of materials handling was the moving line, which had already been introduced in the Old Shop. Now, timing and coordination of all movement became the single most important management task. Without improved timing and coordination, the potential speed of the moving line would be held back. Consequently, engineers regarded layout and handling as more important in the New Shop than in most earlier factories. Speed became a production priority, and use of time a predominant concern of Henry Ford and his engineers. Workers were constantly prodded to use time well. A typical message in *The Ford Man*, the company paper, reminded them that:

> "Time is the Most Valuable Thing in the World" Shorten the time required to perform an operation. To save one minute in each hour worked means a saving of 1.6% in the wage bill. True efficiency means making every *Minute* count.[43]

The changes in shop organization had the desired result. In 1915, O.J. Abell wrote that Ford production had increased 15 percent and that the company had reduced its labor force by nearly 2,000.[44] Two years later an article in *Automobile Topics* reported that automobile output had been doubled in many plants by rearranging the shopfloor and providing an adequate supply of materials "properly timed in their arrival at the machines."[45] In addition to the reorganized shop, an increase in the number of foremen helped increase productivity. Even though overall number of workers declined, the ratio of foremen to workers increased from one foreman to 53 workers in 1914 to one foreman to 15 workers in 1917.[46]

The New Shop was organized around a *linear system* of handling and production. The long, narrow, side-by-side buildings of the New Shop accomodated the use of cranes as the basis of the new handling system and extended the use of the assembly line.

Vital to efficient production, layout was constrained by the line shafts that distributed mechanical power throughout the plant. Even as late as 1918, few machines ran on individual motors. Usually medium-sized electric engines provided power for a bank of machines, and as one engineer said, "you had to lay your departments out to utilize the line shaft overhead that drives the machine."[47] The shafts and belts not only made layout difficult, they also created safety problems, and generally interfered with movement through the shopfloor.

Nevertheless, New Shop layout significantly improved materials transportation throughout. Continuing Old Shop practice, engineers placed machines in the new shop as close together as possible to minimize necessary transportation between machines. But the timing demands of the moving line also required innovations in materials handling to meet timing needs. Without a ready supply of parts, the line, moving at a set speed, could not function efficiently. Mechanized materials handling became the key to assuring Fordism's success. The old manual methods of moving parts, materials, and assemblies in process created so many bottle-necks that the moving line could not live up to its capabilities. Because it depended on human beings instead of machines, the older method of materials transportation was harder to control than the later mechanized system. The old system used a large number of workers, at one time as high as 1,600, whose jobs could now be eliminated.

The craneways helped to reduce the amount of slow and troublesome carrying of materials around the factory. However, much of the remaining horizontal transportation—the movement across factory floors as contrasted to vertical movement from one floor to another—still depended on the pushers and shovers to deliver parts and materials to the appropriate work stations. Under the new system some manual handling remained, but it now supplemented the mechanical.

In addition to the cranes, the New Shop made full use of gravity slides, conveyors, and rollways, which were customized for each job.[48] They varied in shape, length, width, and function. A slide might carry a finished piece just a few feet to the inspector or it might be twenty feet long and hold the work of several workers. Some slides carried work from one worker to another and some moved work to the next work area, sometimes to the next floor. (See Figure 6.) For example, in the machine shop, conveyors and carriers transferred parts from one operation to the next so that pieces barely touched the

Figure 6. Model T body on wooden slide, demonstrating one of the many uses of slides in the Highland Park factory. (FMC Archives, Edison Institute, Neg. 833-28371)

floor and never accumulated in receptacles as with earlier practice. This resulted in a dramatic reduction of stock in transit, and eliminated the piles of partly finished material at each station.[49]

Ford engineers believed that "conveyors should be installed wherever they will displace enough hand labor to pay for the investment."[50] The in-house publication *Ford Industries* later reported that "the day the first big conveyor went into operation seventy men were released by the transportation department [materials handling] for other work."[51] Other companies, less convinced of the utility of conveyors, argued that "in many cases material can be conveyed in crates or boxes on trucks and elevators with great economy." "In general," the critics argued, "the efficiency of conveyors is apt to be overstated."[52] The critics were proven wrong. Company after company adopted conveyors, and production in most auto factories underwent a transformation similar to that in the Ford Motor Company. The companies that continued to use the older manual system could do so because they were small-scale producers.

In 1914, with the first buildings of the New Shop completed, Ford engineers knew that the moving conveyor would become one of the most important time-saving tools in the factory. A decade later, a Ford spokesman wrote that "conveyors on which assembly or other work is done are carefully timed to insure an even output and thus act as a governor on the rate of production . . . To have them move too slowly is sheer waste." He further explained that "correct timing conserves the energy of the men by holding them to a uniform pace without allowing them to exceed it [and] results in a better and more uniform quality of workmanship."

The new complex of conveyors also helped to solve a managerial problem of increasing importance—the ability to predict production output and its cost. The same Ford spokesman explained that the conveyors enabled the company to determine with accuracy the number of hours of labor that go into each car and every part. This permitted the factory to figure its production requirements months in advance, and to regulate the flow of raw materials through the plant in such a manner that there was neither a shortage nor a surplus.[53]

Mechanization of handling, like other steps toward rationalization, sped production and increased management's control over work. But mechanization of handling differed from mechanization of other jobs. The mechanization of a skilled machinist's job created an entirely new job that an unskilled worker with no experience could perform. The job became standardized and very controllable. Mechanizing handling eliminated many jobs, but the remaining transport jobs were unchanged. Those jobs continued to be difficult to standardize and control. Though materials handling was an unskilled job, its mechanization and standardization continued to be important to the success of Fordism in the 1920s.

The River Rouge Plant and Industrial Control

Construction at the thousand-acre site of the River Rouge plant began in 1917 with the erection of huge bins for raw materials storage and traveling bridge cranes that loaded and unloaded the bins. Work on the first blast furnace also began in 1917. Construction on the materials processing facilities stopped in 1918, when the B Building was started and Eagle boat production for World War I had priority. After the war, the building campaign resumed; it continued until the Great Depression.

In 1922 industrial journalist John Van Deventer wrote:

> The experienced observer [sees each Rouge operation as] *part of a huge machine*—he sees each unit as a carefully designed gear which meshes with other gears and operates in synchronism with them, the whole forming one huge, perfectly-timed, smoothly operating industrial machine of almost unbelievable efficiency.[54]

Indeed, Ford and his engineers believed that the River Rouge plant would be the perfect industrial machine. It would, they hoped, overcome the limitations of the Highland Park plant, particularly the inconvenient transportation facilities and lack of space for expansion. Highland Park, though as modern and efficient as any factory of its period, simply could not satisfy Ford's plans for expansion.

The designers of the Rouge set out to build a new kind of industrial plant. The multiple story buildings of earlier plants, including Highland Park, had been arranged with adjoining walls, or grouped around a central yard. The layout at the Rouge resembled neither of those models. To the outsider the Rouge must have looked like an almost random placement of huge buildings. (See Figure 7.) The Highland Park buildings had been placed contiguously to save time and expense of handling. That arrangement, however, had created another problem—there was no easy way to expand departments. With buildings so tightly arranged, each department had to be carefully planned, and if more machines or operations were added, departments had to be moved to new locations. Thus expansion became a very time consuming and expensive operation. By organizing the Rouge as distinctly separate buildings, Ford's engineers assured the economy and potential of future growth, growth they anticipated with confidence. An editor of *Iron Age* wrote in 1918 that "[at the Rouge] practically all construction is being laid out with a view of 100% expansion when necessary."[55] The company also shifted to single-story buildings. By 1922, single-story plants had become at least an unofficial company policy. In responding to an inquiry about plant design E.G. Liebold, Henry

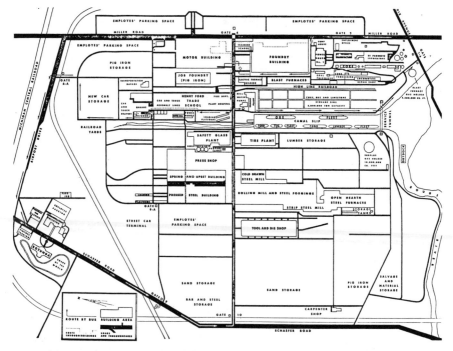

Figure 7. Diagram of the River Rouge plant in 1941, showing dramatically different organization of the plant that resulted from the change in production style and the change in scope of company operations. (FMC Archives, Edision Institute, Neg 75271)

Ford's secretary, wrote "we find that a one-story building for factory purposes with saw-tooth construction is about the most efficient and obviates elevator service and transferring materials up and down."[56]

The diffuse plant layout and single-story buildings were acceptable to the efficiency-minded company only because of the constantly improved system of materials handling. Materials handling was developed to new heights at the Rouge. Every department was equipped with mechanical handling devices and every shop and building connected by a network of overhead monorails and conveyors.[57] According to John Van Deventer, the development of the Rouge's "integrated manufacturing" depended largely on transportation. Integrated manufacturing, he wrote, "ushers in a new era of mechanical handling, announc[ing] the beginning of the exit from industry of manual lifting and shop pedestrianism, and sounds the death knoll of the wheelbarrow and shovel."[58] The continuous flow that characterized the system eliminated "any possibility of loafing or soldiering on the job when each operator is faced with the necessity of keeping up with the procession or else seeing his stock piled up to a point where it becomes distinctly noticeable by the immediate management."[59]

Process and transportation provided the key to understanding operations at the Rouge. Engineers had already improved individual production machines such that the cost of fabrication became a small part of the total cost of production. "The center of thought in the modern plant is therefore no longer the individual machine but the process," wrote Van Deventer. "The biggest cost savings of today and tomorrow are likely to come from moving rather than from making. This is the decade of mechanical transportation."[60]

Engineers at the Rouge designed many different types of materials handling equipment, most of them essentially expansions on ideas first developed at Highland Park. The moving conveyors, cranes, monorails, railroads of the earlier plant persisted, and were joined by overhead conveyors and other new handling technologies. The moving conveyor continued to be a prominent feature of the company's operation. As it was improved and extended to more departments, it continued to speed production and eliminate unskilled jobs just as it had at Highland Park. In a 1929 letter to Charles Sorensen, Ford's head of production, one engineer described the most recent cuts:

> I cabled you today, stating that we had eliminated over 400 men in the B Building, with the installation of various conveyor systems throughout the different departments. In the torque tube department, the conveyor from the department to the shipping dock, has been completed and is in operation, eliminating 20 men for handling stock. The brake plate conveyor from this department to the loading dock completed, eliminating 80 men. The differential gear case forging balcony and conveyor for same from this department to the dock, has been completed and in operation, eliminating 20 men . . . In the steel mill, the front radius rod conveyor has been completed and is in operation, eliminating 20 men. The cold heading conveyor for handling cold heading wire and finished parts will be put in operation Monday, 40 men will be eliminated.[61]

At the Rouge, engineers succeeded in almost eliminating hand trucking. Although Barclay lists it as one of the many methods still in use as late as 1936, hand trucking played only a small role by then.[62] The transportation around the shopfloor, previously done by the hand trucks, was transferred to standard full-size, gas-powered trucks. On the "upper floors of the B building one sees a truck loaded with tools, jigs, fixtures, or supplies, running along the broad aisles, stopping at certain points to unload goods and at others to pick up materials," wrote Van Deventer as he compared the aisles to streets "in a small but busy town."[63]

Overhead conveyors, made possible in the Rouge after the elimination of belting, played the greatest role in displacing hand trucking and improving reliability of handling and speed of production. They maintained a constant supply of parts for the worker, eliminating the necessity of storing parts at each work station and more importantly, eliminating the trucking of parts. At the Rouge, individual motors provided the power to most machines. By eliminating belting, pulleys, and overhead shafting, plant engineers opened the space above the machines, allowing for the installation of overhead conveyors.

Engineers at the Rouge also designed a vast network of railroad tracks and roads and the "unusual high line" that served as a major transport system throughout the plant. The railroad system, which utilized l05 miles of track within the the plant, moved heavy materials between storage bins and buildings. The High Line was a forty-foot high concrete structure resembling a viaduct, carrying as many as five railroad tracks. Van Deventer called it the "backbone of the plant."[64] According to the editor of *Mill and Factory*, "the new River Rouge plant includes the largest completely mechanized installation of handling equipment ever installed in any industrial enterprise."[65]

The High Line was a unique materials handling technology. Similar to the craneways of the Highland Park plant, it provided semi-automatic delivery of parts and materials to several buildings. Like the craneways, it handled the heavy materials and transported raw materials to and from the huge storage bins. To that end, the line was equipped with hoppers and gravity unloading devices which were moved by a remote control system.

In l931 Edsel Ford commissioned the Mexican artist, Diego Rivera, to paint murals with an industrial theme in the courtyard of the Detroit Institute of Art. The Rouge plant fascinated Rivera and he chose it as the subject for his murals. Rivera considered modern factories important as architecture and as cultural symbols. He wrote that "in all the constructions of man's past— pyramids, Roman roads and aquaducts, cathedrals and palaces, there is nothing to equal these [factories]."[67]

Rivera believed in the importance of the factory in modern life, elevating industrial buildings, machine design, and engineering higher than all other historical accomplishments. But he saw the worker as the center of, and the power behind industry. In focusing on people in the factory, Rivera's murals suggest a negative side of factory life. He depicts the machines as larger than life, as dominating the men around them and dictating the pace of work. The activity in the mural is almost too much for the viewer to comprehend. Rivera's Rouge is frenetic, reminding the observer of the nervous condition called Forditis suffered by workers in the early days of the assembly line.

It was fitting that the River Rouge plant become the subject of important works of art. The Rouge was the culmination of three decades of experimentation with factory planning and design. It represented the direction of modern industry, both in building style and production methods. Above all, it reflected the growing recognition of factory design as a means to facilitate the perfection of assembly-line production, and as a way to better manage workers.

The rational factory created by Ford's engineers had a profound impact on the worker. It heralded the stage in industrialization at which the experience of work in the factory had no referents to life outside the factory. The rational factory—special purpose machines, division of labor, the moving assembly line, and mechanized handling—was indeed a mechanical wonder that left the worker with few authorized freedoms.

Edsforth and Asher (with Boryczka),
"The Speedup. . .," *Autowork*, eds.
Ronald Edsforth and Robert Asher
(1995)

THE SPEEDUP:
THE FOCAL POINT OF WORKERS' GRIEVANCES,
1919–1941

....

Ronald Edsforth and Robert Asher
with the assistance of Raymond Boryczka

The speedup was built into the structure of mass production work in the American automobile industry. Throughout the 1920s and the Great Depression, the speedup created an environment in which auto workers experienced an almost continuous stream of implicit, or explicit, threats to their incomes and job security. By the mid-1930s, as Sidney Fine demonstrated in his study of the epochal General Motors sit-down strike, this deeply coercive work environment inspired a critical mass of workers to fight to organize the United Automobile Workers union (UAW).[1] In recent years, many radical critics of the UAW have pointed out that the union never actually won for workers the right to control completely the intensity of their labor. This fact cannot be denied, but it does not mean that the union failed to reform the speedup system. Through collective bargaining, which began at General Motors and Chrysler in 1937 and at Ford in 1941, the UAW forced the management of the Big Three to pay straight hourly wages plus an overtime premium, to guarantee workers' seniority, to provide relief time for rest and bathroom breaks, and to supply extra relief workers when absenteeism or temporary increases in labor intensity overstressed workers. UAW contracts also permitted workers' representatives to review time-study calculations, prohibited alterations in production standards when a job was substantially changed, and established a grievance procedure to ensure workers a voice in the resolution of disputes. Without question, the UAW transformed the structure of auto work in ways that greatly improved workers' lives.

This chapter reviews the speedup and the UAW's initial response to it. A brief overview of the development of mass production work and the industry's labor force is followed by a long discussion of the speedup, its devastating physical and psychological effect on auto workers between 1929 and

1936, and the workers' efforts to combat the speedup without the assistance of a strong union organization. Resistance to the speedup in the years 1937–1941, as the UAW gained a foothold, is analyzed to reveal the dramatic impact of unionization on auto work.

Fordism

As chapter 2 demonstrated, between 1908 and 1916 the Ford Motor Company in Detroit and the Buick Motor Company in Flint, pioneered the use of chutes, conveyor belts, and assembly lines to improve materials flow in automotive production.[2] During these years, new single-purpose machines were also continually developed by industry engineers to increase output. These technologies, and Henry Ford's unprecedented commitment to mass production, led Ford managers to intensify greatly the division of labor in their factories. New job categories in parts production and in the component assembly and final assembly shops multiplied, even as individual tasks were simplified; and as demand for new vehicles continued to soar, tens of thousands of new workers were hired into the industry.[3]

Although a few low-volume, quality car makers did not embrace the Ford Motor Company's widely-publicized new methods, the industry's other large producers were forced to follow Ford's lead to stay competitive.[4] The "Fordist" transformation of automotive production dramatically changed the character of most auto work. Fordism, to use David Gartman's words, "resulted in a catastrophic decline in the overall skill of the factory labor force." Semi-skilled operators of special purpose machines replaced skilled machinists who had operated general purpose lathes, drill presses, grinders, and milling machines. Demand for skilled painters and varnishers, as well as for unskilled workers who did common physical labor, was also greatly reduced. And some traditional vehicle-building jobs, like those of blacksmiths and skilled woodworkers, were virtually eliminated by the 1930s.[6]

During the long auto boom, the greatest job growth came in semi-skilled machine tender and assembly line positions. As early as 1925, up to 40 percent of auto workers were machine operators, while assembly line workers accounted for another 15 percent of the payrolls. In 1925, 5 percent of the industry's workers were classified as semi-skilled inspectors, while only 12 percent worked as laborers, and fewer than 10 percent held skilled jobs as machinists and tool and die makers.[7]

In the mid-to-late 1920s, as the development of new production technology and new automobile technology slowed, General Motors displaced Ford as the industry leader. GM's market strategy was developed by company president Alfred P. Sloan Jr., and is sometimes referred to as "Sloanism," or more disparagingly as "planned obsolescence." It relied on producing multiple lines of cars which offered consumers a choice of models, engines, "sculptured" bodies, and a variety of colors. In addition, GM began to frequently redesign their Chevrolets, Oaklands, Buicks, Oldsmobiles, and Cadillacs, although the annual model change was not regularized until the mid-1930s.[8]

Sloan's strategy of planned obsolescence established a new trend in the automobile marketplace, and it also somewhat altered the composition of automobile industry labor force. Though the basic structure and organization of the Fordist factory remained intact, "flexible mass production" began to emerge under the direction of William Knudsen, a Ford engineer who was hired by GM's Sloan in 1923 to plan production for Chevrolet. Knudsen's plans called for the extensive use of metalworking machines with built-in flexibility, instead of the single-purpose machinery that Ford had installed at the Rouge. Such machines were necessary to meet the varied requirements of Sloan's new market strategy. These machines also required somewhat higher skill levels of their operators, as well as more frequent attention by set-up, maintenance, and repair workers. Although flexible mass production could never be as cost-effective as the singleminded mass production of one product like Ford's Model T, the repeat car buyers, who dominated the market after 1925, seemed eager to pay the additional price premium for General Motor's stylish new cars.[9]

As the choice of body styles and colors offered to consumers increased, and closed cars replaced open cars, vehicle body-making experienced its own Fordist revolution. General Motors and Dodge/Chrysler bought up and expanded existing body-making enterprises, while the big independents, Briggs and Murray, also enlarged and modernized their operations. High volume production was attained by mechanizing materials movement, simplifying jobs, and introducing new machines like paint sprayers and automatic welders. Large numbers of semi-skilled press operators, spot welders, metal finishers, sanders, spray painters, lacquer rubbers, polishers, buffers, and trimmers replaced highly skilled body-makers, some of whom had learned their trade in the horse-drawn coach and carriage industry.[10]

On the whole, flexible mass production represented a significant modification of Fordism. Rather than forcing more de-skilling, it actually increased the significance of some skilled workers. By the end of the 1930s, vital maintenance and repair workers made up nearly 10 percent of the industry's labor force. In addition, toolmakers, die setters, and die sinkers comprised nearly 5 percent of all auto workers, nearly twice their ratio in the 1925 workforce.[11]

Although wage differentials between skilled workers and their less skilled co-workers decreased over time, skilled auto workers did have many

of the characteristics of an "aristocracy of labor." Since they were in relatively short supply, and since they were always needed, *especially during retooling and model changes* when the majority of workers were laid off, most
skilled auto workers earned $2,500 to $3,000 per year during the late 1920s.
By comparison, even the best paid semi-skilled workers, such as metal finishers and spray painters, seldom took home more than $2,000 a year. And in
the same years, the average annual wage for auto workers fluctuated between
$1,600 and $1,700.[12] In addition to higher pay and greater job security, skilled
auto workers also had greater freedom to move around the factory and work
at their own pace. Most importantly, skilled workers were paid to think, to
solve problems, and define the specific tasks which they had to accomplish.
As Steve Babson has noted, the skilled worker did "not need to be told how
to do a job, [and] he positively resented it when white-collar supervision med-
dled in his work."[13]

A Diverse Labor Force

Automobile manufacturing became the nation's largest industry in the two
decades before the Great Depression. The total number of wage earners in the
motor vehicle industry, including its body and parts plants, increased from
less than 76,000 in 1909 to over 447,000 in 1929. Who were all these new
workers? "They came from Mississippi and Arkansas," Joyce Shaw Peterson
has written,

> from Poland and Italy, from Indiana and West Virginia, and from the heart
> of Detroit itself. They were white, black, foreign, native, young, old, male,
> and female. But in the main, they were young and male [and overwhelm-
> ingly white], limited in industrial skills, and eager for a good paying job.[14]

The larger automobile companies and employers' federations like the
Employers Association of Detroit (EAD) advertised widely in the Midwest
and the South for workers. Up to 1919, most job growth occurred in the big
companies, and especially in their assembly plants; overall employment in
these capital intensive facilities actually declined between 1923 and 1929.
During the 1920s, most new automotive jobs were created in the industry's
big body-making plants and in the much smaller parts-making factories where
production remained more labor intensive.[15]

   The automobile industry's growth shifted the industrial center of the
nation to the Midwest, encouraging thousands of young Americans to migrate
from rural areas to the cities of the Great Lakes and upper Mississippi River

basins. Widely held assumptions about gender, race, and ethnicity combined to shape the distribution of workers in the industry. Young white men from the Midwest predominated in the early years of the automobile boom, but many young women also sought employment in the industry after 1908. Some women reportedly even disguised themselves as men to get the famous five dollar a day jobs at Ford before the company openly admitted them to the program in 1916.[16] During the 1920s, women made up about 7 percent of the automotive workforce. Over the complaints of many male workers, in the mid-1930s the industry hired additional women in an effort to cut labor costs. Despite some improvements initiated by the National Recovery Administration's code authority, in 1934 86 percent of female auto workers remained concentrated in the industry's lowest wage category (earning less than 60 cents per hour) compared with just 23 percent of male auto workers. On average, women were paid just two-thirds of what men were paid.[17]

By raising minimum wages, the UAW somewhat narrowed the sex-based wage differential after 1937. The average wage of women working in body-making and assembly plants was 74 percent of the men's average wage in 1940; in parts-making factories women averaged 70 percent of male wages.[18] By 1940, there were over 30,000 female auto workers, or nearly 11 percent of the industry's workers. Most of these women actually posed no threat to male jobs since gender stereotyping, established early in the automobile boom, continued to shape hiring practices. Before World War II, women were excluded from foundries, engine-making, and large parts (transmission, axle, wheel, etc.) manufacturing; and only a handful were hired into the big assembly plants. Instead, female auto workers were heavily concentrated in body-making and small parts factories in jobs that paid less than "men's work." In the body plants, they worked as sewing machine operators, trim bench hands, assemblers and trimmers, and in factories like Flint's AC Sparkplug, they were used extensively in operations that required what one trade publication described as the "integration of small parts into small, precision assemblies; . . . [and] dexterity and exceptional skill on high repetitive tasks."[19]

By the mid-1920s, large numbers of white Southerners and significant numbers of black Southerners were joining the continuing stream of rural Americans who were finding work in automobile and automotive parts factories. However, the industry was not racially integrated. With the exception of Ford, which employed over half the black workers in the industry in the mid-1920s, the big automobile companies did not recruit black workers. In fact, as late as 1937, General Motors only employed 2,800 black workers in all of its Michigan factories. These workers were assigned the lowest paying jobs, such as sweepers and janitors, or the most hazardous work in the blast furnaces,

foundries, and paint shops. Ford management permitted some black workers
to take jobs at higher levels on the occupational ladder, but only at its Rouge
plant in Dearborn. Other Ford factories remained as segregated as the rest of
the industry.[20]

Ethnic stereotyping also shaped the work roles of the immigrants, heavily concentrated in Detroit, who formed a large part of the growing automotive
labor force. At the end of the long boom in 1930, foreign-born whites made
up just over 30 percent of national automobile industry labor force, but 43
percent of Detroit's auto workers. Poles, Russians and other Slavs,
Hungarians, and Italians formed the largest groups of foreign-born auto workers. Workers from these immigrant groups usually found themselves assigned
to less skilled, lower-paying jobs as laborers, machine operators, and assemblers. In 1920, after the heaviest influx of immigrants and first generation
Americans into the industry, nearly three-quarters of all common laborers,
and over half of all machine operatives, were either foreign-born or the children of immigrant parents. Throughout the 1920s and beyond, the best paying
semi-skilled jobs, and the opportunity to move into the skilled trades were
generally reserved for native-born whites and skilled immigrants from
Canada and northwest Europe who shared a common ethnic heritage with the
industry's engineers and managers.[21]

A Systematic Speedup

No matter what their race, ethnicity, or gender, automobile workers found
themselves confronting similar problems: they labored in huge, noisy factories and they were "driven" by managers who cared far more about increasing production than about the welfare of workers as individuals. Between
1935 and 1941, deeply felt resentments about what these workers called "the
speedup" or "the stretch out" brought diverse groups of auto workers together in the successful organizing drives of the United Automobile Workers'
union (UAW). Investigators from the National Recovery Administration who
interviewed auto workers in closed sessions all across the country in 1934
reported,

> Everywhere workers indicated that they were being forced to work harder
> and harder, to put out more and more products in the same amount of time
> with less workers doing the job. There was a tendency to excuse the auto-
> mobile manufacturer for a lack of steady work . . . but when it comes to
> increasing their work loads they are vigorous in denouncing management as
> slave drivers, and worse. If there is any one cause for conflagration in the
> Automobile Industry, it is this one.[22]

Without a doubt, the speedup was the focal point of auto workers' grievances in the 1930s; but it was neither an isolated nor a new problem. Widespread worker complaints about unfair time studies, uncertain pay, excessive hours, increasingly dangerous conditions, lack of seniority, and perhaps most importantly, the lack of a voice with which to respond to authoritarian management, were not a laundry list of discrete grievances. Instead, each of these complaints described a different aspect of the speedup's devastating impact on workers' lives. Moreover, the speedup, and workers' problems with it, did not originate with the Great Depression. Nevertheless, more than any other problem, the speedup was the management practice that united auto workers in their desire to unionize to obtain protection against the pernicious authority of the auto companies. The UAW's attempt to end, or even modify, the speedup after 1935 was nothing less than an attempt to reform the basic structure of work, and to change the relations of production, that had prevailed during the preceding quarter century of auto making.

The speedup was an intrinsic part of Fordist auto work. It originated when Fordism was born. Up to 1929, soaring demand for cars had been the driving force behind the development of the industry's new mass production methods and the growth of its massive blue-collar labor force. Fordist techniques and technology had of course increased output per worker; but production managers also felt compelled to find other ways to raise worker efficiency. Between 1910 and 1920, as company executives pressed factory management to meet continually rising demand, most shopfloor supervisors became obsessed with accelerating the pace of auto work. Alfred P. Sloan Jr., who moved from the Hyatt Roller Bearing Company to United Motors to the presidency of General Motors in this period, vividly recalled the origins of the speedup in his first autobiography, *Adventures of a White Collar Man.*

> Speed! Do what you are doing but do it faster. Double your capacity. Quadruple it. Double it again. At times it seemed like madness. Yet people clamored for the cars. There were never enough automobiles to meet the demand. The pressure on the production men was desperate.[23]

As Sloan's recollection implies, industry executives established a preference for increasing work loads over hiring additional workers at the outset of the automobile boom. The initial impulse for the institutionalizing the speedup came from top management, but lower level plant managers and department supervisors were actually responsible for devising practical methods to increase output per worker without raising wages.

In the oligopolistic market that emerged in the mid-1920s, the speedup permitted auto companies to increase profit margins by reducing their wage costs per unit while holding prices steady. This strategy worked particularly well in the Big Three—Ford, General Motors, and Chrysler—assembly plants, but was less successful in the automotive parts industry which had a higher percentage of skilled workers and more price competition. (See Table 1.) Also, for a variety of reasons, including the later implementation of Fordist methods, workers in the industry's body plants were still resisting the speedup before Great Depression began.

By the end of the automobile boom, plant managers and department supervisors at the major car companies had achieved significant increases in labor productivity. Of course, new plant designs, new machinery, and the reorganization of production processes all contributed greatly to improved productivity. But increased worker effort also added to gains in labor productivity. Ford management took great pains to hide this fact from the thousands of schoolchildren and tourists who visited the Rouge plant each year. "You see the line over there," a worker explained to Robert Dunn in 1925,

> It moves slow. That is the line the visitors go by. If it is going fast and visitors come in they will slow it down as sure as hell. I once worked on that line myself and visitors would come by and they would say, "Why these men aren't working hard."[24]

During the 1920s, increased work effort did not necessarily result in higher pay. While average output per worker rose between 1919 and 1929, average real wages actually fell from 1919 to 1922 before recovering to their postwar level in the last years of the boom, 1927–1929.[25] By the end of the decade,

TABLE 1
Percentage Share of Wages in Value
Added by Manufacturing, 1914–1929

	Motor Vehicles	Motor Vehicle Parts and Bodies	Motor Vehicle Combined
1914	31.8	53.1	36.8
1919	38.6	54.2	43.1
1923	40.0	56.4	45.0
1927	33.5	57.0	41.8
1929	27.8	54.0	36.6

Source: J. Steindl, *Maturity and Stagnation in American Capitalism.* (Oxford: Blackwell, 1952), 105.

plant managers had perfected six tactics to increase the pace of parts production and assembly line work without giving workers higher pay:

1. increasing production quotas and/or line speeds when new machinery was installed or an existing process was redesigned,
2. setting special (i.e., higher than average) daily production goals,
3. retiming jobs to establish new basic production standards,
4. recalculation of piece rates and bonus pay,
5. designating the fastest workers as leaders or "straw bosses" of gangs of hourly workers, and
6. constant exhortation and intimidation by foremen.

During the early years of the Great Depression (1929–1933), when auto sales dropped 75 percent, and payrolls in the automobile industry were slashed by 65 percent, management used various combinations of these speedup tactics in a relentless attempt to get more production from of each worker.[26] There seemed to be no end to this process. In 1934, the Automobile Labor Board, which had been created by President Roosevelt to administer the NRA code for the industry, reported that,

> Under the speedup system, each time a job is made slightly over 100 percent efficiency, it is re-timed. Speed, more speed, and the impossible is expected.[27]

Of course, time study had been resisted by auto workers almost since it was first brought into the industry by the Ford Motor Company in 1907.[28] Long before the Great Depression, management tried to prevent workers from restricting output during time studies. "There has *never* been any suggestion of fair dealing at all in regard to studying the time of a job," a veteran worker told government investigators in 1934.

> "In fact the usual rule was to put a timekeeper behind a post or some department head behind a post some place and time a man."[29]

In general, a combination of booming automobile sales, management uncertainty, and workers' resistance to time study had tempered the exploitation of production workers before the Great Depression. For example, L.W. Haskell, an engineer at Dodge later recalled,

> In 1921 time study men were put on . . . The thing was new at the Dodge plant—the time study men naturally wanted to keep their new jobs—as a result [piece] rates were slashed right and left. There was much dissatisfaction among the workers—the Dodges were not yet in control . . . the policy

> was reversed . . . As a result the aim of the Time Study department became one of concentrating on higher production [per hour] rather than reducing rates—which brought about lower unit costs and raised [total] wages [earned].[30]

Unfortunately, when the Great Depression devastated the automobile market, workers could not easily defend their wage levels with the kind of informal, spontaneous resistance that Haskell described. Workers were simply too vulnerable to being fired. By 1934, the Automobile Labor Board found that "production schedules have been increased in many cases 60 percent," while "wages are 40 percent less than 1929." A primary reason for this outcome was the corruption of time study itself. In 1935, the National Recovery Administration's Research and Planning Division reported,

> The competitive conditions of the past few years have reached down to the time study men. *They have been forced to show how to make inequitable reductions in working time to hold onto their own jobs*, and from setting jobs on an efficient basis, they have come to set them on a speed-up basis that puts *production demands beyond human capability to produce day after day.*[31]

The automobile companies' abuse of the time-study method during the Great Depression ultimately had important political consequences. In the 1940s, as the UAW-CIO solidified its bargaining position with the Big Three, it won the right to monitor and verify management's time-study calculations.

There is no question that new machines and redesigned production processes also contributed to the industry's rising productivity in the mid-1930s. General Motors, which returned to profitability in 1933 and had record earnings in 1937, led the way. For example, in 1935 GM launched a $50 million dollar program to "reorganize, readjust, and expand manufacturing operations." As Douglas Reynolds has shown, this program was actually a two-edged sword, which was aimed at increasing productivity while simultaneously eliminating workers who had demonstrated a willingness to organize a union.[32]

Most often the introduction of new technology became the occasion for a new intensification of workers' labor. For example, at AC Sparkplug, new punch presses installed in 1934 allowed 300 workers to maintain the same production that had required 500 workers the previous year. Nonetheless, Delmar Minzey, an experienced worker from that shop estimated that "pure sweat" accounted for at least a one-quarter of the productivity increase.[33] Margaret Clark, a sparkplug gapper in the same plant, told NRA investigators a similar story. In her first year on the job, 1927, she was required to turn out 4,500 sparkplugs in a ten hour day. For this production she was paid $4.50 a day. Clark used a machine was powered by a foot pedal. She had to depress the pedal twice to gap each sparkplug. Thus, she had to lower her foot on the pedal 9,000 times a day. In 1934, after the company brought in redesigned machines, Margaret had to turn out 10,000 sparkplugs in an eight hour day for just $3.20 a day. Her daily 20,000 foot motions were more than double her previous effort. "It is harder work . . . but you can turn more out," she explained. But the financial benefits of higher productivity went to her employer.[34]

As Margaret Clark's case indicates, pay problems and the speedup were intertwined throughout the 1920s and 1930s. The piecework pay and bonus systems, which most automobile companies maintained until the mid-1930s, greatly intensified the unsettling impact of the speedup. Frequent changes in line speeds and production quotas, and frequent recalculations of piece rates and bonuses, meant that auto workers were constantly being presented with new wage-effort bargains (i.e., the amount of effort a worker agrees to exchange for a particular sum of money). Of course, auto workers learned that revisions in piece rates almost always meant they had to put forth a greater effort to maintain total weekly earnings. For example, when management cut piece work rates in Buick's fender department in July 1928 from 9.8 cents to 8.46 cents per fender, workers quickly complained that they had to turn out 97 rather than 88 fenders a day to maintain their income.[35] During the early 1930s, these types of complaints proliferated as management used the threat of unemployment to raise production standards while trying to hold down wages and investment in new equipment.[36] Testimony gathered in 1934 from hundreds of workers in automobile production centers throughout the Midwest by the NRA's Research and Planning Division reveals that workers repeatedly had to find new energy and increased stamina to meet their quotas and maintain wage levels. For instance, Ralph Amy, a machinist in Flint's Chevrolet crankshaft department, told NRA investigators how production tolerance limits had been reduced from two ounces on the 35–40 pound shafts he had turned out in 1929 to one-half ounce on the 45–50 pound shafts he was making in 1934. Amy admitted that the NRA's automobile code had increased his earnings because the company had switched from piece rates to the recommended hourly wage standard, but he continued, "it is not a question of that [wages]. It is a question of the endurance of the man."[37]

The group bonus pay systems that prevailed in most large automobile factories compounded the wage problems generated by the speedup.[38] Workers were paid a flat hourly rate and a bonus on top of that when the group's production exceeded a base level. Group bonus pay systems had proliferated in 1920s because they utilized peer group pressure to speed up individual workers' production. Not coincidentally, group bonus schemes also shifted some of the onus of work discipline from management to each work group, since the group as a whole had to break in new workers quickly to maintain output and earnings. Workers' difficulties in figuring the real costs of each particular speedup were compounded by the group bonus system. Bonus workers often complained that when they worked harder, increasing the number of units they produced in a given pay period, their pay "would be less."[39] For example, in South Bend in 1935, Studebaker workers who investigated discrepancies in group bonuses reported finding "lost work" (i.e., uncounted, ostensibly accidentally, by management) that represented as much as 50 percent of the group's bonus output.[40] These workers, and many others like them, resented being cheated out of the wages they believed they were due.

The perception that management cheated workers was very widespread. Bonus formulas were complex and managers often refused to provide details of the formulas to workers. The bonus pay systems thus added to workers' sense of being powerless. A skilled worker at Studebaker who made crank-shafts summed up the problem in 1935. "Group work is absolutely unfair," he explained.

> It is unquestionable that it takes a certified public accountant to figure wages, and you never know what you make until three or four days after the pay period is ended, when the pay sheet is posted, and then you don't know whether you have made it, whether they are stealing, or what . . . It should be a bonus, but it is bogus.[41]

Raymond T. McNiff, who had been a foreman at the Chevrolet plant in St. Louis, told National Recovery Administration investigators that time-study engineers in his factory did not want to listen to foremen who tried to explain that some job assignments were too much for a single worker. When McNiff brought his men's complaints about group bonuses to the plant superintendent and the time-study men who had set the bonus rate, they told him,

> "Well, we can't do that. If they are not satisfied, tell them to get their ass out." [McNiff continued,] They would not give it [the actual bonus formula] to you. When you got it on the sheet . . . you could not figure it out . . . I was a foreman there for years and I could not figure it out.[42]

Management had earlier learned to offer workers what appeared to be higher pay to facilitate direct increases in line speeds and/or production quotas. For example, when labor economist Robert Dunn studied the Dodge plant in Hamtramck, Michigan during 1926–1927, he noted that management gave workers who kept their jobs a modest wage increase when,

Force on the body assembly line cut from 31 to 20. Production increased from 177 to 202 [car] bodies.

But Dunn also concluded that "this [increase] is not enough to cover the wages of those who were fired. Nor enough to take care of the increased production [effort]."[43] During the Great Depression, promised wage increases were often not given for weeks after they were announced to the press. One group of Ford workers grew impatient with the delay in implementing a 10 percent raise promised in early 1934. Finally, as Matthew Smith told NRA investigators,

> This particular night when I was in the motor building . . . there was just a continual uproar started, shouting by the men, continuing to work, not stopping, but shouting, just a continual, "Ho, ho, ho," and this continued over a long period, almost three-quarters of an hour.

Spontaneous job actions like this one were sometimes effective. Two days later, the men reported, but stood around not working. They then told the foreman they would not work until they got the promised raise, and they "made tracks to go out of the building." At this point, the plant superintendent arrived and authorized the pay increase. It was a small victory, but the workers still had to accept the increased work pace.[44]

It should be clear by now that pay systems were designed by management to facilitate the speedup. At the same time, complicated piece rate pay formulas and group bonuses often made workers feel powerless in their dealings with management. For example, Edward Joyce, a worker at the St. Louis Fisher Body plant, reported that after layoffs in 1931, management required 65 stock workers to do the work previously done by 125 workers. A five dollar increase in the group's bonus was paid for four weeks, but then without prior notice, the stock workers found their bonus reduced to the pre-layoff level. When these workers confronted one of the plant's time-study men about the reduced bonus, they were told,

> I understand a lot of you men think you got fucked on your last pay. Maybe you did and maybe you didn't. Whenever you don't like the pay you are getting, go out to the gate and get your check. There are four hundred men out there every morning willing to work for less than what you men are working for.[45]

These comments clearly illustrate the arrogant and abusive manner of management during the early 1930s. Without a union, individual workers could do little to prevent such abuse. They had to find ways to perform their jobs while

containing the anger and despair brought on by the recognition of how management dealt with them.

These feelings were compounded by the widespread use of the other
major speedup tactics: the appointment of work group leaders, special daily
production quotas, and direct pressure applied by foremen. Such tactics,
which in combination are sometimes called the "drive system," created an
extremely coercive work environment. In most plants where the foremen had
the absolute authority to hire and fire workers, there was nothing subtle about
this coercion. For example, in 1927, a woman who worked at the Hudson
Motor Company's Gratiot Avenue plant in Detroit told labor economist
Robert Dunn that her foreman,

> stands by 300 women and yells "More Speed. If you girls don't speed up,
> I'm going to fire you." This is all we hear all day long. I was a healthy girl
> before I started at Hudson's, but my nerves are all shot to pieces now.[46]

Dunn also reported that workers were often coerced into greater effort by
the threat of a worse job assignment. "When a group on repair work . . .don't
step it up," he wrote in his field notes, they are threatened with being sent
to the foundry. In the foundry, they can be given a worse job if they don't
step on it.[47]

During the Great Depression, the drive system became even more bluntly coercive. As a foreman who worked at the Flint Chevrolet plant throughout the 1930s later recalled, it "was predicated on getting every bit of work
out of a person . . . that he could stand."[48] The mass unemployment and widespread destitution of the 1930s heightened the effectiveness of management's
threats and intimidation. Frequently individual members of a work group
were victimized to scare the rest of the group into accepting more intense
labor. "If they [the foremen] thought the particular gang was not speeding up
sufficiently strong enough," a worker told NRA investigators,

> they would pick a man out of that particular gang and fire him for the pur-
> pose of putting more fear into the particular men who were left, to gain
> speed-ups."[49]

Physical abuse was even used by foremen to supplement other forms of coercion. For instance, when Buick foreman W. A. Snider was asked, "And you
would have to pound the men?" by a NRA investigator in 1934, he replied,
"Yes sir. Right on the back."[50]

The selection of one worker to act as a group or line leader was another
common strategy which predated the Great Depression. In 1934, a trimmer
who had worked in the industry for eight years testified,

> They [the foremen] have always been able to find a man or two out of each group that they can scare, and the rest have to follow in order to stay in business. If they don't they are on the outside.[51]

The group leader might be then held up as an example by the foreman. Or acting as a "straw boss," the designated worker might actually perform the most abusive part of the foreman's job, personally exhorting the members of the group to work up to his or her speed. "Our manager [the foreman] steps on his straw boss and the straw boss goes onto the men and pounds you right on the back," one worker told NRA investigators in 1934.[52]

Nelson Lichtenstein has described the typical straw boss of the inter-war years as a "combination pusher, relief man, spy, and all around foreman substitute."[53] "They treated us like a bunch of coolies," F. R. Palmer of Flint's Fisher Body 1 later recalled,

> "Get it out. Get it out. If you cannot get it out, there are people who will get it." That was their whole theme. That was all the knowledge you had to have to be boss . . . or a foreman.[54]

As Palmer's recollection indicates, hard-driving straw bosses and foremen were despised by most workers. In a real sense, this proved they were doing their job. Foremen in particular served management as "flak catchers" who deflected workers' resentments about the speedup away from the engineers and white-collar executives who actually designed and directed the work process.

Often described as a "man in the middle," the automobile industry foremen of this period were in a particularly difficult position. He had to be, in the words of a 1933 General Motors Executive training manual, both a "representative *to* management" and a "representative *of* management." Typically, foremen were recruited from the blue-collar work force, were constantly on the shopfloor, got their hands dirty, were paid by the hour, and often wore the same type work clothes as the rank-and-file. Yet for all practical purposes, until the rise of the UAW, they retained the managerial power to hire, send home, and fire workers.[55] Some foremen tried to avoid unduly pressuring the workers in their shops, but most could not avoid the pressure to turn out more production. "There are some people . . . if you give them enough power they will abuse it. But the majority . . . had been workers themselves," explained Orvel Simmons, a buffer at Flint's Chevrolet plant. But

> actually they didn't want to be that way . . . fear was driving them to those things. Each one of those guys if they didn't get [production] . . . might be right back on the damn line himself so he is passing it right down to the bottom and there is the worker who is really getting it."[56]

The extraordinary empathy expressed in this statement by a worker who also admitted loathing foremen is perhaps only the product of hindsight. Contemporary worker testimony, and subsequent oral histories, make it clear that foremen were more commonly resented as class traitors. Statements like "First we had to cut down the size of those hard boiled foremen," the initial reaction of a Dodge worker to the company's recognition of the UAW, probably better expresses the hatred which a great many workers felt toward their foremen.[57]

The fears and resentments of Depression-era auto workers were not irrational; they were in fact deliberately cultivated by management. By continuously threatening workers' incomes and jobs, and even their physical well-being, automobile managers were able to maximize production in the short run. The large number of unemployed auto workers enabled managers to ignore the long-term effects of the speedup on their work force. The special daily production quotas which were widely used during the 1930s regularly tested the limits of this strategy. In 1934, one foreman told NRA investigators how special quotas worked in his plant.

> When we got our orders in the morning, we would set our production for 15 jobs per hour, that would be our daily production. They [the general foremen] would come in at about 10 o'clock and ask for an additional 25 jobs for that day. It was our duty to turn up that line to speed to produce those additional jobs without increasing manpower on that line.[58]

Historian James McDonnell has reported that "It was a common practice of the foremen to increase the speed of the line whenever possible" at the General Motors Axle Division plant in Buffalo.

> The practice was to turn the speed up for fifteen minutes or until the men showed signs of extreme fatigue and began to fall hopelessly behind. Then the speed was reduced to normal for forty-five minutes. This process went on every day, all day.[59]

Workers who had been told that their jobs were likely to be eliminated learned to be especially alert for signs of a speedup. An imminent layoff was often signaled by a brief speedup which pitted worker against worker in a competition to avoid unemployment. John Riley, a worker at Ford's vast River Rouge plant, later recalled that:

> anyone working knew when a speedup or layoff was near. You could see the foreman with a white card in his hand [on which he recorded the identification numbers of those not laboring at the increased pace], watching some of

the boys, that is all of those except those he knew . . . would work 'till they dropped at his command . . . Then without notice, or a chance to check on your seniority, [you] would be tapped on the shoulder and told . . . you were being laid off..[60]

In addition, workers throughout the industry had to endure brief speedups that occurred during the last hour of their shifts. If they could not keep up during this final rush hour, they knew they might not be called into work the next day. This end of the day speedup was especially dangerous for workers because, as numerous studies of industrial accident frequency have shown, accidents reach their daily peak during the last hour of work.[61]

A Killing Pace: The Ordeal of the Workers

The physical and psychological toll exacted by the speedup appears to have been extremely high. But it is difficult to determine just how much damage was inflicted on auto workers. Throughout the inter-war period, the companies denied they were using speedup tactics and injuring workers. Most of the major companies' personnel records from the pre-union era have either been destroyed or closed to outsiders. As a result, auto workers' testimony gathered by the NRA, various oral history projects, and investigations conducted by other government agencies and individual scholars, remain the best sources of information on the physical and psychological effects of the speedup.

As early as 1926–27, Robert Dunn tried to document the price paid by just one worker who struggled to keep up with the speedup at Dodge's Hamtramck plant. His field notes contain the following record:

Increased operations per individual . . .at first only one operation; then after 3 months has four. His particular job causes continual bending and stretching. No time for rest . . . Causing physical and nervous relapse. Was off work Thursday. Unable to get up. Could hardly walk. Strain on leg and back muscles causing great pain. Afraid to tell boss about it; "If you can't do the job there are plenty of men who will." Cannot eat his lunches because of bad physical effects.[62]

Intense physical effort and constant psychological stress were the principal elements which shaped workers' daily on the job experiences during the inter-war period. Over the long run, it seems clear that the speedup left workers physically and mentally exhausted. In the 1930s, as the speedup became ubiquitous, America's automobile workers suffered from a pandemic of chronic fatigue and shattered nerves. In 1934, one worker described the syndrome to NRA investigators in these terms:

> You work until when you get home you are so nervous you can't go to sleep.
> You are screwed right down to the last notch.[63]

Another worker who complained about the government's failure to ameliorate the speedup put it this way, "The way the [NRA] code is working is terrible. When a man goes home at night he is so tired that he cannot see." [64] Joseph Kinecki, a Fisher Body trimmer from Buffalo, later recalled:

> After working ten and eleven hours even with a small hammer, you got through and went home and sat down and tried to read the newspaper. In fifteen minutes you were sleeping, in twenty minutes you were knocked out. And this was when I was young and in top shape.[65]

During the peak production period which usually extended from January through March, workers typically put in very long hours that undoubtedly compounded the detrimental physical and psychological effects of the speedup. This was especially true during the mid-1930s when the auto companies extended overtime rather than adding an extra shift. For example, Myrl Reed, a veteran worker, reported that his Fisher Body plant in St. Louis had worked "thirty consecutive days" in January 1933,

> from seven o'clock in the morning until eight or nine in the evening . . . I would get home at ten o'clock and I would be so tired I could not eat my supper. I would drop in a chair and cry myself to sleep.[66]

Obviously, workers such as Myrl Reed could not enjoy life outside the plant; there was, at least during peak production periods, simply no time for family, friends, or relaxation.

Even when companies scheduled eight hour shifts, preparation and clean up often extended workers' actual work days with *unpaid* labor. In 1934, an A. F. of L. official familiar with conditions at the Ford Highland Park plant testified that,

> The speed on the final assembly line was so terrific that the men could not cope with the production in eight hours [for which they were paid]. These men went in sometimes a half an hour or three quarters of an hour before the starting time and had all the material laid out that they wanted to work with and everything ready to go, and it took them just about the same time at night to get the stuff away.[67]

Similarly, Fayte Shearer, who worked on the chassis line in a St. Louis plant, explained that she had to start laying out stock half an hour before the line actually started, and she had to sacrifice twenty minutes of her lunch break to get ready for afternoon production.[68]

Although the seasonal and cyclical rhythms of the automobile marketplace had always generated concerns about job and wage security among the industry's work force, the intensified speedup of the mid-1930s greatly magnified those insecurities. As we have already seen, during the Depression, layoffs and firings were regularly used by management to force acceptance of new production quotas and wage bargains. In addition, as the many historians of the UAW have shown, pivotal "sparkplug" unionists were frequently fired for their organizing activities.[69] But most importantly, the problem of age discrimination increased dramatically during the Great Depression. In those years, even relatively young workers in their mid-thirties began to worry about whether or not they were too old to keep their jobs.

Experienced workers had at least two good reasons to be anxious: the automobile industry's history of discriminating against older workers, and way the speedup prematurely aged its work force. From the onset of its Model T program, the Ford Motor Company had always preferred "young, vigorous, quick men not past the age of thirty-five," whom its managers had believed were best suited for mass production work. When the other major producers adopted Fordist methods during the long automobile boom, they also adopted the preference for younger workers.[70] But while the industry was still growing, and its workforce was still relatively young, discrimination against older workers was not a major problem. However, once mass layoffs and systematic work force reductions began during the Great Depression, automobile workers thirty-five years and older became especially vulnerable.

The accumulated physical and psychological effects of the speedup accelerated the aging of many workers. And those workers made "older" by the speedup invariably lost their jobs when layoffs were announced. As one foreman frankly confessed in 1934,

> After these men have served ten years in this work, they are burned up. They have not got the capacity to compete with outside labor . . . [management] brings into the city, therefore *a man who is beyond forty years old is beyond the age of earning.*[71]

In 1935 the NRA's Research and Planning Division reported that,

> When a man who has reached the age of 40 is laid off . . . it becomes increasingly difficult to get back on the next rehiring period . . . Men over 40 who are still on the rolls feel in many cases that they are working on "borrowed time" as they express it.[72]

Only very young workers, and those skilled tradesmen who were able to escape the worst effects of the speedup and who were not so easily replaced, could believe they would remain immune from age discrimination.

Evidence from August 1934 collective bargaining sessions between the UAW and White Motors Company, Cleveland, Ohio, suggests that even in jobs that did were not physically taxing, like stock room jobs and parts salespeople, older workers were let go in favor of younger workers. Getting inexperienced workers at lower pay seems to have been management's goal. One such worker had started at White in 1915. In 1934 he was "doing a two-man's job" when he received a discharge slip. He testified that his foreman had candidly explained that the lay-off was necessary to decrease expenses. When the worker presented his layoff slip to the Personnel Department, someone there changed the notation on the lay-off slip to "inefficiency."[73]

Many auto workers testified that the physical exhaustion they experienced was compounded by poor ventilation, a year round problem in the foundries and paint shops where black workers were often concentrated, and a seasonal (mid-summer, mid-winter) problem for other workers. "Under this excessive work and physical exertion with lack of ventilation in the plant," one worker told NRA investigators in the winter of 1934–35, "when you come out and hit fresh air, it just knocks you groggy, dizzy."[74] Clayton Johnson, a metal finisher in Flint's Fisher Body 2 plant, recalled that when he collapsed from heat exhaustion on June 30, 1936, "The foreman grabbed me by the shoulders and told me to get to my god-damn feet." Johnson tried to stand and work, but collapsed again. Several other workers also collapsed, forcing management to temporarily shut down the line, an action which probably saved Johnson's job, and perhaps his life.[75]

Foremen also forced workers to endure obvious (i.e., bloody) injuries so as not to hold up production. Under the speedup regime, enduring pain was part of the price many workers paid to keep their jobs. For example, in 1934 a running board installer told NRA investigators that in his department,

> men have cut themselves, torn by pieces of jagged steel, or had tools fall on their feet and injure them, and they would be bleeding and in a position so that really demanded first aid, and there was no one available, and these men have been threatened [for complaining].[76]

Auto workers' apparent willingness to routinely suffer physical pain and injury reveals the extent to which management's systematic intimidation was internalized in the pre-UAW era. When he entered the industry in 1936, Ken Bannon, who would become the head of the UAW's Ford Department in 1947, worked on large Bullard lathes that machined heavy metal castings containing many sharp, rough spots. Handling these castings was inherently dangerous, yet Bannon and his fellow lathe operators had to accept mutilation as part of the job. As he later recalled,

> after a few hours on this job your fingers would bleed. They would bleed from the beginning of the week really until the end of the week. You were not allowed to wear gloves. *Gloves were supposedly a safety hazard*, although today [1963] people who run machines . . .wear rubber gloves . . . We would get cloths and make bandages out of them and wrap them around out fingers and then from a dime store buy a package of rubber bands . . . to put around the bandage so that it would hold our fingers . . . However we were always fearful of a foreman coming by and seeing us with the cloths on our fingers, for which we were subject to discharge or some other type of penalty.[77]

Intimidation also forced workers to regularly labor without necessary bathroom breaks, a situation which we all know causes both intense physical pain and a great deal of psychological humiliation and stress. A surprisingly large number of Depression-era auto workers specifically mention this problem in the testimony they have left in the historical record. For example, in 1934, a skilled toolmaker told NRA investigators,

> The foreman keeps after us every minute of the day, driving us to greater and greater speed every year. Only the other day I was called down for going to the wash room for a few minutes.[78]

Again, this problem seemed to be most widespread during peak production periods. J. G. Kennedy, a forty-three year old final assembler at Chrysler, testified in 1934 that work on a new model began at 15 cars per hour, rose to 25 per hour as the peak period approached, then was further increased to 37 per hour—a 50 percent increase in production, which the company mitigated with just a 10 percent increase in the work force. At this point, Kennedy stated that "conditions on that line were unbearable," and that "in the majority of cases [workers were] without relief for hygienic purposes."[79]

Throughout the 1930s, auto workers usually cheered when their line broke down. There were undoubtedly many reasons for these expressions of collective jubilation, but it seems fair to surmise that at least some of the workers who cheered recognized a breakdown as their chance to get to a toilet. What happened in the absence of this kind of opportunity? George Scheitinger, who worked in the Fisher Body plant in Buffalo in the mid-1930s, recalled that

> People in our plant I know, who'd dirty their pants because they didn't feel they could go to the men's room in time. There was one guy who'd go into the toilet and went without ever taking his pants completely down. He had

these suspenders that were real springy and he would run back up to the john
and push them down and sit down and get off, and pull them up and run out
to the line again.[80]

It is impossible to for us to know how common the humiliating behaviors
described by Scheitinger really were during the pre-union era. His testimony
supports the conclusion that management's relentless intimidation was internalized by some auto workers in deeply repressive and self-destructive ways.

In *Modern Times*, Charlie Chaplin portrayed an assembly line worker
who, even after he was fired and was walking on the street outside the factory, kept moving his hands in the circular motions he had used when he
was tightening bolts with a wrench. Frank Marquart, an auto worker who
organized for the UAW in the 1930s, recalled that even after the Dodge
Main plant was unionized, many workers had been so conditioned by the
drive system that

> We often had a hard time getting our own people to slowdown; they had
> been so used to working as a fast speed that they couldn't adjust to a slow-
> er pace. So we told them to take a walk from time to time and not turn out
> more work than the rest of us did . . .[81]

Dr. I. W. Ruskin, who had been treating Detroit automobile workers for
thirteen years, reached a similar conclusion in 1934. In testimony presented to
NRA investigators, Dr. Ruskin maintained that since the Depression had
begun,

> These are not the same people I once knew. They have not the same tem-
> peraments, they have not the same dispositions, they have not the same stan-
> dard of living . . . It has been amazing to learn of the high percentage of neu-
> rosis and psychosis which has been revealed among these workers.[82]

Even more compelling insights into the psychological effects of the
speedup can be found in an article written by an unusually perceptive and
articulate twenty-three year old auto worker, Gene Richard, who described
one week of peak production for *Atlantic Monthly* in April 1937. Richard
noted that the long winter shifts meant living without ever seeing the sun:

> Each day I go to work in the dark and leave in the dark. I haven't seen day-
> light since Sunday, and it Saturday afternoon.[83]

The speedup was often compounded by this inherently depressing condition—life brightened only by artificial light. To survive it, Richard recognized

that he, like other workers in his plant, were making severe psychological adjustments which numbed him to his everyday work environment.

> When I come in the gate in the morning *I throw off my personality and assume a personality which expresses the institution of which I am a part* . . . The only personal thing required of me is just enough consciousness to operate my body as a machine . . . We are working so fast I don't see how anyone can think of quality . . . I seldom make a mistake, yet I never have my mind on my work . . . my subconscious is more capable of this monotony than my personality.

Richard's striking observations indicate that auto work in the 1930s could be an intensely alienating, traumatic experience. Indeed, Richard's description of how he desensitized himself in order to perform his job under the speedup regime brings to mind the psychological coping strategy that Robert Jay Lifton discovered in his work with American veterans of the Vietnam War.[84] Of course, speedup trauma was not as severe as combat trauma; auto workers did not have to deal with either an enemy out to kill them or the psychological consequences of killing other human beings. However, Gene Richard and many other unskilled and semi-skilled auto workers seemed to have faced a crucial problem very similar to one Lifton found among Vietnam veterans—*the problem of distancing themselves from personally meaningless and often repugnant actions that they regularly performed on the orders of authority figures.*

Like soldiers, pre-union era auto workers had to find ways to avoid taking personal responsibility, escape feeling guilty for "choosing" to tolerate work hazards, and to labor at a killing pace that they would not otherwise have been willing to endure. Like soldiers, auto workers had to avoid succumbing completely to the emotions of victimhood. However, unlike the more extreme cases of American soldiers who killed and wounded other people in Vietnam, the auto workers' despised actions were production tasks that often mutilated their bodies and stressed their psyches.

The speedup/military analogy also helps to illuminate management practice. The coercive practices of hierarchically organized personnel management in most Depression era auto plants resembled those employed by the military. Like military officers, auto company supervisors and foremen wanted workers to do what they were told, in the way they were told to do it, when they were told to do it. Management clearly preferred an intimidated work force to workers who questioned orders, so like the military, they employed coercive techniques including some designed to elicit a gender-based response to demands for more work. Most significantly, like Army drill sergeants, foremen and straw bosses tried to make the workers in their over-whelmingly male work force suppress their individual personalities by combining verbal and physical abuse with frequent challenges to male honor. Of course, unlike soldiers, auto workers were not subject to court martial and execution or imprisonment if they disobeyed orders.

"When a man insinuates by any action that he is an individual," Richards reported, "he is made to feel that he is not only out of place but doing something dishonorable." From management's standpoint, this strategy would ideally transform the speedup from a group experience of manipulation and exploitation, which might lead to group resistance to managerial policies, into a situation in which a worker might feel that he or she was letting down his or her fellow workers if he or she did not obey managerial orders. Management would profit from this type of group loyalty. But of course this ideal response was not always realized in practice.

Workers frequently rebelled against the speedup regime in both collective and individual ways. Work slowdowns and wildcat strikes increased after 1933, and especially after workers felt empowered after they forced management to recognition of the UAW in the late 1930s. Less confrontational and less productive expressions of rebellion also punctuated auto work during the Great Depression. Occasionally, Richard, as well as other observers of the speedup like Matthew Smith in 1934, discovered workers' psychological isolation would break down. Macabre, but cathartic group protest followed:

> The work will not absorb the mind of a normal man, so they must think . . .
> Suddenly a man breaks forth with a mighty howl. Others follow. We set up
> a howling all over the shop. It is a relief, this howling.[85]

Frustration, anger, and pain were all expressed in these spontaneous "animal-like" outbursts on the shopfloor. Other responses to the speedup and management intimidation included outright denial and the creation of sometimes bold, but ultimately false personalities. "Some of the men develop a surprisingly self-important air . . .," Richard observed. "Their outward front expresses an ownership of all those things they haven't got."

More commonly, like the American and British soldiers that Paul Fussell describes in *Wartime*, some of whom were probably speedup survivors, auto workers constantly used foul language as a coping strategy. "We cuss and talk filthy," Richard reported. Swearing undoubtedly expressed the bitterness and anger which stemmed from workers' recognition of what Fussell calls "constant victimhood." It was also an acceptable form of rebellion. If it did not directly challenge the speedup, expressing anger by swearing enabled workers to be more alive and manly. To paraphrase Fussell, if you couldn't resist the speedup any other way, you could always say, "Fuck it!"[86]

The UAW and the Speedup

After the passage of the National Industrial Recovery Act in June 1933, many auto workers had hoped that conditions in their industry would be improved by a combination of federal action and union organization. The National Recovery Administration's (NRA) Automobile Code did move average hourly wages upward by encouraging employers to shift from piece rates to regulated hourly rates, even as it reduced the hours of work by establishing a forty hour standard work week. (See chapter 6.) Several factors, including the Ford Motor Company's refusal to sign the national Automobile Code and the National Automobile Chamber of Commerce's control of code enforcement, prevented the NRA from ending the speedup. But most importantly, the NRA itself failed to compel employers to bargain with emerging unions which actually challenged the speedup.[87] For example, in December 1934, Al Cook, president of the A. F. of L.'s ill-fated union at the Flint Fisher Body plant, got a hearing but no effective action from the Automobile Labor Board when he told them:

> We have had some conferences with the management, or we have protested as far as the seniority and . . . piecework prices, and pointed out to the management where this [problem] could be eliminated without hardly any additional cost . . . The management's reply was "Cook, you are full of shit."[88]

Despite this failing, NRA did *indirectly* contribute to the rise of an independent auto workers union. First, many sparkplug unionists, who would become leaders of the UAW-CIO's local organizing drives after 1935, gained valuable experience during the NRA period. And secondly, by increasing the share of value added going to wages, NRA undoubtedly increased the pressure on plant managers to pursue new productivity increases via new speedups. (See Table 2.)

The NRA Automobile Code did not discourage the speedup. The initial interventions of President Roosevelt in auto labor relations undermined the efforts of auto workers to form a strong industrial union, the kind of organization that could fight the speedup. Historically, skilled workers, semi-skilled machine operatives, and lower-skilled assembly workers and laborers had often been reluctant to join together in the same union. Skilled workers were especially afraid of joining in a union with lower-paid workers, since the likely result would be a narrowing of the wage gap between the better paid and their less fortunate peers. Common employment experiences during the Depression—the speedup, dangerous machinery that was not repaired, and the virtual abandonment of seniority protection, which was a particular shock to the skilled workers who had accumulated more seniority than other work-

TABLE 2
Percentage Share of Wages Added by
Manufacturing, 1929-1937

	Motor Vehicles	Motor Vehicle Parts and Bodies	Motor Vehicle Combined
1929	27.8	54.0	36.6
1931	30.1	45.3	36.9
1933	31.6	46.5	38.9
1935	37.7	60.2	39.8
1937	45.6	55.7	51.0

Source: Joseph Steindl. *Maturity and Stagnation in American Capitalism* (Oxford: Basil Blackwell, 1952), 105.

ers—brought the skilled and less skilled workers together. What use was their advantaged wage position, reasoned skilled workers, if they were working so hard they were shortening their lives? If joining a union with less skilled workers was the only way to obtain credible seniority rights, and avoid the favoritism of foremen, it appeared to worth taking the risk of future wage compression. By the mid-1930s these considerations unified the labor force in the auto industry as it never had been previously. Militant auto workers, many of them skilled workers, would take the decisive steps that brought industrial unionism to the auto industry. Staging sit-downs in Cleveland, Ohio and Flint, Michigan, these workers, with the backing of the CIO and the timely intervention of President Roosevelt, forced GM, and then Chrysler, to initiate collective bargaining with the UAW.[89]

During the six difficult years which followed its founding convention in South Bend in 1935, the new UAW-CIO promised to provide deeply aggrieved workers with a potent rebellious response to the speedup. A half century later, it is easy to look back to those years and discover the inadequacies of that response. Quite simply, the union did not destroy Fordism, nor did it establish an effective way for workers' to actually make production decisions. However, union leaders and rank and file activists did wage a sustained struggle that cut into management's monopoly of power in the work place. General Motors' chairman Alfred P. Sloan Jr. certainly remembered it that way. In 1964 he recalled,

> What made the prospect [of a unionized work force] seem especially grim in those early years was the persistent attempt to invade basic management pre-

rogatives. Our rights to determine production schedules, to set work standards, and to discipline workers were all suddenly called into question.[90]

Although tempered by his recognition that the company did not ultimately lose its "the right to manage," Sloan's recollection indicates the intensity of the union-management battles of 1936–1941 with its invocation of a union "invasion" and the "grim prospect" of a management defeat.

To better appreciate the dimensions of this struggle, and what the union actually accomplished, we must also listen to the voices of activist workers who fought for union recognition, and of the workers who sustained shopfloor struggles to implement the rights and procedures defined in the UAW's first national contracts. Only then can we put today's more critical evaluation of the union's performance into proper historical perspective. And what do the voices of those workers, as they have been preserved in contemporary documents and oral histories, tell us about those struggles? Inevitably, these workers speak especially of a union which established *security*, and restored workers' *dignity*. In other words, they describe a union which successfully reversed some of the worst psychological, as well as physical and material, damage created by the speedup.

As we have already seen, for most pre-union era auto workers, *accumulated experience meant less, not more, security in their jobs.* In December 1933, the National Recovery Administration's Automobile Code established the principle of seniority for workers with more than six months of service. But as the NRA's own investigators discovered in late 1934, the seniority principle was ignored at most plants when workers were rehired after layoffs.[91] Between 1936 and 1941, UAW-CIO organizers repeatedly discovered that the promise of contractually guaranteed seniority rights was a key to successfully organizing the majority of workers who were not militantly pro-union.[92] Carl Swanson, a UAW leader at Flint's giant Buick plant, later recalled,

> There was no problem at all to get people to join the organization . . . People were longing for some kind of security in line with their work. We had seen so much discrimination on the basis of people who had a lot of service and had been laid off.[93]

During the UAW's successful campaign at the Ford Rouge plant in 1941, union organizers stressed seniority and its connection to the CIO's policy of racial equality . "The seniority rights of all workers are respected equally," the union pledged in a full-page ad in *Ford Facts*, "irrespective of race, color, or creed."[94] In fact, as Carl Gersuny and Gladdis Kaufman have pointed-ed out, seniority provisions which discriminated against blacks and women were written into many local contracts in this period. These scholars conclude that seniority became "the keystone of their [auto workers] moral economy . . . an anti-laissez faire morality against the unrestrained labor market freedom of employers who acknowledged no limitations based on the rights of employees."[95]

Most labor historians have treated seniority as a distinct issue involving aging and job security, but the UAW-CIO's insistence that length of service established a worker's right to a job was actually part of the union's complex response to the speedup. Contractual seniority provisions were essential for creating a new sense of dignity for auto workers in the workplace. Moreover, in combination with formal grievance procedures, seniority rights changed the balance of power on the shopfloor. Foremen were stripped of their power to arbitrarily hire, fire, and layoff workers. This change strengthened the foremen's sense that they too were workers. In the Detroit area, foremen at Ford, Chrysler, Briggs, Hudson, Packard, and Kelsey Hayes actually organized their own ill-fated union, the Foremen's Association of America, in the 1940s. Elsewhere, the change was less dramatic, but still important. Buick worker and UAW activist Arthur Case later explained that over time,

> "It [the union contract] brings the foreman closer to the men . . .There is a lot more 'will you' and "how about it' where there used to be 'do this' and 'do that.'"[96]

Of course, a new relationship between foremen and workers did not emerge immediately. The 1937 UAW-CIO contracts, which established seniority and grievance procedures, not only weakened the foremen, but simultaneously gave workers the right, and the confidence, to talk back to management. In the new union shop, workers were released from the external and internalized constraints which had prevented them from effectively protesting the speedup. With company spying curtailed, and the victimization and blacklisting of union members ended, workers angered by years of intimidation could express a rebellious response to the speedup more freely and more frequently. Not surprisingly, open resistance to the speedup spread quickly after the UAW was recognized at General Motors and Chrysler. "When the employees came back to work," Fisher Body 1's Everett Francis recalled, they expected immediate action on their grievances. Number one on the list was an end to the speedup. They simply would not work at their former unnatural pace.[97] Shop stewards and shop committees were elected from the ranks of union activists. UAW members initiated at least two thousand sit-downs, slowdowns, and other work stoppages in the twenty-six months between March 1937 and May 1939.[98]

Not all workers participated equally in this war against the speedup. Age, not ethnicity, race, or gender, was the primary determinant of activism. Confrontations with management were largely a young men's, and, as Nancy Gabin has shown, a young women's game.[99] Indeed, a distinct generation gap emerged among the membership at many plants. "Attitudes of the first-generation workers remained unchanged, while those of the second-generation were dramatically transformed," Peter Friedlander reported in his now classic study of Local 229.

> The first-generation worker exhibited feelings of fear and submissiveness, in spite of an equally strong hatred and resentment. When a foreman approached a first-generation worker the latter if not working, hurriedly and furiously began. If working, he sped up his pace. . . . On the other hand, the second-generation worker ignored or talked back to the foreman and went to the can when he wanted to. If not working when a foreman passed by, he returned to his machine or task but in a more leisurely manner.[100]

The union theoretically empowered all workers, but the overwhelming majority of activists were in their twenties and thirties. Younger workers dominated most of the newly elected shop committees. Many of these activists were also political radicals (Communists, Trotskyites, or Socialists) who had enthusiastically seized opportunities to organize workers. But Left politics did not really define the UAW's early presence on the shopfloor; demands for an end to the speedup and the establishment of minimum security and dignity did. For example, it was Catholic supporters of Father Coughlin who led the campaign for "fair play" at Chrysler's Dodge Main plant, and dominated Detroit's Local 3 in 1937–1938. Perhaps Stephen Meyer's recent description of the Communist stewards who controlled UAW Local 248 (Allis Chalmers, Milwaukee) best sums up the significance of the many shopfloor radicals during the UAW's early years. They were dedicated idealists, Meyer explains, who spent four to six hours a week doing unremunerative union work because they "possessed a deep commitment to both unionism and to their fellow workers."[101]

Whatever their politics, shop stewards generally believed the newly recognized UAW would protect them if they staged direct action protests against a new speedup or a perceived violation of the grievance procedure. For example, the 1938 records of Local 25 at Fisher Body, St. Louis indicate that workers repeatedly stopped production to protest work speed and production standard changes initiated by management, and that the union's shop committee consistently supported the workers' grievances. In fact, by November 1938 it was urging the officers of Local 25 to negotiate a new agreement because of the "seriousness of the speedup and the lack of settlement of grievances."[102] At other plants, like GM's Ternstedt plant in Detroit, workers used the mass-slowdown tactic effectively.[103]

However, local unions did more than simply protect activist workers. The UAW's collective bargaining records indicate that union grievance committees frequently used the grievance procedure to challenge production standards that workers believed forced them to work harder to maintain their earnings. Typically the UAW grievance committee, consisting of contractually recognized "committeemen" who acted as chief stewards for groups of as many as 500 workers, demanded increased numbers of workers on line work and new time studies on bench work that allowed workers to maintain existing work intensity and earnings. UAW committeemen also insisted that "after [a] line is set up to a certain speed . . . that the speed of the line not be increased or decreased in the course of a day."[104]

The details of one such instance of collective bargaining—a meeting between managers of the Briggs Corporation plant in Detroit and representatives of UAW Local 212 on April 21, 1938—reveal the significant ways that union recognition had altered the politics of the speedup. Briggs' cylinder shop workers had recently staged a "slow-down" because, as UAW negotiaor Ray Burke explained,

> the men get so fed up with the speed-up and the antagonistic tactics of supervision—"get to work on your job, you've got no grievance"—that they have provoked these [slow-downs] . . . that we've been talking about.

Not surprisingly, Briggs' managers insisted on uninterrupted production, and the UAW representatives at Briggs did not really disagree. Burke and the other union representatives conceded they could live with a grievance procedure that did not settle all worker complaints immediately after they arose on the shopfloor. Thus production would not be stopped while a steward or union committeeman debated the merits of a worker grievance with supervisors.

However, Ray Burke took exception to one aspect of this policy. *"Except in the speed of it,"* he asserted, *"We maintain the speed up grievance should be settled immediately."* To defend this stance, Burke described a typical situation faced by workers on a moving line:

> What we do when the company increases the production by, say adding an operation to a line and the Chief Steward goes down and says he wants two more men to take care of that added operation and the company says there is no speed-up, they've got sufficient manpower to do the job, somebody has

got to do the job until such a time as the grievance procedure has gone through. And . . . on long, drawn out cases it would last for a couple of weeks before they get a decision and after they get a decision, the company comes back with an argument like this—"Well, they have been doing it for two weeks now."

Plant manager Fay Taylor responded to this argument by insisting that many workers did not work hard except at times when management could not quickly redesign a production process that needed improvement. "We have given you examples," Taylor declared,

hundreds of them where the question of production stepping up, or added operation, *we have hundreds of men here who do not—and we can't help ourselves—do a day's work*, and we are not asking them to, [we] can't do because of the line up of the operations. Now if production steps up or if there is an added operation sometimes in those cases it is possible to work it out and they work the same as the other men along side of them . . . Now, if you stopped every time that condition came up, we wouldn't be operating here at all. You men know that just as well as we do.

The UAW's Burke ignored this old fashioned attack on workers' willingness to work. Instead, he replied by emphasizing instances in which workers were asked to work harder as management added new tasks to their jobs instead of hiring additional workers whose time could not initially be fully utilized. Burke elaborated,

You see the way the increased production . . . comes out where the work is not enough to add another man, yet they expect that man to do that, they add another operation in the same manner which may be that they only need 10 percent of a man, and they keep on adding these until, *the men get so fed up that they can't stand it, and they go down.*[105]

In this exchange between Briggs' Fay and the UAW's Burke, it is clear that both sides recognized the difficulty of maintaining a constant work load. But what the company's representatives either did not understand, or simply refused to recognize, was the union's insistence that *fair play* was more important than production imperatives. If the UAW simply accepted the managerial argument about the priority of increasing production, some workers would always end up with an unfair burden, which meant more fatigue, a greater risk of injury, and an acceleration of the aging process. These were lessons auto workers had learned in the pre-union era, and the early UAW did not forget them. After 1937, auto workers refused to be sacrificial lambs for the industry's god of greater productivity, and the union backed them up. Although in any large plant, at any given moment, such "over-worked" workers were usually in a minority, there were at least two compelling reasons for trying to protect them from the dangers of a speedup. First, these workers were vulnerable human beings who had a right to protection against overwork. Second, union officials knew from their own experience in the auto factories in the 1920s and early 1930s that the cumulative effect of small but incremental increases in work load multiplied the numbers of workers affected and magnified the overall increases in work intensity achieved by management.

The negotiation at Briggs in April 1938 did not settle disputes over increased work loads and proper manning of assembly lines. This should not be surprising, nor should it be interpreted as a union failure to achieve "workers' control." As the Briggs case illustrates, the UAW placed a high priority on the immediate adjudication of speedup grievances. This response was not confined to Briggs. For example, in the fall of 1939, when 105 workers were fired for refusing to meet new production standards, the UAW authorized a strike vote at Chrysler's huge Dodge Main plant. On October 12th, workers voted overwhelmingly—13,751 to 1,324—for a work stoppage. When Chrysler capitulated on November 29th, it reinstated the fired workers and granted UAW shop stewards both super seniority and the right to leave their job, without loss of pay, to discuss worker grievances with foremen and plant managers.[106]

For a long time, union dissidents and labor historians critical of the UAW leadership, have suggested that the union's early acceptance of national contract language which outlawed unauthorized (wildcat) strikes reflected the leadership's abandonment of the auto workers' struggle against the speedup. While it is true that a ban on unauthorized strikes was accepted as early as September 1937 by the union's General Motors bargaining team, and that language implementing such a ban was included in the 1938 General Motors and Chrysler contracts and the 1946 Ford contract, these facts alone do not describe the totality of the union's policy regarding speedups and worker protest.[107] As this essay and subsequent chapters in this book illustrate, the UAW developed a policy of using grievance bargaining and authorized strikes to resist management efforts to increase work loads and to direct workers' anger into lawful procedures which would not endanger the union's acceptance by management. As Walter Reuther, then head of the UAW's General Motors Department, explained in an October 30, 1939, interview,

> We have no choice, even if we chose to delay or evade—which we do not—
> we would be forced to do something by the rank and file, by the men on the
> production lines. [Otherwise] They would turn to measures of resistance

such [as] . . . slowdowns and kindred weapons. This would result in *the wrecking of the union*. [Emphasis added.]

In this interview, Reuther insisted that shop stewards conduct the initial negotiations with management over production standards because their participation was "a condition necessary for acceptance with the least friction by the workers." Reuther continued, explaining that a shop steward had special knowledge since he or she was "one of those who will work under the standards so set." But since management would never tolerate too much militancy on the shopfloor, Reuther also asserted that, "such a plan should not prevent the stepping in of higher officials in cases where stewards are hopelessly disagreed with company representatives."[108]

General Motors actually facilitated the development Reuther described in this interview because, unlike Ford and Chrysler, its labor policies offered workers an important benefit: managerial consistency. Once production standards were set at a GM plant—and they were certainly demanding standards—the company generally stuck to them. It did not alter assembly line speeds and production standards for bench workers and machinists during the life of a particular model. This policy strengthened GM management's credibility, making GM workers less likely to start wildcat strikes than their counterparts at Ford and especially Chrysler. At the latter companies, management manipulated production standards frequently, often violating agreements made with UAW locals. So naturally Ford and Chrysler workers viewed their bosses as hypocritical and untrustworthy. Between 1939 and 1956, the result was a far higher incidence of slow downs and wildcat strikes at Ford and Chrysler plants than at GM factories. And, as chapters 4 and 5 demonstrate, UAW leaders supported many of these worker protests, particularly when they were responses to flagrant management violations of local agreements.

In both the pre-union and early UAW periods, the speedup remained the focal point of auto workers' grievances about their jobs. The lessons workers had learned about management's speedup tactics and their detrimental effects on individual lives were part of the political wisdom shared by the UAW rank and file and their national leaders. In their unique position as both the executive officers of a highly vulnerable institution and the elected representatives of an aggrieved workforce, UAW leaders could neither endorse a level of militancy that would bring the union down, or refuse to resist the speedup that so angered their membership. UAW leaders thus accepted management's goal of uninterrupted production, but also insisted that management, as well as workers, had to honor contracts that defined production standards and stipulated that they would not be altered capriciously.

Too much recent labor history has emphasized the ways that the UAW disciplined its most militant members. Collective action directed by the union also disciplined management whenever it violated the contract. Over time, the result for auto workers was greater job security, improved conditions on the job, expanded protection of worker health and safety, longer work lives, and perhaps most importantly, power with which workers could contest unilateral management decisions. Between 1937 and 1941, the UAW made great progress toward its goal of establishing a new political regime that recognized and protected the humanity of workers.

Acknowledgment

The authors' research was funded by grants from the Henry J. Kaiser Family Foundation. Robert Asher's research was also funded by the Research Foundation of the University of Connecticut.

4

AUTO WORKERS AT WAR: PATRIOTISM AND PROTEST IN THE AMERICAN AUTOMOBILE INDUSTRY, 1939–1945

....

Kevin Boyle

Late in the afternoon of March 9, 1945, Republican senator Homer Ferguson, Michigan's representative on the Senate Special Committee Investigating the National Defense Program, paid an unannounced visit to the Packard Motor Company plant on Detroit's lower east side. The plant, contracted to produce marine and aircraft engines, was hardly abuzz with activity when the senator walked in. Half an hour before the end of the day shift, a number of production workers idly cleaned their machines, a wheel polisher slept face down on an air conditioning unit, and two gear grinders played checkers. Appalled, Ferguson demanded that the men explain themselves before the Senate committee the next Monday.[1]

When the checker players, Freddie Goggin and Purdy Irwin, Jr., came before the committee, they were unrepentant. In the early days of World War II, Goggin explained, "the foreman would come up to us and tell us that they needed more gears [and] we were willing to give them to them [sic] . . . . I say that not only for myself but for all the men. They would go all out . . . . But then it was getting to the point there where they started cutting down on hours and they started cutting down on the number of workers, and naturally everyone figured . . . that they were working themselves out of jobs."[2]

Goggin's attitude was hardly unusual. Shopfloor conflict, both large and small, was endemic in the auto industry throughout the war years, as workers resisted a wide array of management initiatives, from the retiming of a job to the upgrading of newly-hired blacks. The struggle peaked during the latter half of the war, when a staggering 65 percent of Michigan United Automobile Worker (UAW) members participated in wildcat strikes, shutting down some of the most pivotal war plants in the nation for days at a time. "The situation in some of these plants is so tense," an exasperated Walter Reuther admitted in early 1945, "sometimes just the slightest spark will ignite the powder keg."[3]

The auto workers' wartime militancy has received a substantial amount of scholarly attention in recent years. Once dismissed by labor historians as little more than the unruly behavior of workers unwilling to abide by union discipline, the shopfloor struggles and wildcat strikes of World War II increasingly have been portrayed as one of the most intense moments of "a protracted conflict with the bosses over . . . distribution of power in the factory." Building on David Montgomery's pathbreaking work, historians Nelson Lichtenstein, Martin Glaberman, and others have argued that auto workers, under the direction of militant shop stewards, took advantage of favorable wartime conditions to extend the rank-and-file's relative control of the shopfloor. Although often devoid of overt political content, World War II job actions, according to this view, had the potential to reshape the American factory regime along social democratic lines. "The wartime struggles over factory discipline," Lichtenstein contends, "seemed to lay the basis for a decentralized system of post-war industrial relations in the auto industry that would incorporate . . . effective shop floor bargaining over production standards. . . . This system would not have been far different from that which in fact came to characterize large sections of the British industry of the postwar era."[4]

This sense of "shopfloor syndicalism" was undercut, the argument runs, by both institutional and cultural forces. Anxious to formalize their place in the American political economy, the UAW leadership vigorously opposed the rank-and-file's militancy as contrary to the centralized, highly bureaucratic, "responsible unionism" that the union hierarchy favored. At the same time, the government's unremitting appeals to patriotism, typically couched in the appealing promise of cultural pluralism, undermined the auto workers' sense of class aggrievement. By so doing, the government made it all but impossible for the rank-and-file to develop "an oppositional social vision" that might have infused the workers' job actions with ideological legitimacy. Buffeted by these forces, the auto workers' militancy, it is argued, collapsed in the immediate post-war years, falling victim to the pull of Cold War consensus politics on the one hand, and to management's re-assertion of its shopfloor prerogatives on the other.[5]

This essay offers a substantially different interpretation. Undoubtedly, there were shopfloor activists—members of the Trotskyite Workers Party, for instance—who hoped that the workers' job actions could be transformed into a broader struggle against management and union policies. A good deal of evidence indicates, however, that for rank-and-filers like Freddie Coggin, the factory-level conflicts of World War II were generally defensive moves, designed not to push the boundaries of worker control, but rather to prevent erosion of traditional practices or newly-won union rights. Far from undercutting that defense, the hyper-patriotism of the period actually contributed to the intensity of rank-and-file's reaction to management. As Gary Gerstle has shown in his fine study of Depression-era textile workers, ordinary people could define and use "the political language" of Americanism to serve their political, economic, and social needs. Wartime auto workers, I contend, did precisely that, with explosive results.[6]

World War II transformed the American automobile industry in many ways. Most obviously, from early 1942 onward, the industry served as the nation's leading producer of military material, turning out a staggering array of aircraft, tanks, jeeps, shells, and rifles for the war effort. Assured of a comfortable profit through the federal government's cost-plus contract system, the industry launched a massive expansion campaign, retooling old plants and constructing new facilities. Between 1940 and 1944, for example, General Motors built nearly $900 million in new plants, a sum greater than its total capital assets in 1939. As government orders poured in, the industry also added almost five hundred thousand new workers to its payrolls, pushing the total number of auto workers above the million mark. Unable to find enough white males to fill the available slots, auto makers drew many of their new hires from groups, especially women and blacks, which had heretofore been largely excluded from auto work. The change was dramatic. By 1943, every second auto worker in Detroit was new to the auto industry.[7]

When they walked onto the shopfloor, the new hires stepped into a world of rights and regulations created by generations of auto workers determined to exercise at least some control over their work lives. Those rights and regulations took two forms. For decades, auto workers had taken direct action at the point of production to challenge management's control of the pace of work. In the late 1930s, the factory hands, working through their new union, had established detailed work rules and grievance procedures designed to check management's shopfloor disciplinary system.

Auto workers had not gained these rights easily. A host of scholars have detailed the devastating effect the establishment of assembly line production in the early twentieth century had on auto workers. By subdividing the production process and gaining control over the pace of work, auto makers were able to break the power of the skilled craftspersons who had dominated the infant industry. As a result, workers were forced to endure a relentless work pace that left them, in the words of one spouse, "all played out."[8] Managers buttressed the new regime with a strict, and often arbitrary and brutal, disciplinary system. A web of foremen, supervisors, and security personnel enforced petty prohibitions against smoking and talking; regulated lunch breaks, rest periods, and the speed of the line; and, most importantly, controlled the right to upgrade, transfer, and fire workers at will. A production worker of the pre-union era captured the essence of the system. "When he

goes to work at Ford's," he explained, "a man checks his brains and his freedom at the door."[9]

Despite the triumph of Fordism, however, auto workers, particularly the
majority of factory hands who did not work directly on the line, managed to
maintain at least a minimal degree of power on the shopfloor. Adapting the
skilled craftsperson's traditional control of the pace of production to the new
factory conditions, auto workers covertly established their own "stint." At
times they exercised their power in a negative way: sabotaging parts or
destroying tools, for example. At a more sophisticated level, auto workers
intentionally slowed their work pace while being subjected to time studies,
held their daily output to a level agreeable to their fellow workers, and stashed
away completed parts for use when they felt like slacking off.[10]

Experienced hands quickly inculcated new hires into the system, typically taking them aside and telling them to slow the pace. Workers who refused
to cooperate could be treated harshly. "They were ostracized," a gear cutter
and political activist in the Continental Motors plant explained in his mem-
oirs. "Every time one of them went for a drink of water or to the washroom,
the belts on his machine were cut, his personal tools were damaged, the word
`RAT' was chalked on his machine in block letters. . . . I remember that two
of the speed kings could not take it any longer and quit Continental."[11]

Auto workers used the same tactics to exercise a minor veto power over
their employers' hiring practices. The auto makers obviously controlled the
hiring gate, and foremen often enjoyed exclusive power to bring new hands
into their work crews. Workers, however, often harassed and abused new
hires they found unacceptable. When an immigrant-born "learner" refused to
buy World War I war bonds, for instance, his fellow workers beat him, covered him with yellow paint, and insisted that the management dismiss the
worker. White workers reacted particularly vehemently on the rare occasions
that management attempted to cross the color line that relegated blacks to
foundry, janitorial, and similarly unsavory jobs. "They [company officials]
always say it's not company policy to put coloreds on machines," a white
worker explained in 1940. "Coloreds have worked on machines years ago.
But they're have been 'accidents.' A colored fellow gets pushed into a
machine or something else happens. That's probably one of the reasons why
they don't work on machines now."[12]

Auto workers' power over the pace of their work should not be exagger-
ated. Throughout the pre-union era, the factory hands' stint amounted to little
more than "silent and opaque resistence," in David Montgomery's words,
small acts by men and women pushed to the edge of their endurance. That was
particularly the case in the early and mid-1930s. Struggling to maximize productivity while reducing the number of hands, auto manufacturers quickened

the speed of the lines. Desperate to hold onto their jobs, auto workers had no choice but to keep pace. The brutal work regime quickly took its toll. "My husband, he's a torch solderer," a woman in Flint, Michigan told a reporter. " . . . at night in bed he shakes, his whole body, he shakes." With the triumph of unionization in the late 1930s, however, auto workers asserted more strongly than ever their traditional right to take informal action over work pace. As Nelson Lichtenstein has argued, "shopfloor . . . confrontations, slowdowns, and stoppages proliferated after the sitdown strikes of 1937." General Motors alone experience 435 unauthorized work stoppages between mid-1937 and mid-1939.[13]

The UAW likewise gave the hands the leverage they needed to check management's shopfloor disciplinary system. Until 1937, a Flint Fisher Body worker recalled years later, "no unions, no rules: you were at the mercy of the foreman. I could go to work at seven o'clock in the morning, and at seven fifteen the boss'd come around and say: you could come back at three o'clock. If he preferred someone else over you, that person would be called back earlier, though you were there longer." In their earliest contracts with the auto makers, consequently, workers insisted on the detailed classification of jobs and wages, the strict application of seniority in transferring and upgrading, and carefully negotiated procedures for timing jobs and breaks, all to be enforced through an elaborate grievance procedure.[14]

The record of grievances filed by workers at one Detroit plant, the Chrysler Corporation's Jefferson Avenue facility, illustrates the point. No single plant is representative of the auto industry as a whole, of course, but Jefferson Avenue is fairly typical of the large production plant that served as the UAW's backbone in the union's formative years. Built in 1908 on Detroit's east side, the factory employed some 7,000 workers by the late 1930s. Union sentiment had been widespread in the plant throughout the Depression years; despite Chrysler's adamant opposition to meaningful unionization, both the American Federation of Labor and the Coughlinite Automotive Industrial Workers Association made at least some inroads in the factory. In the wake of the Flint sit-down strike, the Jefferson hands threw their lot in with the UAW, occupying the plant for seventeen days in March 1937 until the corporation recognized the union. The UAW chartered the plant as Local 7.[15]

Local officials began keeping grievance records in December 1939, after Chrysler formally recognized the procedure in that year's contract. Over the next twelve months, rank-and-filers at the plant, undoubtedly enjoying the opportunity to address long-simmering problems, pursued 413 grievances to the third stage. Over one third of these came from groups of workers, often entire departments. Even by conservative estimates, then, approximately one in every four workers in the factory took advantage of the grievance process during its first year, a remarkably high level of activity. The numbers fell off precipitously the next year, when workers filed only 150 grievances. Once again, however, one third of these complaints came from groups, so like the year before a substantial minority of rank-and-filers, approximately one in every thirteen hands, participated in the process.[16]

In both years, wage issues were the single greatest cause of grievances, accounting for 30 percent of grievances filed between December 1, 1939 and December 1, 1940, and 22 percent of those filed during the next twelve months. After wages, rank-and-filers were most likely to grieve over questions of upgrading, seniority, and safety. Taken together, these four issues accounted for three fourths of all grievances filed at the plant in the first twenty-four months that the system was in place. On the other hand, workers rarely grieved questions of work pace: the issue accounted for only 8 percent of grievances filed during the 1939–1940 period, and 4 percent of those filed in 1940–1941.

TABLE 3
Grievances Filed at the Jefferson Avenue Assembly Plant, December 1939–December 1941

	Upgrd	Wages	Disc	Sfty	Wkpce	Contr	Senr	Misc	Total
				Issues					
Dec–Dec	98	124	24	37	34	46	42	8	413
1939–1940	23.7%	30.0%	5.8%	8.9%	8.2%	11.1%	10.1%	1.9%	100%
Dec–Dec	14	33	31	33	6	10	31	2	150
1940–1941	9.3%	22.0%	14.0%	22.0%	4.0%	6.6%	20.6%	1.3%	100%

Source: Grievance files, Local 7 Collection, Walter Reuther Library.

Key to Grievance Issues in Tables 3–5
Upgrd — Job Upgrading
Disc — Discipline
Sfty — Safety and Job Conditions
Wkpce — Work Pace
Contr — Contract Violations
Senr — Senority
Misc — Miscellaneous; Typically Plant Wide Issues such as Smoking Rules, Shift Changes, etc.

Auto workers thus saw the grievance process as a way of enforcing work rules and correcting abuses, not as an avenue through which they could challenge managerial control of the production process. Seemingly mundane and inherently bureaucratic, the system was of fundamental importance to rank-and-filers, as a high-level UAW staffer explained in a 1972 interview. "Even though it has given just a limited kind of freedom," he said of the grievance procedure, "it brings enormous satisfactions . . . to a guy who is on the job, you know, and has some son of a bitch misuse him and then is able really to do something about it."[18]

By the time the United States entered World War II, auto workers had already developed a two-pronged response to corporate authority on the shopfloor; employing subterfuge, and even sabotage, to maintain some control over work pace while insisting on grievable work rules, and job classifications as a check on management's arbitrary use of power. The pattern did not change during the war years, despite the social tensions and economic shifts that the conflict engendered.

Local 7's grievance records again serve as a benchmark. Like factories throughout Detroit, the Jefferson Avenue plant experienced dramatic changes during the war. In the months after Pearl Harbor, the plant switched to total war production, manufacturing guns, tank parts, fire trucks, marine motors, and airplane wings. To meet the new schedule, Chrysler boosted the factory's work force from its pre-War level of 7,000 to a wartime peak of approximately 9,500 in mid-1943. Facing an increasingly tight labor pool, the corporation filled many of the new slots with workers who heretofore had been denied access to production jobs during the first year and a half of the war, Chrysler doubled the number of blacks and tripled the number of women in the plant.[19]

These changes undoubtedly altered many social relations in the facility, but they did not affect the rank-and-file's perception of the grievance process. Like their pre-War predecessors, the wartime workers at Jefferson Assembly continued to make wage issues their primary complaint. For example, wage concerns accounted for one third of all grievances filed in 1942. The majority of those were filed in the first half of the year before the Roosevelt administration imposed wage restrictions. The number of wage grievances declined thereafter, while the number of grievances over the upgrading of job classifications, the surest way for a worker to secure a pay boost without violating the federal wage guidelines, increased.[20]

Safety and seniority issues likewise continued to be common causes of grievances. As in the pre-War years, safety concerns consistently accounted for at least 10 percent of grievances filed during the war, though at times the numbers rose dramatically. In March 1943 alone, for example, workers in the plant filed fourteen safety grievances: workers in the dynometer room complained of inadequate ventilation; spraymen demanded overalls; women working on the airplane wing job requested chairs; and the like. Concern over seniority, meanwhile, fluctuated during the war years, peaking during 1942 and 1945, when Chrysler was laying off workers, and ebbing in 1943 and 1944, when jobs were plentiful.[21]

If specific wartime conditions affected the mix of issues grieved, however, it did not affect the overall pattern set prior to Pearl Harbor. Just as in 1940 and 1941, wage, upgrading, seniority, and safety issues accounted for two thirds of all grievances filed. The number of grievances filed over the pace of work, on the other hand, actually declined during the war: there was only one such grievance filed in the plant in 1944, for example, and none filed in the first eight months of 1945.[22]

Even the most confrontational of grievances, those filed over questions of shopfloor discipline, did not break the trend. Most disciplinary cases involved workers who believed that they had been unfairly disciplined by their foremen for some shopfloor offense. By filing such grievances, the plant hands directly challenged their supervisors' ability to set work rules. It seems reasonable to expect, therefore, that a substantial number of these grievances resulted from conflicts over work pace, perhaps the most volatile of shopfloor issues. That was not the case, however. Of the fifty-eight disciplinary grievances

TABLE 4
Grievances Filed at the Jefferson Avenue Assembly Plant,
January 1942–August 1945

	Upgrd	Wages	Disc	Sfty	Wkpce	Contr	Senr	Misc	Total
				Issues					
1942	47	62	12	19	6	9	26	5	185
	25.3%	33.3%	6.5%	10.2%	3.2%	4.8%	14.0%	2.7%	100%
1943	51	38	19	23	3	9	14	2	159
	32.0%	23.9%	12.0%	14.5%	1.9%	5.7%	8.8%	1.2%	100%
1944	39	18	22	19	1	10	5	1	115
	33.9%	15.7%	19.1%	16.5%	0.9%	8.7%	4.3%	0.9%	100%
Jan.–Aug.	8	12	5	4	0	2	5	1	37
1945	21.6%	32.4%	13.6%	10.8%	0%	5.4%	13.5%	2.7%	100%

Source: Grievance records, Local 7 Collection.

rank-and-filers at Jefferson Assembly submitted in the three and a half years from Pearl Harbor to V-J Day, only thirteen involved work pace issues.[23]

It is impossible to generalize from Local 7 to the UAW as a whole; specific conditions in other plants undoubtedly affected the type of grievances workers in those facilities filed. There is reason to believe, however, that Jefferson Avenue's wartime grievance pattern was fairly representative. In February 1943, the UAW Research Department asked a random sample of the union's Detroit area members a series of questions designed to give the International a better sense of shopfloor tensions. Asked to name to most common cause of grievances in their plants, 43 percent of the 174 respondents cited wages, and two thirds cited wages, upgrading, safety and seniority issues. Wage complaints, in turn, fell into two broad categories. Many workers simply believed that they were being underpaid for the work they performed, a perception made all the more galling by high wartime inflation. "The company don't want to pay the money it shoulde [sic], a millwright at the Chevrolet tank plant in suburban Warren wrote. "So I wont [sic] more money." An inspector at the Detroit Micromatic plant offered a similar complaint. The primary source of grievances in his plant, he explained, was "money, money, and more money." Some factory hands, meanwhile, insisted that workers in other plants or other departments were receiving higher wages for comparable jobs. "We are not getting paid the wages that other manufacture [sic] are paying," a machinist at Packard complained, a charge echoed by workers at Chrysler, Cadillac, Dodge, Plymouth, Ford, Hudson, and Briggs. In contrast, only 3 percent of the workers polled said that work pace was the major point of friction.[24]

This is not to say that wartime auto workers had no objection to the pace of work, though it seems likely that by the onset of war most companies no longer maintained the brutal speeds they had established in the 1930s. When conflicts arose, however, rank-and-filers simply dealt with the issue, as they had in the past, by taking matters into their own hands. It is impossible to doc-

TABLE 5
Source of Grievances in Detroit-area Plants, 1943

| | *Issues* | | | | | | | | |
	Upgrd	Wages	Disc	Sfty	Wkpce	Contr	Senr	Misc	Total
Number	19	76	19	10	5	10	11	24	174
Percent	10.9%	43.7%	10.9%	5.7%	2.9%	5.7%	6.3%	13.7%	100%

Source: UAW Research Department 1943 postcard survey, Box 14, UAW Research Department Collection, Walter Reuther Library.

ument incidents of the informal "stint" systematically, but a substantial amount of anecdotal evidence indicates that they were quite common during the war years. The Automobile Manufacturers Association (AMA), the industry's leading trade group, conducted the most in-depth examination of work pace conflict at the point of production. Appearing before a Senate investigating committee in March 1945, AMA spokespeople claimed that by refusing to meet management's output goals, shopfloor "drones and militant hotheads" were "destroying the industry's productivity." To prove its case, the AMA presented the senators with an extensive catalogue of work pace conflicts in Detroit area plants. Though neither objective nor comprehensive, the AMA's list does offer a feel for the variety of ways in which wartime auto workers, like their predecessors, set their own "stint."[25]

Workers whose jobs permitted it often simply set the pace that suited them best. In August 1944, for example, supervisors at one General Motors plant discovered that welders on a truck job were averaging ten rather than the required twelve pieces per hour. When the supervisors investigated the shortfall, they found that the welders typically produced sixteen pieces the first hour they were on the job, then gradually eased their pace, so that by the hour before lunch they were producing only two or three pieces. They followed the same procedure after lunch until they reached their daily average of ten.[26]

Rank-and-filers who did not enjoy such autonomy over their work often employed more covert tactics. During the Foreman's Association strike of mid-1944, workers in one unnamed plant reduced their work pace by failing to notify management of stock shortages, assembling only one side of a two-piece part, claiming that they did not know how to turn on air lines and lights and, in perhaps the least sophisticated of measures, hiding fixtures and stock. Welders at Briggs used an even more subtle strategy. When foremen complained that they were spending too much of the day away from their jobs, the welders increased the amount of time they spent at their stations, but reduced the flames on their torches.[27]

When management actually tried to change long-standing production standards, deception could give way to confrontation, as workers, undoubtedly emboldened by the wartime labor shortage, simply refused to follow company directives. Furnace operators at Ford ignored a company order that they run two furnaces rather than one, and machine hands at Briggs refused to increase their output of gasoline tanks even after the corporation re-arranged the line to make the job easier. Workers at Chevrolet's gear and axle plant, on the other hand, followed their time-study instructions to the letter. During the first two years of the war, the hands in one department produced eight axle joints per hour. In mid-1944, shop managers re-timed the job to 8.6 joints per hour, but by a clerical error, they informed the rank-and-filers that they were to produce 6.6 parts per hour. The workers immediately reduced their output accordingly. Two months later management discovered the error and demanded that the department pick up the pace. The workers refused.[28]

As in the pre-War years, experienced rank-and-filers trained new hires in the system, a role that took on added importance as thousands of workers new to industrial labor flooded into the auto factories. At times the new hands enjoyed the lessons. "Oh, I met all those wonderful Polacks," a migrant from Kentucky recalled years later. "A whole new world just opened up. I learned to drink beer like crazy with 'em. They were all very union-conscious. I learned a lot of things that I didn't even know existed." Not all encounters were as pleasant. In one case, the Fall Spring and Wire company hired a small number of women to make bomb bodies. Management insisted that the women could produce 520 bodies a day. The UAW disagreed, claiming that the new employees could make a maximum of 360 bodies a day. When the women exceeded the union's figure, their fellow workers insulted them and told them, as one of the hands described it, to "cut down or else." Production quickly dropped.[29]

Although they follow patterns established in the years prior to Pearl Harbor, incidents such as these could have carried the tremendous political potential that historians have ascribed to them. By filing a grievance or enforcing a slow-down, after all, auto workers were challenging management's absolute control of the shopfloor. In that regard, they were developing the sense of "shopfloor syndicalism" that Lichtenstein has described. It is not particularly difficult to imagine rank-and-filers wanting to move beyond these practices to demand a less *ad hoc* and more comprehensive say in factory-level decision making that would give shop stewards the right to bargain over production standards and work rules.

Some auto workers undoubtedly did want to see such a fundamental transformation of shopfloor relations. Most rank-and-filers, however, seem to have harbored no such goals. The opinion of every wartime auto worker cannot be documented, of course, but the UAW Research Department's 1943 membership survey provides at least a sample of rank-and-filers' attitudes toward their jobs. Forty-three percent of the 242 workers surveyed indicated that they were unhappy with the war production in their plants. Despite this high level of dissatisfaction, only three of the workers surveyed—a minuscule 1.2 percent of the total—favored a drastic restructuring of labor-management relations: a worker at the Chevrolet Drop Forge plant thought the federal government ought to take over the plants; an aircraft repairman at Briggs insisted that "labor should be taken in [to the war effort] as a partner and not as an interested spectator"; and a material handler at the Ford Highland Park plant argued that if "good union men" were in charge, production could "be doubled with half the force."[30]

The vast majority of rank-and-filers, on the other hand, offered more mundane suggestions for shopfloor improvements. A grinder at Packer wanted more money; a plater at Continental Motors called for more stock and better cafeteria service; a rigger at Willow Run wanted more efficient foremen; a laborer at the American Brake Block company demanded that blacks be put on production jobs; an aircraft assembler at Murray Body thought the hands should work more hours; and a machinist at the Dodge Lynch Road facility insisted that the corporation should "concentrate on quality rather than quantity." Thoroughly practical, such ideas simply proposed to fine tune rather than dramatically alter shopfloor relations.[31]

The unprecedented level of shopfloor turmoil in the auto industry during World War II cannot be explained, therefore, as a consequence of the rank-and-filers' desire for greater control over their work lives. But why did auto workers so often turn to tactics as militant as the wildcat if they simply wanted to maintain the patterns of labor-management relations worked out in the pre-war years? To answer that question, it is necessary to look beneath the rank-and-file's actions to examine the meaning that workers gave to those actions. As William Sewell and others have argued, "the language of labor"— the words, rhetorical conventions, and symbols through which workers shaped their experiences—offers one of the most effective tools for reconstructing that meaning.[32]

Throughout the pre-union era, auto workers insisted that they had not only an economic, but a moral right to control the work pace by limiting production. Writing in 1931, Antioch College professor Stanley Mathewson recounted a scene he witnessed while working in an Ohio truck plant. Management had decided to switch the workers in an assembly department from hourly to piece rate. In the weeks before the time-study men arrived, the workers agreed to drop their daily output from twenty to fifteen pieces. Two men in the department worked together assembling parts for the driver's cab. One of the two killed as much time as he could, but despite his efforts, the pair still completed seventeen pieces at the end of the day. "The dilatory worker was angry about this," Mathewson reported, "and insisted that they alter the time cards to show only fifteen for the day's work. He argued fluently that it was a matter of food, clothing and shelter, and he would stand for no refusal."[33]

Similarly, as Steve Jefferys points out in his study of the Chrysler corporation's Dodge Main plant, many auto workers understood the seniority and grievance procedures won in the 1930s as mechanisms securing them their basic rights as Americans, rights long-denied by management's arbitrary disciplinary regime. "This country was founded . . . to get away from the brutal treatment the British gave [the colonists] and us true Americans intend keeping it so," the wife of an auto worker wrote Franklin Roosevelt in 1939. "We need men of wealth and men of intelligence but we also need to make labor healthy and self-supporting or our nation will soon crumble. . . ." Another worker put the matter more succinctly. He and his shopmates joined the union, he explained, because "we wanted to get away from tyranny." By explicitly employing this republican rhetorical tradition, the rank-and-filers were able to imbue their contractual gains with a profound legitimacy. Seniority lists, grievance procedures, and the rest were not simply the result of union power, the auto workers implicitly insisted. They were, rather, a natural extension of the auto workers' birthright as Americans.[34]

It is not particularly surprising that auto workers interpreted their victories in such a way. Earlier in the century, auto plants had been dominated by immigrant workers, many of whom were more interested in maintaining their ethnic identities than in adopting the ideals of "Americanism." By the late 1930s, however, the industry's work force had changed dramatically. In 1914, for example, only 29 percent of the Ford Motor Company's hourly employees had been born in the United States; by 1940, 70 percent of Ford's workers were native-born. A large number of these workers were the sons and daughters of immigrants and they still retained strong ties to their parents' ethnic communities, but as second generation Americans, they had also adopted large parts of American culture.[35]

For its part, the UAW did its best to reinforce the workers' linkage of unionism and Americanism. Union officials always made sure that there was at least one, and often more than one, American flag at a UAW parade or rally; UAW organizers provided picketers with signs declaring "The Union Way is the American Way"; and UAW locals often started their meetings by singing the national anthem. Even when the rank-and-file was at its most militant, as during the 1937 sit-down wave, the union pressed the theme. "The men in the plants seem to be good Americans, good citizens," the Dodge Main strike bulletin declared in typical style. "They want to have real collective bargaining which rightfully belongs to them. . . . They want to have fair play with the management." Conversely, UAW spokesmen insisted that corporate officials who opposed unionization were un-American. When management proved recalcitrant during the 1937 Guide Lamp strike in Anderson, Indiana, for example, union organizers demanded that the city be "re-annex[ed]" to the United States.[36]

UAW leaders had more than the rank-and-file in mind when they made such claims. From their perspective, it was even more important to convince the general public that unionism was well within the American tradition. As any number of labor historians have noted, the CIO enjoyed phenomenal success in the late 1930s in large measure because the federal government was willing to undergird union claims to collective bargaining. Union officials realized that the support was very tenuous, however. In the wake of the sit-down wave, for instance, conservatives in both parties condemned the tactic as "ominous" and "un-American"; Franklin Roosevelt denounced the CIO after the bloody Little Steel strike of 1937; and in 1938 and 1939 a number of congressmen introduced measures designed to roll back the Wagner Act. Given this situation, UAW leaders believed, the union simply could not afford to project anything less than the most patriotic of images.[37]

That strategy took on even greater importance with the outbreak of war in Europe, and particularly after the fall of France in June 1940, when public opinion shifted strongly behind the Roosevelt administration's call for a massive defense build-up. UAW leaders immediately seized on the growing concern. The auto workers, they insisted, stood squarely against fascist aggression, unlike the auto makers, who were willing to compromise the nation's defenses in order to maximize profits. "Labor wants national defense because labor is America," UAW president R.J. Thomas declared in February 1941. "Labor has the experience, the brains, and the patriotism to solve our defense problems. If industry does not do any better than it has been doing it will have to take a back seat and let those who want to do the job take the wheel."[38]

The auto makers did little to counter the UAW's charges. Despite the mounting European crisis, the manufacturers resisted government exhortations to convert their facilities to defense production. As late as June 1941, the major auto producers had reduced passenger car production levels by a mere 20 percent. Consequently, the industry gobbled up substantial amounts of steel, nickel, chrome, and other vital war material. Moreover, once the auto makers switched to war production, they funnelled much of the federal funds they received into the construction of new plants rather than the much more rapid re-tooling of existing facilities. Over 60 percent of the $1.9 billion in defense contracts awarded to the major auto makers by Autumn 1941 was earmarked for the construction of new factories, none of which would be operational until the next year.[39]

Throughout 1940 and early 1941, union spokesmen pressed, both in the public arena and at the factory gate, the contrast between the union's and the manufacturer's commitment to the war. In his widely-publicized "500 Planes a Day" plan of December 1940, UAW Vice-President Walter Reuther compared the UAW's desire to immediately launch defense production with the manufacturers' desire to stall on military orders until the federal government built the companies new plants. Similarly, during the April 1941 Ford strike, UAW organizers, playing on Henry Ford's friendliness with Adolph Hitler, distributed picket signs attacking "Ford and Fascism" and demanding that Dearborn, home of the company's massive Rouge complex, be "brought back into the U.S."[40]

Such rhetoric undoubtedly reinforced the rank-and-file's linkage of patriotism and shopfloor militancy. At the very least, there is no indication that auto workers checked their militancy in the face of the European crisis. On the contrary, General Motors workers in Flint threatened a major walk-out in September 1940 when G.M. disciplined seventeen union activists for wildcatting; Michigan's governor had to dispatch state troopers to Saginaw in January 1941 to keep order after UAW picketers and city police clashed at the Wilcox-Rich plant of the Eaton Manufacturing Company; and the same month 8,000 workers walked out of the Allis-Chalmers plant in Milwaukee, a major military contractor, when the company fired six union members. Such incidents were unusual, of course, but even on a more routine level, workers displayed a high degree of activism. From December 1939 to June 1940, for example, workers in the Jefferson Avenue plant filed 277 grievances, far more than they would file in any other six month period in the course of the next twenty years.[41]

In mid-1941, however, the situation changed. Public sentiment had been shifting against union militancy for some time. In September 1940, Americans polled by the Gallup organization did not even include unions among the forces causing defense production delays: Four months later, they ranked unions as the second most common cause. In late May, Franklin Roosevelt, exasperated by the labor turmoil, added his powerful voice to the chorus, warning union leaders that the administration would "use of all its power" to prevent disruption of military production, which, he hinted, was being caused by fifth columnists. Early the next month he backed up his threat by asking Congress for legislation empowering him to prevent strikes in defense plants.[42]

Recognizing the danger that the growing anti-labor sentiment posed to the union, UAW leaders quickly moved to dampen the rank-and-file's militancy. In one of the best known incidents of the period, union officials squelched a June 1941 strike of 4,000 workers at the North American Aviation plant in Inglewood, California. The UAW leadership had been trying to organize the plant since late 1940 and had authorized a strike vote in May 1941, but had hoped to avoid a shut-down as too provocative a step. The workers did not agree, and on June 4th, the night shift walked out of the plant. By the next morning, pickets, aided by a substantial contingent of communist organizers, circled the complex. The Roosevelt administration was outraged at the action. The shut-down halted 25 percent of all fighter plane production, and the administration privately threatened to take over the plant. The UAW leadership, desperate to avoid such an embarrassment, pleaded with the strikers to return to their jobs, but their efforts failed, and on June 9, FDR, acting with R. J. Thomas' full knowledge, dispatched 2,500 soldiers to Inglewood to break the strike.[43]

For the most part, however, the UAW leadership did not resort to such extreme measures. Rather, they simply added a new wrinkle: the message they had been presenting since the war began in Europe. Auto workers, UAW spokesmen declared, were the most important component in the nation's defense structure, a point the union drove home by posting in plants a raft of posters, cartoons, and slogans extolling the workers' contribution to the mobilization effort. One widely re-printed cartoon, for example, showed a vigorous Uncle Sam turning a crank on the side of a factory, out of which poured defense production. The caption read, "We're Helping, Uncle Sam." Given their pivotal position, the union leadership insisted, auto workers had to be willing to make the sacrifices necessary to maintain production. All the union asked in return, they concluded, is that corporate America overcome its inertia and pick up a fair share of the burden. " . . . If sacrifices are to be made," UAW Secretary-Treasurer George Addes told the November 1941 CIO convention, "management and big business ought to set aside once and for all the idea of 'business as usual.' The automobile workers appeal to government and appeal to management to give us the work, and we will produce the necessary munitions of war."[44]

In the weeks after the Japanese attack on Pearl Harbor, this rhetorical approach hardened into a policy that would guide the union for the duration of the conflict. Immediately after the United States declared war, both the American Federation of Labor and the CIO issued no-strike pledges. UAW leaders joined their fellow unionists in abrogating the right to strike, of course, but they insisted that the auto workers' pledge be imbedded within a broader program calling for "equality of sacrifice." More specifically, UAW leaders pledged unconditionally to forego both strikes and double time for Sunday and holidays. The union insisted, however, that "the winning of the war requires more than these sacrifices on the part of labor." Accordingly, the UAW called on the federal government to impose strict ceilings on prices, to limit corporate profits to a 3 percent return on investment, to cap salaries at $25,000 a year, and to begin postwar economic planning. Local leaders at the Ford Rouge plant captured the essence of the program. "All sections of our population must . . . unite in this [war] effort," they declared in the local's newspaper, "but to us, the men and women who work in our factories and fields, American democracy is more important than [to] any [other] single group. This war is our war to protect *our* democracy." By so arguing, the UAW leadership continued to lay claim to the patriotic high ground, while at the same time trying to eliminate shopfloor militancy. This was a coherent and politically sophisticated position, but it had one serious flaw: it encouraged, rather than dampened, rank-and-file activism.[45]

This is not to say that most rank-and-filers opposed the no-strike pledge. On the contrary, 71 percent of UAW members polled in 1943 believed that the union was correct in promising to forego strikes for the duration. A few workers supported the pledge for political reasons. A sprayer at Murray Body backed the pledge, for instance, because "reactionary and labor-hating congressmen would use [wartime strikes] to pass anti-labor legislation." Most rank-and-filers, however, agreed with the no-strike policy out of a sense of patriotism. "I think we can't do enough for our boys in service," a hand cutter at Ford's Highland Park plant insisted. Similarly, a filer at Plymouth declared that "we should all do our part here for the boys in the field." And a lathe operator at a small parts plant simply asserted that "we are working for [the] U.S. now." A trucker at the Chevrolet Drop Forge plant summed up the prevailing sentiment. "I believe that all men in the plant are # 1 Americans," he wrote.[46]

As the UAW leadership argued, most auto workers had every reason to believe that World War II was their war. By the time of Pearl Harbor, thousands of auto workers had already been drafted, and countless others had sons, brothers, and husbands in the service. Workers therefore contributed wholeheartedly to the war effort: contributing to plant-wide blood drives, buying war bonds, mounting letter-writing campaigns to men overseas, carefully saving scrap from their machines, and other patriotic measures. Even the most militant segments of the union contributed to the cause. The members of Briggs Local 212, for example, had won a wide-spread reputation for radicalism in the 1930s. Nevertheless, 75 percent of the 17,000 local members contributed to the War Chest Fund in 1942.[47]

In the months immediately after Pearl Harbor, many auto workers came to believe that such patriotic fervor was decidedly one-sided. To be sure, the Roosevelt administration tried to project the impression that the economic transformation to total war would be fair and equitable. Perhaps the most important gesture came in January 1942, when the White House placed the mobilization effort under the direction of Donald Nelson. A former Sears, Roebuck and Co. executive, Nelson was acceptable to the business community. As head of the Supply Priorities and Allocation Board in 1940 and 1941, on the other hand, he had developed friendly relations with a number of labor leaders, including Walter Reuther. His appointment thus served, in the words of one historian, as a "symbolic accommodation to those labor-liberal forces that feared big business domination of the wartime economy."[48]

It proved to be little more than symbolic, however. Both Nelson and the White House wanted to coax rather than coerce business into all-out military production. As Nelson later explained, he wanted "to establish a set of rules under which the game could be played the way industry said it had to be played." Accordingly, the administration provided manufacturers with a guaranteed profit by offering defense contracts on a "cost-plus" basis; it liberalized tax laws for those firms that expanded existing or built new plants, and it left procurement policy in the hands of the military, which was traditionally sympathetic to business and hostile to labor concerns.[49] No matter how well attuned to the demands of a capitalist economy, this policy invited abuse. The results, when contrasted with the UAW's rhetoric of equal sacrifice, simply heightened the workers' sense of aggrievement.

The sharpest blow came immediately after Pearl Harbor, when the auto companies laid-off over 100,000 workers while the plants finally began to retool for wartime production. Many workers reacted bitterly to the corporations' actions. " . . . some of the manufacturers would rather have bussiness [sic] as usual and have the war effort last a long time," a 28-year old Ford worker wrote to the UAW in February 1942. A 35-year old driver at a Detroit-area plant agreed. "It is a shame the way the manufacturers are getting away with murder by stalling on war orders," he charged. A 38-year old polisher at the Lansing Fisher Body plant put the matter even more harshly. "There's 6,000 hand skill [sic] men in Lansing out of work that can make material with their hands and heads, they can *think*," he complained. "If the working people must sacrifice and fight to save Ford's plant in Singapore, and Standard Oil wells in the Far East, and G.M. Opal plants in Germany, I think the industrialist and capital should do their part. They are sabatogers [sic]."[50]

The lay-offs were short-lived, of course; by mid-1942 the industry was employing almost twice as many workers as had been employed a year earlier. Once they returned to the plants, however, workers found new reasons to doubt their employers' commitment to the war effort. By late 1942, a number of Detroit area plants had begun to hoard labor, hiring more hands than they needed in expectation of future shortages. Consequently, many workers spent the work day with little or nothing to do. A tool and die maker at the Hudson Naval Ordnance plant in suburban Detroit expressed the resultant sense of frustration in an August 1942 letter to FDR. "I have followed your request and policy of increasing production," he wrote, "and when men and machines were standing idle, I made tools so the men and machines could produce with the stock on hands. Certain people representing the Hudson Motor Car Company and the U.S. Navy did not agree with this policy. I discovered this when . . . I was fired for making tools against company orders. . . . The union suceeded [sic] in getting me re-instated."[51]

Rank-and-filers likewise objected to the manufacturers' attempts to ensure against shortages of supervisors by hiring large number of inexperienced foremen. According to company records for 1943, 42 percent of General Motor's 19,000 foreman had been on the job for less than a year. "The lack of a skilled management is worse than sabatizing [sic]," an aircraft construction worker insisted. "Instead of sending experienced union men to get the job started," a die leader at the Ford Rouge plant complained, "they sent men who did not know [the job]." Another die leader put the matter bluntly. There is "too much red tape and damn fools trying to boss the job," he charged.[52]

Other workers bridled at the military's often high-handed approach to shopfloor issues. An incident at the Ford Rouge plant illustrates the tension. Shortly after Pearl Harbor, plant managers agreed to give tool and die makers a five-minute wash-up period before lunch and at quitting time. A few weeks later, the plant procurement officer, upset that Ford was paying the men for time not actually worked, ordered the agreement abrogated. When the order reached the Sunday night shift, seven of the men refused to comply, instead taking their break. Company officials responded by sending the seven home for the rest of the shift. The next morning the workers stepped up the protest, as two hundred tool and die makers insisted on taking their break. Management likewise raised the stakes, telling all of the several thousand die-makers in the complex to leave for the day. Virtually all them refused, demanding that they be allowed to return to work. " . . . when they were told they were laid off and not being paid for working," local officials reported, "they replied that they would contribute their services to the United States government." The protest continued through the next three shifts, until the procurement officer re-instated the wash-up period.[53]

Given their perception of the production situation, some workers strenuously objected to the corporations' patriotic propaganda blitz. Much of the propaganda, to be sure, extolled the workers' contribution to the war effort, but a significant minority of material presented in both the plants and in the national media, blamed production bottlenecks on the workers. One day, a machine tool manufacturer charged in one of the harshest of such advertisements, returning soldiers "will want to know why you insisted on your 'rights' at the expense of their weapons and lives." The editors of the UAW tool and die makers' newspaper responded in kind to such charges. "THOSE ARE OUR SONS, MR. MONEYBAGS, NOT YOURS," they wrote. "You have claimed and received exemptions for your sons and given them nice cushy jobs in the front office or in some non-combatant spot in Washington. . . . You also forget that by far the great majority of your workers . . . who are over the draft age were the heroes of World War I and have already contributed more to national defense than you ever will." A polisher offered a terse evaluation of both the companies' and the union's efforts to sway opinion. "There is too much political ballyhoo, too much pep talks, songs and propaganda," he explained.[54]

These were not simply the grumblings of a few disgruntled auto workers. According to a 1942 federal government survey, a majority of Detroit workers thought employers would try to use the mobilization process to roll back union gains. And only 30 percent of UAW members surveyed by the union the same year believed that the mobilization was being handled satisfactorily, whereas 50 percent declared themselves dissatisfied with the war effort. This is not to say that auto workers opposed the war itself. On the contrary, when the UAW asked its members why they were unhappy with the mobilization, the most common response, offered by 28 percent of those surveyed, was that military production needed to be increased. A stock checker at Plymouth even went so far as to call for a return to "those good old car production days" when "we were really busy." More importantly for our purposes, 25 percent of the respondents insisted that the war effort was lagging because industrialists were not patriotic enough, and another 13 percent considered "government confusion" to be the root cause of their dissatisfaction with the mobilization.[55]

The UAW did not indicate how it conducted the rank-and-file survey, so the union's findings must be read with caution. Even if the percentages cannot be considered accurate, the study does confirm the general trend: even in the early months of World War II, many auto workers believed that their patriotism far surpassed that of their employers, who, in fact, seemed much more interested in exploiting the national emergency than in sharing in the sacrifices of wartime. This perception obviously reinforced the auto workers' pre-War view that they, rather than their employers, supported basic American

TABLE 6
UAW Rank-and-File Satisfaction with the War Effort, 1942

Response		Percent
Satisfied		30.0%
Dissatisfied		49.6%
More Must Be Done	28.4%	
Companies Not Patriotic	25.4%	
Government Confusion	18.9%	
Labor Not Given a Voice	4.1%	
People Too Apathetic	3.0%	
Specific Plant Problems	3.0%	
Too Many Strikes	1.8%	
No Comment	15.4%	
No Response		20.4%
Total		100.0%

Source: UAW Research Department survey, n.d. (1942), Box 30, UAW Research Department Collection.

values and, by so doing, made many rank-and-filers even more sensitive than they had been to the defense of those values on the shopfloor. "We want to show the world that labor will win the war in the plants and on the field of war," a riveter at Briggs wrote. "I would like to know what the manufactors [*sic*] gived [*sic*] for war." Similarly, a trimmer at the Dodge Truck plant insisted that workers must "make management understand that they can't destroy our union by using the war as a club over our heads. This is our war. We fight it. We pay for it. We make the tools of war." Far from dampening militancy, therefore, the patriotic fervor of the war actually heightened tensions at the point of production.[56]

A minor incident illustrates the point. On February 2, 1942, a machine repairman at the Jefferson Avenue Gun Arsenal let a gear fall from a handcart he was pushing. His foreman, who was standing nearby, grabbed the worker by the shoulder, swore at him, and accused him of sabotage. The worker immediately filed a grievance with his steward, who phrased the complaint in the most dramatic of terms:

> These acts and deeds [he charged] are certainly contrary to the statement of our great President, F.D. Roosevelt, that the morale of the people of the United States of America shall be the greatest factor in winning this war to preserve our Democracy and so that all of the people of the world shall enjoy our freedom. . . . We do not believe that just because a citizen is employed by the Chrysler corporation . . . he surrenders his inalienable rights guaranteed by the Constitution of the United States and any man who arbitrarily seeks to take these rights away is guilty of moral sabotage, a crime much greater than the destruction of our arsenals. . . . The management must bear in mind that a man cannot . . . work or fight for a Democracy that does not exist. We know that this is a Democratic State in a Democratic country, so let's have Democracy in the Gun Plant.[57]

Confrontations like these, now infused with such significance, led many rank-and-filers to believe that their shopfloor rights were in danger. By early 1943, the concern was widespread: two thirds of the UAW members surveyed in February of that year expressed some fear that their employers were trying to roll back the workers' gains while the no-strike pledge was in effect. "Due to [the] no-strike pledge," an inspector at Chevrolet Gear and Axle charged, "it is harder for our men to get justice in many cases." An assembler at Jefferson Avenue agreed. "Looks to be that some of the manufacturers are taking advantage of the workers' cooperative attitude," he wrote. Similarly, a sprayman complained that "the companys [*sic*] sure are taking advantage of that pledge." A scaleman at Chevrolet was even more blunt in his assessment. " . . . we're taking a lot of crap," he declared.[58]

In particular, many workers claimed that the auto makers, immunized from strikes, were refusing to process grievances. "Management would not settle grievances," Jess Ferrazza, wartime president of Briggs Local 212, explained years later. "They would tell us to take them to the War Labor Board. The War Labor Board, although they tried to do the job, was not properly staffed to do the job that had to be done . . . . Many of the workers thought that this was the long course around. They . . . became impatient when their grievances became unsettled." Two rank-and-filers put the charge more succinctly. "Grievances pile up and are ignored," a machine repairman at Ford Rouge told the UAW in early 1943. "[There is] no cooperation from management." A painter at the Chrysler Tank plant offered a similar interpretation: " . . . the company takes advantage of [the pledge] and reject [sic] lots of our grievances."[59]

Hamstrung by the no-strike pledge, the UAW leadership could do little to assuage its members' fears. To be sure, union spokespersons complained of management's uncooperative attitude and urged the federal government to punish corporate abuses. Such a response obviously did not impress the increasingly frustrated rank-and-file. As the war entered its second year, many auto workers began to take the defense of their rights into their own hands, turning to the wildcat as the quickest and most dramatic response to perceived management provocations. "The strike is still the only real weapon labor has," an inspector at Packard told the UAW. "It still must be used when the manufacturors [sic] are not patriotic."[60]

A comprehensive overview of the industry's wartime wildcats cannot be constructed, since there is no complete list of the walk-outs, many of which involved a handful of workers and lasted only a few hours. It is possible to draw a very rough picture of the wildcats, however, by examining the 1944 strike record of one major manufacturer, Chrysler. According to company records prepared for the 1945 Senate investigation of defense production, Chrysler workers were most likely to wildcat after management took disciplinary action against an individual or group of rank-and-filers. Wage concerns, shop rules, and disputes over job assignment followed discipline as the most common causes of walk-outs. The corporation cited two 1944 wildcats as typical. In August, workers struck after a truck driver was given a one-week suspension for reckless driving. The next month rank-and-filers walked out of the Detroit DeSoto plant to protest the firing of a probationary employee. Together, the two wildcats cost the company over 26,000 man-hours of production.[61]

Chrysler's statistics obscure as much as they illuminate, however. As a number of wartime observers noted, disciplinary actions often precipitated wildcats, but they were rarely the walk-outs' root cause. Take, for example, a

September 1943 wildcat at Dodge Main. Ostensibly, workers struck when the company suspended C. Kelly, a millwright. The trouble began when Kelly, a twelve-year man in the plant, finished training a newly hired woman to run his milling machine. The foreman then told Kelly to turn his machine over to the new employee and to operate a different milling machine. Although he would not be required to change classifications, Kelly refused, insisting that the first machine was his. The foreman responded by ordering Kelly to leave the plant, but the millwright instead returned to his work station. Shortly thereafter, the shop committeeman, the shop steward, and the department supervisor arrived on the scene. The supervisor reiterated his foreman's demand that the rank-and-filer leave for the day. Unimpressed, Kelly again refused, at which point the supervisor summoned plant protection officers. The union officials advised Kelly to ignore the officers, but after a short discussion with the guards he thought the better of it and walked out. The committeeman and steward then marched through the department waving their arms, a signal to stop working. A number of the workers complied.[62]

The resultant grievance explained the underlying issue. Chrysler maintained that the corporation had the right to transfer workers, particularly when

TABLE 7
Causes of Wildcats at the Chrysler Corporation, 1944

Reason	Number	Percentages
Discipline	86	34.0%
Wages	28	11.1%
Shop Rules	25	9.9%
Refuse Assg. Job	21	8.3%
Work Conditions	19	7.5%
Promotion/Transfer	19	7.5%
Supervision	18	7.1%
Manpower	13	5.1%
Refuse to work with other employees	14	5.5%
Working Hours	8	3.2%
Union Jurisdiction	1	0.4%
Misc.	1	0.4%
Total	253	100.0%

Source: U.S. Congress, Senate, Special Committee Investigating The National Defense Program, *Hearings* (Washington, D.C.: Government Printing Office, 1945), 13603.

the move did not require a change in classification. The workers insisted that according to "custom and practice in the Dodge plant for a great number of years" no senior employee would be removed from a job to make room for a new employee. The Dodge hands wildcatted, then, not simply to protest Kelly's suspension, but to protect what they believed to be a long-established, albeit unwritten, principle.[63]

The defense of shopfloor tradition took on even greater urgency when rank-and-filers believed management was challenging the "stint." In July 1944, for example, 7,000 auto workers shut down five General Motors plants for eleven days after the corporation suspended five rank-and-filers for "failure to produce a full day's work"; in November 1944, workers struck Chrysler when fellow employees were laid off for leaving their jobs before the end of the shift; in December 1944, Dodge Main hands again wildcatted to protest the firing of an employee who reacted violently when his foreman told him he would not be paid for time he did not work; in January 1945, rank-and-filers at both the Rouge and Willow Run plants struck when Ford suspended employees for "slowing down production"; and in March 1945, workers again shut down the Dodge Main plant to protest the discharge of five men for not meeting production standards.[64]

White auto workers likewise staged a number of wildcats to protect another long-standing shopfloor tradition: the color line. The first recorded "hate strike" occurred at the Packard Motor plant in Detroit in the fall of 1941; white workers walked off the job to protest the upgrading of blacks into heretofore "white" classifications. Similar walkouts occurred in a number of auto plants throughout the first year and a half of the war, the trend peaking in the Packard "hate strike" of June 1943. Packard had employed blacks for years, but had restricted them to jobs in the foundry or as janitors and material handlers. After the 1941 hate strike, Packard management resisted the federal government's demands that it break the color line. The company finally gave in to the pressure in February 1943, upgrading three black women to drill presses. The white women in the department immediately struck, refusing to return until the blacks were removed. The company capitulated. Three months later, however, management tried again, this time placing three black men on the aircraft assembly line. The white workers again demanded that blacks be removed, but management refused. "At this point," a government official reported shortly thereafter, "the 25,000 white workers, shop and shop and shift after shift, walked out."[65]

Despite such dramatic incidents, most wildcats probably were not caused by violations of shopfloor traditions. Rather, Chrysler's 1944 strike record seems to indicate that most wartime strikes were staged in response to the same contractual issues—wages, seniority, safety, and the like—over which workers filed grievances. Indeed, two-thirds of the 126 Chrysler wildcats staged in the latter half of 1944 began as conflicts over these seemingly routine issues. In the highly charged atmosphere of wartime, however, no issue was particularly routine.[66]

The city-wide Chrysler wildcat of May 1943 provides a case in point. Chrysler's Detroit-area workers, convinced that the corporation was stalling on grievances and violating contract provisions, had grown increasingly restive during the early months of 1943. A Dodge Main committeeman explained the growing sentiment in the March 15 edition of the local's newspaper. ". . . management . . . by their [*sic*] labor-baiting tactics," he wrote, "are [*sic*] attempting to undermine our union and destroy our hard-earned gains under the guise of furthering the war effort. Since when has it been necessary to destroy our promotional set-up to whip the Axis? Is it necessary to abrogate our seniority set-up to increase production? . . . . Our rights are something the boys coming home from the battlefronts of the world expect to find intact . . . ."[67]

The strike itself began when two rumors spread through the May 20 morning shift at the Jefferson Avenue plant. According to one story, the plant's labor relations director had rejected union demands for a wage increase, insisting that "employees who had purchased $90,000 worth of war bonds had plenty of money." Other rank-and-filers reported that the labor relations director had answered a request to repair a leaky roof in an area where workers were operating an electric hoist by asking, "Do you expect me to stop the rain?" Indignant, the workers walked off the job and established picket lines.[68]

The wildcat quickly spread to Dodge Main. There, five thousand workers attended a lunch-hour rally in the plant to protest the hiring of new employees, rather than the upgrading of senior employees, to fill jobs in the radio mount department. Someone in the crowd yelled that the speakers could not be heard. Another worker shouted that the rally should be moved to the local union hall. The crowd agreed and marched out of the plant.[69]

It is difficult to determine the extent to which the Chrysler walk-outs were spontaneous expressions of shopfloor frustration. Chrysler management charged that the workers did not want to strike, but were being forced to by the local leadership. Local union officials, on the other hand, denied having any role in organizing the walk-out. The truth probably lies somewhere in between. Local leaders undoubtedly helped to facilitate the strike, but they did not foment the discontent the led to the wildcat. "There had been rumors among the men at Chrysler's for several days that there was going to be a walkout demonstration," a rank-and-filer explained during the first day of the wildcat, "but the rumors were passed around by the workers themselves. . . .That's all I heard—rumors—until the men on the first shift . . . quit work. The guy next to me said that everybody was cleaning up their benches and going home. Well, that's what I did too. I wasn't going to be called a scab."[70]

The wildcat won swift condemnation from politicians and the press. Accusing the strikers of demanding "blood money," the *Detroit News* brutally charged that "somebody somewhere will die" because of the walk-out. The *Detroit Times* followed suit, claiming that the "so-called American workers" were "little better than traitors to their country and to their sons and their brothers who are fighting for that country." In Congress, meanwhile, Missouri Republican Marion T. Bennett claimed that the industrial strife had "greatly delayed our winning of the war." "Is labor willing to be patriotic only at a price," he asked. Local 7 president Ed Carey countered the attacks in a detailed letter to Detroit Congressman George Sadowski. No one had the right to question his members' commitment to the war effort, he wrote. In just over a year's time the 8,000 workers in the Jefferson Avenue plant had donated over 20,000 pints of blood, contributed $22,000 to the Red Cross, and had spent more than 12 percent of their wages on war bonds. If Chrysler was "half as patriotic as the workers," he insisted, the strike could have been avoided. Instead, the corporation ran the plant "like a prison" rather than as a "free American factory." Nevertheless, he concluded, the hands had stayed on the job because "we are in a war and the workers did not want to endanger the war effort." But finally they could take no more.[71]

The rank-and-file's linkage of patriotism and militancy made it all but impossible for the UAW leadership to develop an effective response to the wildcats. The union certainly could not expect to lead the workers into the plant by waving the flag. Shortly after the strike began, UAW Chrysler Department director Leo Lamotte, the union official under whose jurisdiction the plants fell, told the press that 95 percent of the Chrysler hands were patriotic and never would have walked out had they not been led astray by a handful of radicals. Appalled at the suggestion that they were being manipulated to undermine the war effort, the strikers immediately demanded that Lamotte be fired. [72]

As the walk-out entered its fourth day, the UAW leadership tried a different tack. Speaking at a mass meeting in a Hamtramck football stadium, UAW president R.J. Thomas acknowledged that Chrysler was violating its contract, but he insisted that wildcatting would not solve the problem. Rather, he explained, the union would do its best to correct management abuses. The strikers, placated, returned to work the next day, but Thomas had not found a permanent solution to the problem wildcats posed to the union. As the UAW president undoubtedly knew, the union's commitment to the no-strike pledge made it all but impossible for the UAW to confront the auto makers with the rank-and-file's charges. On the other hand, UAW leaders realized that if they abrogated the pledge and struck the auto manufacturers, they risked alienating the federal authorities who controlled the nation's collective bargaining system. By promising what he could not deliver, therefore, Thomas was doing nothing more than buying time.[73]

Unable to develop an effective response to the rank-and-file's discontents, the UAW leadership continued to be plagued by wildcats throughout the balance of the war. According to one estimate, one in every four auto workers participated in a work stoppage in 1943; the next year the percentage rose to one in every two. As the war entered its final year, shopfloor militancy had becomes so widespread that federal officials feared the UAW leadership had lost their ability to influence the rank-and-file. In fact, one knowledgeable observer reported to the War Production Board, the auto workers seemed gripped by a "mood of rebellion . . . ."[74]

It would take the end of the war to end the wildcat wave. Shortly after V-J Day, the UAW abrogated the no-strike pledge, thus freeing the union leadership to realign themselves, at least rhetorically, with the militant patriotism of the rank-and-file. When the auto makers began laying off workers the day after the Japanese surrender, the UAW issued a swift and harsh denunciation. "During the hour of our nation's greatest crisis, [the auto workers] gave unstintingly of their strength and their effort," UAW Secretary-Treasurer George Addes announced. "It would indeed be a negation of the very principles for which this people's war was fought . . . if those to whom the victory belongs should become casualties of the peace."[75]

The UAW International's attempt to regain control of its rank-and-file through aggressive union action peaked in late November 1945, when General Motors department director Walter Reuther brought the union's 350,000 GM workers out on strike. Reuther, the most politically sophisticated member of the UAW's high command, skillfully incorporated the wartime mix of militancy and patriotism into the union's demands. Proclaiming that "the GM workers' fight is the fight of the American people," Reuther insisted that the giant auto maker grant the workers a 30 percent wage increase while maintaining current price levels—a brilliant coupling of private and public interests. He reinforced the point by making liberal use of patriotic symbols sure to resonate with the rank-and-file: staffing picket lines with uniformed veterans, providing strikers with signs reading, "We whipped the Axis, now we fight GM," and the like.[76]

Despite its militant tone, Lichtenstein and other scholars have argued that the GM strike marked the end of the wartime upsurge of rank-and-file activism. In the course of the strike, they contend, Reuther used the power of the International to "manage" the auto workers' discontent, successfully channelling them away from shopfloor struggles and toward the bureaucratic "service" unionism of the postwar era. In the process, the argument runs, Reuther robbed the UAW of the vitality and democracy that had made it one of the most progressive of American unions.[77]

As the auto workers' experience during World War II indicates, however, most rank-and-filers did not fear bureaucratization. They expected the union to act as a bureaucracy, as long as it effectively protected their hard-earned shopfloor rights and fought for their economic interests. Similarly, it seems unfair to criticize the postwar UAW for not extending workers' control over the production process. Wartime grievance records seem to show that rank-and-filers did not expect their union to deal with work pace issues on a regular basis, It is clear, however, that auto workers did want to preserve the informal "stint" that they had established in the pre-War era. It has long been assumed that the system collapsed in the postwar years, but Steve Jefferys' recent work suggests that auto workers, in at least one plant, continued to exercise a degree of shopfloor control into the 1960s. Ben Hamper's recent memoir of life on the line indicates that workers in Flint continued to practice the stint well into the 1980s. Further research should indicate whether these examples can be extended to the UAW as a whole.[78]

Even if it did not aim to reshape labor relations at the point of production, the auto workers' wartime militancy should not be discounted. By insisting that they had distinct rights as workers and citizens, and by defying both their employers and their union to defend those rights, auto workers asserted the ability of ordinary people to assert their sense of self-worth. In the midst of one of the most brutal and de-humanizing of wars, that was no small achievement.

Acknowledgments

The author would like to thank the wonderful staff at the Archives of Labor and Urban Affairs, Wayne State University, particularly Warner Pflug, William LeFevre, and Sandy Kimberly, who made the search for this essay possible. Robert Asher, Kathleen Canning, Ronald Edsforth, Martin Hershock, Michael Smith, David Sowell, and Victoria Getis improved the essay with their comments. The author is grateful to them all.

5

THE 1949 SPEED UP STRIKE AND THE
POST WAR SOCIAL COMPACT, 1946–1961

....

Robert Asher

I

"You talk about bargaining in bad faith. Any bad habits we may have we learned from you." *(Ken Bannon's remarks to Ford management during 1955 contract negotiations)* [1]

By the end of World War II, management in the auto industry, with the exception of the Chrysler Corporation, had accepted trade unions as institutions essential to achieving production stability. Some writers have coined the term "social compact" to describe post-World War II management's recognition of "responsible" unions, which were the unions that eschewed unpredictable production interruptions and acknowledged a general managerial prerogative to control the production process. Although most American auto manufacturers tolerated the UAW, and did not try to destroy it, the Big Three car and truck producers frequently contested auto workers' sense of legitimate work effort standards. In 1948 and 1949, the Ford Motor Company began to refuse to honor many existing plant-level agreements on production standards and balked at negotiating written production standards agreements with the UAW's large Ford locals. Ford's new offensive confronted the UAW with an especially serious challenge to its power to enforce contracts and to protect worker welfare. The outcome of this contest, analyzed in this chapter, undoubtedly influenced auto industry labor relations for at least a decade. Had the UAW lost the Ford Speed Up Strike, the power of all industrial unions in the United States would have been threatened.

Since 1927, Ford Motor Company plants had been run along the lines of the "drive"[2] model by Harry Bennett, a Detroit gangster whom Henry Ford had hired to handle personnel matters. Foremen and Ford Service Department thugs used violence and the threat of dismissal to force Ford workers to increase the intensity of their labor. The end of the Bennett era began in April 1941, when striking Ford workers forced the company to recognize the UAW. The advent of unionization, and the next four years of war-time labor relations, enabled Ford workers to challenge company power on the shopfloor. Above all, worker militancy led to a *steadier pace* of work. Ford workers no longer had to endure the kinds of pre-union, Depression practices described in chapter 3—the arbitrary manipulation of bonus rates, line speeds, and production standards, whether at the end of the day, or when consumer demand surged, or when management wanted to compensate for line breakdowns or material shortages that stopped the line.

By 1940 General Motors, clearly the most powerful of the auto companies, had established an extremely strong position on the shopfloor. Production standards were tight, but were not altered once they had been set for a particular car or truck model. Workers who staged wildcat strikes, and workers who were caught engaging in sabotage and production slowdowns, were disciplined. Throughout World War II, and until 1952, shopfloor labor relations at GM remained relatively stable. By contrast, at Chrysler, a confused management labor relations structure, and management's fears of losing market share to GM and Ford, allowed militant Chrysler workers, especially those in the Detroit area, who were supported by a dense network of labor union institutions, to challenge Chrysler successfully when management tried to manipulate production standards to its advantage. Consequently, Chrysler workers won the least intense production standards in the industry.[3] Ford workers were as militant as their counterparts at Chrysler, but they faced a management that was better organized and was determined to recover the shopfloor authority it had lost during World War II.

In 1946, Henry Ford II took control of the family business. He removed Bennett, ending terrorism on the shopfloor. Ford accepted the UAW as the collective bargaining agent for his employees. But Ford, and the new corporate officers he selected, were not happy with the way production was being managed at the firm's factories. Striving to reverse the company's massive loss of market share in the late 1920s and thereafter, the new Ford management made a maximum effort to design cars with fewer defects, to improve the efficiency of the car-design processes, to buy more modern production machinery, and to increase the effectiveness of the deployment of auto-making technologies on the factory floor. Ford management also felt that it had lost too much of the control it wanted to exercise over its workers' labor effort. Determined to recapture control, Ford management began to apply to all jobs new, scientifically determined production standards based on time study. In the process, Ford's management, whether inadvertently or by design, tried to push assembly workers to accept management's *unilateral* power to determine assembly line speeds and production standards.

Conversely, Ford workers wanted to build on their post-1941 gains and secure palpable, formal rights for worker representatives to influence assembly line work intensity. Auto workers sought collective bargaining agreements that specified co-determination of production standards, or banned any alteration in line speeds once production started on a new model and set ratios of relief workers to production workers, which would provide additional workers when production standards were increased by putting additional assembly jobs on the conveyor belt.

The 1946 Ford national contract included a strict management rights clause empowering the Ford Company to make all decisions about the methods of production used in its plants.[4] The Ford contract also included a system of binding arbitration. Workers were barred from striking if they did not like the decisions of the Ford umpires. Of course, when the national contract expired strikes were legal. But Article VII, Section 18 of the 1946 Ford national contract, which dealt with production standards, exempted from the jurisdiction of the umpire and from the no-strike rule the vital issues of adverse health and safety conditions and production standards. When production standard disputes that affected or involved these areas were not settled by negotiation between union representatives and management, including the third step of the grievance process which involved the UAW Ford Department and the Ford Industrial Relations Department, local unions could take a strike vote. If the vote was positive, the International Executive Board (IEB) could authorize a strike.

Between 1946 and 1949, the Ford Motor Company constantly tested the power of its production workers and the authority of the UAW. Ford ignored local agreements that had been made between management and the UAW plant organizations. Ford managers also repeatedly refused to tell workers what the basic line speeds and product mixes would actually be. Without such a baseline, it was hard for workers to obtain public sympathy for authorized production standard strikes when management violated its *own* standards, since Ford could make any counter-claim it wanted without fear of contradiction.

To combat Ford management, the UAW used *authorized* local strikes in a large number of successful efforts to force management to put production standards in writing and to abide by the national and plant contracts Ford officials signed. Some of these strikes forced Ford to compromise or to rescind its contract violations. But even after 1949, indeed throughout the 1960s, Ford often violated contractual agreements on relief time for production line workers and deviated from the production standards management promulgated.

The Ford story demonstrates that the "social compact" was hardly a labor-management armistice; it simply signalled the end of auto manufacturers' insistence on waging all-out war to prevent workers from maintaining their own collective bargaining institutions. In 1948 and 1949, Ford tried to force the UAW to accept a virtual "unconditional surrender" of the rights of workers to bargain with management on production standards. It was a major offensive. The UAW counterattacked. Ford lost the battle.

II

After the 1946 Ford contract was signed, the introduction of new production standards did not go smoothly. Between July and August 1946, some production standards, without any changes in production technology, went up by 25 to 39 percent.[5] Ford's foremen, superintendents, and labor relations officers often moved with ruthless speed to discipline workers who did not immediately meet new standards. In some cases, workers were not even formally informed of the content of their newly designed jobs. At the River Rouge complex and at the Detroit Lincoln plant, the UAW rank-and-file and the union's national officers vigorously resisted attempts by Ford management to intensify the labor of hourly workers without offering them extra pay.

The problem facing Ford and its workers was complicated by the fact that it took a decade for the central Ford management to rid the company of many of the managers who had been hired by Harry Bennett. Trying to exert centralized control over labor policies, to make them uniform, was not an easy task for Henry Ford II, Ford's President, Ernie Breech and John Bugas (Ford's director of Industrial Relations). In some instances Ken Bannon, the head of the United Automobile Workers' Ford Department from 1947 to 1969, cooperated with the Ford Company's top brass to put pressure on "Neanderthal" plant managers who were holdovers from the Bennett era.[6] However, this kind of cooperation was not possible until after the 1949 Speed Up Strike, which demonstrated to the corporation's leaders that its workers insisted that management make explicit agreements about production line labor intensity, and then abide by the main elements of those agreements. Assembly line workers especially craved certainty. If they were going to perform unpleasant, alienating labor, they wanted a steady work pace, and a work pace that was not frequently increased to the point where workers were seriously fatigued.[7]

The River Rouge Ford complex was the largest factory complex in the world. Located in Dearborn, Michigan, just across the city line from Detroit, the Rouge was a fully-integrated manufacturing facility, complete with steel mills, parts factories, and assembly plants. The Rouge was also the domain of UAW Local 600, the biggest, and one of the most militant, locals in the UAW. In 1949, Ford employed 106,000 workers nationwide; 62,000 worked at the Rouge. Along with the Detroit Lincoln plant, where UAW Local 900 represented the labor force, the Rouge facility would be involved in the 1949 Speed Up Strike.

The 1946 Ford contract did not prohibit company initiatives to speed up production lines; but it gave workers the right to grieve when they believed production standards were not fairly set *and maintained.* Frequent disputes over line speeds, production standards, and Ford's policies on bathroom relief for workers on assembly and production lines flared up in late June 1946 and then exploded in the May 1949 Speed Up Strike. In the June 29, 1946 issue of *Ford Facts,* an anonymous veteran steward explained that:

> When the union first came in (1941) we had 10 minute rest periods on my line plus relief men when you needed them. As far as the guys in this department are concerned the way men are forced to work [now] is certainly hazardous to their health. None of us want to wind up on the scrap heap when we hit the 40 year mark. . . .

The crucial issue at this time was that Ford foremen often assigned designated relief workers to regular production jobs that "they couldn't leave for most of the day." The consequences of the shortage of relief workers were far more serious than worker discomfort at having to wait to go to the bathroom. Line workers believed that "When you gotta go . . . you gotta go."[8] But when workers left the line without being replaced by a relief worker, the entire production line was often disrupted,

> throwing other operations and employees into the hole from which supervision expects them to catch up on their own accord, without additional help, which is just another method of speedup used by supervision.[9]

In August 1946, complaints about higher production standards came especially from the Rouge plastics plant and the "B" building. Articles in *Ford Facts* claimed that the speedup in plastics was substantial, and had not been accompanied by any improved production technologies. A union columnist sarcastically observed that the workers "were trained to be grinders—not rhumba experts."[10] In the "B" building, individual foremen were singled out for raising line speeds, especially during the last hour of production, and the Ford Labor Relations Department was castigated for disciplining workers for not meeting production standards, even though the union had not been given a chance to check the standards, as allowed under Article IV, Section 4 of the national contract. Two specific speedup figures were cited by Leo Osage, union president for "B" building: an August 12, 1946 increase from 301 to 311 cars per day on the NO. 1 Ford passenger line, and a one hour increase from 17 to 23-24 cars per hour on another line.[11]

In October 1946, workers in the Rouge steel mill complained about the speedup, characterizing Ford policy as "Kill a mule, buy another, kill a man, hire another."[12] An article about time-study personnel in the plastics plant claimed that the industrial engineers were given output targets *before* they started time studies on a particular job.[13] In 1946, the only public threat of a strike in the Rouge complex came from open hearth workers, many of them blacks, who were enraged when Ford reneged on a promise to get an expert to look into the use of poisonous sodium fluoride, which the workers claimed had been discontinued at the nearby Great Lakes Steel plant in 1941.[14] A column in the October 12 issue of *Ford Facts* warned the Ford management that by pushing workers too far, it was actually destabilizing labor relations at the Rouge:

> . . . workers realize that wildcat strikes are in violation of the contract, but what can the workers do when the company keeps forcing these strikes by refusing to bargain in good faith.[15]

This was the kind of warning UAW president Walter Reuther often delivered to auto company executives during off-the-record negotiations.

In the broadest sense, auto workers had a more complex moral code than their employers. Auto workers believed that management had only one value: efficiency. Most auto workers, like other wage earners, were not opposed to efficiency *per se*. They understood that if their employers did not make a profit, there would be no jobs. Auto workers invariably felt that their managers and company executives were grossly overpaid, and were unfairly rewarded, even when they had failed to meet earnings targets. They realized that all foremen and managers were under pressure to make their plants or work areas profitable, under pain of dismissal or demotion. But production workers' moral sensibilities told them that human values had to be factored into decisions about what constituted a fair day's labor effort. Women and men had to be protected against injury, against a debilitating and enervating work pace, and against arbitrary dismissal if they protested against specifically unfair treatment, or if they violated factory rules because the frustration of performing alienated labor made it impossible to contain their anger and aggressive impulses.[16]

UAW pressure in 1947 led to new contract language that barred any disciplinary action against Ford workers for failure to meet production standards unless the workers had been notified about the standard four days in advance of its initiation. The four-day warning allowed workers to call in UAW shop stewards to help them formulate objections to any new standards that the workers believed were unfair. In 1947, Ford also agreed to allow union representatives to inspect the studies and computations used to formulate work standards.[17]

In July 1947, local UAW officers and Ford agreed on line speeds on four of the assembly lines of the Lincoln plant. The line speeds were "nailed", i.e., Ford wrote Local 900 a letter that specified the line speeds and committed Ford to *completely constant* line speeds "for the balance of this particular production schedule."[18] This was the kind of guarantee General Motors gave to its workers. The Ford deal did not last long.

In March 1948, John Bugas, Ford's Director of Industrial Relations, wrote a confidential letter to plant supervisors, telling them that on new models they could compensate for production delays by running production lines as much as 25 percent above normal speeds.[19] On April 12, 1948, the UAW obtained a copy of the Bugas letter. Ken Bannon, head of the UAW's Ford Department, interpreted the memo as an indication that Ford management would no longer, as it had in 1947, "negotiate or discuss in any way whatsoever the production that the FMC have in the plants."[20] On July 7, 1948, the Ford Department's Negotiating Committee sent all Ford locals a letter that warned workers that Ford's offensive was dangerous:

> The old system of slave driving with Simon LaGree foremen may have eased up in some instances, but the attitude of the top brass in negotiations proves to us that they have the intention of returning to those times as soon as they can gain more favorable public opinion.[21]

Ford workers were angered by this refusal to honor the contract. Moreover, the UAW would maintain that as time passed, "the [1947] settlement was destroyed by the practice of the company not replacing manpower" as the normal turnover of labor reduced the number of workers on the lines. Lincoln managers even required workers to keep working after they had finished producing the agreed upon quota of 135 cars per day. Eventually, 27 Lincoln workers were fired or given temporary layoffs because they refused to keep up with their work when the line was running above its normal pace.[22] On April 28, 1949 the UAW's International Executive Board (IEB) concluded that an illegal speedup existed at the Lincoln plant. President Walter Reuther was very annoyed by Ford's flaunting of the specific, written agreements on constant line speeds. Without hesitation, the IEB authorized the Lincoln workers of Local 900 to strike on May 5 because "the speed of the line in the Lincoln plant is excessive in proportion to the manpower being used."[23]

At the larger Rouge complex, the March 1948 directive from John Bugas led local managers to continue to make decisions that created numerous disputes over undermanned production lines. The speedup persisted, especially in the Rouge's "B" building, where final car assembly took place. Ford managers combined the job classifications of relief workers and utility workers. At the beginning of the work day, many relief workers were assigned to production jobs, including those that needed manning because of absent workers. Some relief workers were also assigned to train new employees—labor turnover was high on many lines. Consequently, the relief workers were not available to provide relief for regular production workers—the 1947 contract guaranteed workers 24 minutes of relief per day. While the officers of Local 600 cooperated with management in trying to reduce absenteeism, they complained that the workers "that do come in to work should not be penalized and be denied relief just because of a shortage of help."[24]

It appears that Ford's lower-level managers were not always consistent in administering company policy. Tom Riley and Bill Hood, the editors of *Ford Facts'* "B" Building column, complained in February 1948 that

> . . . some foremen have no knowledge of balancing their lines and....[sometimes] their superior insists on a man to be loaned, [the foreman] loans a man and then finds himself short, whereby he has to tie up the relief man.

In June 1948 workers in the "B" Building continued to complain about line speeds and the lack of adequate relief men. In July, Ken Bannon, Local 600 President Tommy Thompson, and the Rouge building chairmen met with national Ford officials and Ford's top Rouge managers to discuss the problem of production standards. Ford agreed that

> no one would be penalized for "riding the job" or "not able to keep up." Along with this, the company tried to enforce estimate[d] Time Study. This was turned down by the union to this extent, that [when the company failed to set work standards based on *actual time studies*] . . . the employee was the sole judge of the speed of his job so long as he was honestly giving a fair day's work.

On July 15, the "B" Building Bargaining Committee and "B" Building President Mike Donnelly met with the new building superintendent, Russell Burd. Burd had replaced Frank Watza, who the Ford workers had found very abrasive. The UAW rank-and-file leaders praised Burd as "a man whom we could at least talk to and not [have] needle the [bargaining] committee about outside union problems." Burd agreed to a new policy requiring foremen who wanted to discipline a worker to call the District Committee and to try to settle the problem before sending the accused worker to the Labor Relations Department, which invariably disciplined the worker.[26]

Despite this auspicious start, by October, Tom Riley, a member of the "B" Building Bargaining Committee and editor of the "B" Building column in *Ford Facts*, complained bitterly that the old problems persisted: relief was chronically inadequate; line speeds fluctuated at "the foreman's whim"; and plant officials ordered line speedups to compensate for assembly line break-downs.[27] On November 27, Tom Riley noted that at the beginning of the work day General Foreman Gabbord had been commandeering relief men from lines that had no absentees. Riley observed that production workers "wonder why they should drag themselves to work to help out on the no-absenteeism record and then have the relief men loaned out and get no relief when they need it." Riley also pointed out that the speedup on the Ford Metal, Ford Feed, Mercury Metal, Mercury Feed, and Mercury Weld Flo Lines was obvious to the workers.[28]

A meeting of Local 600 leaders with the top officers of the Rouge Labor Relations Department did not produce any changes in the conditions that Rouge workers were finding so galling.[29] But then management did an about face. On December 11, *Ford Facts* announced the company had agreed that in the "B" Building, which had been renamed the Dearborn Assembly plant, relief workers would do only relief work and that line speeds would be locked, with the keys necessary to change line speeds held only by the plant superintendent, who would change line speeds only in the presence of a district committeeperson. A January 22, 1949 story mentioned a recently negotiated verbal agreement to lock, at the beginning of each work day, two production lines in the plant. The motors that drove the lines had locks on the compartments that contained the speed controls. Of course, these procedural agreements offered no guarantee that the plant superintendent would not decide to set line speeds, body mixes, or manning schedules at levels that the production workers found undesirable. After the January agreement, Dearborn Assembly Building President Mike Donnelly was quoted as saying he would not "acknowledge any work standards on any line that is not locked." Ford workers were clearly getting tired of Ford management's frequent violation of verbal agreements,[31] and unresolved complaints about speedups remained in other parts of the Rouge complex.[32]

Between January 22 and April 16, 1949 *Ford Facts* did not carry any news about relief workers, assembly line speeds, or production standard disputes. Perhaps Local 600's leadership was trying to give Ford management a chance to show it would abide by the main principles of the accords that had been reached in the fall of 1948. Perhaps the leadership reasoned that a "cooling off" period would undercut the arguments being made by factions within the local that wanted, for political or ideological reasons, to stage unauthorized strikes.[33]

Ford's corporate-level management apparently decided to test the will of the workers and the UAW leadership. In late 1948 and early 1949, the economy was weak, auto sales were down, and auto workers were being laid off in large numbers. At the Rouge, Ford and the leaders of Local 600 were negotiating on assembly line production standards. Local 600 president Tommy Thompson, who was a supporter of the Reuther faction in the UAW, was emphatic about Ford management's devious tactics as he testified at a closed session of the UAW's International Executive Board on April 28, 1949:

> ". . . when we have felt that we have been coming close to an agreement, they would come along, up the schedule another eight or ten jobs, fling some more men in [but not enough to prevent labor intensity from being increased], and throw the negotiations all out of whack again.

The workers were asking for the equivalent of a written constitution, an explicit set of rules and standards:

> . . . give us an agreement as to what speed the line would run. If we are satisfied with that speed. . . then we want to find out how many men are involved to take care of these operations, the question of relief . . . the question of spacing and the question of when the line can be speeded up.[34]

In the absence of written agreements, Ford was playing games.

Tom Riley, the President of the "B" Building at the Rouge, reported that in mid-January 1949, he and the workers had made a "verbal agreement" with Ford managers to lock the final assembly lines. In Riley's department, the workers "had *more or less agreement with supervision* there that we would set it [cycle time] at 1.50 [emphasis added]." Since the time study on the line's most difficult job indicated that the workers could finish it within a cycle time of 1.47, the UAW was satisfied with the arrangement. Then the Ford management unilaterally changed the rules. It did so by spacing production jobs closer together on the assembly line. "In some instances the jobs were so close together they couldn't open the deck lid of the rear for hitting the front grill of the next car . . . ." This change effectively set the cycle time at 1.36, a 9.33 percent speedup. The result, Riley explained, was a serious morale problem:

> That's what we are hearing all the time of our workers, that they are being treated unfairly, and Lord knows that in the years to come, we have got workers on the line there that I have moved [to other jobs] that were good men, and they were just burnt out. . . . .[35]

Riley had his facts right. During arbitration hearings in June 1949, *Ford's Malcolm Denise conceded that at the "B" Building about 36 percent of the 927 workers on the lines were being asked to work at a rate higher than the 480 standard minutes that constituted a normal production day.* At the Lincoln plant 32 percent of the 458 line employees worked more than 480 standard minutes.[36] The UAW demanded that the lines *never* be run at a rate higher than the rate needed to produce the daily quota or production target of cars. This was the number of cars that would be produced if the line ran, without ever halting, at the speed that had been used to calculate each workers' production standard. Even if the line was stopped, and workers had a chance to rest, the UAW demanded that when work resumed, the line speed not be increased to make up the lost production time unless management provided *additional relief workers.*

Ford contended that this policy would require a 10 percent increase in manpower. Ford wanted to be able to compensate for production interruptions by "stepping it [line speed] up until that interruption had been overcome and then leveling off." Ford argued that the rest time employees had when the line was down allowed them to work harder when the line speed was increased. This line of reasoning assumed, although no evidence was offered by either side to sustain or controvert the point, that rest enabled a worker to deal with the stress of moving faster than the normal production work speed. Speaking for the UAW, Jack Conway, Walter Reuther's right-hand man, and Ken Bannon insisted on strict adherence to normal line speeds *unless Ford agreed to share power by meeting with committees of plant workers to negotiate variations in line speed as variations in production conditions arose.*[37]

The manpower issue had another dimension, as Ken Bannon explained in a May 29, 1949 speech. Since the end of World War II, Ford had been modernizing its plants at a fast clip. New equipment was increasing productivity, a trend that threatened to displace many workers from their jobs. However, Bannon maintained that since 1946, "the biggest portion of this curtailment of manpower is due to the increased work load that was placed upon the production man." By demanding that assembly line workers not be overworked, the UAW was hoping to create more jobs for auto workers.[38]

Most labor historians have believed that once Walter Reuther was burned by the UAW's unsuccessful attempt during the 1945–1946 GM strike to encroach on managerial prerogatives to set prices and allocate labor resources, he subsequently abandoned the effort to achieve some kind of co-management in the auto industry. The stance taken by Conway and Bannon demonstrates that as late as 1949 the UAW, given the strategic opportunity, advocated giving the union a significant share of managerial power. Even if this was simply a bargaining tactic, the radicalism of the demand is significant.[39]

As the previous figures cited suggest, the work intensity issue immediately affected about *one-third* of all *line* workers at the Rouge. This was because it was impossible for management to arrange job content, matching workers with the available tools and production tasks, to provide a full 480 standard minutes of work per day to all workers. Since many workers, with the lines at normal speeds, had slack time (seconds when they did not have to be using a tool or moving to a work position) when the line was speeded up, only a *minority* of workers would be asked to speedup their work to the point where they had no slack time, and therefore had to work *faster* as well as steadier. The UAW was especially concerned about the impact of such speedups on workers at times during the day when they were likely to be fatigued and were therefore more likely to make mistakes that could cause injury.[40] Of course, the majority of workers must have known that if they did not back the minority who were affected most adversely by the speedup, in the future the company might change job design to make a higher proportion of the labor force work closer to, or faster than, the 480 standard minutes per day. Ford assembly workers, with the backing of the workers who did not work on the line, went on strike to fight these conditions.[41]

III

To understand the ultimate decision of the UAW's national officers to authorize a strike over the speedup at the Rouge, we need to examine the internal politics of the UAW. In 1949, UAW President Walter Reuther, who had been elected in 1946, was still working to consolidate his position. In 1947 Reuther had appointed one of his supporters, Ken Bannon, as National Ford Department Director. Local 600, the largest Ford local, was divided into several competing factions. Small numbers of Communists were very active in Local 600. Anti-Reuther faction candidates, many of them non-Communist activists, received 38 percent of the votes in Local 600's 1949 elections. A large number of faction leaders and their followers had strong animosity towards Reuther: some disagreed with his decision to support compliance with the Taft-Hartley law; some disliked Reuther's endorsement of President Truman's foreign policy; some believed, accurately, that Reuther favored a union structure that concentrated authority in the hands of national leaders, while reducing, but not eliminating, the power of local presidents, shop stewards and groups of rank-and-file production workers.[42] The umpire system, which drastically limited auto workers' right to strike while a national contract was in force, aroused significant opposition within the UAW, and especially among many members of Local 600. Undoubtedly, some of Reuther's foes used the charge that the leadership of Local 600 was "soft" on the speedup as a political weapon against the Reuther leadership.

A vocal minority of Local 600 members, including several executive board members, wanted unrestricted authority to stage wildcat strikes and other job actions. On January 28, 1949, the issue was broached at a meeting of Local 600's executive board. Seventeen board members voted in favor of a resolution that affirmed the UAW's Ford contract, which banned unauthorized work stoppages. But three members of the board—Speed, Lacey and Locke—indicated their displeasure with the vote by abstaining.

However, in a December 9, 1948 memo, UAW-Ford director Ken Bannon had told Walter Reuther that "only one complaint" about speedups at the Rouge plant "came from the 'parties' who constantly make that claim." Bannon identified the source of the "one complaint" as Ed Locke, a leader in the plastics building. The import of Bannon's memo was that most complaints about the speedup were legitimate and were not politically motivated.[43]

On April 15, 1949, Local 600's General Council approved a strike over the speedup, as allowed in the health and safety clause of the Ford contract. At the Dearborn assembly plant, the strike vote was 2,905–92; overall, Rouge workers voted 31,926–4,400 to walk out.[44] On April 28, the IEB held a strike authorization hearing. The members of the IEB, all Reuther supporters, were well aware of the factional battles in Local 600. Failure to *authorize* a strike by Local 600 would have undoubtedly strengthened the hand of the militants. But the IEB members also were aware that the Ford company had *flagrantly violated its written agreements* with the Lincoln workers represented by Local 900, and appeared to be reneging on oral contracts at the Rouge complex.

Some Ford workers, at locals that were not on strike, were concerned that the Speed Up Strike might adversely effect the upcoming national contract negotiations with Ford. Addressing these issues in a May 7 appearance before Local 400, Highland Park, one of the largest non-striking locals, Ken Bannon maintained that:

> the present strike in no way impairs our bargaining position with the Ford Motor Company when the negotiations open on the entire contract on May 16. We know that for the past month and a half the Ford Motor Company has been storing cars [i.e., stockpiling cars].

Ford had enough cars on hand to satisfy consumer demand during the critical May to July period, when sales volumes were high. If the UAW struck on July 15, when the national contract expired, it could do little to cripple Ford sales. Although Bannon did not make the argument, it is clear that by depleting

Ford's reserves of cars ready for sale, the Speed Up Strike actually strengthened the UAW's hand in the forthcoming national contract negotiations.[45]

Reuther, whom the *Wall Street Journal* and some historians believe was hesitant to back the Speed Up Strike,[46] gave no indication of any desire to undermine a challenge to Ford's speedup policies at the IEB meeting on April 28. Without blinking, he backed the strike authorization for the Lincoln workers in Local 900. Confronted by Ford's claim that a speedup strike would entail a contract violation because it would not be a health and safety-related strike, Reuther candidly told the IEB,

> I would like to make it clear that the language of the Ford contract is not as clear as the language of some other contracts [especially the GM contract] about the right of the union to strike on a production standard.

Yet Reuther aggressively maintained

> . . . it is our position that . . . we clearly have the right to strike the plant if in our judgement that is the course of action we ought to follow, so we are just dismissing the Company's claim that we have no contractual right to strike.

If Reuther had been adamantly opposed to the strike, he would hardly have made this statement. Rather, he could have used the ambiguity in the contract to argue against a strike.

But, before launching the offensive against Ford, Reuther insisted on dealing with strategic concerns. He told the IEB that there was some uncertainty about whether or not Ford had agreed at the Rouge to allocate specific numbers of workers to specific work stations. Reuther speculated that it was possible that even central Ford management was not clear about all the details of the agreements at the Rouge:

> I don't think the Company knows, because what the Ford Motor Company doesn't know about running an automobile plant will also fill a fairly large book, because for years and years and years, the Ford Motor Company, instead of developing efficient management procedure, just drove the guys. You didn't have to be efficient—just kick the guys along when they were behind, so that they have not developed rational, modern, efficient managerial techniques.[48]

To resolve the confusion, the IEB decided to send a team of top officials into the Rouge plant to study the line speeds. This was necessary to protect the union's image in the public relations battle that would erupt during any large strike, and especially during a strike while a contract was still in force.

The UAW team included Secretary-Treasurer Emil Mazey, the second highest officer in the union and one of the most militant members of the IEB, Ken Bannon, Tommy Thompson, Ken McCusker, UAW director for the Detroit region, Tom Riley, the chairman of the "B" Building bargaining unit, and Robert Kanter, an industrial engineer who was the UAW's time-study expert.

Some newspaper reports maintained that the IEB committee found that on April 28, Ford had slowed down the "B" building assembly lines whose speeds were the source of worker anger. On May 1, Mazey's committee pressed Ford, without success, to submit a *written policy* on maintaining constant ratios of levels of line manning to line work loads. At a May 3 meeting of the Local 600 Executive Board, President Tommy Thompson reported that on Friday April 28, Ford had said that it would only agree, in Thompson's words, "to run the lines as slowly as they possibly could." From April 28 to May 2, most of the lines were running at the slower speeds, which the UAW believed were reasonable. But on the morning of May 3, the lines in the "B" building were speeded up.[49]

On May 3, the *Wall Street Journal* reported that Tommy Thompson had charged Ford with violating an oral agreement to keep assembly line speeds at their April 28 levels while negotiations were in progress.[50] With rank-and-file workers seething with anger and pressing their leaders to sanction a strike, the Local 600 executive board voted to give the International two more days to settle the dispute in return for an IEB promise to sanction a strike if Ford did not "deliver a policy on actual line speed."[51] Ford stood pat. Ford's central management had clearly decided to oppose the UAW's basic demand, which most labor-relations experts endorsed, that policies on assembly line production standards—line speed, manning, product mix, component spacing, and relief—be put in writing. The IEB authorized a strike by Local 600. On May 5, the twenty-four day Ford Speed Up Strike began at both the Rouge and the Lincoln plant.

IV

The Ford Company charged that the strike was a "political" event. Henry Ford II baldly denied that his company had instituted any speedup, making the absurd, erroneous statement that "speedups are silly from the view-point of any sane management."[52] In a May 16 strike bulletin, the UAW Ford Department presented the workers' case to the public.

> The Union says: The company can select its [line] speed, can determine the spacing of the cars—but once it determines the speed and the spacing of jobs, they [sic] must be constant speeds—it cannot machine gun the work-

ers in the plant with concentrated short bursts of speedup spread out through the day.

The release also argued that it was wrong for management to "speedup workers as fast as it wants, to make up for time lost by its own mismanagement and bungling . . . " On May 20, Walter Reuther issued a public statement charging that Ford was managing its assembly lines in a manner entirely different from the other major auto companies. Reuther claimed that some companies were willing to weld lugs on conveyor lines to prevent closer spacing of car bodies [by foremen and plant managers seeking higher production rates].[54]

The UAW's Executive Board maintained that the speedup was part of a larger issue involving social policy on work and production technology. Appreciating the interrelationship between the quality of work experiences and the quality of workers' lives as family members and consumers of products and leisure, the UAW explained that it endorsed the idea that the standard of living of [consumers]

> . . . can be raised only by reducing unit costs and making available more goods at lower prices. However, we insist that reductions in the unit cost of production must be made possible by improved technology and production processes...and not by placing an unfair work load on workers...we...will resist . . . any efforts on the part of management to reduce costs and expand profits by speeding up the workers.[55]

During the strike, the UAW broadcast a propaganda play on a local radio station. The story was set on an assembly line. Joe Smith, a worker who had to tighten engine bolts, thought he heard Abraham Lincoln talking to him from inside the cylinder block. The Lincoln voice told the worker,

> Well, son, I got word in heaven that things weren't going so good down here. As a matter of fact, the rumor was that they were making slaves out of men again . . . .

Joe explained that "I sure wish that I would have had time to let Mr. Lincoln out, but you haven't got time to play around when that line is moving." The narrator told the audience that:

> "Perhaps this experience *didn't* happen to Joe Smith, but it gives you an idea of what can happen on an assembly line nowadays . . . this thing that the workers call a "speedup" isn't a propaganda catch-phrase for these men; it's a concrete fact. *You* have all heard of the word, but you have to see it, feel it live it 8 hours a day YOURSELF to really *know* what it means.[56]

Ford workers insisted that they had a right to production standards that could not be not altered whenever management felt it needed more production. Since they were not slaves, Ford workers had considerable latitude to take a stand for a production standards policy that they believed was just and reasonable, a policy that General Motors, the industry's largest employer, had been following since 1940.[57]

After twenty-four days, the Speed Up Strike was "settled" on May 30. Ford agreed to reinstate 35 Rouge and Lincoln plant workers who had been disciplined for resisting the speedup. The company also pledged that during each production day it would "maintain each line at a constant speed...[and would] space units to provide a uniform flow of work for individual employees." In short, *once the production day began, assembly line speedups would not be initiated.* The ratio of relief workers to regular workers would be 1:19.[58] When regular line workers were absent, the company agreed it would take the steps necessary—reducing line speed or assigning utility workers—to prevent an increase in the work load of the workers who had come to work. When the mix of body types *changed*, increasing work loads, Ford would add more workers, increase the spaces between the units being worked on, reduce line speed, or stop the line momentarily. These actions would result in the agreed upon "uniform flow of work for individual employees." Getting these terms accepted, *in writing*, was an important gain for Ford workers.[59]

There was still one important unresolved issue. Ford had accepted a policy of not varying line speeds *during* the course of any given production day.[60] But on any particular day, Ford wanted to be able to increase line speeds at the start of the day to compensate, in advance, for expected interruptions in production, especially when new models were being made for the first time or at times when demand was very heavy and lines regularly broke down or had to be stopped because parts suppliers did not make deliveries. Under these circumstances, Ford wanted its managers to be able to set line speeds that were higher than the standard.

If Ford plant managers decided that the above-standard rate was going to be maintained throughout the entire production day, some workers would have to complete their tasks in *less time than the company's own time study had allotted.* Ford maintained that there were so many production interruptions under normal circumstances, that few workers would ever end up having to perform more than 480 standard minutes of work during the course of the whole 8 hour production day. *The UAW did not want to allow the company to ever be able to require workers, for any given period of time, to complete their jobs in less time than allowed by their production standards.* The UAW and Ford turned this issue over to a panel of three arbitrators, agreeing to be bound by their decision.[61]

This was not an issue that either management or the workers took lightly. The arbitration hearings took three days and generated a 500 page transcript. Management believed its right to manage was at stake. It insisted on unilateral authority to set line speeds at the start of any given production day. The UAW sought to protect workers against the danger this policy could pose to worker safety, health and sanity if management chose to set unreasonable line speeds. Auto workers feared that unchecked managerial authority could easily be abused.

During the arbitration hearings the UAW's representatives argued that Ford should not be given the authority to establish a line speed that would give *any* worker less time to complete a job than the amount of time that had been allocated by the time-study determined standard on that particular job, unless some method was found to provide *frequent* relief breaks to the worker.* Speaking for the UAW, Jack Conway argued that if Ford adjusted for lost production time by increasing line speeds only 5 percent above standard, instead of 10 percent, production efficiency would improve, since there would be fewer workers who would be unable to complete their jobs at the lower temporary above-standard line speed.[62]

The arbitrators, in a 2–1 decision, allowed management to set all line speeds at the start of the production day. Management negotiators had indicated that they believed that overworked workers could get adequate rest time during the "short intermittent recurring interruptions" of production that occurred "every day throughout the day and from day to day."[63] But the arbitration award also stipulated that Ford had to come up with "appropriate solutions," most typically relief workers, when *increased line speeds increased a workers' job content to the point where the worker had more than a minute's worth of work content in each available work minute.* This ruling was not as specific as the UAW negotiators would have liked. It left some ground for disagreement and further bargaining over the character of the relief to be provided to workers. Nevertheless, the arbitrators had accepted the spirit of the UAW's position: *overworked workers deserved relief.*[64] The Ford Motor Company could manage technical production, but it also *had to manage to preserve worker health and safety.*

The Speed Up Strike was a significant victory, perhaps the most important gain of a degree of workers' control on the shopfloor in the auto industry in the post-World War II era. All the new contract language achieved in

---

* In unique situations the UAW accepted this solution. For example, in a Ford foundry the union agreed to let core makers work at a faster pace than that allowed per core by the time study, *provided* that the worker be allowed to skip every seventh core, thus providing frequent rest to compensate for the faster work pace. *Arbitration Proceedings,* 198.

the strike settlement and arbitration ruling provided workers with a new defense against being exhausted by overwork. The 1949 national Ford contract (Article IV, Section 4) applied the terms of the Speed Up Strike settlement to all the UAW's Ford locals. By forcing Ford management to establish written standards for labor intensity, Ford workers defended themselves against being overworked. Because the rate of work flow, line speeds and density of jobs on the line could not be changed during the day, *workers would know what was expected of them at the beginning of the production day.* Therefore, workers who felt they would need relief could, at the beginning of the production day, ask union representatives to present the case for relief to management.

Clearly the strike settlement did not allow the UAW to share in the daily decisions to set production rates. The UAW had sought this radical arrangement during the arbitration hearings, although it is hard to believe that IEB expected the arbitrators to order such a radical diminution of managerial authority. Achieving written production standards was a major gain for Ford workers. In the real world of industrial production, there were so many instances of managerial violation of agreements with workers that union action to reduce management's latitude for arbitrary and capricious decision-making served the interests of production workers, making their work environment more stable and less debilitating.[65]

In the national contract negotiations that followed the Speed Up Strike the UAW built on the precedent established by the arbitrators' award, getting Ford to agree to include allowances for worker fatigue in the time-study calculations that were made on most jobs. The UAW would quickly bring fatigue experts into the Rouge. They began by studying the assembly line jobs and then examined the jobs of off-the-line workers. In December 1949, Local 600 would challenge Ford's method of calculating fatigue allowances, taking the dispute to independent arbitrators.[66]

In August 1949, Ford negotiators proposed that workers participating in *unauthorized* strikes be subject to dismissal. *Walter Reuther refused to accept this demand.* Reuther told the Ford negotiating team that they could expect more stability in labor relations—faster settlement of grievances, fewer wildcats and authorized strikes—when there were *fewer company violations of local contracts.* Reuther pointed out that at General Motors, more tranquil labor relations existed precisely because plant managers had reduced company violations of local and national contract provisions.[67] But the UAW negotiators accepted a revision in the grievance procedure that ended the right of individual locals to take a grievance directly to arbitration. Now locals had to submit a grievance impasse to the UAW's Ford Department, which would decide whether or not it would be presented to the umpire.[68]

IV

How did the outcome of the 1949 Speed Up Strike influence the actual practices of Ford's managers? Securing uniform compliance with any kind of central office directive in a company as large as Ford always took time, and even
then some managers and foremen resisted implementing new rules and procedures. Workers at the Rouge continued to complain about some types of
speedups, although the details are not always clear. Pressure from Local 600 in
December 1949 led the management of the Dearborn Assembly plant to provide relief workers for the repair personnel who worked on moving lines.[69] On
Friday, March 31, 1950, the Ford final assembly line in the Dearborn plant was
speeded up. Workers "marched to the final assembly office during their lunch
hour, endeavoring to take matters into their own hands." The plant bargaining
committee was summoned by management. The committee told the workers to
return to work after their break and let the committee negotiate on their behalf.
The committee gave management "an ultimatum of turning the speed of the
line back to where it was or [the committee] . . . would not be responsible for
what happened." The company slowed down the line until a union representative checked each job and made sure the operation was "balanced properly."[70]
Clearly continued union vigilance was necessary to enforce the terms of the
1949 settlement. But it appears that the union was often successful in this
endeavor. Thus, in August 1950, negotiations led to the settlement of six grievances filed by workers at the Dearborn Assembly plant. Ford agreed to install
regulators on all Mercury intermittent and feeder lines to "provide constant
speeds on such lines. The company also agreed to provide additional manpower constantly until installation of the regulators" was completed.[71]

At the Lincoln plant, Local 900 also had to fight to get Ford to adopt
equitable production standards. In November 1949, the UAW challenged
management on a production standard the Ford workers claimed was one "we
have checked and double checked . . . ." Two impartial engineering consultants, called in to arbitrate the dispute, sided with the UAW. But the Local 900
Bargaining Committee remained unhappy about the adequacy of the staffing
levels on some production lines. Unfortunately, we have limited amounts of
information about the subsequent history of disagreements over line manning
levels at the Lincoln plant.[72]

In 1951, the Ford managers at the Rouge complex continued to test the
UAW's mettle. One day, after the Local 600 Executive Board issued a leaflet
protesting various speedups, the company gave two UAW committee persons
a thirty day disciplinary layoff because they told workers that production on
a job in the Pressed Steel mill was 217 units daily and the workers should not

exceed this limit. Ford alleged that this directive constituted a work stoppage. Local 600 President Carl Stellato was firm with the Ford management: "I told [them] . . . that this was one case that wasn't going to the Umpire." Ford then reduced the layoff to two weeks.[73]

In his discussion of the speedup situation at the Rouge complex at the June 10, 1951 meeting of the Local 600 General Council, Stellato, who was independent of the Reuther faction but clearly was not a communist, spoke candidly about the politicization of the speedup issue within the UAW: "For a period of time all of us that ran for office [in Local 600] at some time or another played politics with this." But, Stellato added, "We have been united for the last year on the question of speedup." Stellato then offered his interpretation of the settlement of the 1949 Speed Up Strike and the experience of Ford workers thereafter: "The contract is very specific and clear and states no employee shall be made to work over 100 percent."[74] Ford had been required to provide adequate relief so that production line workers did not have to work at a rate that exceeded 60 standard minutes per hour. When Ford's local foremen and managers violated this stipulation, the UAW acted to enforce the contract. Without access to Ford's industrial relations records, which exist but are closed to researchers, it is impossible to determine how many of Ford's contract violations were part of a centrally determined strategy to occasionally test the mettle of the UAW, and how many were the result of local Ford supervisors disregarding central office directives on labor relations.

Three years after the Speed Up Strike, M. W. Welty, the manager of the Ford Industrial Relations Department, delivered a speech to Ford plant managers that suggests that by 1952, Ford's central office executives were making a *bona fide* effort to implement the terms of the 1949 strike settlement. Welty urged Ford managers to attempt, at the beginning of each model year, to establish temporary production standards that were as close to using a full 480 standard minutes of work as possible. Loose temporary standards subsequently had to be raised. Human nature led production workers to be "more apt to shout "speedup" under those conditions than if he had originally been given approximately 480 minutes of work to perform." Welty then warned his audience that he was

> sure that the union—the National Ford Department, in particular—is going to be quite vigilant in watching for infractions of the so-called strike settlement agreement . . . if your plant is to "stay out of the grease [avoid strikes]," you are going to have to be equally vigilant to see that you are living up, literally, to that portion of our contract. Put real emphasis on maintaining the proper body mix—and if the body mix goes sour in spite of your best efforts— know where and when to throw the necessary manpower into the job.

Welty also urged his plant managers to give union officials accurate information about production schedules:

> In notifying the union of your line speed and manning be sure you give them your *internal* schedule. For example: If your production schedule is 200; and the line is set at 3 percent overspeed. You must man for 206 jobs—not 200—and you are entitled to 206 jobs if everything works right that day.[75]

This speech suggests that the 1949 Speed Up Strike and the general actions of the men in Locals 600 and 900 had convinced Ford's central management that it had to discipline its "troops" to honor the written agreements negotiated with the UAW. Order and stability meant that management had to make more of an effort to honor the basic contractual agreements that were negotiated.

VI

Ford workers continued to challenge the company when they believed management allowed the work environment to become dangerous, unhealthy, or when workers concluded that specific production standards were unfair. From 1950 to 1955, Ford workers staged more wildcat strikes than GM workers, but walked out less frequently than did Chrysler workers.[76] In 1953, unauthorized strikes by Ford workers accounted for 2.2 lost man hours per employee; in 1954, the figure was 1.5. The average of lost man hours per employee for GM workers, 1950–1954, was 0.42. The comparable figure for Chrysler workers was a stunning 18.6.[77] The figures on wildcat strikes indicate that the Chrysler workers used wildcat actions as negotiating weapons much more frequently than their counterparts at Ford and GM. But the Ford workers often combined wildcats and *authorized* strikes to pressure management to respond positively to worker grievances.

In 1953, the Ford Motor Company sent the UAW a detailed report on the year's *unauthorized* strikes. (See Table 8.) Most of these wildcat strikes lasted less than one shift. The number of workers involved was generally less than 50. When complaints about workplace temperature (too hot, too cold) led to wildcat strikes, there is no record of any disciplinary action taken against the strikers. Most of the 33 heat strikes were simply allowed to run their course—3–6 hours in most cases; one was 8 hours. Corrective action was taken in response to only 2 of the heat strikes, whereas management responded positively to worker demands in 2 of the 4 strikes involving cold workplaces.[79]

There were 17 strikes over other health and safety issues,[80] with Ford management taking corrective action in 12 cases, agreeing to investigate one

TABLE 8
Unauthorized Ford Strikes, 1953[78]

# Workers Striking	# Unauthorized Strikes
1–10	15
11–50	43
51–100	16
101–200	7
201–500	6
501–1,000	4
>1,000	5

complaint, and taking no action in 4 instances. The largest and longest was a successful 2-day wildcat at the Monroe, Michigan parts plant, involving 2,018 workers. Five strikes involved work standards, pay scales, and staffing. The largest was a 15 minute wildcat at the Monroe, Michigan plant. Two small actions, involving 4 and 7 worker rolling crews at the Dearborn rolling mill, lasted one day and saw workers added to crews the workers claimed were understaffed. Sixty-three employees at the Dearborn mill walked out for a day to get a new incentive plan, while 36 workers at the Dearborn transmission plant refused to work for 35 minutes when a worker was disciplined for failing to meet a production standard. This strike was settled when the UAW committeeperson agreed to compel the worker to meet the standard. None of these wildcatters was disciplined. In fact, while 1953's 127 wildcat strikes involved 20,603 strikers and 7,120,056 lost production hours, including non-strikers idled by these actions, the Ford document indicates that only 1 striker was fired and 8 others were disciplined.[81]

Perhaps Ford management did not want to exacerbate tensions in these situations. Ford seemed especially amenable to correcting the hazards that were the cause of the health and safety wildcats. Perhaps Ford did not want to call additional attention to these hazards by disciplining the workers who complained by striking. Moreover, grievance decisions by the Ford umpire had established the right of workers to leave their work positions to avoid intolerable cold, to get fresh air, and in general, to avoid an "undue health hazard." While workers who exercised this right could not be disciplined, they did lose their pay for the time they were not at work.[82] Overall, it seems likely that Ford's industrial relations managers were willing to allow workers to release some of their anger and frustration through short work stoppages. It is also significant that with one exception, Ford did not give way in situations where the cause of the strike was management insistence that a worker uphold a production standard. Ford's concessions on staffing at the Dearborn rolling mill involved very small work groups.

In the 1949 Speed Up Strike, the UAW International, after trying to limit shopfloor job actions to protest Ford's contract violations, had concluded that the Ford Motor Company was aggressively sanctioning such serious violations of union-management agreements that an *authorized* strike was necessary. After 1949, the Ford management avoided such direct, all-out assaults on union power. But Ford *frequently tested the UAW's power in more limited, but significant situations.* It is revealing that in 1955 the manager of Ford's Lincoln-Mercury Division bluntly told Ken Bannon that while Ford had learned to live with the UAW, "[We] don't mean to live up to the agreements we enter into with you." As the case studies that follow indicate, the UAW's Ford Department met such intransigence with authorized strikes and bargained at the national level to try to make such strikes more effective.[83]

Early in 1953, the management at Ford's Monroe, Michigan plant unilaterally doubled a work standard that had existed for fourteen previous months on a job involving polishing part of the tail light assembly of Mercury cars. Local 723 got nowhere in pressing grievances over the increase in the production standard from 400 to 754 pieces per day. Other production standards had also been increased on about 25 percent of the jobs in the plant. The Monroe workers began the direct action phase of their struggle against increases in work loads at the plant on April 1, at 3:30 PM, when 2,208 workers launched a *wildcat* strike. One week later, the strike was transformed into an *authorized* strike by the IEB. The strike lasted until April 15. Overall, 41,207 workers were idled and 953,872 "manhours" were lost.

The strike settlement restored the disputed production standards at the Monroe plant to their former levels and stipulated that the standards were *permanent* ones. Under the national Ford contract, which Ford had clearly violated, no permanent standards could be changed unless there was a change in part design or job design. New local contract language gave Ford 75 days after production began on a new model to change a preliminary standard into a permanent standard. Ford also agreed to pay for an extra local union representative to handle work standard issues. To protect workers against speedups to compensate for parts shortages and mechanical failures beyond their control, the settlement stipulated that when down time occurred during the absence of the immediate supervisor, "the employee's statement of such down time will be accepted unless proven to be false." Workers who finished their daily output quotas before quitting time were to be allowed to leave their work stations to wash up, shower, and dress in the locker room. At the Monroe plant, unionized workers, backed by the UAW's national leadership, had used militant action under their contract's health and safety strike clause to force Ford to honor the basic terms of its national contract.

UAW Local 542 represented workers at the company's Canton, Ohio forging plant. In 1950, the company set a standard on the forging of Ford and Mercury axle shafts that was acceptable to the UAW's skilled forge workers. Then the company made five changes in the way the forging was performed. A dispute arose over the new production standard, which the forge workers claimed was too tight. In February 1951, the UAW sent a time-study expert from its Research and Engineering Department, Robert L. Kanter, to Canton to investigate the dispute. He concluded that the weight of the forgings that workers had to handle had not been considered when the fatigue factor of the job was computed by the Ford engineers. Kantor recommended a new standard of 117.21 pieces per hour instead of the Ford standard of 137 pieces per hour. During the next two years, there were disputes over production standards and significant underpayment when jobs were re-designed by combining two job classifications, which substantially increased the skill base and amount of work required. The foundry workers at Canton also had a large number of complaints about inadequate ventilation, dangerous machinery, and uncomfortable work environments (e.g., concrete floors instead of wooden boards that would produce less strain on lathe operators who had to stand for long periods of time). After three years of unsuccessful attempts by the leaders of Local 542 to use the grievance procedures to combat these management actions, an authorized plant-wide strike was initiated on April 19, 1953. It lasted 36 days. The strike settlement rectified most of the workers' complaints and committed the Ford Company to paying the salary of a full-time union health and safety representative.[85]

Ford workers often used their right to authorized strikes on health and safety grievances to pressure Ford management to settle outstanding production standard grievances. During the 1955 national contract negotiations, a Ford Motor Company spokesperson complained bitterly that during plant level negotiations to prevent or end strikes called under the terms of Article VII, Section 23, the UAW frequently insisted on bargaining on non-strikeable issues:

> Since 1949 not a single negotiation of an authorized strike notice has been restricted to the so-called strikeable issue. In almost every instance the strikeable issue has been insignificant in the negotiations . . . [86]

Ford negotiators also tried, but not as vigorously as they tried to get rid of Article VII, Section 23, to get the UAW to relinquish its right to strike over production standards. Commenting on this management stance at the May 9,

1955 meeting of the National Ford Council, UAW-Ford director Ken Bannon
pointed out that the bargaining committee had told Ford that:

> our new contract most certainly is going to have a clause in there so we will
> have a right to strike [about production standards] . . . They complain bitter-
> ly about the [UAW] position . . . because we have refused arbitration in
> almost every instance where we have had these disputes with the Company.
> We told the Company [during negotiations] . . . "By damn, that is going to
> continue to be our position. We are not going to let a person [i.e., the arbi-
> trator] who does not know the problems of a worker set the standards for the
> people in the shop."[87]

After the 1955 contract was signed, there was continued friction between
Ford workers and management over the way the company manipulated production standards. There were also ongoing disputes about the techniques
used by Ford to calculate fatigue allowances when jobs were time studied.[88]
In June 1960, 48 workers at the Wayne Assembly plant were disciplined for
staging five unauthorized work stoppages related to health and safety issues
and production standards. The Ford Department backed up the plant's 2,037
workers and subsequently requested authorization for an Article VII, Section
23 strike that began on July 7. The strike lasted until August 18. The strike
appears to have been successful. However, Ken Bannon told the May 24,
1961 meeting of the National Ford Council that "a month later the very standards that we corrected are violated again." Ford Council president Gene
Prato noted that this was a recurrent problem:

> We struck the Indianapolis plant last summer over work standards . . . and
> the same jobs which we struck on were in dispute again. The standards were
> tightened up. In Local 1250 we were close to a strike on work standards, and
> on the health and safety issue. We got out of there with a settlement . . .
> It wasn't a month later and the same thing was in dispute again.

Prato concluded that only strikes or the threat of strikes could combat this
management tendency: "If you think that [improved contract] language is
going to convince Ford, you should know better." [89]

On November 16, 1960, 223 workers at Ford's Des Moines, Iowa, implement plant began an authorized work stoppage to protest the work standard on
a welding job. Two workers had been laid off for 17 days when they refused
to meet the disputed standard. The strike resulted in at least 49,000 lost man
hours before it was settled. The Ford Department sent UAW staff members to
aid the strikers, who forced Ford to abolish the standard and restore the jobs
and lost pay of the two workers originally disciplined.[90]

Walter Dahl, representing Ford Local 325, St. Louis, told the delegates at the May 24, 1961 National Ford Council meeting that the members of his local had used unauthorized job actions to force Ford *to comply with contract provisions* for bathroom relief. If the relief worker could not give relief to one of the 19 workers he was supposed to relieve, local management replied, as Dahl phrased it, "That is just too bad. We are not going to tolerate people walking off their jobs." But many militant members of Local 325 simply left their work stations when they did not get bathroom relief. Some were penalized. "Finally they agreed that everyone is entitled to relief...," Dahl reported.[91]

Throughout the 1960s, the UAW encountered frequent problems with violations of the contract's production standard grievances, especially at Ford's medium-sized plants. Members of Local 249 complained that line workers were often overloaded and then given only occasional or part-time help, "keeping pressure on the permanent operator to perform the complete assignment without help." They also reported that Ford's plant supervisors conceded that "operators were overloaded," but admitted to the union that they "had no right to take the work off of the operator." Local 249's officers speculated that "there are internal battles going on between [plant] management and the "work standards" department of the Ford Motor Company as to what constitutes a normal work standard for the operator."[92] This split is similar to the conflict that raged between many General Motors plant managers and the hard-nosed personnel of the General Motors Assembly Division in the the late 1960s and the early 1970s.

VI

Ford workers and union officials understood the maxim, "Eternal vigilance is the price of liberty." The available evidence suggests that Ford workers consistently struggled to maintain their liberty, often paying the price in lost wages and, sometimes, dismissal. UAW leaders clearly did not back all unauthorized strikes against managerial shopfloor policies. But the UAW records indicate that at critical junctures, union officials at all levels provided a great deal of support to production workers in their resistance to management-initiated speedups, especially when these speedups violated local labor-management agreements. The struggle was never an even match. Ford's financial power, and the national legal and political climate, limited the amount of pressure that unionized automobile workers could bring to bear on management when the UAW bargained to control the intensity, degree of risk, and level of pay on auto jobs.

When the UAW forced management to set and adhere to a *steady* work pace, the job environment became more stable and predictable. Auto workers also won *specific* gains in the realm of health and safety, job security, and relief from work fatigue. Without individual and collective worker resistance, auto workers would have been treated less equitably in all regards.

It is a measure of the political tenor of our times that today many contemporary labor relations specialists and general observers would question this conclusion. Shortly after he was appointed Secretary of Labor by President Bill Clinton, Robert B. Reich, a lawyer who had never been directly involved in labor relations, maintained that it was unclear whether or not unions are useful institutions. Certainly the auto workers at Ford found their union very useful in combatting the pattern of managerial agreement-breaking that was endemic during the early post-War years and continued, albeit at a reduced rate, in the 1950s and 1960s. Militant worker pressure, aided by local and national officials of the UAW, prevented Ford management from turning the "social compact" between labor and capital into an unconditional surrender of hard-won worker rights.

Acknowledgments

The author would like to thank Ken Bannon, retired Director of the UAW's Ford Department, for sharing his knowledge of labor relations at Ford from 1945 to 1960. Carol J. Williams was kind enough to critique the chapter. The author's research was funded by grants from the Henry J. Kaiser Family Foundation and the Research Foundation of the University of Connecticut.

6

WHY AUTOMATION DIDN'T SHORTEN THE WORK WEEK: THE POLITICS OF WORK TIME IN THE AUTOMOBILE INDUSTRY

....

Ronald Edsforth

I

During the first three decades of this century, work time standards in the automobile industry were set by management without consultation with workers. In general, work time reforms were initiated to maximize the productive potential of new technology and techniques, not enhance the quality of workers' lives. The Ford Motor Company, the industry's technological leader, introduced the most important work time reforms of this period. Other automobile manufacturers were slow to follow Ford's lead in work time reform.

Prior to World War I, the industry's standard schedule consisted of two ten-hour shifts, six days a week. In 1914, when the Ford Motor Company introduced the moving assembly line, it also reduced the normal work day from ten to eight hours, and moved from a two-shift to a three-shift schedule. The eight-hour day allowed Ford to run its heavily capitalized factories round the clock to keep up with soaring demand for its Model T. General Motors and other major automobile manufacturers also reduced work time as they entered the mass-production era; but throughout the 1920s these companies stayed with two shifts of nine hours each, adding overtime to workers' schedules whenever market conditions warranted it. Ford had limited total hours worked to twelve in any twenty-four hour period since 1912. However, in practice, the industry as a whole placed no limits on overtime and paid no premium for hours worked beyond the daily standard. As Joyce Shaw Peterson has noted, in the 1920s "workers were expected to work overtime for as long as the company required and to do so at the regular rates."[1]

In 1925, the United States Department of Labor reported that all auto workers averaged at least forty-eight hours per week; 70 percent of the industry's workforce averaged a minimum of fifty hours per week.[2] These averages are extremely misleading because actual hours worked fluctuated widely during the typical year. In the spring, when demand for new cars usually peaked, workers would often have to put in sixty or more hours per week. Similarly, weekly schedules would be reduced to five days and less than forty hours during the slack season in mid-winter. In addition, unanticipated changes in demand for a factory's product frequently led management to announce work schedule changes without advance notice. Thus, the industry's prevailing work time policies greatly contributed to pre-Depression auto workers' most consistent grievances: the uncertainty of employment and constant fluctuation of weekly earnings.[3]

The five-day, forty-hour work week was introduced by the Ford Motor Company in October 1926. Although the company promised workers would take home what they had previously made in six days, most workers actually suffered weekly pay cuts from $36 to $30 or $32 when they moved to the five-day week. Moreover, as demand for Ford's new Model A grew, the company asked more and more workers to report to their jobs on Saturdays. For all practical purposes, Ford had reinstituted the six-day week by January 1929.[4]

In 1926, when Henry Ford announced the five-day week, he had explained his company's new work time policy as a necessary adjustment to the ever-increasing productivity created by technological progress, and as a way to assure the continued expansion of mass-consumption. "The country is ready for the five-day week," Ford proclaimed.

> It is bound to come through all industry... The short work week is bound to come because without it the country will not be able to absorb its production and stay prosperous... Well-managed business pays high wages and sells at low prices. Its workmen have the leisure to enjoy life and the wherewithal to finance that enjoyment. The industry of this country could not long exist if factories generally went back to the ten-hour day because the people would not have the time to consume the goods produced.[5]

As Henry Ford recognized, to ensure the continued growth of mass consumer society, business had to both raise wage levels and reduce the average work week when it introduced productivity-enhancing technology and techniques.

In the late 1920s, very few industrialists were as prescient as Henry Ford about the long-term requirements of a true mass consumer society, and very few major corporations followed his lead on work time reform. By 1926, the eight-hour day had been widely adopted by American business, but Saturday shifts remained part of the standard work week in most industries, including automobile manufacturing. No other major automobile company instituted the forty-hour week in the 1920s. Moreover, besides Ford, only three other U.S. corporations employing more than two thousand workers had adopted the forty-hour week by the end of 1927. As Benjamin Hunnicutt has observed, by the mid-1920s, "the shorter-hour movement had outrun its appeal for most employers and managers."[6]

Nonetheless, the Great Depression soon forced many major companies to reduce standard work time to spread employment out and to sustain their needed skilled and semi-skilled work forces. In 1931, Goodyear became the first major corporation to establish a thirty-hour work week for this purpose. As the Great Depression worsened, other rubber companies adopted the thirty-hour week, and it was later incorporated into the industry's settlement with the new United Rubber Workers union.[7] But in most industries, including automobile manufacturing, elimination of Saturday work, and adoption of a standard five-day, forty-hour week, was by far a more common response to the Depression. This pattern was ratified and extended by the Federal Government during 1933–1934. Most of the various code authorities established in over 500 different industries by the National Recovery Administration (NRA) mandated a forty-hour week for all signatory firms. In addition, NRA authorities required member companies to pay a time and a half premium wage for hours worked in excess of the code's standard week.

In 1932, auto workers who were lucky enough to have kept their jobs, averaged 30.8 hours per week. The NRA's original national Automobile Code would have required member firms to adopt a thirty-five hour standard work week at a time—June 1933—when the average work week in the industry had recovered to forty-five hours. The original Code included no provision for overtime pay.[8] General Motors, Chrysler, and most other important firms in the industry's trade association, the National Automobile Chamber of Commerce (NACC), refused to adopt the thirty-five hour standard, and appealed to NRA chief Hugh Johnson for relief. On January 8, 1934, a compliant Johnson announced a new forty hour standard work week for automobile manufacturing using the manufacturers' dubious claim of labor shortages as a justification.

Johnson's action was unique; no other NRA code was amended in this way. The upward revision of the Code's work time standard heightened labor unrest among automobile workers who were already angry about the speedup and victimization of union activists. Over 200 officers of the Federal Labor Unions (FLU) the A. F. of L. had established in the industry sent telegrams to President Roosevelt protesting Johnson's action.[9] In January, tens of thousands of militant workers signed up with the FLUs. On February 3, 1934, reluctant A. F. of L. leaders responded to this "pressure from below" by threatening a national automobile strike. Neither the A. F. of L. nor the manufacturers wanted a showdown at this time. The Federation's William Collins and Francis Dillon helped defuse workers' militancy and forced President Roosevelt to intervene and affirm their right to organize independent unions. On March 13, 1934, the NACC recommended that member firms reduce the standard work week from forty to thirty-six hours, and offer workers a 10 percent wage increase. This recommendation facilitated Presidential intervention. On March 25th, Franklin Roosevelt announced a settlement of the dispute in the automobile industry that included the NACC's hours and wage recommendation, as well as the establishment of a special Automobile Labor Board chaired by Leo Wolman, which would investigate future violations of the Automobile Code. Workers' wages were subsequently increased, but the industry ignored the recommended thirty-six hour standard.[10]

On January 31, 1935, a final revision of the Automobile Code established the principle of overtime pay, calling for time and a half for hours in excess of forty-eight per week. This amendment to the Code had little effect, since the major manufacturers were able to insist that hours be averaged over the whole model year—September 5 to September 4—including the weeks most workers spent laid off for model change retooling. The Supreme Court's decision, declaring the NRA unconstitutional in May 1935, also had little effect on hours worked in the automobile industry. Auto workers averaged 37.1 hours per week in 1935, 38.5 hours per week in 1936, and 35.9 hours per week in 1937.[11] These averages, of course, disguise the lengthly overtime worked in peak production periods and the short weeks worked when orders dropped. It should also be noted that the Ford Motor Company, which had never signed the NRA's automobile manufacturers' code, nonetheless conformed to the prevailing work time standards throughout this period. Thus, by the time the new UAW-CIO had launched its first major organizing drive against General Motors in the second half of 1936, the five-day, forty-hour week schedule, with time and a half premium pay for overtime, had become well-established industry standards.

As the market for cars recovered in the mid-1930s, the industry's Big Three—General Motors, Ford, and Chrysler—restored production with labor forces significantly smaller than they had employed in the late 1920s. Workers with very little experience and usually very young, those with a history of disciplinary problems or relatively poor production records, and individuals deemed "too old" by their supervisors were not rehired. The car companies were able to increase productivity with their remaining workforces by introducing new technology, and by intensifying the pressure for greater output on the shopfloor.[12] When orders for automobiles were strong, as they often were in the years 1935–1937, foremen drove workers very hard to increase production, and production standards were frequently revised upward. Mandatory overtime and the speedup were commonplace. But when the auto market slumped, or when a factory was retooled for a new product, or to introduce new labor-saving technology, workers were simply laid off with no guarantee they would ever be recalled.

Organized labor's basic programatic response to the employment and working conditions created by the Great Depression had been a renewed call for sharp reductions in the standard work week. As early as 1930, the American Federation of Labor had asked Congress to enact legislation establishing a five-day, thirty-hour standard work week with no reduction in pay. Senator Hugo Black of Alabama, and Representative William Connery of Massachusetts, introduced a thirty-hour bill into Congress in 1932. In April 1933, the Senate actually approved the measure, but the Roosevelt Administration intervened and blocked passage in the House of Representatives. Despite this setback, labor leaders continued to demonstrate great enthusiasm for the thirty-hour week. It seemed the most direct way to deal with workers' most deeply felt Depression-related problems, especially unemployment, uncertain employment, and the speedup. With organized labor's support, the Black-Connery bill was repeatedly, and unsuccessfully, reintroduced in Congress during the mid-1930s. Many historians view the sustained popularity of the thirty-hour bill as the spur which forced the Roosevelt Administration to introduce some of its most important New Deal reforms, including the National Industrial Recovery Act,[13]

The demand for a thirty-hour week also played an important role in the revival of the labor movement after 1932, and especially in the rise of the CIO unions in basic industry in the years 1935–1940. Reduced work time was an extremely important issue in the UAW-CIO's momentous sit-down strike against General Motors in the winter of 1936–1937. The union's strike demands, presented in its "Proposed [General Motors] Agreement" dated December 1936, called for a five-day, thirty-hour standard work week with double time pay for all weekend and holiday work. If "Proposed Agreement" is read as a priority list, shorter hours ranked just after recognition and the establishment of a secure seniority system among the union's demands.[14] Yet, despite its great victory over General Motors in the Flint sit-down strike, the UAW-CIO did not win a single work time concession from the company in either the initial contract, which ended the conflict in February 1937, or the longer supplementary agreement it negotiated with the GM a month later.[15] General Motors recognized the UAW for collective bargaining purposes, established a seniority system, and a grievance procedure, but simply refused to alter its pre-strike work time standards. Sidney Fine's authoritative account of the 1936–1937 sit-down strike leaves no doubt on this point. "With regard to hours," Fine declares,

> the [GM] agreement confirmed the existing corporation policy—the forty-hour week, the eight-hour day, and time-and-a half for overtime—rather than meeting the UAW's demand for the thirty-hour week, six-hour day.[16]

General Motors' ability to resist the initial UAW effort to shorten the work week in 1936–1937 had enormous significance as a historical precedent within the industry as a whole. Having agreed to a five-day, forty-hour week for GM workers, UAW leaders found it impossible to reduce work time standards at the other major companies when they subsequently recognized the union. And as years passed without any real reform of work time standards, those same UAW leaders found it increasingly difficult to counter the presumption that the existing standards were fair, and indeed in some way, "natural."

Nevertheless, prior to World War II, rank-and-file auto workers and local union activists continued to demand shorter hours. Members of the union's International Executive Board (IEB) tried to respond to this demand by bringing the issue to the negotiating table, but when the organization split into rival CIO and AFL factions from 1938 to 1940, the auto makers generally refused to bargain over hours, or anything else of consequence. During the war production boom, the drive to maximize military production made the thirty-hour week unthinkable, but the issue remained alive as part of the UAW's institutional memory.

In the early Cold War era, when technological unemployment created by automation first threatened the jobs of production workers in the industry's engine-making plants, a surprisingly persistent rank-and-file movement quickly resurrected the union's original demand for a thirty-hour work week. However, throughout the 1950s and early 1960s, UAW President Walter Reuther repeatedly deflected the new call for shorter hours, even as he made public statements endorsing the logic of reducing work time in response to technological progress. The rank-and-file movement for shorter hours finally disintegrated in the mid-1960s. Since then, although there have been occasional calls to revive the shorter work week demand, UAW leaders have not renewed the labor movement's historic struggle for work time reform. Today, nearly six decades after the call for a thirty-hour work week was raised as one of the UAW's five founding demands, most American auto workers still labor under contracts that mandate a standard eight-hour day and forty-hour week with time and a half overtime pay. As part of their most recent modernization programs, the Big Three have tried to introduce a four-day, forty-hour week, which gives management greater flexibility in scheduling extra shifts, but nowhere in the industry has the most recent introduction of new labor-saving technologies led to real reductions in work time standards.[17]

II

Walter Reuther had been a consistent advocate of shorter hours in the years preceding World War II. In 1936–37, UAW organizers, including Reuther, repeatedly argued that a shorter work week would force management to provide more jobs and more predictable year-round employment. They also presented the thirty-hour week as a direct remedy for the physical and psychological strain of the speedup.[18] At that time, Reuther was still a member of the Socialist Party and the Progressive caucus within the highly politicized UAW leadership circle. His political radicalism was undoubtedly genuine. In the mid-1930s, he believed the new CIO unions would bring about a radical transformation of American capitalism.[19] But Reuther's advocacy of a thirty-hour week was not a matter of Socialist politics. Instead, it reflected his immersion in organized labor's traditional work time ideology, especially the idea that labor value is embodied in new technology, and that the productivity gains created by the introduction of new machinery should be returned to workers in the form of both higher wages and shorter hours. In the late 1920s, the American Federation of Labor had campaigned for a five-day, forty-hour week stressing the belief that reduced work time was the appropriate response to technological unemployment, as well as the idea that shorter hours were a necessary compensation for mass production work that was dehumanizing and exhausting.[20] And as we have already seen, the AFL had endorsed the thirty-hour week as its principal political response to the mass unemployment of the early 1930s.

The new UAW-CIO was unable to win the thirty-hour week in its original contracts with General Motors in February/March 1937, or from Chrysler when it recognized the union in June 1937, but rank-and-file pressure led union leaders to renew the fight for a shorter work week in the second half of that year. Reuther was one of a "Committee of 17" leaders who petitioned GM President William Knudsen in September 1937, asking the corporation to reopen its contract with the UAW. A seven-hour day/thirty-five hour work week, increases in overtime pay, and paid vactions were three of the eleven demands this committee placed before GM.[21] In the summer of 1937, the demand for shorter hours was also prominent in the union's drive to organize Ford's gigantic production complex on the River Rouge. UAW Vice Presidents Walter Reuther and Richard Frankensteen suffered severe beatings at the hands of a company-organized goon squad during this organizing drive.

This so-called "Battle of the Overpass" contributed to the demoralization of
the UAW effort at Ford that fall.

As 1937 ended, the national economy slid into a severe recession, and the
UAW split into two feuding organizations: the larger, more radical one affiliated with the Congress of Industrial Organizations, and its smaller, conservative rival affiliated with the American Federation of Labor. With unemployment in the industry soaring, and the rival factions exchanging political
charges and physical blows, union membership declined drastically, collective bargaining ceased, and the contractually mandated forty-hour week, with
time and half for overtime, took root as an industry fixture. Thus, in the automobile industry as in so many other major U.S. industries, the Fair Labor
Standards Act of 1938 did not really establish the forty-hour week norm so
much as it buttressed management's insistence that there be no further reductions in weekly work time standards.

In 1939–1940, as the UAW-CIO faction secured its place as auto workers' sole bargaining agent through National Labor Relations Board elections,
the union's leaders took to the stump to rebuild the dues-paying membership.
Their speeches from that era reflect a recognition that work time reductions
remained an important concern of the rank-and-file. For example, at a mass
membership meeting of his own West Side Detroit Local 174, Walter
Reuther called on the UAW to take "the initiative within the CIO for the
launching of a national campaign for the thirty-hour week with forty hours
pay."[22] Both the 1939 and 1940 UAW conventions endorsed the shorter work
week—or "thirty for forty" as it was popularly known—as a top bargaining
priority, and the issue remained very much on the union's agenda when the
war emergency began.

As the industry finally began to convert to war production in early 1941,
GM Chairman Alfred Sloan suggested that its contract with the UAW be
amended to make a six day, forty-eight hour work week standard for the duration. This transparent attempt by the corporation to avoid overtime wages and
hold down its payrolls was vehemently denounced by Walter Reuther, who
was by then Director of the UAW's General Motors Department. He told a
conference of GM's local union delegates in February 1941, "we are not even
thinking of working more than 40 hours at the present time, other than on the
basis of overtime provisions." He added that in the future, when the military
boom ended, and unemployment soared again,

> we ought to be prepared to make a fight—and I mean a fight-for a 30 hour
> week and 40 hours pay in order to fill that gap.[23]

There can be no doubt that Walter Reuther was still a serious advocate of "30
for 40" and the work-spreading logic which informed that demand on the eve

of America's entry into World War II. Yet, after the war, when union activists resurrected the "30 for 40" demand in response to the threat of technological unemployment brought on by automation, Reuther refused to make work time reductions a top priority. The explanation for his complete reversal on the "30 for 40" demand is complex; its ideological, political, and economic dimensions are fully explored later in this chapter. It is sufficient to note that by refusing to act upon the demands of the "30 for 40" movement in the 1950s, Walter Reuther, in effect, became a defender of the status quo five-day, forty-hour standard work week.

III

World War II had revived the fortunes of the Big Three automobile corporations, as well as the many smaller firms that made up the industry in the 1940s. However, the production of weapons, armored vehicles, and other war supplies from 1941 to 1945, did not prepare the industry for a smooth return to the mass production of private automobiles and trucks. Reconversion was a difficult process that involved an almost total retooling of many facilities, and enormous turnovers in the labor force. Many historians have noted how the automobile industry drastically reduced the numbers of women and black men on their payrolls during the reconversion period. In retrospect, it is also clear that the biggest companies, General Motors and Ford, saw reconversion as an opportunity to significantly increase productivity, and reduce labor costs, by installing new types of automatic production equipment.

Using government-granted tax incentives, GM was able to set up the first successful automated transfer line in its Buick engine plant in Flint, Michigan in 1946 shortly after the settlement of the longest strike in industry history. As described by Stephen Meyer, these Ingersoll, NATCO, and Greenlee machines were equipped "with individual tools that performed from six to nineteen separate operations on the cylinder blocks. Once placed in a transfer machine, a piece moved from tool to tool until it finished its sequence of operations."[24] The new Buick engine operation represented a significant step toward full automation, but still retained operations that required considerable physical labor to unload and load individual blocks, and to inspect and move them from machine to machine via gravity rollers.

The real breakthrough to what became known as "Detroit Automation" actually came at an engine-making complex Ford built in the Cleveland suburb of Brook Park. This new plant, with its totally redesigned engine lines and an automated foundry, showcased a $2 billion modernization effort, which Ford pursued from 1946 to the mid-1950s. The plant's six cylinder production

line was opened in 1951, and its eight cylinder line began regular production
in 1954. By the mid-1950s, Ford's Cleveland engine plant had become a
national symbol of automation after many industry, labor, and government
officials were given highly publicized tours of the plant.

Ford's fully automated 350 foot long eight cylinder line in Cleveland was
capable of turning out 100 finished eight-cylinder engine blocks an hour,
while requiring the attendance of very few workers. Human labor was
required in the loading process, but from there, all materials handling and
positioning, machine operations, lubrication, removal of scraps, and inspection of machine performance was done automatically. This eight cylinder line
automatically performed 555 separate tasks—including 265 drilling, 6
milling, 21 boring, 56 reaming, 101 countersinking, 106 tapping, and 133
inspection operations—on each block.[25] As Walter Reuther later recalled,
"about all the few workers had to do was watch the panels of red, yellow, and
green lights that indicate whether the machine is getting tired."[26]

Automation proceeded rapidly in the automobile industry in the mid-
1950s. As early as March 1954, at least 119 different companies were producing automation equipment for the automobile industry.[27] About a year after
Ford finished its Cleveland engine plant, GM's Pontiac Division unveiled a
70,000 square foot facility in Michigan that included fully automatic production of cylinder blocks, cylinder heads, pistons, connecting rods, camshafts,
and crankshafts. Both of Pontiac's 1,300 foot long, S-shaped engine block
lines had the capacity to automatically store pieces in holding bins when any
of their thirty separate machines were temporarily overloaded. Chrysler and
Packard completed similar, though smaller engine-making facilities in 1954.[28]
In 1955, Norton introduced special transfer machines that for the first time
mechanized "all operations necessary for accurately grinding the bearings of
crankshafts automatically" to the extremely close tolerances required to eliminate human intervention in the mating of parts. That year Studebaker-
Packard was the first company to adopt this soon standard equipment.[29] By
1957, Udylite machinery, which automated the industry's nickel and chrome
plating processes, and produced uniform products that required little final
buffing, was also becoming standard equipment in the industry's body-making plants. This particular innovation no doubt contributed to the soaring
numbers of chrome plated "dinosaurs" that roamed America's roads in 1958
and 1959.[30] Overall, a survey done in 1957 of the automobile and automotive
parts industries reported that 12 percent of the facilities with fewer than 100
employees had introduced some automation, while 30 percent of the larger
factories employing over 500 workers had begun automated operations.[31]
Automated production continued to spread, especially in the industry's body
plants, in the early 1960s.

Automation was celebrated as unmitigated progress by automobile company spokespeople. Ford, the self-proclaimed leader of the automation movement, was particularly aggressive in getting its message out. Increased output, reduced labor costs, and better quality were always stressed when company representatives addressed the public. Ford Vice President Ray H. Sullivan succinctly summed this approach up in October 1953 when he told a meeting of the Associated Industries of Cleveland,

> The result [of automation] is much higher quantity of production at considerably lower costs. That means that, over the long run, we can offer the customer more and more for his money.

But the company did not ignore widely voiced concerns about the impact of automation on workers. In general, industry spokespeople responded to the fear of displacement and job loss with well-rehearsed arguments that stressed the overall growth of employment in the industry, and the simultaneous creation of a more highly skilled work force. Thus, during the same Cleveland speech, Sullivan explained that the "Ford Motor Company has by far the highest employment in its history, and we are still having a hard time finding all the workers we need." He continued, striking the keynote of the industry's case,

> We may need fewer sweepers, fewer unskilled workers with monkey wrenches, but we need many more engineers, electricians, mechanics, electronics experts, tool and die designers and makers, and the hundred and one other specially skilled workers required to keep the tremendously complex production lines in working order.[32]

As they perfected this argument, industry spokespeople also stressed the growth of skilled employment in firms making automation equipment, and in the wider national economy. Speaking in Akron in 1955, Ford's Executive Vice President for Basic Manufacturing, Del Harder, the man who coined the term "automation," explained,

> With more and more mechanization, and automatic machines being installed all over the country, skilled technicians will be in great demand. Industry will need increasingly larger numbers of men trained in design, hydraulics, machine tool building, and electronics engineers; specialized craftsmen of all kinds who can service and operate large complicated batteries of machines.

Company spokespeople also predicted automation would bring productivity-based, real wage increases for workers, and they extolled automation as a way of improving plant safety by eliminating physical labor. For example, in the Akron speech cited above, Del Harder claimed, "that we have found wherever the installation of automation devices *increased*, our severity and frequency rate of accidents *decreased greatly*."[33]

The auto industry's defense of automation was vigorous and often well-founded, but also somewhat misleading, particularly in regard to workers' fears about technological unemployment. In the years between the Korean and Vietnam Wars, *total* blue and white collar employment in the automobile industry did increase, heavy physical labor was reduced, more skilled and technical positions were created, and plant safety did improve. In addition, productivity gains were partially translated into wage increases, thanks in large part to the UAW's insistence that an "annual [productivity] improvement factor" be included as standard features of its contracts with the Big Three. Nevertheless, in the same period, automation was greeted with skepticism, fear, and hostility by many of the industry's unionized workers, especially those who worked in engine plants and body shops where the trend to automation was most advanced.

Like management's defense of automation, the negative reaction of many auto workers was also generally well founded. Automation did displace workers and eliminate jobs. Domestic automobile and truck output rose 90 percent between 1947 and 1963, while the number of production jobs in the industry actually declined 9 percent. In 1963, 146,000 fewer production workers turned out roughly the same number of cars as the industry had produced in 1955.[34] Often management was not fully prepared for the transition, and workers suffered. For example, the entire work force at the Holmes Foundry in Sarnia, Ontario, which manufactured engine blocks for Ford's Canadian assembly operations, was laid off for most of the second half of 1956. Management discovered its newly automated plant had produced more blocks in six months than the whole industry in Canada could use in a year.[35]

At the plant level, manpower changes often occurred quickly, sending shock waves through an entire work force. In 1953, when Ford modernized its cylinder block operations in the Dearborn iron foundry, approximately 1,000 jobs were eliminated. In the effected shops, labor force reductions disrupted established work groups producing resentment among those who lost their jobs, and anxiety and isolation among those who remained. For example, in one shop in the Dearborn foundry, teams of two men each had set the drags, the bottoms of molds, on conveyors in a shop employing twenty-seven men per shift before automation. After new equipment was installed in 1953, one man working alone operated a unit that automatically performed all the operations previously done by those twenty-seven workers. Management could rightly claim that this new position required more skill and less heavy physical labor,

but as Stephen Meyer has pointed out, new jobs like these were still production jobs, and they frequently offered workers none of the psychological/social
compensations that were an integral part of daily life in larger work groups.[36]
    Given the extensive character of Ford's post-War modernization pro-
gram, it is not surprising that Ford workers at the huge Rouge River complex
in Dearborn, Michigan, and the new Cleveland engine plant, were the first
UAW members to articulate a "bottom up" critique of automation. The critics
were members of the Rouge's Local 600, the largest unit in the UAW, and
Cleveland's Local 1250. From the onset of the Ford modernization program,
the elimination of job categories was perceived by workers in both places as
causing technological unemployment and a new speedup. In mid-1953, five
members of Local 600 issued a public invitation to union President Walter
Reuther to visit the Dearborn engine plant, where he would, in their words,
"see how hundreds of jobs are being eliminated" by what they called "push-
button automation.[37] This initiative was the first step in the emergence of a
significant challenge to Reuther's leadership of the UAW, and more particularly, to the bargaining priorities he had established several years earlier.

IV

During the two decades following World War II, when the American union
movement was at its zenith, Walter Reuther was widely regarded as organized
labor's leading liberal spokesperson. Reuther served as President of the
Congress of Industrial Organizations from 1952 to its merger with the
American Federation of Labor in 1956, when he became head of the new
AFL-CIO's Industrial Union Department. But it was his long tenure as
President of the UAW, a union that included over one and a half million members by 1969, that provided him with both a platform, and a power base for
his national political activities.
    Reuther had gained the top spot in the UAW after a bitter political fight
in 1946–1947. At that time, the union's leadership coalition split into two
warring factions: an anti-Communist "Unity" caucus led by Reuther, and a
"Progressive" caucus, led by the UAW's wartime President R.J. Thomas that
opposed the Cold War at home and abroad. Reuther was elected president at
the union's 1946 convention, but the delegates also gave the rival Progressive
caucus a narrow majority on the union's governing body, the International
Executive Board (IEB). During the next twelve months, factionalism at the
top once again preoccupied UAW leaders just as it had before the war. Walter
Reuther won this factional feud and was re-elected UAW President in 1947
after an extremely acrimonious campaign. The 1947 convention also voted

Reuther's "Unity" caucus a healthy majority on the IEB. Reuther used that majority to consolidate his control of the union's central bureaucracy, and extend his influence at the local union level. With his political base in the union secured by 1948, Walter Reuther was easily re-elected as UAW President for the next twenty-two years.[38]

Throughout his tenure as UAW President, Walter Reuther emphasized bargaining issues that would alleviate the insecurity, and uncertainty that had been built into auto work since the turn of the century. Reuther always insisted that job, income, and lifetime security remain the UAW's top bargaining priorities. Under his direction, the UAW developed, and successfully bargained, for cost-of-living and productivity factor wage adjustments, fully funded pensions, supplementary unemployment benefits, as well as life, health, and dental insurance. UAW wages and benefits put auto workers in the material vanguard of America's working class in the 1950s and 1960s.[39]

Walter Reuther's power to deliver these material rewards was rooted in his institutional positions with the UAW and the CIO. But his stature as America's leading labor liberal was also derived from charismatic personal characteristics—a combination of good looks, intelligence, ambition, and incorruptibility—as well as his connections with important liberal Democratic insiders like Eleanor Roosevelt and the Kennedy family. Reuther was always eager to put new ideas on the public agenda. In the long run, he hoped the Democratic Party would become more clearly committed to the working class and to economic planning. He believed organized labor should have a major voice in Federal policy making, and that the government had a duty to force major corporations to adopt socially responsible investment and pricing policies. From the time he issued his famous "500 Planes a Day" war production plan in 1941, Reuther had involved himself in national politics and the formulation of labor's agenda within the Democratic Party. After the war, the new UAW President became a familiar public figure, who was often asked to express his political-economic views in magazines, radio speeches and debates, and in the 1950s via the newest mass media, television.

By the time he was elected President of the UAW, Walter Reuther had changed his basic political philosophy from socialism to a labor-oriented form of Keynesian liberalism that stressed national economic planning to create full employment and sustained economic growth. As summarized by Nelson Lichtenstein, this "labor-liberalism" included:

> an assault on management's traditional power made in the name of economic efficiency and the public interest, and an effort to shift power relations within the structure of industry and politics, usually by means of a tripartite governmental entity empowered to plan for the whole economy.[40]

Reuther's labor liberalism also included a very strong emphasis on the need to build and sustain mass-consumption. For example, as early as a nationally broadcast speech in October 1945, he proclaimed,

> The war has proven that production is not our problem; our problem is con-sumption. . . First, there must be jobs for every American willing and able to work. And second, such jobs must provide the purchasing power to match our ability to produce.[41]

Disappointed by the final settlement of the long General Motors strike in 1946, especially his failure to gain union access to the company's books and some control over product pricing, Reuther backed away from his strategy of directly reshaping the national political-economy through collective bargain-ing.[42] But the UAW leader continued to articulate a distinctive labor version of liberalism.

The new UAW President's frequent appeals for public support repeated-ly combined attacks on Communists, abroad and in the labor movement, with calls for full employment through job creation, greater income security through programs that guaranteed annual wages, equal pay for equal work, and full access (via affordable prices) to consumer goods. "How do we stop Communism?" Reuther asked in *Collier's* magazine in 1948,

> There is no formula. There is only the never-ending task of making democ-racy work, keeping it alive and fighting injustice; expanding an enriching it by tangible achievement.[43]

In the late 1940s, by fusing anti-communism, social justice, and a commit-ment to mass-consumer abundance for all, Walter Reuther earned a lasting reputation as labor spokesperson who transcended parochial union interests, and addressed the problems of the nation as a whole. Thus, it did not seem surprising to find Reuther putting the resources of the UAW squarely behind the Civil Rights movement in the early 1960s. Since his tragic death in a plane crash in 1970, no other liberal union leader has attained the national promi-nence which Reuther earned in his heyday.[44]

V

In the 1950s, Walter Reuther had both the institutional positions and national stature to shape the industrial labor movement's response to automation. Even before Local 600 challenged Reuther to visit the Ford's Rouge complex to see the problems created by automation firsthand, he had begun to formulate that response. As early as 1949, Reuther had been alerted by MIT's Norbert Wiener to the changes in production technology that automotive engineers were planning.[45] In that same year, in a special conference on economic objectives, Reuther had also rejected the idea that the UAW's pre-War demand for a shorter work week be revived as the primary goal of post-War collective bargaining. At that meeting, in his response to delegates who urged him to renew the "thirty for forty" struggle, Reuther clearly explained the new consumer-oriented logic of his program. "The 30 hour week is a popular demand," he acknowledged,

> The day will come in America when it must be a major demand of the American Labor movement . . . But what is our problem when we talk about workers needs. Is our problem that we have too many things in terms of clothing and housing, radios, automobiles, educational opportunities? . . . All these things that we need and we want and are still fighting to get have to be made in America. Our fight isn't between having too many material goods and not having enough leisure. Our fight is we still don't have enough material goods . . . Our basic fight is to get the purchasing power to buy the things we make. Not to make less things, but to make more things and to get more money to buy the things we make. When we get to the point we have got everything we need, we can talk about the shorter work week, but we are a long way from that place.[46]

These views were undoubtedly popular among the UAW's post-War rank-and-file and the wider working class public. Walter Reuther continued to espouse this kind of consumer-oriented Keynesianism until his death in 1970.

In 1953, Reuther visited the new Ford engine plant in Cleveland, and heard the local membership's fears about technological unemployment. In fact, for years after he often recalled the visit and how he had countered a Ford engineer's remark that "not one of those machines pays dues to the United Automobile Workers" with the observation that "not one of them buys new Ford cars either."[47] Reuther's official response to the rising tide of worker concern about automation in the mid-1950s was perfectly consistent with the logic of this anecdote and with his 1949 remarks on the need to expand consumption. Shortly after visiting the Cleveland engine plant, he announced a five-point plan designed to combat the threat of technological unemployment by increasing demand for cars and other durable goods through a redistribution of income to be achieved via a combination of collective bargaining and Federal initiatives.[48] This program reflected Reuther's confidence in the problem-solving potential of Keynesian growth policies that he had embraced during the national debate over post-War planning in the mid-1940s. The plan's emphasis on raising real wages also nicely complemented the UAW's campaign for a "guaranteed annual wage" which he had inaugurated in 1951. Unfortunately for Reuther, this plan did not satisfy a vocal group of critics in Ohio and Michigan UAW locals who insisted that the union should revive the "30 for 40" campaign to counteract technological unemployment.

For a decade after 1953, the "30 for 40" advocates formed a surprisingly resilient rank-and-file movement to reduce work time standards in the automobile industry. They confronted a UAW president who had once championed the work time reductions, but was now adamantly opposed to a showdown with the Big Three over shorter hours. Although he sometimes gratuitously played up the Communist Party connections of some of the leaders of this rank-and-file movement, Walter Reuther never dismissed their arguments. In fact Reuther agreed with most of their analysis. He recognized the extent of automation and realized workers' fears of technological unemployment were well-founded. Indeed, in most of his public statements on the issue, Reuther affirmed the same causal link between automation and unemployment as his critics. For example, during an televised interview in a 1957 *See It Now* television documentary on automation, host Edward R. Murrow asked Reuther, "What has automation done and what is it going to do to the automobile industry?" Reuther replied,

> Well, I think I can say, Ed, that automation has already had some impact upon the employment opportunities in the automotive industry. Based upon the best figures that we can get, we've lost, roughly about a hundred and fifty thousand jobs during the last nine years, but I think we need to understand that automation is really just in its infancy; that we've just begun this whole mechanization of the manufacturing and assembly processes.

Murrow then followed up his initial question, asking, "But what's going to happen to the men who are displaced by the machines?" Reuther answered,

> This is a big problem and I don't believe that we can truly measure the impact of automation upon the displacement of labor yet because it's too early, but certainly, based upon what has already happened, this will become an increasingly serious problem unless we begin to project plans into the future.[49]

As this excerpt shows, Reuther readily accepted the fact of technological unemployment, but he also tended to push its full impact, as well as its solution, off to a distant tomorrow. For the immediate future, he always urged bargaining for greater income security and more goods, instead of bargaining for shorter hours and increased leisure. This rhetorical strategy complemented the delaying tactics he employed against the "30 for 40" movement. For a more than a decade beginning in 1953, the UAW leader followed a strategy that first diverted, then co-opted, and ultimately splintered and undermined the rank-and-file movement for shorter hours.

The "30 for 40" movement had its origins in Local 600, where fears about technological unemployment were especially well-grounded. Ford's huge Rouge complex had employed as many as 92,000 people during World War II. In the immediate post-War period, employment at the Rouge had stabilized around 62,000 workers. Then in the early 1950s, despite the Korean War boom, average Ford Rouge area employment dropped 20 percent from the levels of the late 1940s. The Rouge's share of total Ford employment in the U.S. fell from 62 percent in 1949 to just 38 percent in 1953.[50] Activists in Local 600's "30 for 40" movement tended to blame Ford's modernization program for these dramatic job losses, but the company was also pursuing a policy of decentralizing production that contributed heavily to the loss of jobs at the Rouge.

Concerns about the link between automation and job losses at the Rouge had crystallized in the demand to revive the UAW's historic commitment to a thirty-hour work week. As the movement developed within Local 600 during 1953, the demand for a thirty-hour work week without reductions in take home pay, or "30 for 40," was coupled with calls for earlier retirement at age sixty, and for lower production quotas. Within the union's Ford Council, Local 600 delegates were joined by delegates from Cleveland's Local 1250 in pushing the "30 for 40" program forward, and bringing it to the attention of the union's International Executive Board.

Recognizing both the genuine character of rank-and-file concerns about the impact of automation on employment, and the influence of the big Ford locals within the organization, the IEB established a special Committee on Automation. This group worked under the direction of Jack Conway, one of Walter Reuther's closest assistants. The appointment of Conway reflected Reuther's perception that automation could be a serious problem for the union, but it also showed the UAW President's determination not to allow the sentiment for shorter hours to overwhelm his ongoing campaign for a guaranteed annual wage, which first emerged as the Supplemental Unemployment Benefits (SUB) plan of the 1955 General Motors contract.

The Committee on Automation quickly took on a life of its own. Using the resources of the union's increasingly professional research department, it produced a preliminary report in October 1954 that concluded automation was already causing significant job loss, deskilling, and reassignment of workers. Ken Bannon, Director of the union's Ford Department, collected data for the committee that showed a net reduction of at least 4,320 jobs in Ford plants alone due to automation in the period 1949–1953.[51] With this and other compelling evidence in hand, the committee tentatively endorsed the logic of the shorter hours movement of the 1930s which had insisted that spreading work through general reductions in work-time was the best way to counter technological unemployment. The committee recommended that "After the guaranteed annual wage, therefore, the shorter work week takes its place at the top of the bargaining agenda along with the continuing fight for higher living standards."[52] The Committee on Automation's 1954 report seriously analyzed automation and work time reductions, while it simultaneously postponed a confrontation with Big Three management over those issues. In other words, the report confirmed the positions Walter Reuther had already staked out.

Delegates from Local 600 and Local 1250 pressed for a commitment to shorter hours at the UAW's next special economic conference at Detroit's Masonic Temple in November 1954. On this occasion, the "30 for 40" advocates forced Reuther to extend the debate on work time reductions. But he adamantly refused to do more than recommend the issue for further study. Using sarcasm to shut off that debate, the union president exclaimed,

> I would like that thirty-hour week with forty hours pay. I would like to go them [the "30 for 40" advocates] even one better. As a matter fact, I'd like a twenty hour week. But I know damn well we are not going to get it in 1955, and I don't want to make any worker believe we are even going to try, *because we know we can't.*[53]

Since failing to force GM to open its books in 1946, Walter Reuther had recognized the extreme difficulty of getting the Big Three to concede new ground to the union in collective bargaining. The anti-union political climate of the Cold War era, highlighted by enactment of the Taft-Hartley and Landrum-Griffin Acts, also tempered Reuther's militancy. The idea that the UAW could not win a strike for shorter hours was seldom voiced by Reuther or his staff in public, but it seems to have been the unspoken conviction of everyone Reuther entrusted to study the work time issue.[54]

Reuther's opponents in the two key Ford locals continued their fight for "30 for 40" in 1955, getting a shorter hours resolution adopted by the union's Ford Council, and pressing a debate on the matter in the national convention. In 1955, Reuther's temporarily muted his pragmatic opposition to the "30 for 40" movement, and the convention affirmed the shorter work week as the union's next priority after the guaranteed annual wage was secured.[55] The IEB then followed up the Convention's action by extending the mandate of the

Committee on Automation, and by directing the research department's staff to put more effort into the study of automation and its impact on employment. The Committee on Automation met for the next two years in preparation for the 1957 convention, gathering more information on the extent of technological unemployment, and discussing expert opinions about the way to cope with what appeared to be an increasingly serious problem.[56] As the committee readied its next recommendations, it repeatedly discussed liberal ideas about retraining displaced workers, and solving unemployment problems by stimulating economic growth. The end result of this bureaucratic process was the long and complex resolution (Number 14) entitled "Automation and the Second Industrial Revolution" which the Executive Board and the whole UAW Convention supported without serious dissent in April 1957 in Atlantic City.[57] Resolution 14 technically committed the union's leadership to making shorter hours a bargaining priority, but this point was only made after many other recommendations including the establishment of a permanent federal "Commission on Technological Change" made up of labor, farmer, industry, and government representatives; increased Supplemental Unemployment Benefits; and the establishment of special government programs to assist areas hard hit by technological unemployment. The resolution also stressed a Keynesian approach to reducing unemployment caused by automation. It called on the UAW

> to press for governmental programs which will enable our economy to expand as the full rate which increasing productivity makes possible and will ensure the fair sharing of the vastly expanded wealth of goods and services which can be produced by the new technology.[58]

In subsequent years, Reuther and most of the executive board showed no enthusiasm for the shorter hours provision of Resolution 14, but were able to say they had followed up its other more prominent liberal recommendations.

The sharp recession of 1957–1958, which caused 150,000 layoffs in the automobile industry, and a drastic decline in UAW revenues temporarily slowed the rank-and-file movement for reduced work time even as it divided the IEB. At the special bargaining agenda conference held in January 1958, Walter Reuther took advantage of the recession, and the national uproar over Sputnik, to force postponement of action on Resolution 14's call for the shorter work week over the objections of board members Emil Mazey, Ernest Dillard, and Harold Grant. Reuther argued it was a time when more, not less productive effort was needed to restore the economy and surpass the Russians in the Cold War arms and consumer goods races. In lieu of bargaining for work time reductions in a recession when there seemed little hope of success,

Reuther convinced the delegates at the bargaining conference to accept a compromise resolution calling for the establishment of joint labor-management committees on automation.[59]

Two years later, as economic recovery restored full shifts and mandatory overtime, rank-and-file frustration with Reuther's continued unwillingness to implement a shorter hours bargaining strategy fueled a renewed challenge from below. As early as September 1960, Dodge Local 3 in Detroit passed a resolution calling on the union's executive board to adopt a "30 for 40" bargaining strategy.[60] In early 1961, GM Local 45 in Cleveland, long a left-wing center of opposition to Walter Reuther's leadership, provided the focal point for this new attempt to obtain a shorter work week. The dissidents at Local 45 were joined by the leaders of Fisher Body Local 1045, Ford Local 1250, and Chrysler Local 122, all of the Cleveland area. This group quickly found allies in the Ford and Chrysler locals in Detroit, and some General Motors locals in Flint, where sentiment for early retirement with full pensions at age sixty ran strong. At a meeting of the Local 45's executive board on January 22, 1961, President John DeVito outlined the plan to present a resolution calling for thirty hours for forty hours pay, plus a sixty years and out retirement program to the special bargaining agenda conference called for the last week of April. "The two-headed dragon of automation and flight to cheap labor markets of the world has knocked many an American worker off his job," DeVito explained, and only significant reductions in work time, accomplished through collective bargaining and legislation could solve the problem.[61]

The renewed rank-and-file movement to reduce work time spread quickly as DeVito and his Cleveland area allies gave speeches, mailed out literature, and held meetings with other local union leaders. The movement had soon answered requests for thousands of "30-40-60" bumper stickers, priced at $7.50 per hundred, made by fifteen different locals in Michigan, Ohio, Indiana, Wisconsin, and California. It even sold out a recording of a song titled "30-40-60" which was played by radio stations in Cleveland, Detroit, and Flint.[62]

Despite its remarkably rapid growth, the "30-40-60" movement failed to carry the day at the 1961 bargaining conference. There were several reasons for its failure. First, Reuther continued to refuse to seriously consider what he believed would be a futile and costly struggle against corporations that would never agree to reduce the work week.[63] Secondly, given Reuther's control of the union's bureaucracy and his influence in most UAW locals, the "30-40-60" movement needed nothing short of a political revolution inside the UAW to succeed; and this was beyond its capabilities. Finally, the movement was actually split between the "30 for 40" group in Cleveland and Detroit, which included longtime radical opponents of Reuther like Leo Fenster of Local 45, and early retirement advocates in Flint, who were not generally dissatisfied with Reuther.

The UAW President understood the limits of support for the "30-40-60" movement in advance of the 1961 bargaining convention. Earlier that year, he had union Vice President Leonard Woodcock engage the Lou Harris organization to poll the union membership in Flint and Cleveland, two movement centers, and in Janesville, Wisconsin, a place where there seemed to be little enthusiasm for shorter hours. Of the nearly 2,900 auto workers who were interviewed, almost all acknowledged a strong desire to reduce the work week, but a large majority also revealed a clear preference for Reuther's bargaining emphasis on income security.[64] Thus, as the next special bargaining convention drew near, Reuther went on the offensive, renewing promises to work for early retirement, better pensions, and improved SUB pay, while railing against his critics as left-wingers out of touch with the union's mainstream.[65]

Two years later, in 1963, when the union was preparing for yet another round of contract bargaining, the Cleveland locals again tried to revive the "30-40-60" movement. However, this time, they were far less successful because Reuther adopted a limited work time reduction strategy of his own. Nat Weinberg, Reuther's Director of Special Projects, and Irving Bluestone, one of the UAW President's special assistants, had developed a program that combined early retirement, longer vacations, more paid holidays, and increased relief time to respond to continued rank-and-file concern about employment, work loads, and mandatory overtime. In 1963, when surging orders for cars had led management to step up pressure on workers for increased output, this program was presented as the leadership's alternative to the demand for a shorter work week.[66]

In preparation for the 1964 negotiations, which would implement this new modified work time reduction strategy, Walter Reuther went on the stump to rally a membership that had become increasingly restive. Speaking in Flint in November 1963, he emphasized the need to create "maximum job opportunities for the unemployed and the younger people coming into the labor market." That night, Reuther was deliberately vague about how this would actually be accomplished through the upcoming negotiations with General Motors, but he explicitly and adamantly rejected the shorter hours route. "The last time we had a collective bargaining," Reuther recalled,

> there were certain guys that had a short work week idea. I never get too excited about a shorter work week. I just think that automation and the technological revolution that . . . nobody is going to be able to stop, is going to give us the shorter work week. That if you ask me—if I thought this was number one priority right now, if you ask me that question—I would tell you no.[67]

Although he was planning to push for modified work time reductions, in 1963 Walter Reuther had not changed his basic thinking about the practicality of a shorter work week bargaining strategy.

Reuther's unwavering opposition, and the accelerated national economic growth of the early 1960s, combined to undermine the "30 for 40" movement. Automobile sales increased steadily from 5.5 million units in 1961 to 9.3 million units in 1965. This booming car market forced the Big Three to hire tens of thousands of new production workers even as they continued to modernize the production process and run long overtime shifts. The industry's expansion eased fears of technological unemployment, but it intensified the speedup in many auto plants. The 1964 strike against General Motors, and the twenty-eight authorized local UAW strikes against GM that continued even after the national contract was approved, helped restore confidence in Walter Reuther's leadership of the union at a time when forced overtime, not job displacement, seemed the principal threat to auto workers' welfare. By 1965, the UAW leadership had undercut the dissident movement for shorter hours by adopting bargaining goals that included: a "thirty years and out" retirement plan; paid vacations that increased on a sliding scale, from a basic two weeks for new hires to four weeks for workers with over fifteen years seniority; a 50 percent increase in daily relief time, from 24 to 36 minutes; and a program guaranteeing workers who were displaced by technological change first call on jobs opened by quits, retirements, or deaths.[68] The national contract strikes against Ford in 1967, and GM in 1970, helped the union secure the first three of these demands, but it never achieved a satisfactory policy for coping with the problem of technological unemployment. Since 1970, the continued adherence of the industry to the standard forty-hour work week with time and half for overtime has undoubtedly limited the union's ability to preserve auto workers' jobs in the face of accelerated technological change and increased foreign competition.

VI

Unlike the labor movement in the United States, Western European unions have successfully bargained for shorter hours since World War II. Although European workers also pursued consumer-oriented affluence like their American counterparts, their unions never abandoned the trans-Atlantic labor movement's traditional commitment to reducing work time. After World War II, work time reform in Western Europe was understandably slowed by the enormous task of rebuilding a shattered continent. Forty-five and forty-eight work weeks were in fact standard in Western Europe as late as 1960. But as early as 1956, the International Metal Workers Federation meeting in Paris resolved to make work time reduction a top collective bargaining priority. "Without delay," their resolution on Automation declared,

> we shall proceed towards the realisation of the increased leisure that recent technological advances, including the already widespread application of automation, makes possible.[69]

By the end of the 1960s, workers in Germany, Britain, and most of the rest of Western Europe had established the forty-hour work week through collective bargaining. In the 1970s, European unions won vacation and holiday standards that greatly exceeded the American average. And after 1984, the movement to further reduce the work week was revived with West German trade unions leading the way.

Today, as the result of sustained trade union pressure, the standard full-time work week in most Western European countries, including the United Kingdom, is between thirty-seven and thirty-nine hours long. In many German industries, including automobile manufacturing, it is scheduled to be reduced to thirty-five hours by 1995. IG Metall, the giant German metal workers federation, claims over 500,000 jobs have been saved in heavy industry alone since 1984 as a result of the its work time bargaining strategy. Industry experts do not dispute this figure, although they do contend the work time reductions have slowed national economic growth.[70] Union bargaining has also reduced standard work time in other ways too. Almost all Western European workers currently receive four to six weeks annual paid vacations, as well as more paid holidays and personal leave than American workers. They are also far more likely to retire with full pensions before age sixty-five than the average American worker.[71]

In *Work Without End*, Benjamin Hunnicutt speculates that organized labor's failure to press for shorter hours in the United States after World War II "may have to do with the issue of weekly or annual wages and the political linking of hours and wages together as an either or choice."[72] This study of the politics of worktime in the American automobile industry confirms Hunnicutt's speculation and also reveals the complexities of the political process which shaped the wages or hours choice. In this study, the 1950s emerge as a critical moment in the history of work time reform in the United States. At that time, like their Western European counterparts, American union leaders considered renewing the struggle for a shorter work week when they first confronted automation. But in contrast to European unions, unions in the United States refused to initiate a long-term struggle with management over work time issues.

Walter Reuther's decision to reject the shorter work week as a response to automation was especially important in this regard. Technological change and work time reform were not abstract issues in the trendsetting automobile industry of the 1950s; they were matters of immediate everyday concern to hundreds of thousands of engineers, technicians, and production workers. These concerns were most clearly articulated by the dissident "30 for 40" movement. As we have seen, Walter Reuther repeatedly blocked the "30 for 40" movement's attempts to link acceptance of further automation to shorter hours. Instead, he asked workers to put their faith in a basically apolitical technological process that would inevitably, but inexplicably, lead to the achievement of a shorter work week at some unspecified future date. By 1963, despite a decade of positive recommendations by a committee of his own executive board, the constant pressure of a significant rank-and-file movement, and two national convention resolutions favoring bargaining for shorter hours, Walter Reuther had made it abundantly clear that he would simply not lead a struggle for a shorter work week. Ultimately, given his political power in the union, it was his stand on the issue that mattered most.

In retrospect, Walter Reuther's stand against shorter hours can be understood as a matter of pragmatic politics. However, when viewed in comparison to developments in Western Europe where unions have continued to successfully bargain for reduced work time, the failure of the UAW to institutionalize the principle that technological progress should be translated into a shorter work week looms very large. Indeed, it haunts Detroit, Flint, and the other declining centers of the American automobile industry to this day.

Acknowledgment

The author would like to thank the History Faculty and the Program in Science, Technology, and Society at the Massachusetts Institute of Technology, and the Henry J. Kaiser Foundation for their support of this project.

7

AUTO WORKERS, DISSENT, AND THE UAW: DETROIT AND LORDSTOWN

....

Heather Ann Thompson

Between 1950 and 1980, the demographic profile of American auto workers changed dramatically in urban centers like Detroit. The second great migration of Southern blacks to Detroit, in combination with a dramatic influx of Northern blacks into industrial employment, recomposed the automotive working class. These workers brought to the shopfloor new traditions and expectations that were alien to the leaders of the auto workers union. During the late 1960s and the early 1970s, the different world views of many black auto workers and the UAW collided. Despite its reputation as one of the most progressive, tolerant, and socially democratic industrial unions, the UAW was not well prepared for the racial and ideological reconfiguration of its urban membership. Conflict was almost assured when a growing number of black auto workers found racism in the auto industry intolerable, while their union leaders saw the issue of racism as preeminently a moral and political issue, not a *labor* issue. As an increasing number of black workers insisted on bringing the issue of race to the forefront of the union's labor agenda, the UAW's "labor-liberalism" was severely tested.[1]

Walter Reuther and other top UAW officials had endorsed the 1963 March on Washington, and had provided funds to bail civil rights workers out of Southern jails. In addition, this union had consistently lobbied Congress for the passage of civil rights and anti-poverty legislation, and had worked to elect various Great Society liberals to Congress.[2] But the leadership's response to the racism that thrived on the shopfloor, and within union politics, was far more timid. This timidity angered black auto workers. It sparked the growth of several dissident groups within the rank-and-file, and it fueled a shopfloor-oriented "black power" ideology in a vocal core of these groups. The birth of this revolutionary black nationalist dissent within the ranks of Chrysler's workforce in particular, generated an ideological, political, and generational crisis within the UAW. Though the UAW had weathered the internal battles of the 1940s and 1950s—and had even come out of them unified and strengthened—the internal battles of the late 1960s and early 1970s weakened the union at a critical moment in the industry's history.

II

Like many other urban centers across America, Detroit entered a period of significant social and political transformation, in both the community and the workplace, between 1950 and 1980. During the earliest years of the 1950s, the most noticeable locus of change was in the community. The city, which had been primarily caucasian and of European ethnic descent, with correspondingly ethnic community structures, was transformed as more and more blacks moved to Detroit from the South, both during and after WWII.[3] The percentage of blacks in Detroit's total population jumped from 9.3 percent in 1940 to 44.5 percent in 1970.[4] The story of black migration and white flight is a familiar one, but numbers alone do not indicate the social and political ramifications of such a demographic change. This population shift did not just decide which "race" would live in the city or the suburbs; it also decided where the skills, power, and money of the Detroit area would be located. Soon the suburbs housed "the majority of the important service, professional, and leadership activities . . . [and most] administrative, executive, and other leadership occupations . . . in the auto industry."[5] According to social geographers looking at a cross section of a model neighborhood in Detroit, by 1968 32 percent of this urban population had a median income under $2,000; 32 percent had no telephone service; and 58 percent did not own a car. In contrast to this growing urban poverty, suburban Oakland County had "... the nations highest average household-effective buying income in 1974".[6]

Despite the fact that Detroit's whites moved out of the city-proper in record numbers between 1950 and 1970, taking much of the city's economic base and the most desirable occupations with them, the seats of power, law, and order in the city remained white. The housing market was controlled by whites, the school system was administered by whites, the police department was almost completely white, and city hall was primarily white as well.[7] Whites were also overrepresented among higher paying and more desirable occupations in the city. As late as 1969, 42 percent of whites held jobs considered "professional, technical, or supervisory" as compared with 21 percent of "non-whites" in those same types of jobs.[8] The fact that whites taught, managed, and governed an increasingly black community had enormous political implications at the grass roots level between 1965 and 1973.

The demographic transition in the city of Detroit gradually led to a significant social and political crisis. It was not that blacks and whites inherently could not coexist within one city, but rather that many of the social and political relationships that had undergirded the community and workplace stability of Detroit had also changed dramatically. This was particularly evident by the mid-1960s. Although the community relations system in Detroit had long been premised on the demands and concerns of the white residents, even after the bulk of black migration took place, in 1961 Detroiters elected a white liberal leadership, which became firmly committed to the politics of the Great Society and the War on Poverty. Liberal Mayor Jerome Cavanagh won office, in large part, due to the efforts of Detroit's black civil rights leadership, and in spite of the UAW's endorsement of his opponent. With the election of Cavanagh came the black community's fervent hope that its goal of ending racial discrimination in the city would now be a central goal of the city's government as well.

Because of contradictory political goals and deep social fissures within the liberal coalition of Detroit, the new liberal leadership found it exceedingly difficult to bring substantive change to the racially polarized city. Thus, between 1965 and 1973, many black Detroiters began to rebel against this white city leadership, and against the black civil rights leadership which had always worked closely with it.[9] The grassroots impatience and dissatisfaction with the liberals' program for social change was most dramatically illustrated in the summer of 1967 when Detroit erupted in one of the nation's most violent race riots, which raged for six days. During the July riot, angry blacks directly attacked discriminatory community institutions, like the police and fire departments, and loudly denounced their liberal leaders, both black and white. With many sniper attacks, 43 deaths, and countless injuries and arrests, President Johnson sent in troops to quell the riot.[10]

Between 1950 and the mid-1970s, Detroit's auto plants were transformed in a manner that paralleled the overall demographic changes in the Detroit community. In 1950, auto plants were primarily staffed by a white workforce, the same group that lived in the city-proper at that time. That work force gradually became more racially diverse during the next two decades. The rise in the number of blacks in Detroit, combined with the exodus of whites to the suburbs and suburban plants, created more inner-city jobs for blacks. Moreover, the economic boom of the 1960s created more jobs generally. The federal government gave companies like Chrysler subsidies to ensure increased hiring of minorities, and after the race riot of 1967, the city pressured the auto companies to provide more jobs for blacks. Although GM and Ford each hired increased numbers of black workers, the greatest increase in black employment occurred at Chrysler.

Changes in the racial composition of the workforce at Chrysler had enormous ramifications within each plant. Although the work force was becoming increasingly black, by and large, the plant management and union bureaucracy were not. Chrysler management still placed blacks disproportionately in the least desirable, most dangerous, and lowest paying jobs.[11] Like post-War community relations, post-War labor relations had also long been premised on the demands and concerns of whites, in this case, white workers. But throughout the 1960s, more and more blacks became UAW members and called for the union to respond to their needs.

In a few plants, as a result of heightened awareness among blacks regarding the importance of holding union office, blacks were eventually elected to positions of some power within the union by the early 1970s. By 1973, however, there was still only one black man on the International Executive Board of the UAW, and only a small handful of blacks held local office. Even with the black electoral gains in the union, and even after the activism of civil rights labor organizations within the union, such as the Trade Union Leadership Council (TULC), blacks continued to be victimized by the overt racism of their supervisors and foremen. They continued to be subjected to the worst jobs and thus the worst conditions in the plant. Much like the liberal leaders in the city, who had difficulty responding effectively to the needs of their black as well as their white constituents, the liberal labor leaders in the union found it politically difficult to respond quickly and effectively to ever-present racial discrimination in the same workplaces where whites had elected them. Ultimately, union leaders were also challenged by the most radical of their black constituents, who called for an immediate end to shopfloor racial discrimination with or without the UAW's assistance.

A vocal minority of Chrysler's younger black workers comprised the first wave of dissent in the plants. It was this group that most challenged the status quo there, and most shaped the UAW's relationship with the Detroit rank-and-file after 1971. These young black militants did not accept the inequities where they worked anymore than they had accepted them where they lived. They became threatening to the UAW primarily because they espoused black power politics, and also because they engaged in wildcat strikes which the union vehemently opposed.

By the early 1970s, the power and influence of the young black militants had actually waned, but to the dismay of the union, the propensity of workers on the shopfloor to dissent, and to wildcat, did not. Particularly for workers who had come from the relatively non-industrial and non-union South, immediate protest began to make more sense than following the union's grievance procedure, which often resolved disputes at a glacial pace. Even the black workers who were well versed in union procedures, and familiar with north-

ern factory traditions, began to fight in-plant discrimination. They challenged
both the company and the union by filing charges against their employers
through the Michigan Civil Rights Commission, and by forming dissident
caucuses within the UAW. Over time, white workers and black workers,who
had historically had a tense relationship, began to join together to protest the
state of post-War labor relations in general, and the union's perceived quies-
cence in the face of workplace racism and dangerous working conditions in
particular. In the workplaces of Detroit, it was not a full scale riot, but rather
a series of separate violent altercations, as well as numerous unauthorized
work stoppages, that created a serious crisis. Everything came to a head in the
summer of 1973 when the rank-and-file dissidents on the shopfloor, some revolutionary and some not, fully tested the UAW's commitment to the liberal
principles of social justice and union democracy.

III

Detroit's auto companies profited enormously from the economic boom of the
1960s. They reported record earnings throughout this decade, and they usually ran their plants at full productive capacity. Even Chrysler, which had flirt-
ed with bankruptcy during the recession of 1958–1959, rode high in these
boom years. Although the good times provided employment and job security
for much of Detroit's working class, it also served to exacerbate problems that
had always existed on the shopfloor. The auto companies began to push their
contractually sanctioned control of production to, and sometimes beyond, the
accepted limit. At Chrysler in particular, the effects of this management offensive strained the rank-and-file both physically and emotionally.

Although Chrysler was faced with a rising demand for cars, it steadfast-
ly refused to hire more workers. In order to turn out higher production,
mandatory overtime soon became a rule rather than an exception. Chrysler
workers in Detroit were put on six and seven day work week schedules with
little opportunity for relief. Twelve hour shifts were not uncommon. Chrysler
had the oldest and most run-down facilities, and its plants posed great health
and safety hazards for workers. Not surprisingly, as production quotas were
raised, health and safety conditions deteriorated even further in Chrysler's
plants. A combination of Chrysler's inadequate internal investment, managerial aggressiveness, and inhuman work hours contributed to dangerous working conditions, which in turn made the company a tinderbox waiting to
explode by the late 1960s.

Workers were appalled as on-the-job accidents and deaths began to
mount. On May 26, 1970, for example, twenty-one year old Gary Thompson

was crushed under two tons of steel at Chrysler's Eldon Avenue Gear and Axle plant. A UAW safety director toured that plant after the accident and noted in his report a " . . . complete neglect of stated maintenance procedures in this plant. The equipment is being operated in an extremely dangerous condition".[12] Younger black workers had the least seniority, and thus they were easily pushed into the most undesirable, lowest paying, and most dangerous jobs in the plant. As the plant working conditions deteriorated, these workers were affected to a disproportionate degree.[13]

As tensions escalated over working conditions, in-plant conflicts between workers and managers escalated as well. Everyday there were confrontations between black workers and their white foremen in particular. Black workers, who were tired of being the brunt of racial epithets and threats, responded by filing grievances, suing the company, and physically fighting with offending foreman. In February of 1969, auto worker Rushie Forge stabbed his foreman several times[14] and, in 1973, Regis Lantzy, the General Foreman of Chrysler's Jefferson Assembly plant, was shot to death by an auto worker named Tilden Engle. This murder was not the only one at Chrysler. Earlier, in 1970, another killing had taken place which captured the attention of Detroit's community and its workplaces. An auto worker, named James Johnson, Jr., killed two Chrysler foremen and a job-setter after he had experienced a series of workplace hassles, which he was convinced were racially motivated.[15] In this case, the worker who had wielded a gun became a cause celebre to many black workers in Detroit and he was defended by Detroit's leading Marxist black attorney, Kenneth Cockrel. After Cockrel's now legendary defense—which asserted that Johnson was a victim of American racism and, as a result, was mentally unstable—the jury of Johnson's peers found him not guilty by reason of insanity. Later on, another attorney named Ronald Glotta, actually won worker's compensation benefits for Johnson dating back to the day of his "injury," which was also the day of the murders. The shopfloor empathy afforded Johnson in 1970 was still there for Tilden Engle in 1973. As an editorial in the plant newspaper *The United Justice Train* put it, "Chrysler Corporation is the real killer. The company drives us all mad with its insane push for profits and production".[16]

In the earliest years of the 1960s, inner-city auto workers responded to shopfloor abuses by following the longstanding contractual procedures for conflict resolution. They counted on their union, with its reputation for militancy and a progressive outlook, to fight for them within the grievance system. The grievance machinery became choked with complaints about overtime, safety violations, and racist practices within the plant. When things changed little in the plants, however, critical in-plant newsletters proliferated, and the number of brief wildcat strikes increased as the 1960s progressed.

Many auto workers began to feel that union officials were not sufficiently dealing with issues of racism and safety, or effectively checking management violations of the contract. The more widespread the opinion became that the union was ineffective in ameliorating the problems on the shopfloor, the more young black workers began to take matters into their own hands. In the minds of these rank-and-file dissidents, management was unilaterally changing the contractual rules of the game and violating worker civil rights, while the union leaders refused both to recognize these problems, and also to specifically address the needs of their black constituents.

Throughout the late 1960s, a number of dissident caucuses, both black and white, sprang up within the UAW. The largest of these was the United National Caucus (UNC). The UNC was started by white skilled workers, but over time it became a multiracial and politically diverse organization which had offshoots such as the United Justice Caucus, Strike Back, Shifting Gears, and the Democratic Caucus in various plants.[17] The UNC-affiliated groups were to the political left of the existing union leadership, but they were to the political right of the shopfloor black nationalists. Their membership was composed of both blacks and whites, men and women, and socialists, as well as liberals. Irish born Pete Kelly of Local 160 and Jordan Sims of Local 961 each came to play a major role in the UNC. Together they reflected the multiracial composition of all the UNC groups. First and foremost, these groups advocated the reform of the union in light of the new shopfloor realities. The UNC explained to workers that "The caucus is an organization of members working within the structure of the UAW to make it more democratic and responsive to the needs of the membership."[18] The UNC regularly called on the union to live up to its reputation as a militant and progressive trade union. Their various dissident newsletters pointedly reminded the union leadership of the militant movement of the 1930s, and they called for a return to those days.

In addition to the UNC groups, between 1965 and 1975 several white left organizations in Detroit sent their members into the auto plants to "industrialize."[19] This meant that they would get a job in the plant, right on the assembly line, and work to recruit members to their own group, as well as to assist groups like the UNC affect a degree of change within the plant itself. Each of these white left groups contributed to the growing body of critical in-plant literature as they distributed their own organization's newsletters and newspapers while at work. There were groups who identified themselves broadly as New Leftists, Trotskyists, Socialists, Communists and Maoists. The groups which had most members in the plants were the International Socialists (IS), The Socialist Workers Party (SWP), and the Revolutionary Communist Party (RCP), respectively.

In 1968, another dissident group was born that was not a caucus within the UAW nor was it composed primarily of "outsiders." Although this group was not designed to recruit members into an outside political organization, it also did not *just* want to reform the union. This group advocated a complete overhaul of the existing union and a new type of unionism based primarily on the needs and concerns of black workers. This group, known as the Dodge Revolutionary Union Movement or DRUM, soon had off-shoots in several other plants, all equally critical of the existing auto union. As the preamble of the Jefferson Avenue Revolutionary Movement (JARUM) read, "Just as in the 1930s when the rank-and-file joined in unity from the bottom up to form throughout the country the CIO, the time has come for the Rank and File once again to rid ourselves of the treacherous, back-stabbing union leadership and their phony reforms. We demand that union democracy start from the bottom and go up."[20] The members of these Revolutionary Union Movements or RUMs, were tired of conditions that maimed and killed fellow workers, and above all, they were unwilling to accept the racism in Detroit's auto plants. In 1969, all of the RUMs came together to form the League of Revolutionary Black Workers (the League) in order to coordinate their actions. As they saw it, the League was "...a black Marxist-Leninist Organization..." designed to function as "an integrative body coordinating general policy, political education, and the strategies for its various components."[21]

These RUMs were as hostile to the UAW as they were to the auto companies because they believed that the union did not fight hard enough for black workers. Workers in these radical groups, along with their supporters, felt that the union's insistence on adhering to the post-War collective bargaining system, with its prohibition of unauthorized strikes, prevented workers from having any real power when it came to dealing with management. As members of the RUM at Chrysler's Eldon Avenue Gear and Axle plant put it, "Everyone knows that our grievance procedure is a fraud. . . . And most grievances are settled the company's way because we do not use our strike power to settle them our way."[22] Increasingly the RUMs rejected the grievance procedure as too slow to address their urgent workplace concerns, and too narrow to include their growing concern with in-plant racism.

The problem of racism had certainly been raised within the UAW before. After the so-called "hate strikes" during WWII, for example, the issue of race was unavoidably catapulted to the forefront of the union's agenda. And clearly the formation of the TULC in 1957 was another moment when black workers called attention to the problem of racial discrimination within the UAW.[23] The birth of DRUM in 1968, however, was a different story. DRUM ushered in a new perspective on the origins of urban racism, what perpetuated it, and what could be done about it. The RUM groups, and their supporters in the plants, did not think of the issue of race only in terms of desegregation and greater representation. They believed that a nationalist agenda should play a key role within union and in city politics.

Of most controversy was the fact that the RUM groups argued that the UAW itself perpetuated and fed off of intra-union and shopfloor racism. Every issue of a RUM newspaper had some reference to the union leadership's complicity in the perpetuation of in-plant racism or of sub-standard working conditions. Even further, the RUMs and their supporters injected a brand of radical politics into the discussions of race by insisting on a "necessary" link between capitalism and racism. Because of this shared attack on capitalism, the RUMs had a certain appeal to the white leftists in the plants. The RUMs were concerned primarily with racism and with the future of black workers alone. However, over time, this separated them from much of the white left. Ironically the shopfloor revolutionary black nationalist rhetoric so dramatically espoused by the RUMs, was usually rejected or ignored by most workers, but it was the very thing that the UAW leadership focused on and found especially threatening.[24]

Between 1968 and 1971, RUM groups sprang up in a number of urban Chrysler plants, one Ford plant, and there was even a RUM group called UPRUM at United Parcel Service (UPS). Of all of these RUMS, however, DRUM at Dodge Main and ELRUM at the Eldon Gear and Axle plant were the most visible and vocal. As Steve Jefferys explains in his book *Management and Managed: Fifty Years of Crisis at Chrysler*, DRUM raised the ire of both the local and the international union when it attempted to educate and mobilize workers around a revolutionary black nationalist platform.[25] At Dodge Main, DRUM members clashed repeatedly with the predominantly white Polish-American union leadership there. Over time, these Polish-Americans, as well as the International union, became deeply alienated by the tactics, demands, and rhetoric of DRUM. Local and international union leaders were similarly alienated at Eldon where ELRUM put out many a newsletter accusing the union of cooperating with, and selling out to, the managers who were just like "slave masters" on a "plantation."[26] Simultaneously, ELRUM accused the company of murdering black "brothers and sisters" whenever fatal on-the-job accidents occurred.

At Dodge Main, Eldon, and various other plants where RUMs existed, the groups were composed of black workers who had a cool, if not hostile, relationship with most whites. At Eldon, for example, there was only one white member, named John Taylor, who felt troubled by the group's refusal to give leaflets to white workers, as well as black workers in the plant.[27] Because of the RUMs' overtly revolutionary ideology, as well as their hostility to white worker support, they eventually became isolated. This isolation made it very difficult for the RUMs to withstand management and union counterattacks. At Dodge Main, for instance, Local union leaders waged a fierce battle against DRUM when DRUM members ran for local office. Union leaders portrayed to the workforce that DRUM was an organization of violent hate-mongers, and the group was seriously weakened after the election.[28] In many ways, it had not been difficult to persuade white workers that the RUM candidates were dangerous. Most white workers had either recently fled the city of Detroit, or were still waging a battle for control within it because in their minds, blacks had become far too radical. White workers' negative feelings about black activism undoubtedly influenced how union leaders themselves chose to handle the RUMS. Union officials already viewed black militants with as much trepidation as white workers did. But their own fears aside, in order to legitimate the grievances of black militants, union leaders would have had to challenge the prejudices and fears of white auto workers. It was also never in their political interests to do so since they were extremely dependant on the support of those white workers when local elections rolled around.

After the elections at Dodge Main, DRUM's numbers dwindled as Chrysler management fired the more vocal members. Not surprisingly, DRUM members and supporters could not count on the wholehearted emotional backing of their union after such a discharge. But even had they not been discredited by the union, or discharged by the company, the credibility of RUM members on the shopfloor was suffering. They particularly alienated older black workers because whenever moderate blacks won union office, the RUM response was to call such officials "Toms" and "sell-outs." Referring to the black president of Eldon's Local #961, Elroy Richardson, members of ELRUM asked ". . . will a brother have to slip and break his neck before those Uncle Toms who run this union take a stand?" and they went on to say, "This is a warning to the racist pigs who run Dept. 71 and the Uncle Tom union, that ELRUM is on the case."[29]

In the end, the union and the company's efforts to dismantle the RUM groups were successful because of the RUMs own resistance to broadening their social base, softening their language, and eliminating their internal factionalism.[30] As Steve Jefferys put it, DRUM was beaten by 1971.[31] The demise of the RUMs, and of the League which followed soon thereafter, left only a handful of RUM members in a few Chrysler facilities by 1972. Despite the short life of the RUMs, the long term impact that these groups had on both the union and the company should not be underestimated. The RUMs had tapped into a preexisting reservoir of resentment in the minds of both black and white workers on the shopfloor. They had made the issue of racism central in ways that the UAW leadership had never done, and they had challenged the assumption that the leadership was always acting aggressively on the workers behalf. In large part, due to the consciousness that the RUMs raised, more moderate blacks were able to win union office in five of Chrysler's plants by the early 1970s.[32] At the Eldon Plant, where a RUM had been quite active, UNC activist Jordan Sims, actually won the Local #961 presidency in 1973.

Although the RUMs played a role in heightening worker awareness, and in paving the way for blacks to hold union office, they had also made the UAW leadership very wary of rank-and-file militancy. These RUMs had questioned, criticized, and verbally lambasted the union as no group had ever done before. They had put the union leadership on the defensive when it came to the issue of race and to the myriad shopfloor problems which continued to exist. Since its inception, the UAW leadership had been quite adept at absorbing, addressing, or at least marginalizing, contending agendas, but the RUMs raised an agenda culturally and politically completely foreign to it. The union leadership was so threatened and alienated by rank-and-file revolutionary black nationalist ideology, both because of its political and "dual-union" implications,[33] that despite its deep-seated belief in liberal tolerance, it could not be accepting of such dissent. When looking at how the union handled shopfloor dissent after the demise of the RUM groups, it becomes clear the degree to which the politics and platform of the RUM groups had circumscribed the UAW's tolerance for any and all rank-and-file militancy after 1971.

IV

By 1973, the problems that the RUMs had called attention to still existed. There were finally a number of black union officials, and a smattering of black foremen, but daily racism went on unchecked. In addition, for both black and white workers, life on the shopfloor had become more intolerable as more speedups and poorer working conditions, took their toll. To all observers, it appeared that Detroit's automobile factories were in a crisis. Shopfloor violence was commonplace, and wildcat strikes occurred with alarming frequency in many of the Big Three plants. The problems were still most severe in Chrysler's aging plants. Like General Motors, the Chrysler Corporation was riding high on the wave of Vietnam War induced economic prosperity. By 1973, the company was still making record-high earnings. Chrysler's sales for April through June of 1973 were $3.18 billion, and it earnings totaled $108.6 million, nearly double the profits of the same period in the previous year.[34] The prosperity that Chrysler enjoyed, however, was largely due to an intense speedup. Rather than investing in, or expanding and updating its facilities, as Ford and GM attempted to do, Chrysler tried to squeeze more out of the workers themselves.[35]

Although the RUM groups were virtually all gone by 1973, dissident groups continued to proliferate in a number of Chrysler plants. In the face of deteriorating working conditions and mounting work hours, workers began to eschew bitter racial antagonisms for class solidarity, and thus, shopfloor dissent not only grew, but it was also becoming multiracial and politically diverse. To management and union leadership alike, however, all dissident groups were equally dangerous. By 1973, they each viewed the rank-and-file members of any dissident group as "troublemakers" with "books of Mao-Tse-Tung falling out of their pockets".[36] The union accused these shopfloor critics of being anti-democratic at best and, at worst, it accused them of being engaged in communist plots. The UAW leadership in particular, did not understand that the nature of rank-and-file dissent had changed significantly over the previous few years, as had the profile of the worker who was willing to dissent. In the summer of 1973, when wildcat strikes rocked Chrysler's Jefferson, Forge, and Mack plants, each in quick succession, the union and the company both began to feel that in order to preserve the labor relations system that they knew and believed in, they had to put a stop to rank-and file-dissent, rather than take a hard, perhaps painful look at what was motivating it.

Like many of the earlier RUM-inspired wildcats at Chrysler plants like Dodge Main and Eldon, the wildcat strike at Chrysler's Jefferson Avenue plant began over an issue that neither the union, nor the company, thought should be handled within shopfloor labor relations: workplace racism. Unlike the earlier wildcats and protests over racism, however, the issue now galvanized a variety of dissidents, not just those sharing a black nationalist ideology. Two Jefferson workers, Issac Shorter and Larry Carter, knew shopfloor racism first hand, and they knew that the labor relations system did little to address this problem. Throughout the summer of 1973, Shorter and Carter, who were admitted socialists but not members of a RUM, complained repeatedly about the racist practices of their foreman, Tom Woolsey. Woolsey was notorious in his department for his overt disrespect of black workers. One worker, Ivory Harris, said that Woolsey had threatened him, and had made several "inappropriate comments about his mother, his heritage, and that kind of thing."[37] Even the company later conceded that Woolsey had indeed "called Ivory Harris a black M-F," and that in addition, he had threatened another black worker with a two by four between his eyes if he did not do as he was told.[38] Although there were still a few members of JARUM left in the plant, it was the in-plant organ of the politically, and racially diverse UNC, whose credibility increased the longer that this kind of daily racism went unchecked.[39]

After Issac Shorter himself had a run-in with Woolsey, he circulated a petition for Woolsey's removal throughout the department. The petition was signed by 214 people—70 percent of the department—and was given to the shop committeeman, Willard Atkins, who then filed a supporting grievance against this foreman. But nothing was done to quickly ameliorate the problem. Woolsey remained in charge, so Shorter and Carter decided to launch their own protest. At 6:00AM on July 24, 1973, the twenty-six year old Shorter, and the twenty-three year old Carter, locked themselves into the six-foot power cage of the metal body shop at Jefferson, cut off all of the power to the feeder line, and demanded the immediate discharge of Tom Woolsey.

Upon hearing of the wildcat, Chrysler's General Superintendent, Jack Riley, sent for maintenance personnel to cut the cable which locked the cage. When maintenance arrived, however, over 150 workers surrounded the cage, and some of them put their hands directly on the cable to prevent the cutting. According to Chrysler's Supervisor of Labor Relations, any attempt to forcibly remove these workers "would certainly have resulted in some bloodshed."[40] The UAW leadership was appalled by this unauthorized action and exerted every "effort to get Shorter and Carter to leave the cage."[41] The workers booed their union representatives out of the area. Shorter and Carter then told the company supervisors that they wanted not only Woolsey's discharge, but also amnesty for all of the wildcatters in writing before they would leave the area.

At 7:15 that same evening, Shorter and Carter emerged from the power cage victorious and carried on the shoulders of their fellow workers. After hours of negotiation, Chrysler had agreed to fire Woolsey. The Plant Manager, Mr. Weiskey, along with the Production Manager, Joe Lazzarre, had even signed a letter granting amnesty to the strikers. Two black auto workers had circumvented the contractual labor protest process and had won an untraditional demand all on their own. Despite what both the company and the union believed, their protest could not be tied to a small group of radical troublemakers. As Shorter said,

> the workers supported us, I'd say 95 percent . . . workers even went to sleep around the cage, and ten minutes after we were in the cage workers were bringing us chains, locks, and even wanted to escort us to the bathroom. Workers stayed there with 25 years seniority, some of them probably retiring in the next couple of months. They were there until we got out.[42]

A few days after the wildcat, it was the United Justice Caucus (UJC), an organ of the UNC, who passed out a leaflet which read, "You are invited to a victory celebration!". On July 29, 1973, at Detroit's Masonic Hall, the celebration took place. Shorter and Carter were the featured speakers and the audience was entertained by the band "Momma's Pride and Joy."[43] The two wildcat leaders answered many questions from workers throughout the night.

Shorter's message to the audience captured the ways in which in-plant dissent had changed over the previous two years when he told them that, "Workers of the world must unite." In a later interview, he elaborated on this by saying,

> In Detroit, the percentage of black workers, just in the Jefferson plant, and in the plants in the city, is the majority. And the black workers should control it. But at the same time there is no such thing as black control. It's workers control. Because it is not a racial thing. . . . I think that the workers should work together, black workers should work with white workers, white workers should work with black workers. That's the only way we're going to accomplish our goals.[44]

Less than two weeks after the Jefferson Avenue wildcat, at 12:00 AM on August 7th, the midnight shift of Chrysler's Detroit Forge plant refused to go to work. Occupational accidents were on the rise at Forge due to speedups and insufficient maintenance. For six months, 60 percent of the plant's workforce had worked seven days a week on involuntary overtime.[45] On July 23, 1973, auto worker Harvey Brooks had his arm crushed in a conveyor belt. On August 5, 1973, thirty-five year old Tony McJennet had his middle finger amputated in a faulty crane. Other cranes sporadically dumped tons of steel into pedestrian areas. In another incident, an axle flew off of a conveyor belt into the chest of an auto worker and, the next day, when the belt had yet to be serviced, Chrysler management told another worker to resume the job. There was still blood on the equipment.[46] It was clear to many workers that the grievance procedure was working too slowly to eliminate the life-threatening hazards that they faced at work everyday. At Forge, as in other Chrysler plants, by 1973 horrific safety conditions had begun to unite workers across the color line and the political spectrum.

Between 1968 and 1973, Forge also had several in-plant dissident groups. For a few key years, it was the Forge Revolutionary Union Movement (FORUM), with its predominantly black membership and its fiery three-pronged critique of contractualism, capitalism, and racism, which had been the most vocal. As FORUM dwindled after 1971, however, old FORUM members, and newer rank-and-file dissidents, firmly believed that despite the large number of blacks in the plant, black workers still held the least skilled and least safe jobs there. In addition, dissidents now felt that the issue of plant safety must be addressed for all workers. Even though FORUM was virtually dead, when the Forge workers went out on a wildcat strike, the issues of racism and safety were still at the forefront. Leon Klea, President of the Forge Local 47, told the wildcatters to go back to work immediately because " . . . we had a contract and we had to go by the contract," but he was " . . . jeered and booed and told they weren't going back to work."[47] Incensed by what he saw as another radical assault, and sensing the seriousness of yet another illegal strike, UAW Vice President Douglas Fraser told reporters that the wildcat was instigated from outside of the plant where "apparently someone has been reading Marx and Engels."[48] After years of dealing with passionate revolutionary black nationalist rhetoric in the various locals where there was a RUM influence, and after having that rhetoric directed explicitly against him, Doug Fraser saw the Forge wildcat as yet another revolutionary-inspired, special-interest insurrection within the ranks. Fraser was blind to the fact that this strike had very little of that rhetoric, and that it had black and white, as well as left and center, support on the shopfloor.

Despite the union leadership's repeated attempts to discredit the strike by blaming it on outside radicals, and by telling the workers to "repudiate these people who are creating a serious problem at Forge,"[49] the striking members stood united. With 1,397 workers now out on an unauthorized strike, Fraser decided to tour the plant himself. On August 11, 1973, he investigated the plant and then told reporters that the conditions there were indeed "abominable." According to Fraser, if the company did not address the safety problems immediately, he would authorize a strike vote for the following Friday. For a moment, workers were heartened, and many of them felt that "victory is assured to us on Friday August 17, 1973 when we meet for a strike vote."[50] On August 12, however, the wildcatters met with the UAW leadership at the union hall of Local 212 hall to discuss the events at Forge. Fraser told them that he would not authorize a vote until all of the workers went back to work. The workers at the meeting argued vehemently against doing this. Eighteen workers had already been fired and they felt that, in light of these circumstances, the vote should be taken immediately.[51]

Eventually, the UAW was able to end the strike when it actively supported the company's ultimatum that anyone who refused to go back to work would be immediately fired. This action did not go unnoticed in the Detroit community at large. As the *Detroit Free Press* commented, the UAW "was lately known for donning the velvet glove instead of the iron fist" when dealing with management.[52] Even though the strike only lasted six days, the rank-and-file at Forge had forced three Chrysler engine plants to cut their production in half. After the strike, it became clear that UAW leaders, while acutely recognizing the degree of power that segments of its own rank-and-file could wield, seriously misunderstood what motivated that rank-and-file, and who these dissidents really were.

During the Forge wildcat, Chrysler had fired fifteen workers. In exchange for local ratification of the pending local contract, Chrysler agreed to rehire twelve of these fifteen workers, while the fate of the remaining three workers would be decided by an arbitrator. The UAW was never successful in getting jobs back for the remaining three workers; Jerome Scott, Karl Williams, and Tom Stepanski—even after arguing before arbitrator Gabriel Alexander that these workers should not be singled out.[53] After the ratification vote, several Forge workers formed a defense committee on behalf of the three discharged workers. Many workers felt that the three men were unduly victimized due to the fact that each of them happened to be one of the few remaining members of FORUM, and because two of them were black. The fact that one of the men, Tom Stepanski, was white was more significant than the UAW leadership grasped. Whereas the early RUM groups had a very hostile relationship with white workers, the remaining RUM members now worked with them. The new rank-and-file dissent groups in Forge, as well as the remnants of FORUM, kept the earlier RUMs' vigilance with regard to attacking shopfloor racism, while also recognizing the pitfalls of excluding almost half of the rank-and-file in shopfloor actions. By 1973, the shopfloor critics had become a more multiracial group and increasingly class, rather than race, identified.

Eventually Scott, Williams, and Stepanski filed a lawsuit against both Chrysler and the UAW leadership for allegedly engaging in a "conspiracy, agreement, understanding, plan, design, or scheme" which resulted in the permanent firing based on their racial and political convictions.[54] During the course of the ensuing trial, testimony revealed that Chrysler's original informal offer to the UAW leadership, had actually been to reinstate the twelve workers "plus plaintiff Karl Williams, if the union would drop its grievances of plaintiff Scott and Stepanski. The union allegedly declined Chrysler's offer because it did not want plaintiff Williams rehired because of his political philosophy."[55] Dennis Baliki, Recording Secretary of Forge Local 47, testified under oath that the Local 47 leadership had, in fact, taken a vote on whether to bring Williams back to work. Three UAW committeemen voted to reinstate him and three voted no.[56] According to Baliki, "It was a 3 to 3 tie and Leon Klea [President of Local 47] broke the tie and voted no to bringing back Karl Williams."[57]

Though the plaintiffs could not prove their case in full, by the end of the trial it was clear that the UAW leadership had made a conscious choice not to bring one of its own members back into the plant, even after the company agreed to do so. The UAW leaders felt that they were saving the union from the "outside" destructive elements of the black nationalist and communist left. Even though the dissidents of the 1970s came from a political and racial cross-section of the rank-and-file, the union leaders believed that they were acting no differently than they had during the McCarthy Era. The union clearly misunderstood, but worried nevertheless, about the ideological influence that workers like Williams had on the shopfloor.[58] Even more than the

Jefferson wildcat, the wildcat at Forge illustrated how the UAW found itself moving closer to the company's position in the face of what it perceived to be a black revolutionary insurgency.

On August 14, 1973, yet another wildcat erupted at Chrysler's Mack Stamping plant. Of all the Chrysler facilities, Mack was the most notorious for its dangerous working conditions. It was the oldest Chrysler plant in Detroit and the plant with the greatest number of work-related accidents. Several serious accidents contributed to the rise of Mack's in-plant dissent groups, and ultimately to the 1973 wildcat. In September of 1972, a die-setter was killed when a bolster plate blew off of a faulty machine and cut off the top of his head. In 1973, a woman working on the cab-back line had fingers severed because the protective guard for the press she was working on was broken, and on August 4, 1973, just days before the wildcat, a press room worker lost four fingers because "the automation device that was supposed to remove stock from the press had never been repaired."[59]

Numerous Mack workers had gone to their union representatives to file grievances about other accidents and about the speedup policy of management, but with little result. In June of 1973, a small wildcat took place when a union steward, Malcolm Woods, was fired for defending his constituents in a speedup dispute. A few months later, on August 10, 1973, a group of Mack workers picketed the Local 212 union hall demanding that a strike vote be authorized because of the safety hazards. All of these protests brought no results. Worker participation in the multiracial United Justice Caucus (UJC) increased as the problems at Mack went unaddressed. Like at Jefferson and at Forge, a number of white left groups, including the Workers Action Movement (WAM) began agitating over speedup and safety issues at Mack as well. WAM openly tied its shopfloor concerns to revolutionary politics, whereas the UJC was concerned primarily with the shopfloor issues. The messages of the UJC tended to resonate on the shopfloor far more than did those of WAM, especially because rather than *just* criticize the union, the UJC also published a newsletter called "The Mack Safety Watchdog" that was informative and actually helpful to workers. The "Mack Safety Watchdog" came out nine times before August 1973, and the workers relied on it to get information about their rights and about the particular hazards in their area of the plant. Significantly, however, the UJC and WAM both were viewed with equal suspicion by the company and the union.

On August 14, 1973, shortly after 5:00AM, a white auto worker named Bill Gilbreth and a black auto worker named Clinton Smith, both members of WAM, went into the Stubs Frame Welding department, sat down on the conveyor belt, and halted production. Gilbreth had been fired days earlier for walking out in support of another discharged union steward who had questioned the speedup. After launching his own sit-down, Gilbreth announced that he would not get off the line until the company rehired him, and addressed the speedup and working conditions in the plant. Workers gathered around Gilbreth and Smith to protect them from forcible removal, but two plant security guards managed to break through the crowd and a bloody battle ensued.

By 7:00 AM, Gilbreth and Smith were still sitting on the line and the two guards, Captain Gene Prince and Captain Paul DeVito, were at the hospital with injuries. The company then sent home the 2,650 workers on the second shift and called the Detroit Police Department to remove Gilbreth and Smith. In the meantime, more workers crowded around the two wildcatters. When the first police officers arrived, they were forced to withdraw, but they soon returned with reinforcements. The workers tightened their ranks around Gilbreth and Smith once again, and thwarted the police department's efforts to break the strike.

An hour after Chrysler had shut its plant down, Gilbreth, Smith, and forty-two other workers went up to the cafeteria to organize a sit-down strike. Once there, these wildcatters elected a committee to represent them to the press. Since many of these workers disagreed with the revolutionary politics of WAM, members of WAM were given very little role to play in the wildcat from that moment on. Meanwhile, outside of the plant, workers and union officials gathered. Rather than attempt to absorb this multiracial dissident impulse and channel it into traditional union methods of redress, the union declared war on it. Doug Fraser told reporters that "the agitators . . . represent only a very tiny fraction of the total Chrysler workers in the Detroit area and I advocate a policy of no surrender."[60] In a telling statement, Fraser later admitted that "it was agreed that these people were not going to take our union and the plants where we represent workers."[61]

Gilbreth's membership in WAM seemed to confirm the suspicion of UAW officials that this was a protest of outsiders. It allowed them to discount the entire walkout by claiming that it was the result of communist masterminding. But other workers at Mack, especially those who were members of the non-revolutionary UJC, quickly rejected the union leaders' charge. In a leaflet titled "Mack Safety Protest" the UJC claimed, ". . . It was not WAM or any other organization that caused the struggle, but rather the anger of Mack workers at our unsafe and inhumane working conditions." They went on to say, "we know why our enemies try to say the whole thing was caused by a few 'troublemakers'. They do this to discredit us. They are trying to hide the fact that it was a genuine workers' protest against the unbearable conditions in the plant."[62]

Because the UAW leadership was increasingly nervous about the wave of wildcats strikes, and about the black radical politics that it was certain was behind them, it did not view events at Mack objectively. It refused to accept the UNC's claim that ". . . we are not a political group, nor are we a substitute for a political party."[63] The leadership's response was grossly disproportionate to the threat that actually existed at Mack. Had the leaders recognized that it was the UJC, not a RUM group, that held sway in the plant, and had they thought through the legitimacy of the workers' grievances about safety and the speedup, they might have seized the opportunity to restore their credibility by authorizing a safety strike. However, the leadership clearly did not recognize the Mack wildcat as "a genuine workers' protest." The union actively supported the company's decision to call in a second group police to end the strike. Sixty policemen in full riot gear—lead by Police Commissioner John Nichols who was also running for Mayor that year—stormed the Mack plant to evict the wildcatters, and to arrest Clinton and Gilbreth. One auto worker recalled what happened next, "the hostility of the police was incredible, when they did come, it was very frightening. It was vicious, like they were chasing anti-war demonstrators, grabbing, yelling, and screaming."[64] Because 28 wildcatters had already gone outside to drum up support, there were only 14 workers remaining in the cafeteria when the policemen charged into the plant. Within minutes, the sit-down was over, but much to the chagrin of the company and union alike, the wildcat was not.

After the police action, the Mack workers outside of the plant immediately went down to their Local 212 union hall where a stormy meeting ensued. According to the *Detroit News*, "during the meeting, the dissidents and their sympathizers, shouted down local and international officials who urged them to return to work, and voted to continue their unauthorized walk-out."[65] Local 212 president, Hank Ghant, pleaded with workers to end their strike. The next day, however, those same workers formed picket lines around the plant. Meanwhile, at 4:30 AM, UAW officials from all over the Detroit area met at the Local 212 hall, and began to plan their strategy for ending wildcats like this one, once and for all. They brought baseball bats and various other weapons with them. After hearing many passionate statements, like Emil Mazey's that "they are a bunch of punks, [and] we are not going to let them destroy everything that we've built,"[66] union officials made the decision to march to each of the four Mack gates in groups of 250. Within minutes of their arrival, over a thousand UAW officials had physically crushed the Mack wildcat. The *Detroit Free Press* reported that Gilbreth, among others, was beaten up by these union leaders. "The men reportedly chased Gilbreth from the Canfield gate to the parking lot, tackled him, and punched him repeatedly until some of his supporters arrived."[67]

At the end of the day, Joseph Areeda, Commander of the Detroit Police Department's 5th precinct, told the UAW officials, "I am glad we're on the same side."[68] Reporter Bill Bonds, from the TV station WXYZ, commented that this was "the first time in the history of the UAW, [that] the union mobilized to keep a plant open."[69] UAW leaders told reporters that they were on-call twenty-four hours a day to go to any other Chrysler plant where workers might decide to wildcat.[70] This unprecedented act demonstrated the depths of the UAW leaders fears. The union had mobilized a thousand officials to keep its critics at bay. With this ominous display of force, the union had no trouble in crushing the Mack wildcat. None of the safety issues at the plant were resolved, and only 35 out of the 75 UAW workers who had been fired were ever reinstated.

IV

To better understand the unprecedented character of the UAW's strikebreaking in 1973, and to better assess the significance of the politics of race in the leadership's political calculations, it is useful to compare the events in Detroit with a better known strike at the General Motors' Lordstown, Ohio plant in 1972. Both the Lordstown strike and the Chrysler wildcats were sparked by similar issues of work place control and the conditions under which workers were expected to labor. UAW leaders handled the Lordstown and the Detroit strikes very differently, however. By comparing these two actions, and the union's responses to them, the impact of the social transformation of the plants in Detroit, and the impact of shopfloor black nationalism on union politics there, can be clarified.

Even before the strike, the Lordstown facility had made news as General Motors' "plant of the future." Its Chevy Vega, introduced in 1968, was to be GM's answer to the growing Japanese competition. Lordstown was one of the most modern and automated plants in the industry. Its production rates were GM's highest. Quite inadvertently, worker discontent and activism at Lordstown drew national media attention. The media portrayed events at Lordstown as evidence of a serious worker rebellion against industrial progress. The fact that the work force at Lordstown was "long-haired, pig-tailed, and bell-bottomed,"[71] as well as remarkably young, only heightened America's interest in the story. When evidence of sabotage surfaced during the strike itself, the event became even more dramatic and newsworthy. The news media framed Lordstown as a picture of working class youth bucking authority and rejecting industrial progress.

Unfortunately a clear understanding of the origins and implications of this strike has been obscured because most observers have accepted the media's picture of the event as historical reality. In fact, the Lordstown strike was about something the media failed to report. It was fuelled by workers' belief that they had the right to work at a humane pace and that they could not allow management to unilaterally abrogate a contract during a plant reorganization.

This strike's dynamics, though traditional, illuminate a pivotal moment between the prosperity of the mid-1960s and the economic crisis of the mid-1970s. Events at Lordstown highlight the serious management offensive taking place during these years, and the particular circumstances under which the UAW was willing to fight back. In addition, this strike raised questions about the character of industrial work in the twentieth century, which served to sensitize the nation to the special concerns of blue collar workers in America.

The Lordstown assembly plant was opened at the high point of prosperity in 1966. Its work force was composed of young, white males who had grown up in the unionized communities of the Ohio Mahoning Valley.[72] The Lordstown work force was young for two reasons. First, General Motors management always favored youth when opening a new facility. Secondly, the prosperity of the 1960s afforded auto employment for young people because there were fewer older unemployed auto workers waiting in line with high seniority to claim the new Vega jobs. These young workers came into the plant to make the Chevy Firebird, and the Camaro, at the unprecedented line speed of 101 cars per hour. This line speed gave assemblers only 31 seconds to repeat a given job.[73] In other auto plants, the line speed was usually 50-60 cars per hour, while in Lordstown's body shop, paint shop and on the feeder lines, the line speeds were sometimes even higher than 101.[74] Even though the line speed was unusually high, GM engineers had used power tools, and vehicle design, to reduce worker effort on the assembly line. In the early years of the plant's operation, the majority of the workers' complaints were not about the intensity of line labor.

Prior to 1972, the Lordstown operation was divided into separate units; Fisher Body and Chevrolet Assembly. The Fisher and Chevy divisions, though under the same roof and only physically separated by a huge column, were run as two separate companies. They had different managements, different local agreements, separate work rules, and separate seniority groupings. According to the then-president of Lordstown Local 1112, Gary Bryner, "they were two [separate] communities of thought, and Fisher was always easier. There was less competition for their product."[75] Fisher made the chassis and Chevy did the final assembly. Fisher always had a customer, Chevy; but Chevy had to deal with outside competition. As a result, Chevy workers felt the squeeze from management more than their Fisher counterparts.

Because it was a new facility and everyone was jockeying for position, things were never that peaceful at Lordstown. There was always a degree of tension in the Chevy division, for example, where issues like intolerable heat, excessive managerial discipline, and perceived lack of concern over safety, often led to workers filing grievances. But overall, the labor relations situation at Lordstown between 1961 and 1971 was quite typical of other plants in the GM system. Although the local union was trying to establish itself as a strong presence in the new plant, it engaged in no actions considered outside of the accepted post-War standards of labor-management relations, and GM never considered Lordstown a problem plant.

In November 1968, GM ordered the General Motors Assembly Division, better known as GMAD, to combine and operate all Fisher and Chevy operations in the country. The company's intention was to increase plant efficiency, while simultaneously responding to the new threat of foreign auto competition. GM was confident that the union would be amenable to most of its suggestions for addressing the new problem of foreign competition because GM believed the union would be fearful of wholesale job losses. Overnight GMAD took over six auto plants, and by 1969, all six were out on strike. According to the UAW, workers struck because GMAD "was unwilling to continue in these plants what many of them had walked the picket line for in 1961, 1964, and 1967–1968."[76]

As the 1960s drew to a close, GM was counting on the union's continued acceptance of its managerial prerogative to reorganize the work process. For certain UAW officials and many UAW members, however, the disturbing implications of GMAD were becoming all too clear. As GMAD took over plant after plant, it was increasingly evident that GM management did not just want to reorganize the work process, which was threatening enough, it also wanted to eradicate key contract language, and erode preexisting union rights in the plant as well.

In October 1971, GMAD management took over and combined the Fisher and Chevy divisions at Lordstown. By now, the Lordstown plant had been producing the popular Chevy Vega for almost two years. GM felt that Lordstown was therefore a profitable plant, which was also a perfect place for implementing GMAD, since the Fisher and Chevy divisions were already in the same building. Perhaps most importantly, however, GM did not expect trouble from Lordstown's rural work force. As the *Cincinnati Enquirer* reported, "GM thought that [it's] effort would be aided by locating the plant in the small northeastern Ohio community where the labor force would be unencumbered by prevailing Detroit antipathies."[77]

When GMAD came to Lordstown, it immediately reduced the work force from 8,500 to 7,700 while keeping the industry's fastest line speed exactly the same.[78] This action deeply angered the autoworkers, but not necessarily because the line was so fast. As Bryner insists, "we could care how fast the line goes as long as there were enough people to do the job and still be able to blow [our] nose without being three car lengths in the hole."[79] Then GMAD unilaterally changed the work standard at Lordstown, cutting back from three to two workers per job, and insisted further, that all previous agreements with Local 1112 be renegotiated. Work rules that workers counted on, such as the provision mandating one relief person for every seven persons on the line, were now in jeopardy.[80] All of these actions angered Lordstown workers, but their hands were temporarily tied because it was too late for Local 1112 to negotiate a new local contract.

Eventually, the Lordstown workers elected a totally new local union slate, which fairly represented the original Chevy and Fisher divisions. Workers from both divisions hoped that this new leadership could deal aggressively and immediately with GMAD, and the drastic increase in required labor effort. Management, however, adopted a very hard-nosed approach with the newly elected shop committee. They refused to increase the work force, and thus shopfloor tensions escalated. Disciplinary Lay Offs (DLO's)[81] were issued in unprecedented numbers because workers often refused to do the work of two, sometimes three, workers. By January of 1972, "there were 1,400 disciplined . . . which meant you had to stand in line to get thrown out of the plant."[82] With so many workers off on a DLO, there were even fewer workers available to produce the required 101 cars per hour. Not surprisingly, the quality of the much-hyped Vega began to suffer. The Lordstown plant's "repair lot [had] space for 2,000 autos, but often [it became] too crowded to accept more. When that happen[ed]...the assembly line [was] stopped and workers [were] sent home payless."[83]

Against the back drop of pent-up worker frustration, evidence of minimal sabotage soon surfaced. In some instances, cars came off of the line with ripped upholstery or loose parts. Despite what many media observers thought, however, the sabotage in the plant was not part of a conscious union strategy to hurt GM. The local was not without a plan to combat management's onslaught, however. Over time, the union decided to have its workers not labor any harder than they had before the GMAD takeover. "We will give them a fair days work", the union argued, "but we will not run to meet management's overloaded standards."[84] The president of the local specifically urged workers "to work at a normal pace"[85] and the Shop Chairman, Paul Cubellis, also "made an appeal to members *not* to work double shifts."[86]

The effectiveness of the "normal pace" strategy led to an impasse at the plant. By December 1971, the line was down almost every afternoon because there was no remaining room in the repair lot for the many damaged and uncompleted cars. Cars were not getting produced, workers were working shorter hours, and there were even fewer workers to meet the production schedule than there had been after the initial GMAD lay off. The leadership of Local 1112 soon realized than a strike against GMAD was necessary.

According to Bryner, "It had to happen. There was no controlling it."[87] But if a strike was inevitable, Local 1112 did not want it to be a wildcat. It worried that despite the possibility of an official strike, workers were too angry to wait for the necessary sanction from the International. In the plant newspaper, and in letters to the membership, Local 1112 repeatedly tried to dilute any support for a wildcat. As the union leaders put it, "Management is now apparently trying to provoke a wildcat strike. Don't be provoked." And, "remember, do not be provoked into a wildcat strike. Your continued cooperation is needed."[88]

At the Chrysler plants, the union hierarchy was suspicious of the militancy in its own ranks, and was attempting to quell dissent when it told workers not to wildcat. In addition, the union leaders at Chrysler were not at all inclined to push for an authorized strike during the term of the contract. The union leaders in Lordstown, however, clearly supported the militancy on their shopfloor and they had every intention of backing a strike. When they told their workers not to wildcat, it was only because they did not want to derail their plans for a more organized, and powerful, legal authorized strike, in the near future.

The International UAW leadership was more hesitant to call a strike at Lordstown than the leaders there were. The International was concerned because the UAW's strike funds were seriously depleted after the drawn out 1970 contract-time strike with GM, and it would be difficult to weather another potentially protracted struggle with the same company. But the International agreed with Local 1112 that the Lordstown workers' grievances were very legitimate and, in the end, it decided to allow a strike vote. As the UAW's GM Department Director Irving Bluestone told the local membership "We cannot give you wild promises, but we can tell you we are and will be with you."[89] Clearly Local 1112 greatly appreciated the International's support. Tony Zone, the Vice President of Local 1112, wrote a special letter to UAW President Leonard Woodcock to tell him "we have the greatest respect for our International. . . ."[90] At Lordstown, unlike at Jefferson, Forge, and Mack, the leadership of the UAW, both Local and International, stood solidly behind the workers who wanted a mid-contract strike. One week after requesting strike authorization, 85 percent of Local 1112 showed up for the strike vote, and 95 percent of those voted "yes."[91]

To make sure that the strike went smoothly, the international kept between 13 and 19 staff members in the area at all times. The UAW local and international leadership hoped that this strike would restore conditions to the pre-GMAD status-quo. They saw the strike as primarily about workplace discipline, the killing pace of work, and respect for union-management contracts. They strove to preserve the best language in both of the previous agreements. As Bluestone told the local leadership, the "purpose with GMAD is to consolidate two agreements, rather than develop new demands."[92] According to Gary Bryner, there was a portion of the membership who opposed the union's position of "maintain" not "gain" because it saw the strike as an opportunity to actually win new gains from GM. Also, there was a vocal group of radicals in the plant who were calling for new ground to be broken in this strike as well. In general, however, the "maintenance" strike goal had the overwhelming support of the workers, the community, and even the local Democratic Party.

The strike was successfully settled within 22 days. The settlement provided for the return of almost all of the jobs lost in the GMAD takeover, and it resolved most of the pending grievances, erasing all of the 1,400 DLO's inclusive of back pay. Some jobs were lost among those workers with less than 90 days service and no seniority due to the merger. Interestingly, of the 3,500 members at the ratification meeting, almost 1,000 voted against the settlement. Yet despite this dissent, the local leadership was able to maintain the upper hand by stressing the success that it had in keeping GM in check, and by reminding the workers how their International had completely supported their fight. Even though some of the dissidents at Lordstown were from the same white left organizations who agitated in Detroit for radical change in the plants, like the IS and the SWP, the union clearly did not feel as threatened in Lordstown as it did in Detroit, where these groups coexisted with and followed on the heels of the remnants of the RUMs. At Lordstown, the UAW, both International and Local, could afford to be more tolerant of dissent and thus, be generally more responsive to the needs of the rank-and-file.

The Lordstown strike was important for a variety of reasons. It was after Lordstown that the UAW and GM both began to recognize the issue of worker alienation, and "blue collar blues", which both became synonymous with what *Business Week* labeled "the Lordstown syndrome."[93] Twenty-nine year old Gary Bryner, the then-President of Local #1112, was even invited to Washington to testify on the existence and nature of worker discontent and job alienation in America. Mainly, however, this strike was significant because it showed that management was indeed launching a new assault on labor during this period, and that there were specific circumstances under which the UAW leadership would fight back. At Lordstown, a new generation of auto workers, with the UAW's blessing, taught the company that management could not always unilaterally change work rules and defy the union with out resistance and cost. It was hardly insignificant that the Lordstown strike cost GM at least $150 million dollars in lost sales.[94]

These auto workers did not take on GM because they were hippies bucking traditional union strategy or authority, nor because they were fighting industrial "progress" per se. They did it because their experience with GMAD had politicized them, and because they recognized GMAD's approach threat-

ened the power of workers to defend even the status quo in working conditions. As Dave Poole, Recording Secretary for Local 1112, told the
Lordstown workers, "Remember that the eyes of your fellow unionists
throughout the country are upon you. And maybe their future in some measure depends on you."[95] The union leaders at Lordstown still had a high degree
of legitimacy so that contending agendas within the local could be addressed,
absorbed, or successfully marginalized. Thus, although the young and hippie-
looking workforce at Lordstown appeared to outside observers to be testing
the union's flexibility and tolerance, the strike itself still fit nicely into the
established the post-War labor agenda of the UAW, and therefore, caused no
problems for the union.

V

The predominantly white workers at Lordstown spoke a similar protest language to that of the UAW leaders, and they kept their demands within a familiar ideological framework. In contrast to this, in 1973 when workers launched
a similar struggle at Chrysler, they were following closely on the heels of militant black workers who had stated unfamiliar demands, and who had spoken
a different protest language—primarily that of Black Power.[96] Unlike at
Lordstown, in Detroit the legitimacy of the Local union, as well as leadership
control, had eroded by the mid-1960s. This, in turn, created a space into which
black dissidents could introduce new labor issues. It was unchecked in-plant
racism and inhumane working conditions that had eaten away at the union's
credibility among many black auto workers, and some militants in that black
rank-and-file stepped in to demand that the union address this racism. Even
after the power of these militants had largely waned, the impact of their message, both on the workforce and on the union leadership, obviously had not.
After the RUMs' heyday, a more diverse group of workers found themselves
dissenting, yet by then, the union leadership was completely threatened by
any and all rank-and-file militancy. The union leaders had worked very dili-
gently to discredit and dismantle the RUM groups. By 1973, then, it was very
difficult for these leaders to look at rank-and-file dissent objectively, even that
which continued to surface as a result of management's flagrant abuse of the
contract, and the insensitivity to black worker civil rights in the Chrysler
plants throughout the early-1970s.

Events at Chrysler between 1967 and 1973, reflect the social and cultural impact of the second great migration and the transformation of the city of
Detroit and its auto plants. These events further illustrate that the voice of
black consciousness was in many ways as alien to the UAW leadership as it

was to Chrysler. It was a perceived echo of this voice that caused the union to choose, what turned out to be, the company's needs over those of the rank-and-file in 1973. At Lordstown, the leadership did not have to make such a choice because the issue of race and a revolutionary black nationalist ideology had not previously threatened it there. At Chrysler, the union leadership actually felt that it had acted no differently in the early 1970s than it had in the 1930s. When referring to the strikebreaking at Mack, UAW's Director of Region 1B, Ken Morris, told reporters, "We have not used these tactics in a very, very long time. This is reminiscent of what happened in the 1930s during our organizational period."[97]

In 1973, the UAW severely underestimated the degree to which the call to combat racism and safety hazards still resonated on the shopfloor, while it simultaneously overestimated the sway held by the groups who espoused militant black power ideology. The death of the RUM groups did not mean the death of rank-and-file concern with racism, safety, and speedup. In fact, it was the UNC, not a RUM, which sponsored a conference on the racism both in and outside of the labor movement on February 6, 1972.[98] It did mean, however, that rank-and-file dissent became more broad-based, involving many more workers with different backgrounds and diverse politics. Although it was true that "In the years since the death of the League, increasing numbers of dissident blacks [had] been attracted to the UNC,"[99] they were only one of several constituencies in that organization.

For the UAW, there were long-term costs for not understanding the nature of rank-and-file dissent in Detroit, and for underestimating the ways in which the issue of racism had become a key *labor*, as well as social or moral concern, when the auto workforce was transformed after 1950. The union leadership had lost credibility with its black workers, both because of its actions in the plants during the years 1965–1973, and because the UAW had refused to endorse the black workers' choice for mayor of Detroit in 1973. More significantly, the UAW had squelched the militancy of its own Detroit-area rank-and-file, both black and white, and this was the very militancy that it would sorely need as the 1970s drew to a close.

By the late 1970s and throughout the 1980s, the auto companies began shutting down plants, laying off workers, and demanding more and more concessions from the union. By then, however, the UAW was in no position to resist. It had already become too cooperative with the Big Three to suddenly shift gears and become adversarial and aggressive and, of course, and there was little shopfloor militancy left to mobilize. Although the weakening economy after 1973, as well as the rise of foreign auto competition in later years, each did their share to reinforce a cooperative relationship between labor and management, it is not clear that such a weakened union posture was inevitable. In the 1930s and 1940s, UAW leaders had utilized auto workers' shopfloor militancy to strengthen the union. In the late 1960s and early 1970s the UAW national office took the initiative in planning strategic strikes against GM. (See chapter 1.) But in the late 1960s, the union's leaders *in Detroit* became increasingly afraid of worker actions that seemed to be totally independent of the union's authority. As historian Steve Jeffreys has concluded, by 1973 most national UAW officials viewed black workers' militancy, even when it was united with white workers' militancy, as a "destabilizing and hostile element."[100]

8

SABOTAGE IN AN AUTOMOBILE ASSEMBLY PLANT: WORKER VOICE ON THE SHOPFLOOR

....

Craig A. Zabala

Introduction

This chapter studies the effects of sabotage on workers and output in a General Motors assembly plant in the 1970s. Sabotage has a profound effect on worker attitudes and union behavior. It also affects managerial responses to production control. I have studied shopfloor sabotage by using participant observer methodology, which allows intimate observations that are at once unobtrusive and telling and provide insight into the relationships between people and technology. This chapter analyzes the phenomenon of worker empowerment, and the yearnings of human beings for autonomy and industrial democracy.

In his 1961 study, *Bargaining in Grievance Settlement: The Power of Industrial Work Groups*, James Kuhn sought to explain why sabotage and the wildcat strike had not atrophied during the post-War era of relative union-management stability.[1] He argued that sabotage was an integral part of the grievance bargaining process, a form of fractional bargaining, which superseded union-management grievance procedures among those groups of workers whose high level of social cohesion and shopfloor solidarity enabled them to organize extra-contractual protest activity. Kuhn called this a *disruptive* grievance tactic.

Geoff Brown, in his study of the British industry auto industry, adopted a broad definition of sabotage, drawing on the views of revolutionary syndicalists and industrial unionists in the early 1900s, "The machinery of capitalism can be clogged quite effectively without the employment of that form of sabotage which expresses itself in destruction."[2] Brown emphasized the slowdown as a trade union tactic to deliberately limit output and to exert pressure on management to affect change, primarily in the effort-wage bargain and the general contest for shopfloor power. During the 1960s, some U.S. auto workers used this type of sabotage. A Detroit worker explained,

> "A plant-wide rotating sabotage program was planned [by workers] in the summer to gain free time. . . . Each man took a period of about 20 minutes during the next two weeks, and when his period arrived he did something to sabotage the production process in his area . . . the entire plant usually sat out anywhere from five to twenty minutes of each hour for a number of weeks due to either a stopped line or a line passing by with no units on it."[3]

At about the same time, Michael Burawoy also found that machinists in Illinois "bargained" on piece rates by staging job-actions to slow down production. This behavior usurped some management control in rate determination, but it did not undermine overall management power or retard the process of capital accumulation.[4]

Mike Davis has traced the origins of modern scientific management to Frederick W. Taylor's preoccupation with shopfloor soldiering. Davis celebrated the Industrial Workers of the World's strategy of *output restriction* to defend unskilled and immigrant workers from factory Taylorism and assembly-line speedup. Davis argues that workers' power emanates not only from the collective voice afforded by unionization, but from the even more potent power of the primary work group. Sabotage, therefore, is not just a key part of the "grieviculture," but part of workers' struggle for power in the workplace.[5]

David Noble argues that because contemporary unions lack sufficient power to use formal collective bargaining to demand and enforce real constraints on the introduction of new technology, sabotage is a necessary alternative to collective bargaining at the shopfloor level itself. Noble has been particularly interested in highlighting the extent to which sabotage has limited the introduction of job-destroying or job-degrading machinery in the current era of microcomputer technology. But Noble does not find that sabotage significantly delayed the introduction of new production technologies in the General Electric plant he studied.[6]

Sabotage has two fundamental effects on the shopfloor: (1) it intentionally restricts output, and (2) it constrains the administration of production. This often results in poor quality product and increased production costs. Sabotage also has high social costs, increasing the volatility of relationships between workers and foremen, workers and the company, foremen and their supervisors, and even worker contempt for the union. These hostilities may result in increased grievances and new labor policies. Such policies redefine factory discipline, production standards, work rules, and wage rates; in other words, they change the effort-wage bargain. A recurrent and widespread phenomena, sabotage incidents are a form of extra-legal bargaining that complements other forms of workplace conflict. Thus, sabotage tactics are likely to have more negative effects on capitalist economic and social relations in the plant than sociologists like Burawoy acknowledge.

J.R. Norsworthy and Craig A. Zabala have estimated the effects of worker behavior on productivity and costs in the U.S. automobile industry for the 1958–1980 period and provide strong evidence that a wide variety of worker behavior imposes profound economic costs on the firm. The behavioral variables (called worker attitude indicators) include grievances, unresolved grievances, unauthorized strikes, and quits, which are collected from plant data. The attitude index changed randomly about 20 percent over the business cycle. In the U.S. auto industry in 1976, the total cost of production would have declined by $5 billion from merely a 10 percent improvement in effects of attitudes. Five billion dollars was more than 5 percent of the total cost of production in U.S. autos in 1976. On average, for the years since 1971, a 10 percent decline in worker attitudes resulted in a 3 percent–5 percent increase in unit costs of production per year. As measured by the attitude index, the industrial relations environment worsened by more than 30 percent overall from 1959 to 1976.[7]

The inclusion of absenteeism and sabotage, when estimating production costs, is based on the premise that the economic impact of shopfloor conflict is substantial. These findings suggest that sabotage can have significant economic costs, with far greater consequences for the workplace. Burawoy's analysis ignores these effects. This essay shows some cause-and-effect relationships of sabotage incidents and why understanding sabotage is important to our broader understanding of political and economic forces over time.

Sabotage and the Shopfloor

The success and durability of sabotage is based on *the strength of both formal and informal work groups and on union power.* Sabotage is part of the work force's collective voice; that is, while sabotage can be an individual act, the saboteur, in most cases, must have the support, if not the active cooperation, of the work group to avoid management reprisals.[8] Thus, individual or small group sabotage involves the entire plant or shop community. Supported by work norms and informal customs and practices, shopfloor sabotage activity weakens the authority of management and enhances the power of the union in their more conventional bargaining relationship. In contrast to Noble and Burawoy, during my years in the plant I found that *union representatives often responded positively to extracontractual forms of shopfloor pressure, defending accused workers in the ensuing negotiations with management.* Of course, this union support usually remains unofficial, but saboteurs nevertheless assume that the union will defend them in subsequent grievance negotiations, or in disciplinary proceedings, if they are caught by line supervisors. If union representatives do not provide satisfactory representation, workmates and work groups apply substantial pressure to protect saboteurs in both these grievance proceedings and during the general course of the workday. These defenses reduce the frequency of management reprisals.

Sabotage is not an alternative to grievance bargaining; rather, it is a supplement. A militant union on the shopfloor may support or invite sabotage activity to gain bargaining power over conservative or inactive local officers, or over management during contract negotiations. A militant local administration may similarly solicit sabotage behavior in response to poor shopfloor representation. And a rank-and-file with a history of independent action might sabotage regardless of the particular people who led its union. The important constraint is the ability of the work group to protect its members and the willingness of the union to represent such workers in these disputes.

GM Van Nuys

General Motors' Van Nuys assembly plant is located in a predominantly Latino community about 20 miles north of downtown Los Angeles. The two-story factory opened in 1947 and was unionized a year later. GM employed approximately 4,800 workers on two shifts during most of the time that I worked there. My first year in the plant marked the beginning of a dynamic period of growth, and 1976 to 1979 were watershed years of record corporate employment, as many new workers, like myself, entered GM's ranks. Until the 1980 recession eliminated the second shift, each year Van Nuys built upwards of 250,000 units of the popular Camaro and Firebird models on a line averaging 60 cars per hour. Large capital investment in the 1980s resulted in significant robotization and expansion of plant capacity. Van Nuys was one of the leading plants in the General Motors Assembly Division in terms of productivity and product quality performance, and the only West Coast plant kept open by the Big Three automakers during the industry depression of the early 1980s.

In the 1970s Van Nuys had the largest Latino labor force, about 45 percent, of any GM plant. Blacks did not work there in significant numbers until the late 1970s, when the elimination of the second shift at the nearby South Gate plant generated a large number of transfers to Van Nuys. The South Gate plant eventually closed, increasing the number of transfers. By 1977, approximately 5 percent of the plant's labor force was comprised of women, blacks, and other non-Latino minorities. Although there was substantial cooperation among workers in making their production rates, and in collective bargaining in the shop, informal work groups were based largely on race and sex, and to a lesser extent on age.

Racial segregation was both a product of the seniority system, which tended to put older Latino and white married men on the day shift, and the choice of workers themselves, who kept the coffee breaks and after-hours drinking and socializing segregated. This pattern held true even among those younger Latin and black workers who labored together in the same departments. Indeed, white and Latino workers commingled to a greater extent than white and black, or Latino and black workers during off-work hours. This was due, in part, to racism. But it was also a result of the recent arrival of black workers at the plant. These newcomers were not immediately integrated into the plant workers' social networks.

On the night shift, younger workers had stronger commitments to their departmental work mates than did older workers on day shift, who were more concerned with "'putting in their time" and going home to their families. Young workers, especially single men, often spent their early morning hours after the shift drinking with their mates in the plant parking lot, or at the Chevy-Ho Bar across the street. Women workers on both shifts socialized more often with other women and with older male workers.

UAW Local 645 has a history of leadership changes based on race. An older Chicano worker once described pre-1978 local politics as "'musical chairs", an analogy accepted by a number of politically active white workers. A shop committee, dominated by older, white skilled tradesmen, repeatedly traded places with an administration of Latino production workers. All local presidents were white workers until Pete Z. Beltran, a Chicano and former committeeman-at-large, won election in 1978. Beltran and the Latinos on his slate came to power because they led a generally successful strike over production standards, working conditions, and disciplinary grievances. During the strike, Beltran had been the workers' main negotiator.

The Latino leadership was known for its militancy, in contrast to previous administrations, but it was also difficult for new workers to enter the leadership cadre. Indeed, younger workers were often discouraged from running for union offices because of political "inexperience". Usually, candidate recruitment was based on family ties—for many workers had fathers, brothers, uncles, and cousins in the plant—and on friendship rather than politics or electoral support from the shopfloor.

These associations often resulted in unsatisfactory union representation in the labor process. Both black and white workers complained that only Latin workers received good support from their committeeman. When I was a new hire, an older white worker told me, "The Mexicans run our local. If you ain't one of them, you might as well not run for (union) office. They take care of themselves in here. Might as well not write a grievance." His work mate added, "Did you ever go to a union meeting? It's all Mexicans. Drinking, Shouting. Why bother?" A black worker, who was transferred from South Gate after that plant was closed permanently, similarly remarked. "I ain't called the union since I came over. It's all Mexicans here. That's why management runs everyone in here. Nobody to stop them. They (the union) don't know how to fight. We ran things at South Gate." Former South Gate workers believed that the South Gate local was stronger than the Van Nuys local. They believed that workers grieved more effectively at South Gate and that foremen at South Gate had less authority on the shopfloor than their counterparts at Van Nuys.

My experience suggests that many of these invidious comparisons were faulty. By national standards, Local 645 was generally militant inside the shop, if not in local administration. Representation in Local 654 was not limited to Hispanics. Some of the former South Gate workers' criticisms may be attributed to racial hostility; but there has always been some unevenness in the effectiveness of local union representation, a consequence of the varying personal abilities of the union committeemen, periodic management intransigence on certain labor policies, insufficient union training programs, friendships on the shopfloor, and political inexperience.

In April 1976, when I started working at Van Nuys, a "folk" history of shopfloor sabotage was already an important part of the collective consciousness of workers, and of training in the use of collective bargaining in the body shop department. The story of a close-knit group of five skilled tradesmen had already assumed mythic proportions. As a group, they were able to control the number of breaks on the second shift by welding the chain that pulls the car on the line to the rails. The welds caused the line to stop, and when this occurred, production ceased for up to 30 minutes, occasionally three or four times a shift. Each time the line stopped, workers sat and talked, while foremen ran up and down the line searching for welds. The result: management added overtime on the shift. This cause-and-effect relationship was not lost on these skilled second shift workers, who found periodic sabotage of the line a convenient way to win additional overtime pay on any particular night.

Many workers in the shop knew about this group, although no worker disclosed their identity to shop supervisors. In fact, these skilled tradesmen had both active and passive support from production workers; and other skilled tradesmen often covered for them when they broke plant rules. As one older black worker remarked, "Nobody dared snitch on those crazy s.o.b.s because they knew we'd be waitin' in the parkin' lot for them. We'd have killed them. We were tight, back then. We was organize a lot of time off cuz of those [workers]."

However, the sabotage ceased when this particular group of skilled tradesmen quit their jobs. The remaining tradesmen were not as militant, nor did they seem to be concerned with the effort-wage bargain of production workers. In 1976, we heard stories that implied that sabotage was possible and rewarding. Older workers often told the new hires that loyalty to fellow workers and the union was the key to successful bargaining, including sabotage where necessary and appropriate. An older Latino worker told me, "We work together. We stick together. Nobody can beat you then. That's what the union gives us."

The notion that a worsening industrial relations environment in the plant often accelerates the use of more serious extralegal bargaining has intuitive appeal and should be examined at the plant level. David Noble and others have suggested that high grievance rates often warn of impending sabotage activity.[9] Also, the idea that workers renegotiate the effort-wage bargain is by now sufficiently accepted, but not fully understood. We must begin to understand if and how this occurs in the conventional collective bargaining framework.

The UAW grievance machinery has four main steps. Each step contains a number of substeps, designed to facilitate an early and even informal resolution of the conflict. The national UAW-GM contract stipulates the number of meetings required before the grievance may be appealed. In each stage of the grievance procedure, the worker is represented by a union representative. Step 1 of the grievance procedure enables the worker to present a grievance to the foreman, based on a charge that some paragraph in the local, or national collective bargaining agreement, has been violated by management. This step has three stages. Step 1a is the informal bargaining between the worker and his or her foreman, and can include the committeeman. Step 1b is the formal step where a grievance is actually written following negotiations between the worker, committeeman, and the foreman. Step 1c enables the committeeman to negotiate directly with the general foreman and/or the shop superintendent. The foreman is removed from bargaining at this step, although informal discussions between the foreman and the committeeman and higher supervision often take place.

Step 2 of the procedure is designed to appeal unsatisfactory Step 1 bargaining. Here, the worker appeals the grievance to the shop committee, which oversees workplace bargaining throughout the plant.

Step 3 is reached if negotiations are unsatisfactory at Step 2. The worker appeals the grievance, and plant representatives are assisted by international representatives from the regional or national offices when they meet to negotiate the dispute with GM's corporate labor relations personnel. Production standard disputes did not go to the UAW-GM umpire after Stage 3. GM workers had the right to conduct authorized strikes over unsettled production standard grievances.

Step 4 is formal arbitration by an arbitrator selected from a list compiled by the Federal Mediation and Conciliation Service. Although almost all grievances are settled before arbitration, they can be pursued before the National Labor Relations Board and the federal and state courts. On average, an arbitrator hears only two cases per year at the local out of thousands of annual grievances. Ninety-nine percent of the cases involve wrongful discharge. On the shopfloor, workers did not view arbitration as woven into the fabric of shopfloor bargaining. It was considered a method of last resort, relevant primarily when a worker was fired, and similar to a law suit against the company—daring, if impractical, and with victory improbable at best. Local 645's officers took arbitration more seriously than did workers because of a bias for top-down bargaining, and because the whole grievance process justified the local's existence.

At General Motors, grievance bargaining has for many years provided the underpinning for the more informal shopfloor bargaining that took place every day. The first rapid increase in grievance handling occurred in the 1952–1957 period, as grievance bargaining replaced strike bargaining as a primary bargaining tactic following the introduction of multi-year contracts. A dramatic long-run surge in grievances took place between 1961 and 1969. 1973 had the second highest level of grievance bargaining for the years 1947 to 1980. Before I started working at the Van Nuys plant, layoffs had already shaken the industry from late 1974 through the spring of 1976. Nevertheless, between 1974 and 1980 worker grievance rates were very high. 1979 was the high point of grievance bargaining for the post-War years, both in actual numbers of grievances and in terms of the intensity of shopfloor tensions.

The Van Nuys plant experienced similar trends. In 1970, for example, workers filed 3,489 grievances. In 1976, my first year in the plant, there were 4,948. Grievances continued to increase in each of my years there. In 1977, there were 7,384 grievances, and in 1979, 19,876 grievances, as three years of record overtime and high output levels increased tension in the plant. Layoffs in 1980 led to a reduction in conflict, with the number of grievances falling to 12,055. But the 1980 grievance figures were still about twice the 1977 level. In 1981, 6,340 grievances were filed.

My years at Van Nuys, 1976–1983, were marked by record output levels and heightened shopfloor tension over the production standards management enforced to make good on the company's output targets. Production standards, or job task-output rates, were a chronic issue at Van Nuys, especially after the annual model change, when management introduced new technology and imposed new standards. For example, a production line worker's job may change by adding more elements, while hourly wages and benefits remain fixed under the contract. Because management was making frequent changes in jobs and job standards, with the local's acquiescence, workers complained, but the grievance procedure proved slow or impotent. In fact, it was not unusual for the local and management to "freeze" grievance processing until changes in the labor process were normalized following model changeover. This eliminated further constraints on new policies and gave managers more autonomy early in each production cycle. Both foremen and committeemen often told workers, "'Give it a try for awhile. You'll get used to it." We called these grievances 78's because Paragraph 78 in the UAW-GM contract asserted the workers' right to challenge management-set production standards, and this was the paragraph we invoked when we submitted these grievances. Workers determined the criteria for challenging management's "right to rule" in the plant. If workers made a production standard complaint, the local usually submitted the grievance to writing. Workers were given a wide berth in complaining when they believed agreed on job standards had been violated by management.

In 1970, Van Nuys workers had filed 519 production standard complaints, 14.9 percent of all grievances filed. During my years in the plant, output rate disputes tracked the factory's increasing output: in 1976, 572 grievances; in 1977, 927 grievances. The record year at Van Nuys was 1979, both in terms of automobiles produced and the 1,569 production standard grievances filed. With layoffs in 1980, the number declined to 709, a significant number with only one shift in operation, and in 1981 and 1983, the figures dropped further to 216 and 149, respectively. In 1983, Van Nuys reinstated two-shift operations resumed. The plant was closed permanently in 1992.

Case Studies

Let us now examine four specific sabotage incidents.

Case One.

Bill, a young Latino, worked on a subassembly job on the door buildup operation. He repeatedly complained about his job because he was isolated from the assembly line, and his job required heavy lifting—up to 5 tons per shift—without the aid of a mechanical hoist. In 1973, GM changed the mix of production from two-thirds mid-size Chevy and Pontiac models and one-third Camaros and Firebirds, *which had heavier doors than the mid-sized models*, to one-third mid-size models and two-thirds Camaros and Firebirds. A single door on the mid-size model ranged from 40 to 60 pounds. A single door on the Camaros and Firebirds weighed more than 100 pounds. In addition, hinges on the 2-door and 4-door mid-size models were preassembled and installed on the line by other workers on remote operations in the plant. Bill's responsibilities included door inventory management, door build-up, and hanging Camaro and Firebird doors on a conveyor rack that fed the door-hanging operation on the line. The new production mix doubled his daily work effort to 10 tons of physical lifting. Bill now had to work twice as hard for the same pay.

Bill made several requests for compensation either in the form of eliminating job elements or a wage rate increase, but to no avail. Bill next filed a production standards grievance. When the grievance was denied at Step 1, Bill expressed bitterness and frustration. Then, with the help of another employee, Bill began to sabotage an automatic drill press that made holes in the door where the outside mirror was mounted. Every door had this mirror defect. Neither management, nor the skilled tradesman called in to make repairs, suspected that deliberate action by the workers had caused the malfunction.

The following week, the foreman removed a few job elements from the door buildup operation to compensate for the perceived substandard operation of the drill. The sabotage continued. Eventually, the general foreman suspected sabotage and suggested that the foreman assign Bill to another operation and assign a new hire, a young white worker, to the door buildup job. Surprisingly, the foreman made Bill his new absentee relief operator (ARO) and kept the new hire on the job as the regular operator. The new hire had no compunction about doing the door buildup job with zeal. He wanted his new job and did everything asked of him by the foreman. The general foreman came over to him shortly after he took the job and said, "You're a good worker. There's room for someone like you in the company. We're always looking for good workers." The new hire smiled and worked even harder. It is worth noting that over the course of the next few years the industrial engineering department installed a hoist to minimize lifting requirements on the door buildup job. But the hoist was cumbersome and slowed production, so workers rarely, if ever, used it.

Case Two.

Sabotage at Van Nuys also formed an explicit part of the strategy whereby some workers negotiated with management to gain more job control in the labor process. A 1977 door line incident demonstrated the extent to which sabotage activity might reinforce more traditional forms of grievance bargaining, and in the process, increase union consciousness within the work force. By the fall of 1977, workers on the door line, who formed an informal but cohesive work group, thought that the local's slow, cumbersome grievance procedure was incapable of resolving any of their 15 outstanding production standards grievances. In general, these door line workers were white and Latino, with less than two years seniority, although they had the assistance of older, experienced workers prior to their struggle with plant management. With strong social ties both inside and outside the plant, these young workers frequently discussed ways to resolve outstanding disputes both at home and at work. I attended a barbecue with seven of these workers. One of the leaders, Maury, a young white absentee relief operator, stated, "We gotta do something about that damn foreman. He doesn't care how the job is done, just so he gets production out." John added, "They don't give a damn about our 78's. Break your back. I just go to Medical [Department] and stick my arm in the jacuzzi for awhile. Beat the line for an hour or so." Maury continued, "I went to Medical the other night. Told the foreman I banged my hand with the hammer. I saw the doctor and told him what happened. He said, 'Light-duty for the night.' Went right back out the next night and told him I still couldn't move my hand. He put me back on [light-duty] for the rest of the week." The workers laughed because Maury had three "'easy nights." Maury concluded, "We should get together and fix the foreman." John interrupted him, "We should flood the damn office with grievances."

Maury and John began organizing a grievance writing campaign on Monday morning. Minutes before the line started, they explained to a group of door line workers how the work group might force the foreman to settle their outstanding grievances by flooding the union office with committeeman calls. Then both the committeeman and the shop supervisors would pressure the foreman to solve the disputes. John suggested, "You guys just write him up for everything he does wrong. Hey! Tell him to try tightening the bolt on the hinge and then write him up for working on the line." GM foremen were not allowed to work on the line due to a contract provision ensuring maintenance of negotiated manning levels and production standards. The workers laughed and nodded approvingly. Maury also suggested, "Hey, let's write group grievances. They want us to carry those doors and hold them up while we drill the bolts. With those hoses on the floor, you could trip and break your neck." This is a violation of industrial health and safety standards, also included in the local contract. "You see those hoses laying out?" He pointed to the air hoses near his work station. "Call the committeeman. We'll write a damn group grievance."

Maury spent most of his lunch and break discussing the issues with his work mates. He was also able to work ahead on his door build-up operation by "banking" extra doors. "Banking" doors meant building up an inventory of extra doors. The doors were stacked in close proximity to the conveyor rack. This meant that he had already handled the doors twice and assembled and attached the hinges. He could sit down and take a break and pick up the door the third and final time when loading the conveyor. Approximately 85 percent of the total tasks for each door had been completed already. He might get a worker to double-up and load doors on the conveyor line, while he talked with the nearby workers. At times, he banked doors, loaded the conveyor line, and left his work area to discuss disputes with a grieving worker. Then, he had five minutes before he was in the hole.

John also sabotaged actively while organizing the grievance writing. He worked on the striker operation so he could not "bank" on the job. The striker operation is a line job. It follows the door hang and door fit operations on the line. The worker installs a striker on the door post. If you open your car door, you'll notice that the lock inside the door closes over a protruding metal bolt, the striker, on the door post and locks on. The worker screws the striker into a threaded fixture inside the door post. First, the striker is screwed in loosely using an air gun. The worker then closes the door to check door alignment with the striker and with the outer lines of the car body. Third, the worker fits the door by bending it against a hand-held ball hammer and, finally, tightens the striker with the air gun. The job enables the worker to work ahead on the line and to spend as much as two thirds of his or her time talking to workers in his immediate work area. Sometimes, the worker would be located two work stations down the line, 30 feet away, talking with work mates about the load of unresolved grievances. The worker did this by working up the line—into his neighbor's work area—and then leaving to talk to the next worker. The worker returned in time to work the next job, but was usually in the hole. John explained how he adapted on the line, "All I could buy was three minutes working like this. But, I got a lot accomplished." He commented about his work quality. "I put out a lot of crap the last two nights. A lot of jobs with loose strikers in there. Management don't give a damn about us. We shouldn't worry about their cars." The sabotage lasted for about two weeks.

Ten door line workers wrote more than 30 individual grievances during the two weeks. They then requested group grievances following infractions by the foreman. With little success, the union committeeman attempted to downplay the grievance campaign. The committeeman warned, "Don't listen to those guys (John and Maury). They're just trying to stir up trouble." But one worker countered, "Hey, I think it's a good idea. Your way ain't working." Workers lodged a dozen group grievances within two weeks, and although the committeeman submitted only a few of these in writing, most were quickly settled with the foreman.

From the workers' viewpoint, the grievance writing campaign was successful. Most of the unresolved disputes were settled to their satisfaction, with 50 cent hourly pay increases for the days worked since the infraction commenced, sometimes up to 20 work days at 9 hours a day and including overtime pay of time-and-a-half, and elements removed from a job. For example, the striker operator did not have to double-check quality fits. Perhaps more importantly, because the door-line work group remained cohesive, the foreman began to negotiate directly with his workers and settle immediate disputes more quickly leading to Step 1a settlements. The shop superintendent saw his foreman's behavior as the loss of authority over the work group, and he was reassigned to another line in the shop. "A foreman can't be too easy with his people," the superintendent told me. He continued, "If he is, they'll tear him apart. You have to keep your distance and have a firm hand. If a man doesn't do his job right, putting him out on the street for the balance [of the shift] is sometimes better than giving him candy." But the door line group maintained its solidarity, and for the next two years they had a new foreman about every two months.

Case Three.

GM's shop rules and the local contract specify discipline standards. Management has a broad set of rights to discipline workers through layoffs (DLOs) and dismissals. Workers can challenge DLOs by filing grievances, usually demanding reinstatement, back pay, and lost seniority. Dismissal decisions are rarely sustained.

Larry was a Vietnam veteran, a "'tough guy," on and off the shopfloor. Managers considered him a "'problem worker" because he was "'independent minded" and "likes to do things his way," as one committeeman remarked. In 1976, during his first year in the plant, Larry had numerous disputes with his foreman, who was the general foreman's nephew, including one that nearly resulted in a fist fight. Larry narrowly avoided a disciplinary penalty, but the tension between himself and his foreman did not dissipate. Larry's workmates were proud of him because it was the first time any worker had stood up to this foreman.

Three years later (1979) the same foreman was now supervising a different operation in the shop on the second shift. Larry worked there now, having been bumped from his previous job on day shift by a worker with more seniority. He was unhappy because he wanted to be on the day shift in order to spend more time with his family. He applied for a job as assistant relief operator (ARO) in the door line work group on second shift in order to bump back to day shift, where the door line absentee relief operator had less seniority.

Bumping is defined in Local 645's local contract as an employee's right to change work shifts. An employee can transfer from his current job classification on one shift to the same job classification on the other shift, in the same department, based on plant seniority. The applicant will displace a worker with less seniority, or a nonseniority employee, in that classification. There are also special provisions in the contract to transfer employees for the purposes of job training, permanent labor adjustments, such as from redundancy schemes, and so on. Employees can also move between departments within the same classification.[10]

Larry grew increasingly frustrated when the general foreman would not allow him to transfer to the ARO job classification. Larry attributed the foreman's refusal to their past friction. After Larry had put in a call to his committeeman, he was taunted by the foreman, "Hey, cry baby! Still on this easy job?" Later in the shift, a car came down the line with a quarter panel kicked in. The boot print was visible. Suspicion immediately turned to Larry. The general foreman took Larry to the office, and Larry was charged with destruction of output and threatened with disciplinary suspension and dismissal.

Larry remained calm and asked for his union committeeman to represent him against the charges. He also threatened the general foreman with a counter grievance for harassment. The union argued that the company did not have witnesses and, therefore, no substantial evidence to prove that Larry was the saboteur. But the company labor relations representative responded, "Come on. We've got the man. [The general foreman] saw him do it." The shop superintendent was agitated and stated, "We aren't gonna let the sonofabitch get away with it. We're gonna kick his ass out of the plant for good." He ordered the supervisor to take a blank piece of paper and ask each doorline worker to put their bootprint on it. He was hoping to determine that only Larry's boot had dented the car door.

But neither the supervisor nor the superintendent could get the workers to step on the paper. This collective resistance by the workers reflected their resentment of management's intrusive, heavy-handed tactics. Nevertheless, the superintendent recommended that the labor relations representative suspend Larry for the balance of the shift and three days. The union committeeman countered that there was no certain evidence Larry had committed the sabotage and that the union would fight the case and probably win, "Go ahead! We'll get the man back at work with back pay. You're just giving him a paid vacation." After a two hour argument between Larry, the committeeman, and the shop managers, Larry was told to return to his job without a formal, written reprimand. The committeeman told Larry, "Keep your nose clean for a few days." The sabotage charges were dropped, and within three weeks Larry transferred to the first shift. Later, Larry remarked, "Sometimes a grievance doesn't do the job." And the committeeman explained further, "The company knew we had them. No witnesses. It was a case of bad blood between the two men."

The union protected Larry for two reasons: (1) he was being psychologically abused; and (2) he was being denied his rights under the local collective bargaining agreement. "If they would have kicked him out for the balance, or fired him, we could have won our grievance. The company knew it," stated the committeeman. Workers later surmised that Larry had kicked in the door panel, although he never admitted it. But the workers sanctioned his sabotage as a "legitimate" protest against the prior violations of his human and contractual rights. In this case, the venting of worker frustration at both intrinsic work alienation and managerial law-breaking was protected by both group solidarity and by the union contract, which prevented management from firing a worker without proof that the worker had committed an infraction.

Case Four.

Negligent sabotage is a term I use to describe the behavior of workers who do not perform all of their assigned jobs. Ken, who worked on the door-fit operation on door-line for six months, ended up practicing negligent sabotage. His job was neither difficult nor involved heavy work. It involved tightening six bolts with an air gun and then adjusting the door fit. Using only a hammer and air gun, he finished one job every 56 seconds. Most workers thought the job was tedious, but easy because there were no challenging job elements. As long as the door build-up operator installed the door hinges properly, and the door hanger installed the door on the car body correctly, Ken's operation was simple, although he remained confined to a small 12 foot work area. He had three tasks: check door-body alignments, tighten six bolts on the hinges, and check door-body alignment again. Problems developed, however, if errors were made by either operator before the door fit. Stripped bolts presented the greatest difficulties. Imperfections in materials and door fabrication at the stamping plant also caused frequent problems.

Ken refused to fit doors with stripped bolts. When he encountered them, he simply shipped the job without a good door fit; "If I get a stripped bolt, I ship the [job]. That's their [management's] problem." When I asked Ken whether it bothered him that the pickup men had to do his work at the end of the line, he answered:

> That's their problem. Their job's to pick up the [repair work]. They have an easy job. Go down there. They'll be sittin' on [their] asses. I ain't gonna do more than I'm supposed to. If the bolts are bad, management can solve that problem before it gets to me. They ain't paying me to think for them.

Ken often shipped cars without tightening bolts to reduce his work load.

> I let a few [doors] go by now and then. I get bored on this job. Bolts might be in OK. But you gotta get off the line. Have a smoke. I'll go buy myself a coke or something. Foreman don't ever catch me. If he did, he'd have my ass. That's how I ease the tension.

Clearly, these actions suggest a link between monotony and the stress that it produces.

But Ken also refused to work harder than he believed was normal.

> If the door alignment is real bad, I don't try to fix it. I just bang on the hinge a little and ship it. Usually, that means the hinge was welded wrong. No sense beating on the door until I get a damn headache. The inspector doesn't like it, but he won't say anything to me.

Because his job was so routine, and he was so disengaged, Ken seemed classically alienated from his work. When problems arose, he felt no obligation to solve them.

> If one comes down without a bolt, and the guy left me an extra [bolt] on top of the job, I'll try to put in on. I'll take it and jiggle it a little, feel around with my hand, and try to get it started. If I can, I'll tighten it up and adjust the door. I ain't gonna give 'em much more than that. The foreman comes down and asks why I shipped the job. I just tell him the bolts were stripped, or the hinge was bent. No problem.

Negligent sabotage of the sort Ken practiced often meant a break from the boredom of assembly-line work and an improved wage-effort bargain. But the effects of such sabotage on production costs and product quality were substantial.

Sabotage in Perspective

Mutilation data can also be used as an indicator of the incidence of sabotage. The data report in-process material and product damage, after accounting for (1) bad material shipments, (2) bad product design, (3) bad job design, and (4) poorly trained and/or inexperienced workers. In 1985, plant management at Van Nuys estimated that mutilation repairs on car bodies averaged 5.3 per ten autos, a significant level. During the 1976 to 1983 period in which this study took place, the rate was much higher. Lower amounts of worker sabotage after

1983 seem to reflect workers' fears that the plant would be closed if product quality were not maintained. In an environment in which workers were terrified that they would lose their jobs, management programs like quality circles and team concept (see chapter 9) undoubtedly lessened worker solidarity and made workers more attentive to product quality.

Although sabotage is a measure of worker dissatisfaction on the shop floor, it also makes collective bargaining work. It is an important dimension of worker voice. Sabotage without collective bargaining can also backfire with substantial costs to the saboteur. Hence the paradox: orderly and predictable collective bargaining can be abetted by disorderly, unpredictable subterranean conflict.[11] That workers rarely make the connection between sabotage and broader economic consequences, and fail to develop coordinated political and economic programs that shape national contracts and expand international strategies, illustrates the major limitation of localized sabotage. Factory sabotage is linked to local contract administration and policy formation at the local level. This study suggests that the durability of sabotage behavior in modern auto plants is even facilitated by the existence of stable collective bargaining relationships.

Acknowledgment

The opinions and conclusions expressed herein are the author's alone. Robert Asher, Paul K. Edwards, Steve Jefferys, J.R. Norsworthy, Katrina A. Zabala, and Maurice Zeitlin provided encouragement and helpful comments at various stages of the research and manuscript preparation.

9

RESTRUCTURING THE WORKPLACE: POST-FORDISM OR RETURN OF THE FOREMAN?

....

Steve Babson

In 1990, forty-one years after the Ford Speed Up Strike, the Dearborn Assembly Plant was still building cars on Detroit's western border. The plant's continued operation made no sense according to the auto industry's conventional wisdom, which favored new factories, new technology, and new work methods. Old factories with Fordist work relations and traditional UAW contracts were supposed to be a thing of the past.

Dearborn persisted nevertheless, even as other pre-1920 assembly plants were shuttered or slated for closing: Dodge Main in 1980, Plymouth Lynch Road the same year, Cadillac Clark Street in 1987, and Chrysler Jefferson Avenue in 1989. Dearborn Assembly not only continued to crank out 200,000 Mustangs a year during the 1980s, nearly two million in the decade, but it did so at a level of efficiency that made it one of the most profitable factories in North America.

Dearborn Assembly is a good starting point for examining auto work in the late twentieth century, not because its operation has confirmed new trends, but precisely because it has lagged behind them. As an historical anomaly, Dearborn Assembly represents what is superseded and latent, alongside what is emergent and triumphant. The innovative Employee Involvement and Quality of Worklife programs that first redefined work practices at Ford and GM in early 1980s also came to Dearborn and changed the tenor of plant management, but with far less impact on the basic structure of operations than initially promised. In the late 1980s, while GM locals faced threatened plant closings and ever more ambitious proposals for restructuring work, Ford, in general, and Dearborn Assembly, in particular, stuck with many of the tools and work practices Henry Ford had developed in the early decades of the twentieth century. Only with the onset of the 1991 recession did the aging plant finally enter the "post-Fordist" era, as some called it, with a new Modern

Operating Concepts (MOC) labor agreement to replace its traditional Fordist work methods. Ford and UAW Local 600 agreed to few specifics in the initial MOC, but the certain prospect of work restructuring brought with it the company's promise of new technology and new models.

Even so, this new lease on life did not guarantee that Dearborn Assembly wasn't heading backwards into the future. Would the vague promises of "worker empowerment" contained in the initial MOC really mark a break with the past? Or was the Japanese model of team concept, which management favored, a sophisticated agenda for restoring supervisory powers? These divergent potentials presented themselves in the context of Dearborn's particular history and work culture, but they also took their meaning from the larger story of the auto industry's global transformation, the rise of the Japanese model, the decline of General Motors, and the consequent turmoil within the United Auto Workers.

Past Practice

"World class" auto factories in the 1980s were supposed to be sprawling green field structures, usually built in semi-rural exurbia, and packed with robots and laser vision devices. The Dearborn plant, by contrast, was a throwback to Detroit's heroic past. Built during World War I for the manufacture of small navy ships, it marked its 70th birthday in 1988 as one of the last multi-story assembly plants in the United States. Body welding was still done with hand-held spot guns and acetylene torches, and painters still wielded hand-held sprayers. Clamping fixtures and welding bucks automatically aligned and completed much of the work, but this was "hard" tooling, not the flexible programing that controlled modern robot welders. Housekeeping was continual in a plant where the roof leaked and the paint peeled from old rafters; parts of the plant were so rat infested that a special provision in the collective bargaining agreement mandated weekly pest control.[1]

Modern assembly plants were supposed to operate with production teams of 10-15 workers, who rotated jobs and met in Quality Circles to improve work methods, as in Japan; Dearborn had no teams in 1989, no job rotation, and no remaining Quality Circles after the Employee Involvement program of the early 1980s petered out for lack of volunteers. Where modern practice mandated a single status for all production workers, each cross-trained for rapid and flexible deployment within the plant, Dearborn, in contrast, still assigned every production worker to one of 65 job classifications specified in the contract, each defined by narrowly prescribed tasks and special pay grades: from the Power Sweeper Operator at $13.63 an hour, to the Chasis

Assembler at $14.02 to the "Dinger", in body repair, at $14.61. The contract also specified the seniority rights that regulated layoff, recall, shift preference, and lateral transfers between these classifications. For older workers, this meant they could bid on job openings that offered more or less overtime, more agreeable supervision or an easier workplace, and the main criteria for such non-promotional transfers was their seniority, not the foreman's assessment or the superintendent's preference.[2]

Flexibility was the byword of factory innovation in the 1980s, but Dearborn Assembly was still governed by contractual rules, and many of these, to a remarkable degree, were still based on the terms of the 1949 strike settlement. Line-speed controlling devices were still to be locked, and Labor Relations was still obligated "to notify the appropriate union representative so that he may be present" when the mechanism was adjusted. When the model mix shifted to include more of the popular fast-backs with their additional door, extra trim, and optional V-8 engine, the contract not only specified the alternative for handing the increased work load, but explicitly cited "the provisions of the 1949 Settlement . . . 1) Addition of manpower, 2) Greater spacing of units, 3) Reducing speed of line, 4) Stopping line momentarily." On the many occasions when these remedies were ignored, UAW workers held to the normal pace and let some jobs pass on to the sizeable repair department.[3]

Accepted wisdom held that these job-control work rules and customs impaired productivity, but Dearborn built cars with fewer labor hours than the Toyota-GM joint venture in California or the non-union Nissan plant in Tennessee, as indicated in Table 9. These results did not require the youthful workforce that non-union transplants favored in their greenfield operations. The average Dearborn worker was forty-four years old and had at least 15 years seniority, much of it accrued at other plants in the Rouge complex. Seventy percent of Dearborn Asembly's workforce was black, but the proportion of women had fallen to less than 5 percent after heavy layoffs in the early 1980s. The plant manager was also black, and so was the plant's UAW officer.

One overriding factor accounted for the unusual success of these aging workers and their ancient factory: despite predictions that the rear-wheel drive Mustang would soon lose its market appeal, consumer demand for the car was surprisingly strong through 1989. Slated for closing in 1984, Dearborn Assembly instead operated at high levels of capacity utilization, with two steady shifts and little change in tooling through the rest of the decade. When these conditions disappeared after 1989, the historical clock spun ahead. Sales slumped in the 1990 model year, and so did prospects for protecting the old contract. In November, 1991, UAW Local 600 agreed in principle to a Modern Operating Concepts plan for Dearborn Assembly that included elimination of many production classifications and reorganization of the work-

TABLE 9
Labor Hours per Car, Selected Assembly Plants, 1987

Plant	Product	Labor Hours[a]
Honda, Marysville, OH	Accord/Civic	19.5[b]
Ford, Louisville, KY	Bronco II, Ranger	19.9
Ford, Dearborn, MI	Mustang	21.8
Ford, Chicago, IL	Taurus, Sable	22.9
Ford, Wayne, IN	Escort, EXP	23.0
NUMMI, Fremont, CA	Nova, Corolla FX-16	24.4[c]
Nissan, Smyrna, TN	Sentra, light truck	25.6
GM, Shreveport, LA	S-10, S-15, Blazer, Jimmy	28.3
Chrysler, Sterling Heights, MI	Sundance, Shadow, LeBaron GTS, Lancer	30.2
Chrysler, Detroit, MI	Aries, Reliant	32.0
Chrysler, Windsor, ONT	Voyager, Caravan	32.1
GM, Wilmington, DE	Corsica, Beretta	32.5

a. Calculations based on hourly/salaried payroll minus unscheduled absenteeism; worker and straight-time output data from companies and UAW. Stamping and molding excluded.
b. Excludes 550 workers for second plant start-up.
c. Excludes 200 workers removed from line by production cuts; peak productivity at full production, 18 hours.

Source: James Harbour and Associates, *Detroit Free Press,* cited in John Lippert, "Racing to Cut Time on Assembly Line," *Detroit Free Press,* February 7, 1988.

force into teams and "natural work groups." The six-page MOC agreement didn't specify any details, but committed both parties to negotiate a future Modern Operating Agreement to build the new-model Mustang. Ford management had made it clear that without a MOC Dearborn would not get the new model, and the plant would close.

The World Turned Upside Down

The world as known to the speedup strikers of 1949 had been turned on its head.

The Rouge complex that surrounded Dearborn Assembly was already littered with empty buildings and weed-covered lots where factories once stood.

The foundry, at one time the world's largest with a workforce of 15,000 people, was long gone. Now the slab mill was closed, and so were the coke ovens. The tool and die building was operating well below capacity, and the stamping plant was half empty. Like GM and Chrysler, Ford had decentralized production in the decades after 1949, in part to follow the expanding national market as it moved south and west, but also to escape the UAW in its Detroit stronghold. Once the epicenter of mass production, the Rouge had become a monument of disinvestment, still making steel and building cars, but no longer the hub of company operations. In 1950, Ford Rouge employed 62,000; by 1987, automation and decentralization had cut the hourly workforce to 16,000.

The Rouge, in turn, was a microcosm of American auto making. When Ford Local 600 waged its Speed Up Strike in 1949, the U.S. made 78 percent of the world's cars and trucks, and imports accounted for less than 1 percent of the North American market. The war-ravaged economies of Japan and Germany together produced only 2 percent of global output, and Japan's 1949 production of passenger cars, totaling just 1,070 units, barely matched two days worth of production at Dearborn Assembly.[4]

All this changed in the years that followed, as German, and then Japanese competition, eroded the Big Three's market share. Rising total demand postponed the impact of this change until the back-to-back recessions of 1979 and 1982, when it hit with catastrophic force. With half the auto industry's capacity idled, employment plunged from all all-time peak of 833,000 production workers in December, 1978, to a recession low of barely 470,000 in the autumn of 1982—a fall of 44 percent. Recovery brought back little more than half these jobs, and as American automakers restructured, and Japanese companies opened U.S. transplants, the non-union sector expanded to 39 percent of total auto industry employment in 1990. Outside the Big Three, the non-union sector grew even more rapidly among independent suppliers, from 41 percent of employment in 1978 to 76 percent by the end of the decade.[5]

In 1989, the Big Three's domestic plants, including joint ventures, produced only 24 percent of the world's total vehicle production, a distant second to the 31 percent share produced in Japan's home-based factories. Japanese competition harried U.S. companies in a wide range of industries, from micro-electronics to machine tools, but imports of vehicles and parts accounted for three-quarters of the U.S.-Japan trade deficit in 1991. In that year, Japanese-made automobiles, including imports and American-based transplant production, captured one-third of the total U.S. market.[6]

Decades before, delegations from Japan had come to see the just-in-time production system that supplied parts to Dearborn Assembly from neighboring plants in the Rouge complex. In the 1980s, Ford no longer used the system. Only a trickle of parts went from the stamping, engine, and glass plants at the Rouge to the Mustang assembly line. Instead, Ford shipped stampings from as far away as New York and Mexico, glass from Tennessee and Oklahoma, and engines from Cleveland and Lima, Ohio. The Japanese model was now the global benchmark of modern manufacturing practice, including just-in-time production; when Japanese delegations toured the Rouge in the 1980s, it was only to place a bid on its decaying assets.[7]

After Japan

Dearborn Assembly's Modern Operating Agreement (MOA) promised to bring worker autonomy, empowerment, even holistic humanism to the workplace. It remained to be seen if Local 600 could negotiate specific language that would realize these lofty goals. There was little doubt, however, that management's agenda in the 1980s included much more than rhetorical commitments to worker satisfaction. "The real distinction between us and the Japanese," Ford's Vice President for Labor Relations, Peter Pestillo, had said in 1982, "is that our labor relations system is law driven, and the Japanese in human relations driven. . . . I'd like to see us move towards that."[8]

The "laws" which Pestillo and others wished to leave behind included most of the contract provisions that had regulated Dearborn Assembly's operations since 1949. In the 1980s, these rules were condemned for the "rigidities" they imposed on an industry trying to accommodate changing market conditions and declining market share. The complaints contained a small truth within a larger evasion. Most of the Big Three's problems stemmed from management practices that subordinated quality and product innovation to cost cutting and short-term profit taking. Work rules became rigidities only when these management practices led to market failure and underutilized capacity. Mismanagement was highlighted all the more by the proliferation of Japanese models and their rapid turnover as import competition penetrated even niche and luxury markets. Unlike Dearborn Assembly, which built a stable product line in relatively high volumes with fixed production technology, a growing number of Big Three plants had to build a wider array of models in smaller volumes with new technology and frequent design changes. Under these more demanding circumstances, both productivity and quality suffered when management pigeon-holed workers in narrow job classifications and ignored their knowledge and input on job restructuring.

"What we're really trying to do," as Pestillo put it, "is change a whole culture." Ford and GM had taken the first substantial steps in the early 1970s, when they negotiated Employee Involvement (EI) and Quality of Work Life (QWL) programs, respectively, with the UAW. Under joint labor-management guidelines, EI and QWL left intact the structure of work rules and shopfloor authority that prevailed at Dearborn and elsewhere, but added voluntary Quality Circles (QC) that took workers off line and solicited their ideas for improving operations. Groups of five to twenty-five workers were to meet with trained facilitators on company time, usually once a week, and focus their attention on such non-contractual issues as plant layout, production methods, and work environment.[9]

Like the MOC, EI and QWL had also promised to transformed the work process, making it "a more satisfying, meaningful, and stimulating experience." These fine words were soon contradicted, however, by the grim reality of collapsing sales and massive layoffs. In this crisis atmosphere, the dominant workplace transformation was not EI/QWL, but labor concessions, beginning at Chrysler with the company's near bankruptcy in 1979–1981. Ford and GM came next with new contracts in 1982 that cut holidays, reduced benefits, and temporarily froze wages.[10]

If these circumstances worked against a happy start for EI at Dearborn Assembly, there were counter tendencies that pushed in the opposite direction. The 1982 contracts established income security for more senior workers, and subsequent agreements promised a version of the "lifetime" job security that some Japanese auto workers enjoyed. The rhetoric of QWL and EI also appealed to the many workers who resented authoritarian management and recognized how their company subordinated quality to quantity. The sheer novelty of sitting at a table and talking about these issues—and getting paid for it—brought additional volunteers, numbering almost one third of the plant workforce at Dearborn by the mid-1980s. Many of these recruits stayed after their efforts produced concrete results—better cafeteria service, improved work procedures, or a new drinking fountain.[11]

"EI is not a passing fad." So said the UAW-Ford National Joint Committee on Employee Involvement in one of its earliest communications to union members. But by 1990, EI and QWL had passed into oblivion in most Big Three factories, including Dearborn Assembly and others where the program left a bitter residue of disappointment. Even where the program survived, the number of volunteers had fallen dramatically and the QC structure had given way to leadership committees with token shopfloor representation. At Dearborn, where EI circles had disappeared by 1989, all that remained were a handful of plant-wide committees with a single union representative.[12]

Among Ford workers interviewed at the Wayne, Michigan, Truck plant in 1986–1987, both supporters and critics saw reason to amend, restrict, or eliminate the program:[13]

> If a man [in an EI group] tells me he needs a fan in his work area, that's a health and safety issue, so I'll tell him to go see his union committeeman or

I'll see the committeemen. If you have too much work, that is also between
you and your committeeman because work standards is a contractual area.

Mander Thornsberry, UAW EI facilitator

When EI first started, nobody trusted management, so only a few people
were involved in it, and most of them were suck-asses that nobody trusted.
To get more involvement, management had each group pick its own EI
leader, rather than have them appointed by the foreman. . . . There is still a
lot of the old shit that goes on. There is still some hostility among workers.
And there are still foremen who boss you around and write you up, who take
an authoritarian position.

Bernard Clifford, welder and elected EI leader

The EI program has opened some doors that will be beneficial in the long
run. But the company controls what the employee will be involved with. To
me, it's just another form of psychology that the company is using as
opposed to its old brute-force days.

Harold Coleman, inspector

I do attend the EI meetings because they pay you for an extra thirty minutes
if you go. But in our EI group we don't discuss the plant. We talk about
what's going on in the world. I only had to make my point one time at the
meetings. We were discussing the little things that we could do to improve
our jobs, and I said, "We are going to be eliminated completely. Why in the
hell should we help them eliminate jobs. Are we crazy?"

Ramon Reyes, spot welder

At Wayne Truck, Dearborn Assembly, and throughout the industry, EI
had promised more than it could deliver. After the first round of easy successes, groups typically confronted a stiffening resistance from middle managers, plant engineers, and supervisors, many of whom resented the program's implicit criticism of their roles. As group members saw a growing
number of their ideas rejected, they often blamed local union leaders who had
promised more from EI or QWL than management was willing to support.
The membership's resentment was all the more acute in cases where management contradicted the spirit of the program by unilaterally cutting jobs or
outsourcing work. On the other hand, even the success of EI and QWL groups
could pose a problem, as local leaders opposed to labor-management cooperation found evidence that it undermined the union. Plant management might
refuse the Bargaining Committee's proposal for an outdoor break area next to
the plant, but grant the same proposal to an EI group, thereby communicating

the clear lesson that EI, not the union, was the favored means for solving problems. Under these circumstances, the formal guidelines that prevented EI groups from discussing contractual issues were frequently violated. As it turned out, most workplace problems had some relationship to the contract, and there were not enough union representatives to monitor how every group discussed these issues. As the EI/QWL agenda widened, there was the additional danger that the collective bargaining agenda would narrow accordingly, hemmed in by the preemptive claims of the new process.[14]

For top management, the bottom line came to this: after the initial easy successes, EI/QWL programs often cost more for training and time away from the job than they generated in measurable improvements. Management was willing to pay for programs that boosted company loyalty and enhanced the skill-base of their employees, but Quality Circles didn't go far enough. "QCs are merely 'off-line' discussion groups," as *Business Week* put it in a 1989 cover story, "and don't reorganize work or enlarge the role of workers in the production process." Something more was needed. "It is now management that is pushing employees in both union and non-union plants to accept more involvement—and not to make workers happy but to improve the company's bottom line."[15]

Post Fordism

The Japanese model, it turned out, required more than adding Quality Circles to existing work relations. At Dearborn Assembly and elsewhere, management now wanted Modern Operating Agreements that completely retooled the plant's work methods and labor relations. The model for change varied from case to case, but in most plants management's operational definition included the core concepts in Table 10's left-hand column; worker and union concerns (right-hand column) focused on the issues that remained problematic, and usually unspecified, in the management model of Japanese work relations.

While some plant managers agreed to partial or piecemeal introduction of these concepts, "best case" practice emphasized the interdependence of the system's elements. Functionally, they would combine to reduce non-value-added labor and minimize the amount of work in progress, with the attendant goals of reducing unit costs, minimizing defects, and increasing throughput. By delegating responsibility for inspection, line-side housekeeping, and preventive maintenance to production teams, there would be a corresponding reduction in the number of indirect workers who specialized in these non-value-added tasks; by combining classifications and flexibly deploying labor within the plant, there would be an upward leveling of work loads as under-

TABLE 10
Core Concepts and Bargaining Issues in the
Japanese Model of Work Relations

Core Concepts	Bargaining Issues
Decentralization of decision-making to the workers closest to the job	Which decisions? Which "workers?"
Continuous improvement of production methods by workers to eliminate waste. Also called "Kaizen."	When does "improvement" become "speedup?" Is there gainsharing of improved productivity?
Single classification and wage rate for production workers.	Are all jobs really the same? Who gets best jobs?
"Electrical" and "Mechanical" classifications for skilled trades, with single wage rate.	Does new technology require more specialization, or less? Who cross-trains?
Flexible deployment of labor within the factory.	What happens to transfer rights? Who decides?
Teams of workers take responsibility for particular portion of work process, including inspection, housekeeping, and routine maintenance.	How big are the teams? What resources do they actually control? How much real initiative? Is pay boosted for added work?
Rotation of tasks among team members.	How frequent? Full-team, or restricted by skill?
Team leaders coordinate tasks, monitor results, trouble-shoot problems, train new members, cover for relief, and facilitate Kaizen efforts.	Who chooses the team leader? What is his/her appropriate role: lead worker, "junior foreman" and/or utility relief?
Build quality in station and stop line to fix problems, rather than pass along to repair department.	Who can pull the cord? How much down time does management really tolerate?
Just-in-time delivery of parts, with small inventory buffers.	Can teams pad buffers? Is JIT a work-pace control?

utilized workers shifted to new tasks. Quality would improve as workers identified and immediately fixed problems "in station," eliminating the cause of the defect and avoiding the potential for subsequent damage as repair workers, also non-value-added labor, fixed the problem. Likewise, just-in-time inventories would reveal defects sooner and reduce the potential for damage during storage and handling.

For many of those who advocated the Japanese model, these innovations marked a qualitative break with the Fordist production system that had dominated American auto making since 1914. Where Fordist practice at Dearborn Assembly emphasized specialization and narrowly defined job titles, the Japanese model put a premium on flexibility. Where Fordist management ruled by bureaucratic fiat, amended only by the union's bargaining leverage, Japanese managers decentralized decision making and delegated authority. Where Henry Ford and Fredrick Taylor had separated conception from execution and made the former an exclusive prerogative of management, Japanese practice made workers responsible for continually reconceptualizing their work methods.

Academics and industry consultants promoted this post-Fordist system as "lean production" a phrase coined by the International Motor Vehicle Program (IMVP) at MIT. *The Machine that Changed the World*, the best-selling book that popularized the IMVP's study of global auto making, described the system as lean because it used less of everything: "half the human effort in the factory, half the manufacturing space, half the investment in tools, half the engineering hours to develop a new product in half the time."[16]

All this would be good for workers according to MIT. Under Japanese management, the "freedom to control one's work" would replace the "mind numbing stress" of Fordist mass production. Armed with "the skills they need to control their environment," workers in a lean production plant would have the opportunity "to think actively, indeed proactively" to solve workplace problems. This "creative tension" would make work in a lean production factory "humanly fulfilling."[17]

Big Three managers put these claims, and often the MIT book, in front of local union leaders as a selling point for adopting lean production. Ford did so in its negotiations for the Dearborn MOA by selectively quoting the MIT study and emphasizing its promises of worker empowerment. Direct quotes from Toyota's own production manual would probably have been less persuasive:

> Where conventional systems pad the schedule for many tasks with so-called reserve time, Toyota's system is oriented toward eliminating every minute and every second that is not absolutely necessary to generate value.[18]

Toyota's promise of a "stimulating" workplace where "employees can take charge of their own destinies" might have appealed to workers at Dearborn Assembly, though a system that also promised to "enforce a creative tension," "demand continuous vigilance," and inspire "unflagging efforts" would have been harder to sell. Next to these statements, Toyota's acknowledgment that its "employees don't coast" seemed a polite understatement.[19]

The danger for UAW members at Dearborn Assembly and elsewhere was that these sugary phrases simply put a new face on the same problem union members had confronted in 1949: speedup. If the union abandoned the work rules it had won in the 1949 Speed Up Strike, what would prevent the company from using "Kaizen" to intensify the workpace and push workers to levels of physical and mental exertion that could not be sustained over a working life? The MIT study had a ready answer. First, "to make a lean system with no slack—no safety net—work at all, it is essential that every worker try very hard." This dependence on worker commitment was precisely why lean production would be less oppressive than Fordist mass production. "Simply put, lean production is fragile." A wrong move by management and "no one takes initiative and responsibility to continually improve the system." To encourage the necessary worker commitment, management would have to abide by "reciprocal obligations," including the promise of lifetime job security.[20]

Workers, in short, could withdraw their commitment to "continuous improvement" and revert to the rote behavior of Fordist production.

The Real Thing

What these accounts of lean production failed to grasp, or acknowledge, was that under Japanese production management worker commitment was not just the fruit of reciprocal obligations, but also of intense socialization, and for would-be slackers, the threatened loss of wages and promotional opportunities. This meant that for UAW members at Dearborn Assembly and other Big Three plants, the MOC's vague promises of worker empowerment would only be realized if the union could develop an alternative to the Japanese model's coercive potential.

The Japanese model was not so easily transferred to the U.S. in any case, for many of the social and corporate structures that made worker commitment mandatory in Japan's auto industry were unique to the system's home base. Among these institutions of social control, only the last of the five following institutions could be transferred to North America without considerable amendment.

Lifetime Jobs.

As Japanese auto companies grew to world leadership in the post-War era, they recruited the permanent labor force for their assembly plants and first-tier suppliers, roughly one third of the industry's total jobs, exclusively from the graduating class of high school and college students. Despite Japan's chronic labor shortage, auto companies did not hire "off the street" to fill these permanent positions at the top of the job pyramid. Consequently, workers who quit their original employer had no prospect of hiring into comparable jobs in another auto company; if they remained in the auto industry at all, they fell into second and third-tier supplier jobs with low wages and little security of tenure. If, however, they remained loyal to their firm, they could count on a job until mandatory retirement at age 55, which was raised to 60 in the 1980s. Japanese auto workers, in assembly plants and first-tier suppliers, were thereby socialized into the company's norms and expectations from an early age, and those who contemplated a withdrawl of commitment risked their only claim to the job security and high wages paid in auto industry. In the United States, on the other hand, workers and managers jumped from one firm to the next during boom times, with no penalty for their lack of loyalty. After 1979, sputtering sales and high unemployment foreclosed this job hopping for hourly workers, but these same conditions also limited the auto industry's capacity to finance "lifetime" jobs.

Corporate Mono-culture.

In Japanese auto companies, lifetime socialization into corporate norms occurred in an environment where competing loyalties were significantly muted. This stemmed in part from factors unique to Japan as a whole, including the relative absence of ethnic, racial, or religious subcultures. Large corporations reinforced this homogeneity by hiring only men into permanent positions in their main plants, and by housing them in company-owned dormitories and apartment blocks. Since housing remained scarce and expensive outside the corporate estate, many workers viewed company housing as a positive benefit and a further inducement to loyalty. It also reinforced their dependence on the firm, and further isolated them from competing loyalties. The result was a remarkably self-contained world. In a 1985 survey of blue and white collar employees of major manufacturing firms, 90 percent of Japanese workers said they "always" or "sometimes" socialized with co-workers, compared to 48 percent in the United States. In post-War America, the auto workforce was a diverse spectrum of people distinguished by race, ethnicity, religion, region, and gender, most of them living in distant neighborhoods far removed from the plant. Racial and social divisions made a one-dimensional loyalty all the more problematic, for both the corporation and the union, particularly as the UAW's organizational history reinforced a cultural bias against overtly paternalistic management. In this environment, worker commitment to company goals was comparatively weak. In the international survey previously cited, 38 percent of American workers said they had no shared interests with their employer, nearly triple the 14 percent of Japanese workers who expressed similar levels of alienation.[21]

Conditional Pay.

By the 1980s, less than two-thirds of a Japanese auto worker's annual income was paid in base wages: the balance depended on the performance of the individual worker, of his (rarely her) work group, and of the company. Group production bonuses, individual capability indexes, semi-annual profit sharing, and "merit" pay all effectively subordinated the worker to company goals, particularly when the foreman determined each worker's merit rating. Consequently, Japanese workers who didn't "volunteer" for the Quality Circles, or who failed to meet the expected quota of suggestions, paid a heavy price for their lack of "commitment". In the United States and Canada, the acceptable range of conditional pay was growing, but still lagged well behind Japanese norms in the 1980s. The UAW negotiated profit sharing plans in the Big Three, but only Ford paid significant sums, and in most years, these amounted to less than 5 percent of total earnings. Even the Japanese transplants paid high base wages with relatively small bonuses.[22]

Enterprise Unions.

As in Japanese industry generally, post-War unionism in the auto industry took the form of company-based representation, with separate unions in each of Japan's nine auto companies. While loosely allied in a national federation, these enterprise unions had no coordinated bargaining and no pattern agreement across company lines, other than the general wage targets established in the labor movement's "Spring Offensive." Since the early 1950s, when management defeated militant auto unionism and replaced it with the current structure of representation, enterprise unions played no independent role in bargaining shopfloor issues of pressing auto workers' grievances, with the partial exception of Nissan. In a 1981 survey of employees at Toyota City, for example, fewer than 1 percent said they sought union assistance for work-related problems, while 43 percent said they turned to management. There was little to distinguish the two in any case: most union officers were foremen or middle-level managers, and the union's role was primarily one of passive support for company goals and "consultation" on company programs. Inter-managerial conflict occasionally disrupted this cooperative relationship, and the Nissan union's opposition to the productivity campaigns of the early 1980s has been cited as such a case. In 1986, however, a caucus led by the Foreman's Association forced the union's leadership out of office and returned union policy to one of passive cooperation. In the United States, the potential for enterprise unionism grew after 1979, when the Chrysler bailout temporarily breached the auto pattern. But it necessarily took a different form in an industry where a single union represented all organized workers, and where federal law prohibited foremen from joining or leading industrial unions.[23]

Foreman's Rule.

The Japanese model was often invoked as one in which authority is decentralized to the shopfloor and production workers are empowered to make key decisions. What these uncritical claims failed to specify was that in Japanese factories, the actual delegation of authority was to the foreman, not the workers. Peter Wickens, Director of Personnel for Nissan's plant in Britain, was refreshingly blunt of this score:

> Nissan supervisors are responsible for making the decisions on who will work for them; they have full responsibility for quality, housekeeping, and much maintenance. Within obvious constraints they lay out their work area and material arrives lineside where *they* want it to come. They have the responsibility and authority continuously to improve work methods and timing—and to resolve problems. They develop their own process sheets and control their own costs. It is the supervisor who communicates with the group. Above all, they are the genuine leaders of the group."[24]

In contrast to the prevailing practice in western firms, Nissan's approach "has been the concept of giving back to line management and supervisors many of the responsibilities that have been taken away over the years [in British firms] by the bright young people in the indirect departments.[25]

This feature of the Japanese model was often obscured in Western appraisals of the system by the fact that lean production also entailed a reduction in the bureaucratic layering of management. In fact, the two were linked: when the leadership delegated to the foreman, it meant there was less need for additional layers of "bright young people in the indirect departments." The foreman in a Japanese plant was given ample means for enforcing this leadership role. As previously mentioned, the foreman's assessment determined much of the contingent pay for workers in his group. In addition, the foreman exercised discretion over job assignments, training, transfers, and promotions. The committed worker who "volunteered" for overtime, worked off the clock, joined the QC circle, and exceeded his quota for kaizen suggestions was rewarded accordingly. Slackers were punished with lower pay, harder jobs, and less training for transfers or promotions.

Japanese workers were not empowered to change the fundamentals of an assembly-line system based on standardized jobs with cycle-completion times that rarely exceeded 60-100 seconds. In this environment, worker initiative was limited to suggestions that fine-tuned a management-controlled production process. Rather than being *pro*active, as MIT suggested, Japanese workers were reactive: they solved the problems that a lean management system continually forced upon them. In this sense, the range of responsibilities was far wider than their span of control. The promotional literature of the Kaizen Institute of America illustrates the point. Masaaki Imai, President of the Institute, noted with approval that the founder of the Toyota Production System, Taichi Ohno, routinely gave his department managers only 90 percent of the manpower, space, and equipment they needed for straight-time production. Managers and foremen were then expected to implement kaizen. "As soon as a no-overtime equilibrium was met," according to Imai, "Mr. Ohno would come in and would again remove 10 percent of the resources. His way of managing came to be known as the "OH! NO! system!"[26]

Since this "OH! NO!" system minimized overhead costs and contingency buffers—inventory, relief workers, specialized trades—and because it continually pushed the production process to the verge of breakdown in an effort to find this minima, critics described it as "management by stress." It need only be emphasized that in the "MBS" variant of lean production, the particular agent who vitalized this stress was the foreman, empowered by lean management.[27]

Made in the USA?

Contrary to the claims of the MIT study, there was nothing fragile about the system as it evolved in Japan. The question for American management was whether these robust features of lean production could be transferred from their home environment, with all its reinforcing structures of social control, to North America.

If the past was any guide, the answer was yes. It could even be argued that the Japanese system owed much of its pedigree to the "American Plan" of the early twentieth century, when U.S. corporations used company housing, corporate welfare plans, elaborate spy systems, black lists, and private police forces to fend off unionization. But much had changed since Japanese delegations visited U.S. Steel and other open shop employers in the 1920s, and the intervening years had created cultural, legal, and organizational obstacles to the reformulation of such anti-union strategies.[28]

Even so, Big Three management was eager to give the Japanese model a try, with the necessary modifications to suit American conditions. Because GM's initiatives came first and pushed the farthest, its approach set the standard for subsequent efforts at Dearborn and elsewhere. And significantly, when GM launched its first plant-wide restructuring of work relations, it did so in the region where the legacy of the New Deal and the CIO was weakest: the South. In the 1970s, the company implemented "team concept" work methods in several of its non-union southern plants, all "greenfield" sites, where no previous bargaining history barred the way to "unilateral" management action. Supervisors controlled the decision-making process in these plants, serving either as team leaders or as advisors who effectively subordinated the team leader to their agenda. As it turned out, however, these were not lasting initiatives. UAW organizing drives targeted management's use of team concept to keep the union out, and a combination of factors, including the national union's pressure on GM to abide by the neutrality clause it had signed in 1976, put an end to the company's southern strategy by the early 1980s.[29]

GM's next initiative also targeted a new worksite at the fringe of its operations, though in this case the plant and the workforce were recycled from the corporation's previous production system. In 1984, Toyota and GM launched a joint venture in California at the former GM-Fremont plant, closed since the 1982 recession. New United Motors Manufacturing Inc., better known as NUMMI, was touted by GM as a first-hand opportunity to learn the Japanese model from its leading corporate practitioner. True to its billing, NUMMI incorporated all of the core concepts indicated in Table 10, though the supporting institutions of social control were absent or heavily modified. Under a process negotiated with the UAW, NUMMI hired 2,100 former members of the Fremont workforce and promised them it would only resort to layoffs if management cuts and insourcing of work failed to stem catastrophic losses. While something less than a lifetime guarantee, this was a considerable improvement on the previous practice of U.S. industry. NUMMI had nothing comparable to the conditional pay and corporate mono-culture of the Japanese model, but there was an alternative means for generating worker commitment—the previous experience of prolonged unemployment and low-wage labor that had dogged Fremont's workforce after 1982. Workers were happy to return to the plant, particularly as the UAW-NUMMI contract matched, or improved upon, the Big Three pattern of wages and benefits.

Supervision would not enjoy the same unchallenged preeminence at NUMMI as it did in Japan. Yet in practice, some GM planners thought that

NUMMI's particular variant of team concept would still intensify supervisory control. As described by one management study team from GM's Leeds,
Missouri, assembly plant, NUMMI's formal ratio of one supervisor to every
24 workers was only slightly better than the 1-to-30 ratio at Leeds, "This does
not appear to be significant," the report continued, "until you understand that
included in their hourly count are 258 team leaders." After comparing the
leader's responsibilities for continuous improvement, quality control, training, and work planning with the tasks of a front-line supervisor at Leeds, the
study team drew a telling conclusion: "Remove the [supervisor's] responsibility for formal discipline and they are virtually the same job." On this basis,
the practical ratio of supervisors at NUMMI was an astonishing 1-to-4. More
important, as the study pointed out, these "working supervisors"

> aren't dictatorial (sic) and demanding ramrods. They are respected fellow
> workers. They are the cream of the crop—carefully selected using a modified
> GM assessment selection process. They are the most important people in the
> plant on a minute-to-minute, hour-to-hour basis. They are power point #1.[30]

The potential for dramatically extending and enhancing supervisory control made team concept appealing to these GM managers. But there was nothing automatic about realizing this potential, at NUMMI or Dearborn. In fact,
many of the team leader's responsibilities—continuous improvement, quality, training, work planning, relief, etc.—were not intrinsically supervisory,
but instead represented the historic borderline between skilled work and
supervisory control. Their definition as one or the other depended on the balance of power between workers and managers. In the craft production system
that prevailed in metalworking until the first decade of the twentieth century,
skilled workers defended their right to manage the workplace, up to and
including the claim that it was the craft union, not the boss, who should discipline wayward members. In some cases, foremen were recognized members
of craft unions, though in practice their role was more akin to that of lead
worker, a designation retained in contemporary skilled trades (tool and die
leader, maintenance leader, etc.). As scientific management destroyed the
craft system in the years before and after World War I, the foreman's role
began a prolonged evolution from skilled worker to bureaucratic functionary.
By 1947, when the foreman's union lost its strike at Ford, and when the Taft-
Hartley Act denied them protection under the Wagner Act, the process was
complete. The workers in the white shirts had become salaried employees,
and management had secured its exclusive claim to run the factories[31]
    Corporate proponents of team concept had no intention of surrendering
this right-to-manage. Instead, their aim was to make team leaders willing
adjuncts of supervisory practice, without designating them as such. Indeed, all

the better if they remained, at least nominally, "respected fellow workers" of other team members. At NUMMI, they were hourly workers and UAW members, but management made every effort to win their commitment to supervisory goals. First and foremost, management retained the right to choose who would become team leaders. The first 200 were then specially trained for their new role, including three weeks in Japan working under the tutelage of a Toyota foreman. In this respect, NUMMI's initial team structure reproduced the established practice in Japan, where team leaders functioned as sub-foreman. In Fremont as in Toyota City, they helped promote the continuous improvement of production methods by eliminating wasted motion, idle time, and redundant labor. The team leader's identification with NUMMI's goals proceeded all the further as the job took on the symbolic trappings of supervisory practice, including taking attendance, reporting tardiness, and canvassing team members for overtime.[32]

Not all team leaders at NUMMI saw themselves as "junior foremen," and many union leaders balked at suggestions that their local had become an enterprise union. But the pressures in this direction were enormous, especially as layoffs and plant closings put a deep chill on union militancy. At NUMMI, the union's bargaining and district committee members shared an open office with their corporate counterparts from labor relations—an arrangement unthinkable at Dearborn Assembly or most other traditional plants. The number of formal grievances fell dramatically from the high levels that characterized the old Fremont plant, in part because NUMMI's foremen had the authority and training to solve many problems before they became grievances, but also because workers had fewer contractual rights upon which to found a grievance. Even the formal designations given management and union representatives blurred the boundaries between the two: first-line supervisors were not foremen but "group leaders"; the elected union representatives who worked on the line and communicated directly with the members were not stewards but "coordinators." They were expected to handle first-step grievances, but some complained that local union leaders discouraged them from pursuing this responsibility. In an industry where management put a premium on replacing the adversarial designation "We vs. They" with the consensual designation "Us," grievances were an uncomfortable anomaly.

Diffusion Confusion

NUMMI set a precedent for the transformation of labor and work relations throughout the Big Three, but it was not a blueprint the Dearborn Assembly or many other plant locals were willing to adopt with amendment.

Most required a crisis before they could even consider such a massive reformulation of their roles. Most didn't have long to wait. In the volatile market conditions that prevailed after 1979, many popular car models lost their appeal, many new models failed to win a following, and model changeovers came with growing frequency. As Big Three companies lost market share, high levels of excess capacity put any plant that lost its current model at considerable risk of a permanent shutdown, and in this crisis atmosphere, management made it clear that "cooperative" locals stood the better chance of winning new work. In most cases, the litmus of cooperation was whether the local would renegotiate its plant agreement. Because GM had more market failures than Ford or Chrysler, and because the company had retained more of its capacity through the recessions of 1979–1982, the "whipsawing" of one GM local against another was especially pronounced at the number one auto maker.

The competition within GM's far-flung production system generated complex and overlapping antagonisms: between plants in California and Quebec competing for the Camero and Firebird models, between plants in Wisconsin and Michigan competing for GM's new truck models. In the latter case, the Janesville, Wisconsin plant lost the pickup truck they had built in 1987 to the GM plant in Fort Wayne, Indiana. To compete for the new medium-duty truck model that would otherwise go to the Pontiac Central plant in Michigan, Janesville's Local 95 agreed to reduce the number of production classifications from 90 to 3 and to accept 10-hour workdays and the four-day week with no overtime premium. The Pontiac local, by contrast, refused to amend its contract or consider team concept. When Janesville got the work, Pontiac union leaders complained bitterly that Janesville had caved in to GM and allowed the company to pit one local against another. One officer of the Janesville local acknowledged in an anonymous interview that "If we went to Pontiac, they'd cut our throats." But he had no regrets. "If we get that work, it's because we deserve it. GM is putting it where it will get made right."[33]

Local union leaders in Janesville and elsewhere had the backing of many UAW members for this incipient brand of plant-enterprise unionism. Younger production workers with less seniority had fewer options for transferring to another plant and more reason to favor contract changes linked to job security. They also had less to lose if the traditional contract, which conferred seniority-based benefits and rights on older workers, was abandoned. But senior workers could favor renegotiation as well if their accumulated years of service were threatened by plant closure, and skilled tradesmen could even abandon their traditional range of trade lines under such a threat. There were also positive inducements. As with EI and QWL, team concept had a genuine appeal for workers who resented the heavy hand of supervision and hoped the new approach would empower team members—as promised. Many workers also welcomed the symbolic changes that made factory life more egalitarian, including abolishment of such management perks as reserved parking and separate cafeterias. As with EI and QWL, there was often an initial honeymoon period as teams sorted out the new methods and the new models. During this gradual "ramp up" to full production, while teams debugged the system and the workplace was still leisurely, team members had more opportunity for input in the design and layout of their work.

Among the UAW's top leaders, team concept found its strongest supporter in Vice President Don Ephlin, director of the union's GM department in the late 1980s. Ephlin favored cooperation in joint efforts to restructure plant operations, and took unusual steps to establish a non-adversarial relationship with the company. An especially controversial example of the new policy was the joint UAW-GM delegation that traveled to Japan in 1987 to visit auto plants and learn first-hand what lean production was all about. In a press release issued by Ephlin, and GM Vice President Al Warren, shortly before they left, the two expressed their shared hope that "this trip [will] broaden the perspective of the negotiating committee members"—who accompanied the two leaders and their staffs—"as they prepare for the difficult decisions necessary to reach a new labor agreement." Upon their return from Japan, company negotiators agreed to expand the contract's job security provisions along lines the UAW had sought since the 1950s. The 1984 agreement had already established that Big Three workers, who would otherwise be laid off as a result of new technology, outsourcing, or increased productivity, would go into a "job bank" at full wages and participate in training or "non-traditional" work, as assigned, until recalled to a new opening or transferred to another plant. The 1987 agreement went one step further by guaranteeing a minimum plant population in each location, and requiring the company to hire one new employee for every two that retired. GM, in addition, pledged it would not close several plants previously targeted as likely candidates for shutdown.[34]

The goodwill these promises might have generated was soon squandered at GM. Plants the company had pledged it would not close were "indefinitely idled" instead, a semantic distinction that satisfied none of the workers who lost their jobs. Whipsawing continued, and with it, intensified pressure on the union to surrender its independent voice. The outcome varied local by local. With rumors of shutdowns and layoffs in the air, management at GM's transmission plant in Warren, Michigan, proposed in the fall of 1987 that the plant shift to a ten-hour day, four-day week without overtime pay, and that Local 909 members accept a new Bulls Eye agreement that merged company and union leaders into a single partnership team. Department managers would become Business Team Managers, general foremen would become Area

Coordinators, and foremen would become Team Advisors. The UAW's District Committee member would be redefined as a joint business partner with the Business Team Manager, with the two jointly responsible for continuous improvement of uptime and quality. Distinctions between company and union roles were purposefully blurred, but the underlying power relationships were evident in the proposal's fine print. Under the Bulls Eye agreement, the Business Team Manager's augmented powers to set goals and maximize departmental revenues would require that he "force decisions to be made at the lowest possible level." That empowerment had to be forced upon workers did not trouble management's negotiators, who had perhaps heard of Mr. Ohno's "OH NO!" system. That it didn't trouble Local 909's Bargaining Committee, which endorsed the management proposal, was a measure of how far the logic of plant-enterprise unionism had proceeded.[35]

Union Made

After a heated debate that pitted the Bargaining Committee against Local 909's President and Executive Board, the membership rejected the Bulls Eye concept by a vote of 1,868 to 177. Undaunted by this lopsided margin, the Bargaining Committee put the proposal to three more votes in 1987–1988, and each time the president and the executive board mobilized successful campaigns to vote the proposal down.

While the margin of defeat and the repeated number of ratification votes were unusual, the conflict of Local 909 highlighted the wider turmoil over work restructuring within the UAW. Critics pointed to Local 909 and charged that the company was using team concept to undermine the contract and turn the local into an enterprise union. Supporters countered by pointing to successful cases where team concept worked for all concerned. Top on their list was the Pontiac Fiero plant, one of the first to implement on-line work teams and a frequently cited case of genuine company-union partnership. But Fiero took on an entirely different meaning in 1988 when GM suddenly announced it would "idle" the plant and discontinue production of the two-seater sports car. Fiero's workers thought they had done everything asked of them, but top management unilaterally decided, with no input from workers, union leaders, or dealers, that because the model didn't sell at high enough volumes to maximize profitability, the plant would close. "The Fiero decision," as Don Ephlin later put it, "was a total disaster." Supporters of team concept felt betrayed, critics felt vindicated, and opposition to further labor-management cooperation grew accordingly. At GM, where the company's huge overhang of excess capacity made whipsawing a particular source of resentment among UAW

members, the dissident movement grew to special prominence. Ephlin's highly visible role in promoting a company-union partnership also drew an angry
response from those who saw the UAW Vice President as unable, or unwilling, to stem the drift towards enterprise unionism. When many opponents of
these collaborative policies coalesced into an organized caucus called New
Directions, they pitched their approval for renewed militancy to the UAW's
entire membership, but it was in the union's GM locals that New Directions
won its principal following.[36]

The UAW's top leadership turned back the dissident challenge in 1989,
when New Directions ran candidates for Regional Director in two of the
union's 16 jurisdictions: Region 1 in north suburban Detroit, and Region 5
centered in St. Louis. In bitter campaigning characterized by charges and
counter charges of election fraud, the New Directions candidates lost the bal-
loting at the 1989 convention by nearly 2-1 margins. The failure to reelect the
movement's leader, Jerry Tucker, to his post as Director of Region 5 was an
especially hard blow for New Directions. But the intense campaigning also
forced the early retirement of UAW Vice-President Don Ephlin, who cited the
political turmoil within the union as his principal reason for stepping down at
the same 1989 convention. Steve Yokich, his successor as head of the UAW-
GM Department, set a different tone for company-union relations. While
favoring joint programs to reduce substance abuse and improve health and
safety, Yokich told UAW-GM staff to "concentrate on enforcing the collective bargaining agreement, and then worry about quality and productivity."
There would be no more use of GM corporate jets for travel, and no more use
of company office space in the GM headquarters. Rather than accept the company's distinction between plant idlings and closings, the union contested the
company's reinterpretation of the 1987 agreement and took the issue to arbitration. The ruling favored the company. Locals that contested GM's outsourcing decisions were now more likely to get support and encouragement
from the national leadership, up to and including strike authorization.[37]

The company's position hardened as well. In December 1991, GM
announced it would close 21 factories in North America, but left it to rumor
which plants would be shuttered and which would be saved. GM Chairman
Robert Stempel invited each UAW local to compete for its future. "We're
working on them one at a time and that's the way it has to be," he told the
media in February 1992. "We're going to each plant and work individually to
see what that plant wants to do and how they're going to do it." In reply,
Yokich was equally blunt. "If Bob Stempel thinks he can whipsaw us, he's out
of his mind."[38]

Local 600 began negotiating the content of Dearborn Assembly's
Modern Operating Agreement in this contentious environment, though with a

difference specific to Ford. In some respects, the number two automaker had
followed a different strategy during the 1980s than GM, with less emphasis
on new technology, whipsawing, and top-to-bottom restructuring of work
relations. But these differences were a matter of circumstance as much as pre-
meditated policy: Ford's staggering loses in the early 1980s meant the company could not afford to build new assembly plants and install cutting-edge
technology, as GM did. Since its models, new and old, sold surprisingly well,
Ford had no excess capacity during the latter half of the 1980s, and less need
to whipsaw the old plants. These circumstances had only postponed the
inevitable for Dearborn Assembly, which came under the gun when sales
slumped after 1989. The very fact that the MOA negotiations were forced
upon the union as the price for continued operation of the plant underlined the
same lesson learned at GM—no matter how much the UAW and the company explored the common concerns that linked their fate in the market place,
there was still an irreducible inequality imposed on the union by the claims of
private wealth. It was not enough to win market share or even generate
"acceptable" profits; stockholders wanted maximum return on their investment, and the company would deploy its capital accordingly. All other things
being equal, management would also favor the Japanese model because it
intensified the workpace, eliminated idle time, and reduced the number of
work rules that codified workers' rights. UAW members would oppose the
Japanese model for the same reasons, and doubly so since it was they, not corporate leadership or MIT consultants, who would carry the heaviest burden
under such a system.[39]

It remained for Local 600 to define where a union alternative would over-
lap with management's agenda, and where it would differ. Teams would be a
central feature of the new system, and for reasons that the company and the
union might agree on: quality was enhanced when teams shared suggestions
for improving the process and collaborated on the difficult task of debugging
new technology and new car models. But would the teams also serve as focal
points for genuine worker empowerment, with adequate resources, training,
labor power, and authority to get the job done? Or would they become passive transmitters of corporate culture, dominated by newly empowered supervisors, and driven to extremes of physical and mental exertion?

As latecomers to the debate, UAW members at Dearborn Assembly had
the luxury of drawing upon a growing number of homegrown models for a
union variant of team production. And the first lesson of these accumulated
case histories was that team leaders played a pivotal role in defining the nature
of the system. Paid an hourly premium of 50 cents for their added responsibilities, team leaders represented one of the few promotional opportunities
within a team-concept plant. If, as in Japan, they were chosen by manage-

ment, then inevitably they would answer to management when it came to solving problems of policy or process. If, on the other hand, they were chosen by team members, they would have to answer to their fellow workers when it came to implementing kaizen, rotation, or relief. At NUMMI, growing criticism of the intense workpace and the role of team leaders led to reconsideration of the initial selection process, which left recruitment of team leaders under management's exclusive control. In a 1988 agreement, the union won the right to participate in the selection process and in the establishment of a clear set of criteria for evaluating applicants.[40]

At the Mazda assembly plant in Flat Rock, Michigan, the initial selection process in the 1988 agreement included similar criteria for evaluating candidates, with an additional stipulation that management had to interview applicants in seniority order and select the first individual who matched the job's minimum qualifications. Even this system caused resentment among many of the plant's 2,900 UAW members, who complained that supervisors manipulated the criteria to favor their preferred candidates. When new local leaders surveyed the membership before 1991 negotiations, the 2,400 respondents expressed a general unhappiness with the intense workpace, and a particular disenchantment with the process for selecting team leaders. Three out of four indicated they would "likely be injured or worn out before I can retire," and only 16 percent favored the selection process for team leaders. Of the remainder, 48 percent favored election, 14 percent favored rotation, and 16 percent favored seniority. Backed by a 94 percent strike vote, Local 3000 took these results to the bargaining table and successfully negotiated a new selection process: for future openings, team members could now elect the team leader, and recall any incumbent with a petition signed by two-thirds of the team. Lest there be any doubt that the team leader was not a junior foreman, the new contract also stipulated that his/her role was limited to coordinating team activities, and did not include taking attendance, distributing paychecks, or offering overtime.[41]

In the Big Three generally, the UAW negotiated MOAs that made team leaders answerable to election and recall by team members. At the Buick Reatta Craft Centre in Lansing, Michigan, where 700 UAW members built the low-volume two seater, team leaders were initially elected for two-month terms, stretched to four months in 1988. Their role, as specified in the local agreement, included responsibility for maintaining team records, coordinating job rotation, and assigning team members to specific tasks; supervisors were responsible for time sheets, distribution of payroll, and conflict resolution between and within teams. In practice, however, it was left up to the teams whether supervisors were invited to their half-hour Tuesday meetings, and roughly half the teams in the trim and chasis departments excluded them. "If the meeting becomes a bitch session, where people are complaining about each other," observed Dan Lasky, a team leader in the repair bay, "I'll ask the supervisor to leave." In a further departure from the Japanese model of lean production, the Reatta plant retained a reserve workforce of low-seniority workers, one or two assigned to each supervisor, to fill in as absentee replacements; team leaders only had to step into an unscheduled vacancy when these relief workers were not readily available.[42]

The MOA negotiated by UAW Local 900 at the Ford Escort stamping and body plant in Wayne, Michigan, served as another model for Dearborn Assembly. The local agreement mandated election of team leaders and gave teams the option of rotating the position every three months. As at Reatta, there was provision for absentee relief, though at Wayne each team had such a relief worker as part of its normal rotation. Teams met without supervisors and determined their own rotation sequence through jobs that included repair, lineside material handling, and robot servicing as well as direct labor tasks. In addition, the Wayne MOA addressed the problem of transfer rights in a plant that no longer had the array of job classifications in a traditional agreement. "The [MOA's} one classification created difficulty in how someone could possibly move from area to area," as Bargaining Chairman Mike Oblak described it. "We wanted to avoid the problem of supervisors or managers, or teams, moving people from team to team, thus forming cliques, thus creating problems." To replace the old system of bidding by job classification, the new contract specified five production areas within the plant and provided for area-to-area transfers by seniority, with an annual "bump" stipulated in cases where no vacancies existed in the areas chosen by senior workers. The contract also specified three additional off-line areas to be filled by a Seniority Interest survey as openings occurred: dockside material handling, quality control, and an "environmental" area that included everything from cleaning the carpets to cutting the grass—jobs which Japanese plants usually outsourced to low-wage contractors.[43]

These new arrangements required a more concerted union presence in the workplace, not, as some had advocated, a blurring of union-management roles in joint leadership bodies. Joint Steering Committees could make a positive contribution to plant operations by defining common agendas and seeking consensus solutions. But in practice, the non-adversarial spirit that guided these joint efforts only went so far. Management pressure for maximum production at minimum cost eventually collided with the human needs of workers who could not, or would not, subordinate their entire being to company goals. Even the committed worker wanted more latitude, more rest, and more rights than management would freely surrender.

At Dearborn Assembly these issues proved to be far more difficult to adjust than either the company or the union had imagined when the two parties agreed to the initial Modern Operating Concepts in November 1991. It was then assumed that the Modern Operating Agreement that specified the details of the new work organization would be negotiated well before the new-model Mustang came off the line in the fall of 1993. But two years later, after the official launch ceremony celebrating the new car, there was still no new collective bargaining agreement. In fact, MOA bargaining was at an impasse: the two parties had suspended negotiations, and the union had temporarily withdrawn from the Joint MOA Steering Committee.

Generalizations which had promoted consensus in the 1991 MOC now generated conflict when it came to the day-to-day particulars of an MOA. Both sides had agreed in the MOC that team leaders should be elected, but when it came to negotiating details of the election process, there was little agreement on the criteria for determining eligible candidates. The company said it should only be those who possessed the merit and ability for the job, and had been selected for team-leader training; the union agreed that candidates should have good attendance and know the jobs in the team, but it wanted both the training and election of team leaders otherwise open to all who desired a chance at the job. Likewise, both sides had agreed in the MOC that there would be job rotation and an Ability Rate Progression, a pay-for-knowledge system, that rewarded workers who learned additional jobs, but the two sides differed on the particulars: the union wanted full rotation and ample training for all who wished to reach the top rate; the company wanted less rotation and less cross-training, citing concerns for quality and training expense.

Ironically, failure to negotiate the MOA did not prevent a successful launch of the new Mustang. Even as the company and the union disagreed on the overall terms of their new relationship, they implemented several innovations that enhanced quality and increased worker participation. These initiatives included the designation of twenty-five hourly workers who served as Product Specialists during preparation for the model launch; working with plant engineers, they helped design and set of the new jobs on the high-tech assembly line. Together with an equal number of Assembly Specialists who were also drawn from hourly ranks, they then served as peer trainers who helped prepare the workforce for the new production process.

These innovations marked a genuine departure from the past practice of relying exclusively on plant engineers and corporate trainers to define the work practices for a new model. But there was no denying that this fell well short of the wholesale changes promised in the MOC. Dearborn Assembly was building a new car with new technology—with dozens of narrowly

defined job classifications, no job rotation, no cross-training, and no work
teams. The management rights clause was unamended, and so was the 1949
settlement language.

After Germany

The UAW's bargaining position at Dearborn Assembly took the union in a
direction that departed substantially from the Japanese model of lean production. What the union wanted was genuine equality in decision making, not as
an indistinguishable adjunct of enterprise management, but as an independent
force representing the interests of workers. There were some in the union who
believed this joint decision making process should include overall business
strategy as well as shopfloor concerns, and advocates of this union model
looked not to Japan, but to Sweden and Germany, where factory works councils shared decision making responsibilities on a wide range of issues.

In some ways, the UAW's role at the GM Saturn plant in Tennessee
seemed the most akin to this model of labor-management co-determination.
The union's representation at all levels of decision-making, including
Saturn's top policy-making body, the Strategic Action Council, made the
UAW-Saturn agreement unique. At the base of its production system, each of
the plant's 400 teams elected a UAW Counselor to monitor contract compliance and promote two-way communication with the union. To underline the
UAW's augmented role, the agreement did not include the usual management's rights clause that reinforced an employer's legal preeminence in traditional contracts. Instead, the UAW-Saturn contract defined a Consensus
Process that gave both parties the right to block a potential decision, with the
obligation that "the party blocking the decision must search for alternatives."

But to the degree that the UAW-Saturn agreement was unique among all
other local contracts, so was it also fundamentally different from the German
model. Saturn was a single case, an isolated private initiative; Works
Councils, in contrast, converted most of the German economy, representing
a public policy that backed elected worker representatives with the force of
law. In Germany, these laws required employers to bargain with workers
over plant closings, layoffs, hiring, overtime, and other business decisions;
in the United States, where there was no statutory obligation to accommodate
worker interests, corporate management made strategic planning their exclusive prerogative.

The UAW-Saturn agreement took much of its coloring from this free-
market environment. There was ample union representation at Saturn, but the
UAW's independent role was obscured by the codewords of enterprise unionism: Bargaining Committee members were redefined as Business Unit

Advisors and paired with management's Business Unit Leaders as junior partners in the corporate mission. More telling, the next two levels of representation, Crew Coordinators, attached to a particular crew as it rotated weekly between day, afternoon, and night shifts, and Work Unit Module Advisors, coordinating several teams, were not elected by union members but jointly selected by top company and union leaders; management Partners with the same title were also jointly selected, giving the company and the union mutual veto powers over the choice of their mid-level representatives. Defenders of this arrangement argued that concerns for skill, knowledge, and ability would guide the joint selection process, and that this was preferable to the politicized popularity contests that elections provided; critics condemned this indictment of the democratic process and its patronizing dismissal of the membership's judgment.[44]

Corresponding to this top-down structure was a sharp curtailment in the number of union representatives who were authorized to file grievances. However, this did not entirely preclude union initiatives that veered away from the collaborative agenda. The contract provided that the union could call for renegotiation of its provisions at any time, and in 1991 the union did so with an accompanying Quality Campaign that frequently stopped the assembly line for in-process repairs. The local won improved pension rights for some members, but only postponed until 1995 the provision in the original agreement that Saturn workers would be paid 20 percent of their income in conditional wages—the same package of profit sharing and productivity bonuses, minus merit pay, that the Japanese model prescribed.[45]

There was little prospect that Local 600 would negotiate such a pay system for Dearborn Assembly. On the other hand, union negotiators knew they could only go so far in pressing management for provisions that strengthened the union's position in the MOA. Dearborn was an old plant, and management had other options for building new models besides the aging workforce at the Rouge. If the union pressed too hard, would the company take future models elsewhere and close the plant? Such a threat was no abstract matter for UAW members at Dearborn Assembly. Every day they passed the abandoned plants that dotted Detroit's landscape, that surrounded the Rouge itself. They could see the unemployed workers who gathered on Detroit's street corners, some wearing faded UAW jackets. They knew of friends, relatives, and fellow workers who had been laid off and never recalled, or who had taken their last option to save a Big Three job by moving to some distant plant, and resettling their families. They knew that in a widening sea of non-union competition, the UAW's local unions were receding islands of collective bargaining.

It was, in fact, the world outside of Dearborn Assembly that would ultimately determine the nature of the work process inside the plant. The initial MOC agreement had promised "an organizational structure that will serve the needs of our UAW-represented employees . . . through a philosophy of mutual cooperation between management and union." In a society where public policy championed the comparative advantage of Mexico's low-wage production, and where some employers purposefully provoked strikes as a union-busting expedient, these fine words seemed brave, but unconvincing.

In the past, justice and worker empowerment had required independent unions and collective action to make meaningful the promise of a better life. It could be no different with the promises of a post-Fordist utopia.

Acknowledgments

The author wishes to extend thanks to members of Dearborn Assembly's UAW Bargaining Committee and District Committee, and particularly Gilbert Rodriguez, for assistance in researching plant operations and visiting the facility in the fall of 1992.

NOTES

....

Chapter 1

1. *My Life and Work*, written in collaboration with Samuel Crowther. (Garden City: Doubleday 1922), 80, 105, quoted in James J. Flink, *The Automobile Age* (Cambridge: MIT Press, 1988), 119.

2. *The Big Money* (New York: New American Library edition, 1969), 75.

3. The term "on the line" was used by Harvey Swados as the title of his compelling collection of short stories about auto factory work, *On the Line* (Boston: Little, Brown, 1957).

4. Consider the views of Peter Dworshak, a GM worker who was interviewed in the 1950s by the Yale Technology Project, headed by Charles R. Walker. Dworshak was not wild about his UAW local, which he thought was controlled by a "clique." He wanted to be able to earn as much as possible on piece work jobs and felt the UAW allowed pressure to slow down workers who chose high personal output targets. Yet Dworshak did not believe having no union was the answer. He insisted that the working man needed a defense against "speedup," but "not for any cause." Foremen had to be toned down because they used language "that's not fit for pigs. Foremen should have respect for the worker." Foremen talked to the workers "like dogs. That's why working man needs some protection." Dworshak also complained about inadequate seniority provisions in his plant's current contract, demanding a better seniority system that protected him against the arbitrary authority of management. "I don't like [it] because [you] can't go down step by step the way you come up. When cutback, the company can put you wherever it wants you. The foreman can put you wherever he wants you." Field notes, GM 010, Yale Technology Project, Sterling Library, Yale University.

5. Joyce Shaw Peterson, *American Automobile Workers, 1900-1933* (Albany: State University of New York Press, 1987), 37.

6. Stephen Meyer III, "Mass Production and Human Efficiency: The Ford Motor Company, 1908-1921," doctoral dissertation, Rutgers University, 1977, 164. See also Meyer's book, *The Five Dollar Day: Labor Management and Social*

Control in the Ford Motor Company, 1908-1921 (Albany: State University of New York Press, 1981), and his essay, "The Persistence of Fordism: Workers and Technology in the American Automobile Industry, 1900-1960," in Nelson Lichtenstein and Stephen Meyer, eds., *On the Line: Essays in the History of Auto Work* (Urbana: University of Illinois Press, 1989), 73-99.

7. This analysis is based on materials in Meyer, and David Gartman, *Auto Slavery: The Labor Process in the American Automobile Industry, 1897-1950* (New Brunswick: Rutgers University Press, 1986).

8. Huw Beynon, *Working for Ford* (London: Allen Lane, 1973), 89-90.

9. The modern literature on work alienation begins with Marx's early writings in the *Economic and Philosophical Manuscripts*. Robert Blauner was the first American sociologist to develop a far-ranging typology of alienation in the years after World War II, *Alienation and Freedom* (Chicago: University of Chicago Press, 1964). The next crucial work was Harry Braverman, *Labor and Monopoly Capital: The Degradation of Work in the Twentieth Century* (New York: Monthly Review Press, 1974). The best overview of work on studies of worker alienation is in Stephen Hill, *Competition and Control at Work: The New Industrial Sociology* (Cambridge: MIT Press, 1981). An important anthology on American labor process and alienation in the U.S. is Andrew Zimbalist, ed., *Case Studies on the Labor Process* (New York: Monthly Review Press, 1979). A superb, neglected analysis of the underlying philosophy of Taylorism, arguing that it is inherently biased toward increasing the total labor effort of workers, not making life easier for the worker by removing wasted effort from the workers's job, is Ed Andrew, *Closing the Iron Cage: The Scientific Management of Work and Leisure* (Montreal: Black Rose Books, 1981). For studies on the alienation of auto workers see Ely Chinoy, *Automobile Workers and the American Dream* (New York: Random House, 1955), and B.J. Widick, ed., *Auto Work and Its Discontents* (Baltimore: Johns Hopkins University Press, 1976). Three excellent studies of auto workers in other nations should be mentioned: Graham Turner, *The Car Makers* (London: Penguin Books, 1964); Satoshi Kamata, *Japan in the Passing Lane: An Insider's Account of Life in a Japanese Auto Factory* (original Japanese edition 1973, English-language edition New York: Pantheon Books, 1982); and a study of work in a French auto factory, Robert Linhart, *The Assembly Line* (original edition 1978, U.S. edition Amherst: The University of Massachusetts Press, 1981).

10. See Meyer, (1982), 140, on the exclusion of women from the five dollar day scheme. See Nancy Gabin, *Feminism in the Labor Movement: Women and the United Auto Workers, 1935-1975* (Ithaca: Cornell University Press, 1990), 10-11 for statistics and *passim* for a cogent narrative of the discrimination suffered by women auto workers and the actions they took to oppose it. On job discrimination see Ruth Milkman, *Gender at Work: The Dynamics of Job Segregation by Sex during World War II* (Urbana: University of Illinois Press, 1987). See also the interviews with women workers in Alice and Staughton Lynd, eds., *Rank and File: Personal Histories of Working-Class Organizers* (Boston: Beacon Press, 1973); and in the superb recent collection of oral histories, *End of the Line: Auto Workers and the American Dream*, Richard Feldman and Michael Betzold, eds., (New York: Weidenfeld & Nicolson, 1988).

11. Typed mss., "Program for Automobile Industry," Henry A. Kraus Papers, Box 1, Walter P. Reuther Library, Wayne State University. (Hereafter abbreviated WRL) Raymond was a member of the Communist Party.

12. Flink, 257-267.

13. Sidney Fine, *The Automobile Under the Blue Eagle: Labor, Management and the Automobile Manufacturing Code* (Ann Arbor: University of Michigan Press, 1963), 248-257.

14. Steve Jefferys, *Management and Managed: Fifty years of crisis at Chrysler* (Cambridge: Cambridge University Press, 1986), 79-85.

15. The UAW was hurt when a conservative minority of its leaders bolted from the union because they did not want to be affiliated with the CIO. The seceding leaders formed a rival, AFL-affiliated UAW. Dual unionism confused many workers and weakened the bargaining position of the UAW-CIO, which was the largest of the two rival unions.

16. Minutes, GM Conference, November 14-15, 1937, 30-31, Box 1, Stuart Strachan Papers, WRL.

17. It is unlikely that most of the members of the different factions of Local 3 expected to secure this last, radical objective. It was probably included in the strike demands as a sop to some of the more radical minority factions. This conjecture is based on a discussion with Ray Boryczka, an expert on the history of Local 3.

18. Jefferys, 83-95. Our interpretation differs from Jefferys'. He offers no evidence that the particular speedup of September 1939 was rolled back. Jefferys also fails to explore the effect on the thinking of radicals and militant centrists of the failure of the militant Dodge Main workers to obtain the kind of radical co-management they demanded. In his analysis of the post-World War II actions taken against the militants in Local 3 by the International Executive Board of the UAW, Jefferys seems to forget that all the members of the national leadership had lived through the 1937-1947 period and had absorbed the lesson that militancy had its limits and could also lead to significant government repression.

19. Typed interview notes, Walter Reuther, October 30, 1939, Box 10, Edward A. Wieck Papers, WRL. Wieck (b. 1884) was a former coal miner, a Socialist, and an activist in the UAW when it was an AFL union. He had the kind of background that would have made Walter Reuther willing to be candid with him. Wieck was a Research Associate at the Russell Sage Foundation when he interviewed Reuther.

20. Steven Tolliday and Jonathan Zeitlin have examined labor relations in the British auto industry in the years after World War II to test the validity of the assertion the leaders of U.S. industrial unions should have endorsed the model of shopfloor militancy in which shop stewards aggressively mobilized the rank-and-file discontent (through slowdowns, quickie strikes, etc.) to confront management on production standards issues and other questions of equity. Tolliday and Zeitlin conclude that the success of the British militants was sporadic and evanescent. Major gains were made only when the Labour Party was in power, in the late 1950s and mid–1960s. Tolliday and Zeitlin, "Introduction: Between Fordism and Flexibility," 1-25, in Tolliday and Zeitlin, eds., *Between Fordism and Flexibility: The Automobile Industry and Its Workers* (Oxford: Berg, 1992). In the same vol-

ume, see also Giovanni Contini, "The Rise and Fall of Shop-Floor Bargaining at Fiat 1945-1980," 144-167. This analysis confirms the judgement of many American labor leaders that the political climate in the U.S. after WWII would lead to further repression of the labor movement, worse than Taft-Hartley, if shopfloor militancy was promoted without restraint. For a converse assertion, see Nelson Lichtenstein, "UAW Bargaining Strategies and Shopfloor Conflict: 1946-1970," *Industrial Relations.* 24 (Fall 1985), esp. 371, 378.

21. Jefferys, 95, argues that by 1942 all the factions of the IEB had come to support the umpire system.

22. Reuther Speech, February 9, 1941, 9, Folder 17, Box 18, Walter Reuther Papers, WRL.

23. Memorandum on Production Standards, 1964, 7, Box 17, Kenneth Bannon Papers, WRL. Consider also the following example of the latitude to protest that was given to auto workers by the standards of equity enforced by umpires. This example is typical of the occasional "liberalism" of industry umpires. In July 1951, workers on the trim line at the Dodge Main plant refused to work up to the level of new production standards imposed by the company. Two workers were laid off for two days. But the Chrysler umpire ordered their reinstatement, without pay for the period of their layoff, on the grounds that it was unfair to severely punish a small minority of the workers guilty of an infraction. This kind of industrial relations policy allowed workers some latitude in protesting against management decisions workers believed were unjust. And it gave groups of workers considerable latitude to use direct action to protest job conditions at strategic points in time when their company did not want an interruption of production. Faced with the restricted choice of disciplining all the workers, or disciplining none, management often chose to look the other way if the dispute was settled and production was not seriously impaired.

24. UAW officials tried to "educate" Ford managers to these realities. After a major work stoppage at Building 5 at the Highland Park Plant in 1943, the UAW pointed out that it was the "complete breakdown of collective bargaining" that was one of the most important causes of the stoppage. The other factors were abominable health and safety conditions, mismanagement, and racial discrimination against blacks who deserved promotions. "Work Stoppages," typed mss., Box 85, Local 400 Papers, WRL.

25. Nelson Lichtenstein, *Labor's War at Home: The CIO in World War II* (New York: Cambridge University Press, 1982); Howell John Harris, *The Right to Manage: Industrial Relations Policies of American Business in the 1940s* (Madison: University of Wisconsin Press, 1982).

26. Jefferys, 98-100.

27. Robert Dallek, *Lone Star Rising: Lyndon Johnson and His Times* (New York: Oxford University Press, 1991), 288, 303, 314-15, 320-25.

28. See the newly negotiated Article 5, Section 6 of the UAW-Ford contract, 1947, enclosed in Richard Leonard to All Ford Locals, August 11, 1947, Box 12, Emil Mazey Papers, WRL; Although the NLRA had allowed workers to walk off the job if they were asked to work in the presence of an immanent, serious hazard, the legal status of such actions under the Taft-Hartley Act was very nebulous. See the discussion in American Bar Association, *Proceedings of the National Institute on Occupational Safety and Health Law*, 1947, pp. 146-147.

29. Unions, and the UAW, convinced President Truman to back them on a few issues, especially the exemption of cost of living wage increases from wartime wage freezes. Seth Widgerson, "The UAW in the 1950s," doctoral dissertation, Wayne State University, 1989, 147.

30. One could argue that the same would be true even in many socialist systems. Hence, the use of the term industrial system in the text. Consider the fact that during the Popular Front period in France, the socialist labor ministry was at loggerheads with union workers who were building the World's Fair facilities because the workers had slowed down construction to give themselves more days of employment, expecting that in the slack economy they would become unemployed once the World's Fair was completed. Michael Seidman, *Workers Against Work: Labor in Paris and Barcelona During the Popular Fronts* (Berkeley: University of California Press, 1991), 231-65.

31. Beynon, 299-300.

32. William Serrin, a journalist who lived in Detroit and covered the auto beat, argued in *The Company and the Union* (New York: Random House, 1970) that the UAW leaders had essentially sold out the interests of the membership to maintain their cushy jobs and union stability. Serrin did not cite any union records and appears to have been totally oblivious to the national leadership's role in the 1949 Speed Up Strike and to its defense of the right to stage authorized strikes during collective bargaining sessions. Serrin's thesis is too simplistic and lacks credibility. Nelson Lichtenstein's analysis of Walter Reuther's support/non-support of worker militancy during WWII seems to apply a double standard. At times, Lichtenstein criticizes Reuther for being too timid, too conservative in opposing government wage freezes, etc. But when Reuther backed militant challenges to incentive rates and other policies the rank and file supported, Lichtenstein implies that Reuther was simply trying to garner support within the union for his personal ambitions for higher office. (Lichtenstein, supra n. 25) In the post-1945 years, Reuther did not please the militants who wanted more support for shopfloor challenges to managerial authority. He did not please those who opposed long-term contracts with the auto companies. (Reuther himself admitted that the five year contract with General Motors, signed in 1950, was his biggest blunder.) Reuther and his allies did not please those workers who wanted even higher levels of pay and fringe benefits or the workers who wanted to alleviate unemployment with a shorter work week. He did not please all women and black auto workers many of whom wanted more vigorous anti-discrimination action than the action that was being taken by the UAW national leadership. While auto workers had interests in common as wage earners, they also had so many different views on tactics, and so many different formulations of their basic needs, that no leadership could have consistently pleased the entire UAW membership. Considering this reality, the UAW leadership's overall record looks very good, especially when compared to most other contemporary trade union leaders in the United States.

33. Robert Howard, *Brave New Workplace* (New York: Viking, 1985), 177.

34. B.J. Widick, a shop steward at Chrysler Local 5 in the post-War period, said that in six years he had settled hundreds of grievances on the shopfloor and had filed only one formal, written complaint. George B. Heliker, "Grievance Arbitration in the Automobile Industry: A Comparative Analysis of its History and Results in the Big Three," Ph.D. dissertation, University of Michigan, 1954, 390.

35. See the excellent narrative in Jefferys, 104-15.

36. Arbitration Proceedings, June 14, 1949. These are typed, bound minutes, Box 40, Kenneth Bannon Papers, WRL.

37. Jefferys, 109-10. After 1945, management pressed the UAW to reduce the number and authority of stewards at Ford and GM. Lichtenstein, supra n. 20, believes that if the UAW has resisted this pressure more forcefully, auto workers would have had better working standards. Of course, the UAW might have been smashed by management. See the discussion in n. 20.

38. Ibid., 111. Harris, 148, believes that in 1948 Chrysler's productivity was fifteen percent lower than GM's.

39. Wigderson, 43-59.

40. GM Conference, November 14-15, 1937, 64, op. cit. Box 1, Stuart Strachan Papers.

41. See Nelson Lichtenstein, "Life at the Rouge: A Cycle of Worker Control," in Charles Stephenson and Robert Asher, eds., *Life and Labor: Dimensions of American Working-Class History* (Albany: State University of New York Press, 1986), 237-59.

42. James R. Zetka, Jr., *Militancy, Market Dynamics and Workplace Authority: The Struggle Over Labor Process Outcomes in the U.S. Automobile Industry, 1946 to 1973* (Albany: State University of New York Press, 1995), chapter 9.

43. Based on Robert Asher telephone interview (January 26, 1994) with Irving R. Bluestone, Director UAW GM Department, 1970-1980.

44. Wigderson, 168, 178.

45. Frank James, Memorandum on Production Standards, January 9, 1964, 9, Box 17, Kenneth Bannon Papers; Lichtenstein, supra n. 20, 372, 373, 376.

46. Zetka, 186-187.

47. Ibid., 40, 46.

48. Jefferys, 104-29.

49. Ibid., 143-44.

50. Ibid., 143-44.

51. See testimony of Bernard Wallace, Negro American Labor Council of New Jersey, U.S. Senate, Subcommittee on Employment and Manpower of the Committee on Labor and Public Welfare, *Current Unemployment Situation and Outlook*, 87th Congress, 1st Session, 1961, 147.

52. U.S. House of Representatives, Subcommittee on Unemployment and the Impact of Automation of the Committee on Education and Labor, *General Investigation into Types and Causes of Unemployment*, 87th Congress, 1st session, 1961, 761-79; Lichtenstein, supra n. 20, 377-78; *Los Angeles Times*, September 27, 1964, Box 128, Walter Reuther Papers.

53. Wassily W. Leontief, "The Distribution of Work and Income," *Scientific American* 247 (1982), 188-204.

54. Based on Table 8.1 in Zetka, 191.

55. "Recommendations to Assembly Plant Committee—GM Department," January 20, 1964, Box 17, Kenneth Bannon Papers. The conjecture about the internal developments at Ford is based on David Halberstam, *The Reckoning* (New York: Avon Books, 1986), 222-59.

56. Draft #1, Production Standard Study Committee," memorandum, January 9, 1964; "Established Work Standards and Nail Down Work Standard Agreements in No Later than 60 Days from Model Changeover," brief, July 9, 1964, Box 17, Kenneth Bannon Papers.

57. UAW-FORD NATIONAL NEGOTIATIONS, September 26, 1967, rough minutes, 3, Box 24, Kenneth Bannon Papers; Minutes, UAW Production Standards Study Committee, January 13, 20, 1964, Ibid., Box 17.

58. Ibid., 1-2. Second quote from the brief, "Established Work Standards . . . ," supra, n. 56.

59. James Zetka, chapter 9. Much of the narrative on the next two pages is based on a reading of Zetka's excellent manuscript. It appears that the UAW secured changes in the 1961 contract that inhibited GM's ability to use minor disciplinary actions to intimidate workers to increase their labor effort. See Frank James, supra n. 45, 2-7.

60. These standards could undermine "deals" that local plant managers had cut with auto workers. But they also probably worked a hardship on workers whose plants had special conditions that required different standards if workers were not to be "sweated."

61. GMAD also introduced a large number of robot welders, which displaced labor.

62. In addition to concerns about profit margins, GM was worried about federal anti-trust action. By merging the Chevrolet and Fisher units, GM achieved a tighter structural integration, which would enable it to defend itself against an anti-trust action by arguing that any dissolution of Chevrolet operations would create diseconomies in production. *New York Times, Wall Street Journal,* November 6, 1968.

63. Zetka, 234-237; Jefferys, 86. It has not been possible to determine how many of these strikes were successful.

64. Robert Asher, phone interview (January 26, 1994) with Irving Bluestone, head of the UAW GM Department 1970-1980.

65. Feldman and Betzold, 74.

66. Ibid., 231.

67. Ibid., 201, 242, respectively.

68. Ibid., 95.

69. No analogy is perfect, and we do not mean to suggest that the new management paradigm was similar to the one Aldous Huxley described in *Brave New World.* Note the metaphoric use of Huxley's title in Robert Howard, *Brave New Workplace,* supra n. 30.

70. Robert Asher has interviewed an insurance clerk who reported that the elimination of 7.5 minutes of break time in a small office created such a high level of stress for one third of the workers, all of whom were experienced and had taken pride in their ability to accurately enter insurance claims on computer terminals, that the workers quit. One of the clerks actually had a nervous breakdown. This anecdote demonstrates how even very small respites from high-pressure work are important to the mental health of working people. The clerk worked in a small Connecticut office of one of the nation's largest insurance companies.

71. Michigan Department of Labor, Bureau of Safety and Regulation, *Compensable Occupational Injury and Illness Report*, 1982, 1986, 1990.

72. In his study of Dodge Main, Jefferys reports that during the 1960s older Chrysler workers (mostly white) were able to use seniority to avoid night shift work and to transfer to off-line jobs. Jefferys, 149. For an overall assessment of the benefits auto workers gained from contractual language on job classifications and seniority rights see Richard Herding, *Job Control and Union Structure* (Rotterdam: Rotterdam University Press, 1972) and Robert M. MacDonald, *Collective Bargaining in the Automobile Industry: A Study in Wage and Competitive Relations* (New Haven: Yale University Press, 1963).

73. Mike Parker and Jane Slaughter, *Team Concept* (Boston: South End Press, 1988) 190.

74. Feldman and Betzold, 183.

75. See the excellent account of relations of production at the Mazda Flat Rock plant by Joseph J. Fucini and Suzy Fucini, *Working For The Japanese: Inside Mazda's American Auto Plant* (New York: The Free Press, 1990).

76. Barry Bluestone and Irving Bluestone have argued cogently that if management will genuinely share power with workers, productivity and the quality of work life can be enhanced. The problem, of course, is that most U.S. firms still are reluctant to try this mode of production. *Negotiating the Future: A Labor Perspective on American Business* (New York: Basic Books, 1992).

77. (Boston: South End Press).

78. Parker and Slaughter, 200.

79. Stephen Dandaneau, "Ideology and Dependent Deindustrialization: A Study of Local Responses to Flint, Michigan's Social and Cultural Decline," doctoral dissertation, Brandeis University, 1992, chapter 2.

80. Parker and Slaughter, 207-211.

81. Steve Babson, "Lean or Mean: The MIT Model and Lean Production at Mazda," *Labor Studies Journal* 18 no. 2 (Summer 1993), 3-24.

82. Gary Bryner, taped interview (January 16, 1991) conducted by Robert Asher and Heather Thompson, in interviewers' possession.

83. Compare Bryner's remark to Huw Beynon's conclusion that shop stewards in British factories sought "to obtain at least some control over the decisions that management make." Beynon, 101.

84. Mike Parker, telephone interview with Robert Asher, October 25, 1993

85. In September 1994, 12,000 UAW workers at the GM Buick City complex in Flint, Michigan staged an authorized strike to protest GM's insistence on relatively constant amounts of compulsory overtime. The strikers insisted that GM hire additional workers to reduce the stress on the existing labor force. The required extra work hours had been taking an especially heavy toll—in fatigue, mental stress, and injuries—on the Flint workers, whose average age was 45. The older workers pointed out that they could not bounce back from exhaustion and minor injuries the way they could when they were younger. (The labor force at the auto plants in the Midwest has a much higher average age than the labor force at the new plants that were established in the South in the 1980s. During the 1980s, as the auto manufacturers laid off thousands of workers, older male and female workers, who had the largest amount of accumulated seniority, were able to keep their jobs by "bumping" younger workers.)

The Flint strike came at an inopportune time for GM, since demand for cars was strong. Moreover, the Buick City plants were the sole source of most of the transmissions used by GM cars. Threatened with the loss of product in most of its assembly plants, GM agreed to hire additional workers, who would be permanent employees. GM also promised to hire many of the new workers from the ranks of former GM workers who still live in the Flint area, but had been laid off for such a long time that their seniority rights had expired. This episode illustrates two of the themes emphasized in the text of Chapter 1: the increased stress experienced by many auto workers since the early 1980s and the willingness of the UAW to use militant tactics at strategic moments when strikers can exert significant pressure on their employers. *New York Times,* September 29, October 1, 1994.

Chapter 2

1. Letter from Fred Colvin to Sidney Miller, November 12, 1926. Ford Motor Company Archives, Edison Institute (Hereafter cited as FMC Archives), Acc 96, Dodge Estate, Box 3. It should be noted that there were obvious exceptions to the small auto shop, most important were Oldsmobile and Packard.

2. Allan Nevins and Frank Hill, *Ford: The Times, the Man, and the Company* (New York: Charles Scribner's Sons, 1954), 228. The company later added a second floor to the building. Letter from John W. Anderson to his father, June 4, 1903; FMC Archives, Acc 1, Box 114.

3. For details on the way this assembly group worked see David Hounshell, *From the American System to Mass Production,* (Baltimore: Johns Hopkins University Press, 1984), chapter 6.

4. Joyce Shaw Peterson, *American Automobile Workers* (Albany: State University of New York Press, 1987), 46.

5. The lot was 430 feet by 380 feet and the building, at 402 feet by 56 feet, filled much of it. The architects were Field, Hinchman, and Smith.

6. See Reyner Banham, *A Concrete Atlantis* (Cambridge: MIT Press, 1986) for an excellent discussion of the daylight factory. For a treatment of the shift from belting to motors and industrial electification in general see Warren E. Devine, Jr., "From Shafts to Wires: Historical Perspective on Electrification," *Journal of Economic History,* vol. 43 (June 1983), 347-72.

7. Nevins, *Ford,* 364.

8. Hounshell, 220-22.

9. David L. Lewis, "Ford and Kahn," *Michigan History,* 64 (September/October 1980), 17.

10. On Kahn and reinforced concrete construction see Grant Hildebrand, *Designing for Industry* (Cambridge: MIT Press, 1974); W. Hawkins Ferry, *The Buildings of Detroit* (Detroit: Wayne State University Press, 1980); and Moritz Kahn, *The Design and Construction of Industrial Buildings* (London: Technical Journals, Ltd., 1917).

11. William Vernor Reminiscences, FMC Archives, 3.

12. Philip Foner, *History of the Labor Movement in the United States* (New York: International Publishers, 1965), vol. IV, 385.

13. See David Gartman, *Auto Slavery* (New Brunswick, NJ: Rutgers University Press, 1986) for a discussion of discretion in auto work.

14. Hounshell, 235-37.

15. Horace, L. Arnold and Fay L. Faurote, *Ford Methods and Ford Shops* (New York: The Engineering Magazine Co., 1915), 41-42.

16. During these early Highland Park years the company employed few women. Women worked at clerical jobs in the administration building, in the upholstery shop, and a few in small magneto assembly; none worked at the jobs being describe here. In general, Ford felt that "women had no place in the factory." See Kathleen A. Steeves, "Workers and the New Technology: The Ford Motor Company. Highland Park Plant, 1910-1916," doctoral dissertation, George Washington University, 1987.

17. Nevins, 383; Stephen Meyer, *The Five Dollar Day* (Albany: State University of New York Press, 1981), 10; *Factory Facts from Ford*, 1917.

18. Oliver J. Abell, "Making the Ford Car," *Iron Age* (June 6, 1912), 1384. (Note that Abell wrote a series of articles all under this title for *Iron Age*).

19. Arnold and Faurote, 25; Meyer, 57.

20. Harley Shaiken, Stephen Herzenberg, and Sarah Kuhn, "The Work Process Under More Flexible Production," *Industrial Relations*, vol. 25 (Spring 1986), 175.

21. Abdell, "Making the Ford Car," 1388.

22. Oscar C. Bornholt, "Placing Machines for Sequence of Use," Iron Age (Dec 4, 1913), p. 1276.

23. Oliver J. Abell, "Making the Ford Car," *Iron Age* (December 1913), 1276-77.

24. Arnold and Faurote, 25.

25. Harry Jerome, *Mechanization in Industry* (New York: National Bureau of Economic Research, 1934), 188-90.

26. Meyer, 48; also see Fisher Body Corp, Job descriptions, Mary Van Kleek Collection, Box 32, folder 9, Walter Reuther Library, Wayne State University, for general descriptions and wages of auto workers.

27. Arnold and Faurote, 38.

28. See Hounshell for details on the first moving assembly line. Ford was not the only auto maker experimenting with rationalizing production. See for example, Ronald Edsforth, *Class Conflict and Cultural Consensus* (New Brunswick: Rutgers University Press, 1987), 51-52 for the experiments at Buick contemporaneous with the Ford experiments described here.

29. "Production by Years," FMC Archives, Acc 33, Box 41.

30. Figures based on 1909 and 1914 census, cited in *Iron Age* (February 24, 1916), 499.

31. Arnold and Faurote, 386.

32. Hounshell, p. 247

33. See Meyer, chapter 5 for the introduction of the five dollar day.

34. In 1913, the company had a average workforce of 13,624, it hired 52,445 workers to fill those jobs, and had total quits of 50,448 for the year. In 1914, after the introduction of the five dollar day, the average workforce was 12,116, for which it hired 5,071 workers and had total quits of 6,508. See Kathleen Anderson

Steeves, "Workers and the New Technology, The Ford Motor Company, Highland Park Plant, 1910-1916," PhD Dissertation, George Washington University, 1987, 115.

35. Steeves, 135.

36. Oliver J. Abell, "Making the Ford Motor Car," *Iron Age* (June 13, 1912), 1458.

37. Robert G. Valentine, "The Progressive Relation Between Efficiency and Consent," *Bulletin of the Society to Promote Scientific Management*, vol. 1 (October 1915), 26.

38. The manual handling system was a constant frustration to Ford and his engineers; see Oscar Bornholt, "Placing Machines for Sequence of Use," *Iron Age*, vol. 92 (December 4, 1913), 1276.

39. William Knudsen, "Assembly Department Report," 1914-1915, FMC Archives, ACC 1, Box 122.

40. The building measured 62 feet by 842 feet. By 1914, Julius Kahn, an engineer and the architect's brother, had invented a new type of reinforcing rod used in the new buildings.

41. The upper floors had been made strong enough to accomodate the weight of the foundry and heavy machine tools by the increased strength of reinforced concrete.

42. Arnold and Faurote, 25.

43. *The Ford Man*, January 3, 1918, 1.

44. Oliver J. Abell, "The Making of Men, Motor Cars, and Profits," *Iron Age* (January 7, 1915), 37.

45. "The Manufacturer Much to be Admired," *Automobile Topics*, vol. 45 (February 24, 1917), 254.

46. Meyer, 56.

47. Max Weismyer Reminiscences, FMC Archives.

48. See Hounshell, chapter 6, for argument about the origins of some of these handling devices.

49. Abell, "Making of Men, Motor Cars, and Profits," 41.

50. *Architectural Forum*, vol. 139 (1930), 90.

51. *Ford Industries*, 1924, 13.

52. Henry T. Noyes, "Planning a New Plant," *Annals of the American Academy of Political and Social Science*, vol. 85 (September 1919), 87.

53. *Ford Industries*, 1924,13.

54. John Van Deventer, "Links in a Complete Industrial Chain," *Industrial Management*, vol. 64 (September 1922), 131-32, emphasis in original.

55. *Iron Age* (December 10, 1918), 1520.

56. Letter to D. Boyer from E.G. Liebold, July 25, 1922, FMC Archives, Acc 572, Box 23.

57. Hartley W. Barclay, *Ford Production Methods*, (NY: Harper Brothers, 1936).

58. John Van Deventer, "Mechanical Handling of Coal and Coke," *Industrial Management* (October 1922), 196.

59. John Van Deventer, "Machine Tool Arrangement and Parts Transmission," *Industrial Management* (May 1923), 259.

60. Van Deventer, "Mechanical Handling," 196.

61. Unsigned letter to Charles Sorensen, Aug 2, 1929, FMC Archives, Acc 572, Box 23.

62. Barclay, 100.

63. Van Deventer, "Mechanical Handling," p. 196.

64. John Van Deventer, "Links in a Complete Industrial Chain," p. 133.

65. Barclay, 99.

66. ibid. 133, 95.

67. Bertram Wolfe, *Diego Rivera, His Life and Times* (NY: A. A. Knopf, 1939), p. 313.

Chapter 3

1. Sidney Fine, *Sit-Down: The General Motors Strike of 1936-1937* (Ann Arbor: University of Michigan Press, 1969).

2. Although they were hampered by a cautious banker-dominated General Motors board, Buick division president Walter Chrysler and his team of engineers developed modern mass production techniques and technology in Flint during the same years of the "Fordist" revolution in Detroit. Undoubtedly, the enormous popularity of the Model T, as well as Henry Ford's great passion for self-promotion, help explain why Buick's and Chrysler's role in the early automobile boom have been virtually ignored by most historians. See Ronald Edsforth, *Class Conflict and Cultural Consensus: The Making of a Mass Consumer Society in Flint, Michigan* (New Brunswick: Rutgers University Press, 1986), 50-52; and Walter Chrysler, *Life of an American Workman* (New York: Dodd, Mead, 1950), 135ff.

3. Among the best recent accounts of the "Fordist" revolution in automobile production are David Gartman, *Auto Slavery: The Labor Process in the American Automobile Industry, 1897-1950* (New Brunswick: Rutgers University Press, 1986), 60-127; Stephen Meyer, *The Five Dollar Day: Labor Management and Social Control in the Ford Motor Company*, 1908-1921 (Albany: State University of New York Press, 1981), 9-65; and David Hounshell, *From the American System to Mass Production, 1800-1932* (Baltimore: Johns Hopkins University Press, 1984), 217-61.

4. James J. Flink, *The Automobile Age* (Cambridge: MIT Press, 1988), 66.

5. Gartman, 138.

6. Charles Reitell, "Machinery and Its Effect Upon Workers in the Automotive Industry," *Annals of the American Academy of Political and Social Science*, 116, November 1924, 40; and "The Effects of Technological Changes Upon Occupations in the Motor Vehicle Industry," *Monthly Labor Review*, 34, February 1932, 248.

7. Reitell, 40; Gartman, 135; and Joyce Shaw Peterson, *American Automobile Workers*, 1900- 1933 (Albany: State University of New York Press, 1987), 37.

8. Flink, 229-40.

9. After the Ford Motor Company absorbed a disastrous $250 million dollar loss while abandoning the Model T to completely retool its Detroit factories in 1927, the dominance of frequent styling changes and more flexible forms of mass production was assured; see Hounshell, 263-301. Also see Flink, 240-244; and Stephen Meyer, "The Persistence of Fordism: Workers and Technology in the American Automobile Industry," in *On The Line: Essays in the History of Auto Work*, Nelson Lichtenstein and Stephen Meyer eds. (Urbana: University of Illinois Press, 1989), 81-83.

10. Steve Babson, *Building The Union: Skilled Workers and Anglo-Gaelic Immigrants in the Rise of the UAW* (New Brunswick: Rutgers University Press, 1991), 33-37.

11. Gartman, 135-38; and "The Effects of Technological Change," 249.

12. Peterson, 75-86; Edsforth, 83-85; and Babson, 49-53.

13. Babson, 45.

14. Peterson, 9; and William Ellison Chalmers, "Labor in the Automobile Industry: A Study of Personnel Policies, Workers' Attitudes and Attempts at Unionism" (PhD dissertation, University of Wisconsin 1932), 12-13.

15. In 1929, wages comprised just 27 percent of the value added to product by manufacturing in the big assembly plants, while wages were 54 percent of the value added to product in the body and parts plants. These figures compiled from U.S. Census of Manufacturing data collected by Chalmers, 12-13.

16. Peterson, 57.

17. Nancy Gabin, *Feminism in the Labor Movement: Women and the United Auto Workers*, 1935- 1975 (Ithaca: Cornell University Press, 1990), 13-14.

18. Gabin, 29.

19. Joseph Geschlin, "Method Study Promotes AC Operating Economics," *Automotive Industries*, 80, June 1, 1939, quoted in Gabin, 12. Also see Gartman, 254-57.

20. Although the Ford Rouge plant's management gave a few blacks the opportunity to enter the skilled trades, they still had between 60 percent and 70 percent of their black work force employed in the foundry. See August Meier and Elliott Rudwick, *Black Detroit and the Rise of the UAW* (New York: Oxford University Press, 1979), 5-17; and Flink, 126-28; Peterson 24-29; Gartman, 249-54; Chalmers, 183-87, and "The Labor Market in the Automobile Industry," a WPA National Research Project prepared by Blanche Bernstein dated February 1937, Box 2, Edward Levinson Papers, Walter P. Reuther Library, Wayne State University. (Hereafter cited as WRL).

21. Gartman, 139-41, 247-48; Babson, 57-62; and Peterson, 14-24.

22. "Preliminary Report on the Study of Regularization of Employment and Improvement of Labor Conditions in the Automobile Industry," Research and Planning Division, January 23, 1935, Box 1, Entry 31, Records of the National Recovery Administration, RG 9, National Archives. (Hereafter cited as "Preliminary Report.")

23. (New York 1941), 86.

24. Notes on speedup, interview marked "Rouge," Mimms 2, Robert W. Dunn Papers, WRL.

25. Gartman 141-46; and Chalmers, 100-104 and 168.

26. Sidney Fine, *The Automobile Under the Blue Eagle* (Ann Arbor: University of Michigan Press, 1963), 1-43, 96-141, 231-90.

27. "Automobile Industry—Speedups," Wolman Report, Automobile Labor Board," 1; in Records of the National Recovery Administration, RG 9, Box 5, Entry 39, National Archives. (Hereafter cited as "Automobile Industry—Speedups.")

28. Chalmers,120-29 and 160; and Gartman, 50-51 and 155-159.

29. "Automobile Industry—Speedups," 62.

30. Typed notes of interview with L. W. Haskell, Assistant Manager of Operations, Dodge Plant, Detroit, Michigan, November 6, 1939, Box 10, Edward A. Wieck Papers, WRL.

31. "Preliminary Report," 46.

32. Douglas Reynolds, "Engines of Struggle: Technology, Skill, and Unionization at General Motors, 1930-1940," *Michigan Historical Review*, 15, Spring 1989, 79-83.

33. National Recovery Administration. Research and Planning Division, Hearings in the Matter of Regularizing Employment and Otherwise Improving Conditions of Labor in the Automobile Industry (typed transcripts), Flint, Michigan, 378-86, National Recovery Administration Records, RG 9, National Archives. (Hereafter cited as NRA Hearings). Leon Henderson was the head of the NRA division which conducted this investigation. While the first hearing in Detroit was a public session, subsequent hearings in cities in which there were large auto plants were held behind closed doors. The press and other spectators were barred, and only one worker at a time testified. The purpose of this procedure was to protect workers against retaliation by employers or by other workers. Confidentiality was also expected to encourage candid testimony. NRA Hearings, Flint, Michigan, December 14, 1934, 1.

34. NRA Hearings, Flint, 183-91.

35. *Auto Workers News*, vol. 2, no. 3, July 1928, Robert W. Dunn Papers.

36. Douglas Reynolds, 73-75.

37. NRA Hearings, Flint, December 17, 1934, 120. Amy's testimony was corroborated the next day by Dow Kehler who also worked in Chevy's crankshaft department. NRA Hearings, Flint, December 18, 1934, 399-405.

38. Chalmers, 229.

39. NRA Hearings, Testimony of Harold Paget, Detroit, December 14, 1934, 36-40. In some plants, like those of the Bendix Corporation, problems with the group bonus persisted as late as 1941. UAW Local 9, Minutes, Regular grievance meeting between the bargaining committee and the management held on August 20, 1941, 3-5,11, Box 46, UAW Local 9 Collection, WRL.

40. Ibid., South Bend, Indiana, January 2, 1935, 60-63.

41. Ibid., South Bend, January 2, 1935, 114.

42. Ibid., St. Louis, December 28, 1934, 73-74.

43. Notes on worker interview, Dodge—Dept 68, Hamtramck Plant, Box 2, Robert W. Dunn Papers.

44. NRA Hearings, Detroit, December 16, 1934, 264-65. Smith was then president of the Mechanics Educational Society of America (MESA), a shortlived union of skilled auto workers.

45. NRA Hearings, St. Louis, December 28, 1934, 131-33.

46. Dunn notes, "Speedup," 4, Box 1, Robert W. Dunn Papers.

47. Dunn notes, side 2 of card marked Li 1925 (presumably Lincoln factory, 1925), ibid.

48. Quoted in Kenneth B. West, "'On the Line:' Rank and File Reminiscences of Working Conditions and the General Motors Strike of 1936-37," *Michigan Historical Review*, 12, Spring 1986, 67.

49. "Automobile Industry—Speedups," 9.

50. NRA Hearings, Flint, 163.

51. "Automobile Industry—Speedups," 2.

52. Ibid., 5.

53. "'The Man in the Middle': A Social History of Automobile Industry Foreman," in Lichtenstein and Meyer, 157.

54. UAW Oral History Project interview with F. R. "Jack" Palmer, July 23, 1960, 9, WRL.

55. "General Motors Executive Training Program 1933, Section G, 'Employee Relations,'" Box 16, Henry Kraus Papers, WRL [emphasis added]; and Lichtenstein, "'Man in the Middle,'" 155-63.

56. Interview with Orvel Simmons, February 28, 1980; quoted in West, 71.

57. Quoted in Lichtenstein, "'The Man in the Middle,'" 163.

58. "Automobile Industry—Speedups," 11.

59. Treating Men Like Dirty Dogs," *New York Folklore*, 10, Fall-Winter 1984, 74.

60. *Ford Facts*, July 3, 1948, 6.

61. George S. Hagglund, "Some Factors Contributing to Wisconsin Occupational Injuries," (PhD dissertation, University of Wisconsin, 1966), 94-111, 405-47. During the 1930s the auto companies often speeded up the assembly line during the last hour of the work day.

62. Notes on worker interview, Dodge-Dept 68, Box 2, Robert Dunn Papers.

63. "Automobile Industry—Speedups," 14.

64. Ibid, 22.

65. "Treating Men Like Dirty Dogs," 73.

66. NRA Hearings, St. Louis, December 28, 1934, 98-102.

67. NRA Hearings, Detroit, December 14, 1934, 66.

68. Ibid., St. Louis, December 28, 1934, 27-28.

69. Melvyn Dubofsky, "Not So Turbulent Years: A New Look at the 1930s," in Charles Stephenson and Robert Asher, eds., *Life and Labor: Dimensions of American Working Class History* (Albany: State University of New York Press), 218.

70. Allan Nevins and Frank Hill, *Ford: Expansion and Challenge* (New York: Scribners, 1957), 534; also see Thomas Klug, "Employers' Strategies in the Detroit Labor Market, 1900-1929," in Lichtenstein and Meyer, 48-51; and Bernstein, "The Labor Market in the Automobile Industry," supra n. 20.

71. "Automobile Industry—Speedups," 11, [emphasis added].

72. "Preliminary Report," 52.

73. Typed minutes of negotiations, Mr. Kelley's Case, Dept. 996L., Mr. Heistler's Case, Dept. 996L, Box 5, Henry Kraus Papers.

74. "Automobile Industry—Speedups," 4.

75. UAW Oral History Project interview, June 1, 1961, 5-6.
76. "Automobile Industry—Speedups," 44.
77. Kenneth G. Bannon, UAW Oral History Project interview,1963, 2-3, WRL.
78. "Automobile Industry—Speedups," 78.
79. NRA Hearings, Detroit, December 14, 1934, 31-35.
80. Interviewed by James R. McDonnell, quoted in "Treating Men Like Dirty Dogs," 74.
81. Frank Marquart, *An Auto Worker's Journal* (University Park: Pennsylvania State University Press, 1975,) 78.
82. NRA Hearings, Detroit, December 14, 1934, 125-32.
83. "On the Assembly Line," *Atlantic Monthly*, 159, 4, April 1937, 427. All subsequent quotes from Richard are from this article, 424-28 [emphases added].
84. Lifton's called this coping strategy/psychological condition "psychic numbing," and he inferred it was a common among survivors of traumatic experiences. Of course, this analogy between Depression era auto workers and Vietnam combat veterans is merely suggestive. *See Home From the War, Vietnam Veterans: Neither Victims nor Executioners* (New York: Simon and Schuster, 1973), esp. 346-66.
85. Richard, 425.
86. *Wartime: Understanding and Behavior in the Second World War* (New York: Oxford University Press, 1989), 95.
87. Fine, 103-7, 120-25.
88. Stenographic Report—Automobile Labor Board Hearing on Fisher Body Corporation, Detroit, December 16, 1934 4, Everett Francis Papers, WRL.
89. The best account of the upsurge of militant workers is Sidney Fine, supra n. 1.
90. *My Years with General Motors* (Garden City: Doubleday, 1964), 406.
91. NRA, Preliminary Report, 5-7.
92. At Chrysler's Dodge Main plant, job security issues constituted five of the six main demands pressed by the UAW in February 1937. "Chrysler Demands," February 17, 1939, UAW Press Release, March 2, 1937, Box 11, Kraus Papers, WRL. Chrysler's rejection of these demands led to the largest sit-down strike in American history (March 8). The strike gained Chrysler workers straight seniority rights and a work sharing plan. "Agreement Entered Into On This Sixth Day of April, 1937, Between The Chrysler Corporation And the International Union, United Automobile Workers of America," "Agreement Entered Into on This 14th Day of April...", Box 6, John Zaremba Papers, WRL. Hudson Motor Company workers made similar seniority demands in March 1937. UAW Press Release, March 9, 1937, Box 4, Frank Marquart Papers, WRL. The details of organizing and bargaining over these issues are discussed in Raymond Boryczka's long, unpublished essay, "'For Recognition as Human Beings:' The Multifaced Quest of Detroit Auto Workers, 1936-1936."
93. UAW Oral History Project interview, August 8, 1960, 3.
94. Quoted in Carl Gersuny and Gladdis Kaufman, "Seniority and the Moral Economy of U.S. Automobile Workers, 1934-1946," *Journal of Social History*, 18, 3, 1985, 468.

95. "Seniority and the Moral Economy," 464. The struggle to breakdown racial discrimination in job classification and seniority lists is described in August Meier and Elliott Rudwick, *Black Detroit and the Rise of the UAW* (New York: Oxford University Press, 1979), 108-74; separate seniority lists for men and women and protests against such gender discrimination before 1941 are described in Gabin, 36-41.

96. UAW Oral History Project interview, August 4, 1960, WRL, 50-51; and Nelson Lichtenstein, "'The Man in the Middle'," 169-81.

97. Everett Francis, UAW Oral History Project interview, October 13-27, 1961, 37 WRL.

98. Gartman, *Auto Slavery*, 264-65. Also see Nelson Lichtenstein, "Auto Worker Militancy and the Structure of Factory Life, 1937-1955," *Journal of American History*, 67, 2, September 1980, 337-40.

99. *Feminism in the Labor Movement*, 20-27.

100. *The Emergence of a UAW Local 1936-1939: A Study in Class and Culture* (Pittsburgh: University of Pittsburgh Press, 1975), 97-98.

101. *"Stalin Over Wisconsin": The Making and Unmaking of Militant Unionism, 1900-1950* (New Brunswick: Rutgers University Press, 1992), 110; and Jefferys, "'Matters of Mutual Interest", in *On the Line*, 114-19.

102. For example see Shop Committee Minutes, January 13, March 31, November 10, December 12, 1938 in Box 1, GM Local 25 Collection, WRL.

103. UAW Local 212 Executive Board Minutes, April 30, May 1, 1937, Box 24, Local 212 Collection, WRL; Margaret Collingwood Nowak, *Two Who Were There: A Biography of Stanley Nowak* (Detroit: Wayne State University Press, 1989), 103-15.

104. Minutes of Bargaining Committee Meeting, October 30, 1940, in Box 8; and "Union Statement of Unadjusted Grievance, Case No.15, February 25, 1941, RE: Appeal Cases No. 13, 14, and 15," Box 2, Local 25 Collection.

105. Negotiating Minutes, 1938, 473-77, Box 35, UAW Local 212 Collection. [emphasis added].

106. Ray Boryczka, "Militancy and Factionalism in the United Automobile Workers Union, 1937- 1941," *Maryland Historian*, 8, Fall 1977; and Babson, *Building the Union*, 231-35.

107. Proceedings, General Motors Department Conference, November 14-15, 1937, in Folder 16, Box 18, Walter Reuther Papers.

108. Typed interview notes, Box 10, Edward A. Wieck Papers.

Chapter 4

1. U.S. Congress, Senate, Special Committee Investigating the National Defense Program, *Hearings* (Washington, D.C.: Government Printing Office, 1945), 13305-54. See also the *Detroit Free Press*, March 11, 1945.

2. Special Investigating Committee, *Hearings*, 13347-54.

3. Alan Clive, *State of War: Michigan in World War II* (Ann Arbor: University of Michigan Press, 1979), 75; Special Investigating Committee, Hearings,13237-38.

4. For the traditional view, see Joel Seidman, *American Labor from Defense to Reconversion* (Chicago: University of Chicago Press, 1953), 142. The more recent interpretation can be found in James Green, "Fighting on Two Fronts: Working Class Militancy in the 1940s," *Radical America* 9 (July-August 1975), 7-47; Ed Jennings, "Wildcat! The Wartime Strike Wave in Auto," *Radical America* 9 (July-August 1975),77-113; Martin Glaberman, *Wartime Strikes: The Struggle Against the No-Strike Pledge in the UAW During World War II* (Detroit: Bewick Editions, 1980); Nelson Lichtenstein, *Labor's War at Home: The CIO in World War II* (Cambridge: Cambridge University Press, 1982), 117-15; Lichtenstein, "Auto Worker Militancy and the Structure of Factory Life, 1937-1955," *Journal of American History* 67 (September 1980), 335-53; Lichtenstein, "Conflict Over Workers' Control: The Automobile Industry in World War II," in Michael Frisch and Daniel Walkowitz, eds., *Working Class America: Essays on Labor, Community and American Society* (Urbana: University of Illinois Press, 1983); and Lichtenstein, "The Making of the Postwar Working Class: Cultural Pluralism and Social Structure in World War II," *The Historian* 51 (November 1988), 42-63. For a penetrating critique of this view, see Joshua Freeman, "Delivering the Goods: Industrial Unionism during World War II," *Labor History* 19 (Fall 1978), 570-93. For an interesting comparison of the English and American post-war factory regimes, see Steven Tolliday and Jonathan Zeitlin, "Shop Floor Bargaining, Contract Unionism, and Job Control: An Anglo-American Comparison," in Lichtenstein and Stephen Meyer, eds., *On the Line: Essays in the History of Auto Work* (Urbana: University of Illinois, 1989), 219-44.

5. On the bureaucratization of the UAW, see the works by Glaberman, Lichtenstein, Green, and Jennings, previously cited. Lichtenstein, "The Making of the Postwar Working Class," focuses particularly on the wartime patriotic fervor. Gary Gerstle, *Working Class Americanism: The Politics of Labor in a Textile City, 1914-1960* (Cambridge: Cambridge University Press, 1989), 279-318, effectively applies the cultural pluralist argument to the textile workers of Woonsocket, Rhode Island.

6. For information on the Workers Party, Glaberman, *Wartime Strikes*, 76-81; Lichtenstein, *Labor's War at Home*, 194; Maurice Isserman, *If I Had a Hammer: The Death of the Old Left and the Birth of the New Left* (New York: Basic Books, 1987), 44-50, and the WP's newspaper, *Labor Action*. Gerstle, *Working Class Americanism*, 5-15.

7. Clive, *State of War*, 18-34; Lichtenstein, "Conflict Over Workers' Control," 29.

8. See, for example, Stephen Meyer III, *The Five Dollar Day: Labor Management and Social Control in the Ford Motor Company, 1908-1921* (Albany: State University of New York Press, 1981), pp. 9-65; David Gartman, *Auto Slavery: The Labor Process in the American Automobile Industry, 1897-1950* (New Brunswick: Rutgers University Press, 1986), 39-257; and Joyce Shaw Peterson, American Automobile Workers, 1900-1933 (Albany: State University of New York Press, 1987), 30-107. The workers' spouse is quoted in Sidney Fine, *Sit-Down: The General Motors Strike of 1936-1937* (Ann Arbor: University of Michigan Press, 1969), 56.

9. Supra, n. 7.

10. Stanley Mathewson, *Restriction of Output Among Unorganized Workers* (New York: Viking Press, 1931); Meyer, *Five Dollar Day*, 86-89; Gartman, *Auto Slavery*, 155-61; Peterson, *Automobile Workers*, 97-99; and David Montgomery, *Workers' Control in America: Studies in the History of Work, Technology, and Labor Struggles* (Cambridge: Cambridge University Press, 1979), 40-44.

11. Mathewson, *Restriction of Output*, 3; Frank Marquart, *An Auto Worker's Journal: The UAW from Crusade to One-Party Union* (University Park: The Pennsylvania University Press, 1975), 24.

12. On the auto industry's employment practices, see Thomas Klug, "Employers' Strategies in the Detroit Labor Market, 1900-1929," in Lichtenstein and Meyer, eds., *On the Line*, 42-72. Marquart, *Auto Workers' Journal*, 15, describes the rank-and-filers' attack on the suspected radical. The white auto workers' enforcement of the color line is detailed in Lloyd Bailer, "Negro Labor in the Automobile Industry," Ph.D. Dissertation, University of Michigan, 1943, 78-81. Bailer notes that the color line differed from plant to plant. "...everywhere there was an arbitrary limit beyond which they [black workers] could not go. In drop forge shops a negro could be a helper but never a hammerman. In stamping departments, he was a trucker but had no chance to be a press operator. It was not a question of lack of ability—it was simply that "Negroes can't work on presses' was part of plant policy."

13. David Montgomery, 4; Fine, *Sit-Down*, 56; Lichtenstein, "Auto Worker Militancy," p. 338; Kevin Boyle, "Rite of Passage: The 1939 General Motors Tool and Die Strike," *Labor History* 27 (Spring 1986), 194.

14. On the importance of unionization for the formalization of work rules see, for example, Studs Terkel, *Hard Times: An Oral History of the Great Depression* (New York: Pantheon Books, 1970), 129, from which this quote is taken; Philip A. Korth and Margaret R. Beegle, *I Remember Like Today: The Auto-Lite Strike of 1934* (East Lansing: Michigan State University Press, 1988), 192-207; Ronald Edsforth, *Class Conflict and Cultural Consensus: The Making of a Mass Consumer Society in Flint, Michigan* (New Brunswick: Rutgers University Press, 1987), 164-66; and Robert H. Zieger, "Toward the History of the CIO: A Bibliographic Report," *Labor History* 26 (Summer 1985), 506. For an insightful evaluation of work rules — particularly seniority — see Ronald W. Schatz, *The Electrical Workers: A History of Labor at General Electric and Westinghouse, 1923-1960* (Urbana: University of Illinois Press, 1983), 105-61.

15. Charles K. Hyde, *Detroit: An Industrial History Guide* (Detroit: Detroit Historical Society, 1980) 21; Steve Jefferys, *Management and Managed: Fifty Years of Crisis at Chrysler* (Cambridge: Cambridge University Press, 1986), 49-87; Steve Babson, *Working Detroit: The Making of a Union Town* (New York: Adama Books, 1984), 80-86.

16. Grievance records for 1940-1941, no box number [unprocessed collection], Local 7 Collection, WRL. I have estimated the number of workers involved in the grievance procedure by assuming that each department filing a grievance had no more than ten workers. This was an arbitrary figure: many departments undoubtedly employed many more hands.

17. Grievance records for 1940-1941, Local 7 Collection.

18. Carl Gersuny and Gladis Kaufman, "Seniority and the Moral Economy of U.S. Automobile Workers, 1934-1946," *Journal of Social History* 18 (Spring 1985), 463-475; Irving Howe, "The Tradition of Reutherism: An Interview with Brendan Sexton," *Dissent* 19 (Winter 1972), 56.

19. *United Automobile Worker* [Local 7 edition], July 15, 1942; Survey of War Production in Detroit area, May 1943; R.J. Thomas to Harry Truman, June 9, 1945; and UAW Research Department questionnaire, April 1943, all in Box 11, UAW Research Department Collection, Walter Reuther Library. The literature on changing gender relations in the wartime auto industry is particularly rich. See, for example, Ruth Milkman, *Gender at Work: The Dynamics of Job Segregation by Sex During World War II* (Urbana: University of Illinois Press, 1987); and Nancy Gabin, *Feminism in the Labor Movement: Women and the United Auto Workers, 1935-1975* (Ithaca: Cornell University Press, 1990) 47-100. The literature on the black experience in auto during World War II has not been treated as thoroughly. August Meier and Elliot Rudwick, *Black Detroit and the Rise of the UAW* (New York: Oxford University Press, 1979) is a reasonable starting place, but is not focused on shopfloor relations. For more general works, see Robert O. Weaver, *Negro Labor, A National Problem* (New York: Harcourt, Brace and Company, 1946); Philip Foner, *Organized Labor and the Black Worker, 1619-1973* (New York: Praeger, 1974); and William Harris, *The Harder We Run: Black Workers Since the Civil War* (New York: Oxford University Press, 1982).

20. Grievance records for 1942-1945, Local 7 Collection; Seidman, 109-30; Richard Polenberg, *War and Society: The United States, 1941-1945* (Philadelphia: J.B. Lippincott Company, 1972), 22-26.

21. Grievance records for 1942-1945, Local 7 Collection.

22. Loc. cit.

23. On the volatility of disciplinary grievances, see Lichtenstein, "Conflict over Workers' Control," 295. The data is derived from 1942-1945 grievance records, Local 7 Collection.

24. UAW Research Department February 1943 postcard survey, Box 14, UAW Research Department Collection. The Research Department mailed 4,000 postcards to a random selection of UAW members from twenty Detroit-area locals. Each postcard contained a series of printed questions and space for comments. Since only a fraction of the 4,000 members returned the postcards, the survey does not reflect the attitude of the rank-and-file as a whole. Rather, it reflects the most motivated segment of the sample. The survey nevertheless, offers a rare opportunity to examine the opinions of ordinary UAW members.

25. Special Investigating Committee, *Hearings*, 13104.

26. Ibid., pp. 13579-80. When management confronted the welders, the hands changed their tactics. Rather than wandering around the plant, they remained at their work stations, but did not increase their hourly production. The company retaliated by replacing the workers with mechanical welders.

27. Ibid., 13576, 13605.

28. Ibid., 13455-56, 13590, 13594.

29. Studs Terkel, *The Good War: An Oral History of World War II* (New York: Ballantine Books, 1984), 107; Special Investigating Committee, Hearings, 13588. A number of historians have argued that the influx of new, often Southern-

born, workers undermined the UAW's militancy, since many of these workers had no previous union experience. Wartime migration statistics cast some doubt on that argument. For example, two-thirds of the white migrants to Willow Run, perhaps the archetypal wartime community, came from the Northeast and Midwest, whereas only 30 percent came from the South. See Lowell Juilliard Carr and James Edson Stermer, *Willow Run* (New York: Arno Press, 1977 [first published in 1952]), 359.

30. UAW Research Department postcard survey, February 1943, Box 14, UAW Research Department Collection.

31. Loc. cit.

32. William H. Sewell, Jr., *Work and Revolution in France: The Language of Labor from the Old Regime to 1848* (Cambridge: Cambridge University Press, 1980), 5-13.

33. Mathewson, *Restriction of Output*, 72-75.

34. Jefferys, *Management and Managed*, pp. 72-73; Gerald Markowitz and David Rosner, *"Slaves of the Depression": Workers' Letters About Life on the Job* (Ithaca: Cornell University Press, 1987), 161-162; Kenneth B. West, " 'On the Line': Rank-and-File Reminiscences of Working Conditions and the General Motors Sit-Down Strike of 1936-1937," *Michigan Historical Review* 12 (Spring 1986), 82.

35. Meyer, The Five Dollar Day, 77; U.S. Congress, House, Select Committee Investigating National Defense Migration, *Hearings* (Washington, D.C.: Government Printing Office, 1941), 7355. Peter Friedlander, *The Making of a UAW Local, 1936-1939: A Study in Class and Culture* (Pittsburgh: University of Pittsburgh Press, 1975) details the crucial role played by second generation Poles in the UAW's organizational drive. On the Americanization of the second generation, see John Bukowcyzk, *And My Children Did Not Know Me: A History of the Polish-Americans* (Bloomington: Indiana University Press, 1987) 65-84. Bukowczyk explains the assimilationist trend among second-generation Polish-Americans. "Out of the flesh-and-blood lives that they had grown for themselves in America," he writes, "the aging immigrants and their growing sons and daughters were forging a new cultural synthesis. They fused cultural practices and forms brought over from the `old country' with a raft of Americanisms that had come into their daily lives, like Democratic voting patterns or American recreations such as baseball and pool." This is not to say that second generation workers abandoned the cultural traditions of their parents. For a fascinating analysis of the immigrant tradition's impact on workers, see John Bodnar, *Workers' World: Kinship, Community, and Protest in an Industrial Society, 1900-1940* (Baltimore: Johns Hopkins University Press, 1982).

36. Thomas Gobel, "Becoming American: Ethnic Workers and the Rise of the CIO," *Labor History* 29 (Spring 1988), 173-98; Babson, Working Detroit, 86; Warner Pflug, *The UAW in Pictures* (Detroit: Wayne State University, 1971), 45-62; Jefferys, *Management and Managed*, 73; Fine, *Sit-Down*, 215.

37. On the New Deal's contribution to the labor movement, see, for example, the various interpretations offered in Irving Bernstein, *Turbulent Years: A History of the American Worker* (Boston: Houghton Mifflin, 1970); David Brody, *Workers in Industrial America: Essays on the Twentieth Century Struggle* (New

York: Oxford University Press, 1980), 105- 12, 138-46, and Steve Fraser, "The
`Labor Question'," in Fraser and Gary Gerstle, eds., *The Rise and Fall of the New
Deal Order* (Princeton: Princeton University Press, 1989), 55-84. The conservatives quoted are Senators Hiram Johnson of California and Allen Ellender of
Louisiana, quoted in Fine, *Sit Down*, 334. Robert Zieger, *American Workers,
American Unions, 1920-1985* (Baltimore: Johns Hopkins University Press, 1986),
59-60 discusses FDR's condemnation of the CIO; and Lichtenstein, *Labor's War
at Home*, 47-48, details attacks on the Wagner Act. It is important to note that the
New Deal era National Labor Relations Board believed that union rights were not
inherent rights but rather "new" rights, established by statute. See Christopher L.
Tomlins, *The State and the Unions: Labor Relations, Law, and the Organized
Labor Movement in America, 1880-1960* (Cambridge: Cambridge University
Press, 1985), 187.

    38. R.J. Thomas, "President's Column," *United Automobile Worker*
[National Edition], February 1, 1941. For similar sentiments, see UAW-CIO,
Proceedings of the Fifth Annual Convention (July 29-August 6, 1940), 9.

    39. Barton J. Bernstein, "The Automobile Industry and the Coming of the
Second World War," *Southwestern Social Science Quarterly* 47 (June 1966), 22-
33. Also see Bruce Catton, *The War Lords of Washington* (New York: Harcourt,
Brace and Company, 1948), 58-60.

    40. For a transcript of the Reuther plan, see Henry Christman, ed., *Walter P.
Reuther: Selected Papers* (New York: MacMillan, 1961), 1-12. The Ford signs
can be seen in Pflug, *The UAW in Pictures*, 87-89.

    41. Lichtenstein, *Labor's War at Home*, 49-51, 54-55; Clive, *State of War*,
58; grievance records, Local 7 Collection.

    42. George Gallup, *The Gallup Poll: Public Opinion 1935-1971*, vol. I (New
York: Random House, 1972), 243, 257. Only 27 percent of those polled in
January 1941 thought unions should have the right to strike firms working on
defense contracts. Lichtenstein, *Labor's War at Home*, 60-61; Samuel Rosenman,
ed., *The Public Papers and Addresses of Franklin D. Roosevelt, 1941* (New York:
Harper and Brothers, 1950), 181-94.

    43. Lichtenstein, *Labor's War at Home*, 57-63; R.J. Thomas, "President's
Column," *United Automobile Worker* [National Edition], June 15, 1941. 44.
United Automobile Worker [Local 7 edition], November 15, 1941; *United
Automobile Worker* [National Edition], December 1, 1941. 45. For a copy of the
Equality of Sacrifice program, see United Automobile Worker [National Edition],
April 15, 1942. The UAW Local 600 officials are quoted in their newspaper, *Ford
Facts*, December 17, 1941.

    46. UAW Research Department postcard survey, February 1943, Box 14,
UAW Research Department Collection.

    47. *Dodge Main News*, November 15, 1941; *Ford Facts*, March 15, 1943;
United Automobile Worker [National edition], July 15, 1942 and December 15,
1942; *United Automobile Worker* [Local 212 edition], January 1, 1943. According
to the UAW Research Department, 90 percent of UAW members had some family member in the armed forces by 1944. See Analysis of Causes of Labor-
Management Conflict in the Auto and Aircraft Industries, July 6, 1944, Box 14,
UAW Research Department Collection.

48. Lichtenstein, *Labor's War at Home*, 89.

49. For details on the administration's mobilization policy after Pearl Harbor, see Polenberg, *War and Society*, 9-14. Nelson's quote is from his book, *Arsenal of Democracy: The Story of American War Production* (New York: Harcourt Brace and Company, 1946), 208-9.

50. *Wall Street Journal*, December 18, 1941; *Detroit News*, December 18, 1941 and April 22, 1941; Survey of UAW Detroit plants, Box 9, UAW War Policy Division, ALHUA; UAW employment questionnaire, 1942, Box 30, UAW Research Department Collection.

51. The industry employment statistics can be found in U.S. Bureau of Labor Statistics, *Monthly Labor Review* 55 (Spring, 1942), 634. Among the plants reportedly hoarding labor were the Briggs Aircraft plant, Chevrolet Gear and Axle, Chrysler Jefferson Assembly, Ford Rouge and Highland Park plants, and Ternstedt. See Report on Labor Utilization, February-March 1943, Box 11, Folder 4, UAW Research Department collection. Tool and Die Maker Bronson Parrett made his comments to FDR in an August 14, 1942 letter, Box 29, UAW War Policy Collection, WRL.

52. Nelson Lichtenstein, "The Man in the Middle': A Social History of Automobile Industry Spokesmen," in Lichtenstein and Meyer, *On the Line*, pp. 169-170; *United Automobile Worker* [Local 7 Edition], May 15, 1942; UAW employment questionnaire, Box 30, UAW Research Department Collection.

53. Memorandum on the relations of Ford Local 600, UAW-CIO with U.S. Army Officers Stationed in the Detroit Area, February 9, 1942, Box 31, UAW War Policy Division Collection.

54. For details on the corporations' advertising campaigns, see James Tobin, "Why we Fight: Versions of the American Purpose in World War II," Ph.D. dissertation, University of Michigan, 1986, 142-77. The tool and die workers' quote is from *United Automobile Worker* [Tool, Die and Engineering Edition], December 1, 1941.

55. Lichtenstein, *Labor's War*, 73; typescript results of UAW survey, n.d. [1942], Box 30, UAW Research Department Collection.

56. UAW Research Department postcard survey, February 1943, Box 14, UAW Research Department Collection.

57. Grievance # 1197, February 26, 1942, Local 7 Collection.

58. UAW Research Department postcard survey, February 1943, Box 14, UAW Research Department Collection.

59. Glaberman, *Wartime Strikes*, 42-44; Lichtenstein, *Labor's War at Home*, 119-121; Oral History Interview of Jess Ferrazza, May 26, 1961, ALHUA; UAW Research Department postcard survey, Box 14, UAW Research Department Collection.

60. For a typical example of the UAW leadership's rhetoric in 1942, see R. J. Thomas' comments in the *New York Times*, September 8, 1942. Insisting that the War Production Board needed a "transfusion from the energetic labor movement," Thomas charged that the WPB "has been ... staffed by men who believe the war should be prosecuted with sensitive regard for the traditional proprietary interests of our great corporations. Labor does not demand the destruction of own-

ership or management," Thomas insisted. "Labor demands only that all groups subordinate their every interest to the sole purpose of winning the war."

61. Special Investigating Committee, Hearings, 13603. For a partial but more detailed record of wildcats at Chrysler during the period, see Robert Conder to R. J. Thomas, December 13, 1944 and April 16, 1945, both in Box 19, R. J. Thomas Collection, WRL.

62. Lichtenstein, *Labor's War at Home*, 121; grievance # 225, September 11, 1943, Box 2, UAW Chrysler Department Collection, WRL.

63. Grievance # 225, Box 2, UAW Chrysler Department Collection, WRL.

64. Special Investigating Committee, *Hearings*, 13575-13609.

65. Bailer, "Negro Labor in the Automobile Industry," p. 58; Meier and Rudwick, *Black Detroit and the Rise of the UAW*, 166-69. For a partial list of other, less well-known hate strikes, see G. James Fleming to Jack Raskin, July 20, 1943, Box 54, Civil Rights Congress of Michigan Collection, WRL. On race relations in Detroit in general, see Dominic Capeci, Jr., *Race Relations in Wartime Detroit: The Sojourner Truth Housing Controversy of 1942* (Philadelphia: Temple University Press, 1984). Many analysts point out that the "hate strike" wave ended with the Packard walk-out and that plant-level race relations remained calm throughout the rest of the war. It should be noted, however, that the racial hatred of the Packard strike spilled into the streets of Detroit shortly thereafter, when rioting broke out in the city. Recent research suggests that auto workers were well represented among the rioters. See Dominic Capeci, Jr., and Martha Wilkerson, "The Detroit Riot of 1943: A Reinterpretation," Michigan *Historical Review* 16 (Spring 1990), 49-72. Hate strikes occurred sporadically well into the 1950s. See Kevin Boyle, "There Are No Union Sorrows That the Union Can't Heal: The Struggle For Racial Equality in the United Automobile Workers, 1940- 1965," *Labor History* (forthcoming). In contrast, male auto workers did not stage hate strikes to protest the upgrading of women workers into previously "male" job categories. Since both the UAW and management made it clear that women workers would keep their jobs only for the duration of the war, the promotion of women did not pose a threat to shopfloor tradition. See Ruth Milkman, "Rosie the Riveter Revisited: Management's Postwar Purge of Women Automobile Workers," in Lichtenstein and Meyer, *On the Line*, 144.

66. According to the company records made available to the Senate Special Investigating Committee, conflicts over wages, seniority, safety, and upgrading accounted for one third of Chrysler's 1944 walk-outs, while conflicts over discipline accounted for another third. It is impossible to know how many of the disciplinary wildcats were in fact conflicts over production standards and other shopfloor traditions. Work pace issues accounted for only 25 percent of the company's wildcats in the latter half of 1944, however. It seems reasonable to assume that the same pattern held for the first part of the year. See Special Investigating Committee, Hearings, 13603, and Robert Condor to R.J. Thomas, December 13, 1944, Box 19, R.J. Thomas Collection. Unfortunately, neither of these documents details the most important statistic: man-hours lost in each strike. The UAW Research Department also compiled a list of wildcats but it seems woefully incomplete. See Box 32, UAW Research Department Collection.

67. Jefferys, *Management and Managed*, 94; *United Automobile Worker* [Local 3 Edition], March 15, 1943.

68. Minutes of the UAW International Executive Board meeting, June 12, 1943, Box 2, R.J. Thomas Collection. Jefferys, *Management and Managed*, 94-95, argues that the Chrysler wildcat began at Dodge Main, then spread to the Jefferson Avenue facility. Steven Babson and Dave Elsila, *Union Town: A Labor History Guide to Detroit* (Detroit: Workers Educational Local 189, n.d. [1979-80?]), 22, on the other hand, argues that Local 7, the home local of UAW president R.J. Thomas, never experienced a wartime wildcat. The evidence indicates that both Jefferys and Babson are incorrect.

69. Minutes of the June 12, 1943 Executive Board meeting, Box 2, R.J. Thomas Collection; Jefferys, *Management and Managed*, 94.

70. Lichtenstein, *Labor's War at Home*, 130, portrays the strike as an "official" wildcat, organized and staged by the local leadership. For the views of management, union officials, and rank—and-filers, see the *Detroit News*, May 20-21, 1943.

71. *Detroit News*, May 22, 1943; *Detroit Times*, May 21, 1943; U.S. Congress, 78th Congress, 1st Session, *Congressional Record* vol. 89, (Washington, D.C.: Government Printing Office, 1943), 5315-16, 5322.

72. *Labor Action*, May 31, 1943; Jefferys, *Management and Managed*, 94-95; Minutes of the June 12, 1943 Executive Board meeting, Box 2, R.J. Thomas collection; *Detroit News*, May 24, 1943. In particular, LaMotte accused UAW Vice President Walter Reuther and his supporters of organizing the strike, a charge the leadership of Locals 3 and 7 vehemently denied.

73. *Detroit News*, May 24, 1943. The UAW leadership's inability to correct management abuses is nicely detailed in the UAW officers' report, "Analysis of Causes of Labor-Management Conflict in the Auto and Aircraft Industries," July 6, 1944, Box 14, UAW Research Department Collection.

74. Lichtenstein, "Conflict Over Workers Control," 295, estimates the number of auto workers involved in wildcats. The knowledgeable observer is A.H. Raskin, the *New York Times'* labor reporter, then serving with the army's Industrial Services Division. He is quoted in Lichtenstein, "Auto Worker Militancy," 335. The continued wildcat wave touched off a bitter factional fight within the UAW leadership over the no-strike pledge. The conflict is ably detailed in Lichtenstein, *Labor's War at Home*, 194-97, 214-15.

75. Lichtenstein, *Labor's War at Home*, 221-22; United Automobile Worker [National Edition], September 15, 1945.

76. Barton Bernstein, "Walter Reuther and the General Motors Strike of 1945-1946," *Michigan History* 49 (September 1965), 265-77; Martin Halpern, *UAW Politics in the Cold War Era* (Albany: State University of New York Press, 1988), 51-93; Lichtenstein, *Labor's War at Home*, 224-30; John Barnard, *Walter Reuther and the Rise of the Auto Workers* (Boston: Little, Brown and Company, 1983), 101-9; Pflug, *UAW in Pictures*, 108-9; Dave Elsila, ed., *We Make Our Own History: A Portrait of the UAW* (Detroit: United Automobile Workers, 1986), 48-51. The strike settlement fell far short of Reuther's sweeping demands. The UAW settled for an 18 1/2 cent pay raise — far short of the 30 percent increase Reuther had demanded — with no mention of automobile pricing policy

77. See, for example, Lichtenstein, "Auto Worker Militancy," 350-52; Lichtenstein, "From Corporatism to Collective Bargaining: Organized Labor and the Eclipse of Social Democracy in the Postwar Era," in Fraser and Gerstle, eds.,

Rise and Fall of the New Deal Order, 132- 33; Edsforth, *Class Conflict*, 202-19; and Halpern, *UAW Politics*, 76-79, 249-63.

78. Jefferys, *Management and Managed*; Ben Hamper, *Rivethead: Tales From the Assembly Line* (New York: Warner Books, 1991). For other discussions of the continuing practice of informal production slow downs in the postwar era, see Leonard Sayles, *Behavior of Industrial Work Groups: Production and Control* (New York: John Wiley and Sons, 1958); Charles Walker and Robert Guest, *The Man on the Assembly Line* (Cambridge: Harvard University Press, 1952);, Donald Roy, "Efficiency and the Fix," *American Journal of Sociology* 60 (November 1954), 255-65.

Chapter 5

1. Ken Bannon's notes for 1955 contract negotiations, Ken Bannon Papers, Box 42, Folder 10, Walter Reuther Library, Wayne State University. (The Reuther library will be cited as WRL.)

2. This term was coined by Richard Edwards in *Contested Terrain: The Transformation of the Workplace in the Twentieth Century* (New York: Basic Books, 1979).

3. Between March and August 1939, Chrysler management tried to push the weakened UAW to accept a 20 percent speedup at the pivotal Dodge Main plant in Detroit. Since Chrysler had not signed a national contract, Dodge Main stewards were legally free to stage strategic slowdown (September 1939) in two departments of the plant. When Dodge fired 105 of the workers involved in the slowdown, opposition to Chrysler's speedup jelled, with the Dodge workers voting 13,751-1,324 to strike on October 12. On November 29, Chrysler capitulated, rescinding part of speedup, and recognizing the rights of shop stewards to leave their jobs to present worker grievance, on November 29. This strike marked the beginning of an odd labor relations pattern at Chrysler. Management attempts to violate contracts and to speed up production were met with militant strikes at a given plant, followed by management retreats, largely determined by the fear of losing market share if production was down for a long period of time. Raymond Boryczka, "Militancy and Factionalism in the United Auto Workers Union, 1937-1941," *Maryland Historian* 8 (Fall 1977); Steve Babson, *Building the Union: Skilled Autoworkers and Anglo-Gaelic Immigrants in the Rise of the UAW* (New Brunswick: Rutgers University Press, 1991), 231-35; and Steve Jefferys, *Management and Managed: Fifty Years of Crisis at Chrysler* (Cambridge: Cambridge University Press, 1987).

4. Howell J. Harris, *The Right to Manage: Industrial Relations Policies of American Business in the 1940s* (Madison: University of Wisconsin Press, 1981), 114-146. The preceding two paragraphs draw on Harris' cogent analysis.

5. *Ford Facts*, August 10, 1946.

6. Taped narrative made by Ken Bannon, 1991, sent to author.

7. See the demand by General Motors workers in Saint Louis in 1940, during local bargaining with plant management, "that after line is set up to a certain

speed...that the speed of the line not be increased or decreased in the course of the day." [Emphasis added.] "Minutes of Bargaining Committee Meeting, October 30, 1940," Box 8, Local 25 Collection, WRL.

8. *Ford Facts*, June 29, 1946, 1,2.

9. Ibid., January 3, 1948, 4.

10. Ibid., August 24, 1946, 1.

11. Ibid., August 17, 1946, 1, 2.

12. Ibid., October 19, 1946, 7.

13. Ibid., October 19, 1946, 7. This article, by James Simmons and Herbert Johnson, concluded that the use of time study to speed up production could be combatted more effectively if the workers could "negotiate production [standards] on the job."

14. Ibid., October 12, 1946, 1.

15. Ibid., 5.

16. See a somewhat similar analysis in Huw Beynon, *Working For Ford* (London: Allen Lane, 1973), 98-99.

17. See speech by Bugas in late 1947 to a meeting of Ford managers in packet entitled "The New Company-Union Agreement", Box 97, Walter Reuther Papers.

18. Arbitration Proceedings, June 14, 1949, 207. These are typed, bound minutes. Box 40, Kenneth Bannon Papers. The language is that used by Jack Conway to describe the agreement.

19. Ibid., 22-23.

20. Speech by Ken Bannon, May 7, 1949, Plant-wide Meeting Minutes, p. 5, Box 66, Local 400 Papers, WRL.

21. "To: All Ford Local Unions," July 7, 1948, Box 97, Walter Reuther Papers, WRL.

22. Some of the work required involved cleaning up, getting stock ready, and "other things." Ibid., June 15, 1949, 408-11.

23. *Wall Street Journal* (*WSJ*), April 28, 1949, 3; Minutes of the UAW International Executive Board, April 27, 1949, 93-97, 142-45, Box 4, International Executive Board Papers, WRL.

24. *Ford Facts*, January 3, 1948, 4.

25. Ibid., February 21, 1948, 4.

26. *Ford Facts*, August 7, 1948, 3.

27. Ibid., October 16, 1948, 6. See also complaints about the use of relief workers on steady operations in Ibid., September 27, 1948, 2.

28. Even the pro-management *Detroit Free Press* had acknowledged that there were speedups at the Rouge. November 19, 1948.

29. Ibid., November 27, 1948, 5.

30. Ibid., December 11, 1948, 10. It is odd that the editor of *Ford Facts* put the news of this significant agreement on page 10, rather than page 1.

31. Ibid., January 22, 1949, 10.

32. Ibid., December 18, 1948, reported that the Local 600 General Council had condemned the speedup by a 85-45 vote. Eight grievances were mentioned, with six reported as having been settled (terms were not described), and two having been placed in the hands of the National Ford Department of the UAW.

33. I suspect this gap in coverage reflected the intervention of Local 600's President. The question of the best tactics to use in fighting Ford's speedup was clearly dividing the members of Local 600. See the discussion of Local 600's internal politics in the text of the article.

34. IEB Minutes, April 1949, 131-32.

35. Ibid., 134-36. A technological quirk exacerbated the normal problems "B" Building managers had in obtaining steady production. The electric power for the "B" Building's assembly lines came from the power plant of the Rouge complex. The voltage fell and rose through the day as different factories initiated and ended production. These variations caused fluctuations in assembly line speed. Arbitration Proceedings, 230-31.

36. Ibid., 361-62.

37. Ibid., 23, 37-38, 365-68.

38. May 29, 1949 speech, Box 40, Ken Bannon Papers.

39. Nelson Lichtenstein, "Reutherism on the Shop Floor: Union Strategy and Shop-Floor Conflict in the USA 1946-1970," in Steven Tolliday and Jonathan Zeitlin, eds., *Between Fordism and Flexibility: The Automobile Industry and Its Workers* (London: Basil Blackwell, 1986), 121-28.

40. See Walter Reuther's remarks, IEB Minutes, April 28, 1949, 136. Non-assembly workers had the chance to pace themselves. As Jack Conway pointed out during the arbitration hearings, in a "man paced job" the worker "works fast in the morning, slows down just before lunch, works fast after lunch, and tapers off in the afternoon, but still makes his overall production..." Assembly line workers did not have this kind of autonomy. Arbitration Proceedings, 220-21. See also chapter 3, n. 61.

41. Huw Beynon points out that British auto workers in the 1960s were especially riled by speedups that took the form of intra-daily line speed changes. One such worker complained: "You'd be working. Get into a bit of a system and just about keeping the job under control and then you'd find that you'd lost control, like. You'd be working that bit harder again. The bastards had altered the line speed." Beynon, 76.

42. William D. Andrew, "Factionalism and Anti-Communism: Ford Local 600," *Labor History*, 20 (Spring 1979), 232-47.

43. Bannon to Reuther, December 9, 1948, Box 97, Walter Reuther Papers.

44. Ibid., April 16, 23, 30.

45. Local 400, Plantwide Meeting Minutes, May 7, 1949, 7, Box 66, Local 400 Collection.

46. *WSJ* May 4, 6, 31, 1949; Martin Halpern, *UAW Politics in the Cold War Era* (Albany: State University of New York Press, 1988), 198-225, 253-59; Lichtenstein, 127-28. On May 16 the UAW was to begin negotiations with Ford about UAW demands for the national contract, demands that included a costly pension plan, medical insurance, and life insurance. I have not been able to find any specific documents in which Reuther, or any other UAW leaders, discussed the tension between their concern over the developments on the shopfloor and the national contract objectives. Nor have I been able to find any material on tactical considerations by the UAW leadership while the Speed Up Strike was in progress. I have found no documents to substantiate Lichtenstein's analysis of Reuther's

acceptance of arbitration. Lichtenstein writes: "...Reuther told Ford executives 'Have you ever thought that to get control the leadership must fight to get the machinery necessary for control.' He was therefore amenable when Ford executives agreed that the issue go before a special arbitration panel empowered to determine if temporary increases in the line speed were detrimental to worker health and safety. This postponed the issue for several weeks, took the international off the hook, and allowed the union to get on with what Reuther considered his central task: renegotiation and improvement of the national agreement." Ibid., 128.

47. IEB Minutes, April 28, 1949, 138, Box 4, IEB Papers, WRL.

48. Ibid., 141.

49. Local 600, Executive Board Minutes, May 3, 1949, 3, Box 2, Local 600 Papers, WRL. The IEB accepted Thompson's account. IEB Minutes, May 3, 1949, 58-59, Box 4, IEB Papers.

50. *WSJ*, May 3, 4, 1949.

51. Ford Local 600, Executive Board Minutes, January 28, May 3, 1949, Box 2, Local 600 Papers.

52. *WSJ*, May 8, 16, 1949.

53. Bulletin: From the UAW-CIO National Ford Department, 1-2, May 16, 1949, Box 40, Folder 17, Kenneth Bannon Papers.

54. *WSJ*, May 20, 1949.

55. UAW Public Relations Department, press release, April 28, 1949, Box 40, Folder 17, Kenneth Bannon Papers.

56. Script by Bill Friedland, Education Department, Michigan CIO, enclosed in Victor G. Reuther to Ford locals, May 24, 1949, Box 124, Walter Reuther Papers.

57. Appearing before a meeting of Local 400 (Highland Park), which did not strike, Ken Bannon noted that the UAW contended that the policy they were demanding was in force "in the GM plants and other plants throughout the country . . ." Plantwide Meeting Minutes, Local 400, May 7, 1949, Box 66, Local 400 Collection. GM plant managers occasionally tested the UAW on the issue of overwork. Authorized strikes brought an end to these deviations. Jack Conway described the GM situation as follows: "They attempt to squeak and chew and do things here and there. You have to be on your toes to see that they don't do away with it." Arbitration Proceedings, 340.

58. The UAW had asked for a flat 24 minutes of relief time each day. "UAW Proposal to Ford Motor Company, May 5, 1949," Box 40, Kenneth Bannon Papers.

59. "Settlement Agreement," enclosed in Ken Bannon to all Ford locals, May 29, 1949, Box 94, Local 400 Collection; *Ford Facts*, June 4, 1949, 1. A "unit" was the term used to describe a car part, car frame, or actual car that was on the assembly line.

60. Lichtenstein, 141, believes that the arbitration panel ruled that "Ford had no right to run its lines faster than 100 per cent of 'standard' at any time . . ." This is incorrect. Before the arbitration panel met, the strike settlement mandated no change in line speed during the production day. The issue to be arbitrated was could Ford, at the beginning of any given production day, set a line speed in excess of 100 percent of standard?

61. The three were Harry Schulman, who had been the sole Ford arbitrator during World War II, William Gomberg, who had done time studies for the International Ladies' Garment Workers Union before becoming an arbitrator, and Carl T. Dunn. Arbitration Award, Ford Motor Co. and UAW-CIO, 1-8, July 8, 1949, copy in Box 26, Kenneth Bannon Papers.

62. Arbitration Proceedings, 214-15. Jack Conway rejected a hint from the Ford representatives that the dispute be resolved by a pay premium to workers whose output exceeded their standard for a production day. Ibid., 234.

63. Arbitration Proceedings, 201.

64. Arbitration Award, Ford Motor Co. and UAW-CIO, July 8, 1949, Box 26, Kenneth Bannon Papers, 1-9. The crucial part of the decision read: "But at whatever speed the lines are operated, the Company must seek to make the individual employee's work assignment as measured by standard work minutes equal to or within the actual production cycle time available to him, that the Company has done successfully for most work assignments. For those which cannot be made equal to or within the actual production cycle time, it is not a sufficient answer that the employee is not assigned more than 480 minutes of work as measured by time study in an eight hour shift. In such cases, appropriate solutions to fit the conditions of the particular jobs must be worked out." Ibid., 9. Schulman and Gomberg were clearly influenced by a recent arbitrator's decision in a speedup dispute at Ford's Louisville, Kentucky, assembly plant. The decision called for "the use of reliefmen, as required." Ibid., 257-66.

The award represented a split decision by the arbitrators, with Carl T. Dunn dissenting. Dunn, who had been the umpire under the General Motors contract, had been Ford's choice for the panel. The UAW had chosen Gomberg. Gomberg and Dunn had selected Schulman. Dunn tended to be very pro-management. His sharp dissent indicates that the majority decision of the arbitrators, while not giving the UAW all it wanted, gave considerably greater rights to the Ford workers than the Ford management desired. See "Separate Opinion by Carl T. Dunn, Arbiter" enclosed in Ken Bannon to Ford Locals, July 18, 1949, Box 78, Local 400 Papers.

65. In some instances, management may accept contract terms to end a strike without intending to adhere strictly to the terms.

66. Local 600, Executive Board Minutes, November 15, December 13, 1949, Box 2, Local 600 Collection.

67. Robert M. Macdonald, *Collective Bargaining in the Automobile Industry* (New Haven: Yale University Press, 1953), 337.

68. 1949, UAW-Ford Contract. This change was consistent with the centralizing tendencies favored by the IEB, which believed that it had to coordinate grievance bargaining, as well as contract bargaining, to achieve strategic goals like uniform wages and the protection of weak auto makers (e.g., Chrysler). The IEB may also have wanted to diminish the power of Local 600. This local was so large that whatever the politics of the group that controlled it, the local had a tendency to assert its independence from organizational restraints.

69. Ibid., December 31, 1949,1.

70. Ibid., April 8, 1950, 2.

71. Ibid., August 19, 1950, 1. Overall, it seems that after the 1949 strike,

Ford gradually improved a variety of working conditions at the Rouge plant. Local 600's Vice President reported that great progress was quickly made on the safety of machines and the piling of parts. Local 600 was pressing Ford to do more to reduce hazardous smoke and fumes. Local 600, Executive Board Minutes, January 3, 1950, Box 2, Local 600 Collection.

72. *Lincoln Leader* (the Local 900 newspaper), November 1949, 1. I have not been able to locate more than a few copies of this essential source. Chester Olson, the former editor of the newspaper, was kind enough to show me his copies of the *Leader* for July, August and November 1949. Olson recalls that the Speed Up Strike changed the attitudes of many Ford managers, making them less hostile to the UAW. Interview with author, June 8, 1992.

73. General Council Minutes, Local 600, June 10, 1951, 9, Box 250, Folder 5, Walter Reuther Papers.

74. Loc. Cit.

75. M. W. Welty, "Industrial Relations Slants for 1952," copy in Box 17, Kenneth Bannon Papers.

76. Memo, Nat Weinberg to Kenneth Bannon, May 20, 1955, Box 42, Bannon Papers.

77. Memo, Jim O'Rourke to Kenneth Bannon, March 23, 1955, Box 42, Bannon Papers; Jefferys, op.cit., table on 145.

78. Computed by author from charts cited in n. 79.

79. Charts of 1953-1954 Work Stoppages - Ford Motor Company U. S. Area, Box 42, Kenneth Bannon Papers; John Bugas, Ford Vice President for Industrial Relations to Bannon, January 17, 1954, Box 42, Kenneth Bannon Papers.

80. Between 1946 and 1949, there were scores of wildcat strikes at the Rouge complex over ventilation questions, relating to exposures to toxic gasses and particles, and safety issues. For a few examples see *Ford Facts*, July 6, 1946, 1,3, October 19, 1946, 3, 6, 7, and July 13, 1949, 4.

81. Loc. cit. In 1961, 10 members of Ford Local 600 staged a work stoppage over safety issues. Ford management at the River Rouge plant did nothing for ten days and then disciplined three of the militant workers. The Local 600 delegate to the UAW's National Ford Council noted that the management strategy in this instance reflected its concern that disciplining all the workers would disrupt production significantly. This was especially true when the militant workers were skilled workers whose knowledge was essential to efficient production. National Ford Council Proceedings, 1961, typed minutes, 184, 192-93, Box 32, Kenneth Bannon Papers.

82. Memorandum, Unauthorized Stoppages, n.d., n.a., Box 43, Kenneth Bannon Papers, citing umpire decisions A-15, A-116, A-241 and others. GM was also more likely to correct safety violations than other worker grievances. Irving King and Grant Ricks interview transcripts, Labor History Project, University of Michigan-Flint.

83. Negotiation notes of Ken Bannon, 1955, Box 42, Kenneth Bannon Papers.

84. Kenneth Bannon, To the Presidents and Building Chairmen of all Ford Local Unions and enclosures, April 10, 1953; similar letter of April 20, 1953, Box 44, Kenneth Bannon Papers.

AUTOWORK

85. Agreement, May 4, 1953 - Company Proposal Rejected; Agreement, Ratified May 26, 1953; Canton Repository, May 5, 27, 1953; Dan Forchione to Edward Schultz, April 20, 1951; Edward Schultz to Marvin Schoultz, January 9, 1951; Edward Schultz to Kenneth Bannon, February 12, 1951; Ken Bannon, circular letter Re: Strike Action in Canton, Ohio Plant, May 5, 1953; Robert L. Kantor, Report, February 13, 1951, Box 44, Kenneth Bannon Papers.

86. Statement cited without source in Robert M. MacDonald, 338. I believe Macdonald's had read a document, "Study on Work Stoppages" written by an anonymous high level Ford manager. The document castigates the UAW for using Section 23 strikes to raise grievances unrelated to health and safety issues. There appears to be some truth to this assertion, although the specific accounts of strikes in the Ford document are marred by serious misstatements of facts about the legitimate Section 23 issues that generally were the prime causes of the authorized strikes. A copy of the document is in Box 97, Folder 6, Walter Reuther Papers.

87. National Ford Council, Minutes, May 9, 1955, 18, Box 32, Kenneth Bannon Papers.

88. The fatigue allowance issue first emerged in late 1953. *Ford Facts*, November 15, 1953. It was a bone of contention throughout the 1960s. The Ford Department of the UAW found that management made few concessions on this issue, which the UAW leaders felt undermined their attempts to prevent excessive work loads. Production Standards Study Committee, UAW, Minutes, January 13, 20, 1964, Box 17, Kenneth Bannon Papers.

89. Wayne Assembly Plant—Authorized Work Stoppage, document, Box 43, Folder 6, Bannon Papers. This folder contains material on authorized and unauthorized strikes in 1960 at Ford's Cleveland Stamping Plant (12 minutes, 10 workers—unauthorized—to protest exhaust fans that were turned off; 8 days—authorized—to protest disciplining of workers involved in a slowdown to protest company policy requiring workers to stay at their work stations until the end of a shift even if they had fulfilled their daily production standard). Ken Bannon believed that when John Bugas retired in October 1960, the restraint that he had forced upon Malcolm Denise, who was a labor relations hard liner, was removed. This may explain the noticeable increase in Ford's manipulation of production standards in 1961 and the UAW's authorization of three plant-level strikes in the first four months of 1961. Positive strike votes at six other Ford plants produced some concessions. National Ford Council, Proceedings, May 24-25, 1961, 26-32, 61, 64, 115, Box 32, Kenneth Bannon Papers.

90. Ibid., 176; Des Moines Implement Plant—Authorized Work Stoppage, 1 page broadside, Box 43, Kenneth Bannon Papers.

91. Loc. cit.

92. "Some of the Things Which UAW Local 249 Believes Prohibits Honest Negotiations and Settlement of Basic Issues with the Ford Motor Company," memorandum, November 25, 1963; Ira Mays, Chairman Local 249 Plant Bargaining Committee to Tom Bladen, July 20, 1964, Box 17, Kenneth Bannon Papers. Members of Local 560, Milpitas, California had similar complaints. M. A. Williams, Building Chairman, Local 560 to Tom Bladen and Jeff Washington, July 24, 1964, Box 17, ibid. See chapter 1 for a discussion of Ford's increased reluctance to abide by production standard agreements with UAW locals in the mid-1960s.

Chapter 6

1. *American Automobile Workers 1900-1933* (Albany: SUNY, 1987), 50. For Ford see Stephen Meyer III, *The Five Dollar Day: Labor Management and Social Control in the Ford Motor Company* (Albany: SUNY. 1981), 108-9.

2. Robert W. Dunn, *Labor and Automobiles* (New York: International Publishers, 1929), 92.

3. Peterson, *American Automobile Workers*, 50; Dunn, *Labor and Automobiles*, 93-95; and William Ellison Chalmers, "Labor in the Automobile Industry: A Study of Personnel Policies, Workers' Attitudes and Attempts at Unionism," PhD dissertation, University of Wisconsin 1932, 176-79.

4. Dunn reported that two-thirds of Ford's workers were working Saturdays in early 1929; *Labor and Automobiles*, 98.

5. Quoted in Eugene McCarthy and William McGaughey, *Nonfinancial Economics: The Case For Shorter Hours of Work* (New York: Praeger 1989), 174.

6. *Work Without End: Abandoning Shorter Hours for the Right to Work* (Philadelphia 1988), 39. Also see David R. Roediger, "The Limits of Corporate Reform: Fordism, Taylorism, and the Working Week in the United States, 1914-1929," in Gary Cross ed., *Worktime and Industrialization: An International History* (Philadelphia: Temple University, 1988), 145-46.

7. See Woodrow L. Ginsberg and Ralph Bergman, both of the Research Department of the United Rubber, Cork, Linoleum and Plastic Workers of America, "The Worker's Viewpoint," in *The Shorter Work Week: Papers Delivered at the Conference on Shorter Hours of Work Sponsored by the American Federation of Labor and Congress of Industrial Organizations* (Public Affairs Press, Washington, 1957), 36-42.

8. Sidney Fine, *The Automobile Under the Blue Eagle: Labor, Management, and the Automobile Manufacturing Code* (Ann Arbor: University of Michigan Press, 1963), 51-52.

9. The Federal Labor Unions were local unions established at automobile plants by the A. F. of L. These FLUs included workers from all occupations in the industry, but they were not designed to be permanent local units of a new industrial union for the automobile industry. Instead, A. F. of L. leaders hoped to eventually sort out the newly enrolled workers by skill, and assign them to already existing craft unions. For more on the speedup, see chapter 3.

10. *Blue Eagle*, 103-5. Also see Ronald Edsforth, *Class Conflict and Cultural Consensus: The Making of a Mass Consumer Society in Flint, Michigan* (New Brunswick: Rutgers University Press, 1987), 160-62.

11. Fine, *Blue Eagle*, 106-10 and 410.

12. See chapter 3.

13. For example see James MacGregor Burns, Roosevelt: *The Lion and the Fox* (New York: Harcourt, Brace & World, 1956), 180-81; William Leuchtenberg, *Franklin D. Roosevelt and the New Deal* (New York: Harper & Row, 1963), 55-58; Anthony J. Badger, *The New Deal: The Depression Years* (New York: Hill and Wang, 1989), 79-80. This idea is most fully developed in Hunnicutt, *Work Without End*, chapters 5-8.

14. Henry Kraus Papers, Box 8, file 33, Walter P. Reuther Library, Wayne State University, hereafter cited as WRL.

15. Both agreements are located in the Walter Reuther Papers, Box 8, file 1, WRL.

16. *Sit-Down: The General Motors Strike of 1936-1937* (Ann Arbor: University of Michigan Press, 1969), 325.

17. The other original demands were real collective bargaining, abolition of the speedup and piecework, recognition of seniority, and higher wages.

18. For a discussion of the history of the shorter hours demand in the UAW see "Draft Shorter Work Week Resolution for Ford Council" (1955) in the Research Department Collection, hereafter cited as RDC, Box 59, WRL.

19. See Kevin Boyle in "Notes and Documents—Building the Vanguard: Walter Reuther and Radical Politics in 1936," *Labor History*, 30, 3, Summer 1989.

20. Roediger, "The Limits of Corporate Reform," 143-44.

21. "Committee of 17" to Mr. William S. Knudsen" dated September 16, 1937, in Stuart Strachan Papers, Box 1, file 16, WRL.

22. Minutes of membership meeting, March 5, 1939, in Walter Reuther Papers, Box 1, file 37, WRL.

23. Speech to GM Conference dated February 9, 1941, Ibid., Box 18, file 17, WRL.

24. Stephen Meyer, "The Persistence of Fordism: Workers and Technology in the American Automobile Industry, 1900-1960," in Nelson Lichtenstein and Stephen Meyer eds., *On the Line: Essays in the History of Auto Work* (Urbana and Chicago: University of Illinois Press, 1989), 87.

25. "Examples of Automation," Walter Reuther Papers, Box 45, File 15, WRL; and William A. Faunce, "Automation in the Automobile Industry: Some Consequences for In-Plant and Union-Management Relationships," PhD dissertation, Wayne State University 1957, 13-14.

26. Reuther, "What Will Automation Do to Workers?", *Washington Post and Times-Herald*, January 23, 1955, 1ff.

27. Memo: Clarence Weiner to Nat Weinberg, dated March 19, 1954, Research Department Collection, Box 43, WRL.

28. "Automated cylinder-block lines," *American Machinist*, November 8, 1954, 136-40.

29. "Continuous Crankshaft Grinding Uses Transfer System," *Automation*, February 1955, 62-64.

30. Research Department Collection, Box 42, File "Automation— Bibliography," WRL.

31. Faunce, "Automation in the Automobile Industry," 17.

32. What Automation Means to You," *Ford Rouge News*, October 16, 1953; in the Kenneth Bannon Papers, Box 59, folder 12, WRL.

33. "The Challenge of Change," March 23, 1955; attached to memo: Jack Conway to Members of the Automation Committee, May 31, 1955; in RDC, Box 44, folder "Automation," WRL.

34. Irving Bluestone, "Automation, Collective Bargaining, and Beyond," a paper presented at the Conference on Manpower Implications of Automation, U.S. Department of State, December 8-10, 1964, 9; Ibid., box 42, WRL.

35. "Automation-Bibliography, 1953-1957," Ibid., Box 42, WRL. These files contain material compiled for the union's Committee on Automation.

36. "Automation—Reduction of Manpower in the Dearborn Iron Foundry," Kenneth Bannon Papers, Box 60, file 2, WRL; and Meyer, "Persistence of Fordism," 91-93.

37. Soretti, Pierce, Carter, Richberg, Gyurko, "Reuther Shocked By Automation," Local 600's *Ford Facts*, 2.

38. The definitive account of the internal politics of the UAW in this period is Martin Halpern, *UAW Politics in the Cold War Era* (Albany: SUNY 1988).

39. For a complete elaboration of this point see Ronald Edsforth, "Affluence, Anti-Communism, and the Transformation of Industrial Unionism among Automobile Workers, 1933-1973," in Ronald Edsforth and Larry Bennett eds., *Popular Culture and Political Change in Modern America* (Albany: SUNY, 1991), 107-11.

40. "From Corporatism to Collective Bargaining: Organized Labor and the Eclipse of Social Democracy in the Postwar Era," in Steve Fraser and Gary Gerstle eds., *The Rise and Fall of the New Deal Order 1930-1980* (Princeton: Princeton University Press, 1989), 126.

41. Speech on General Motors, Mutual Broadcast System, Friday October 26, 1945, Walter Reuther Papers, Box 541, WRL.

42. Lichtenstein, "From Corporatism to Collective Bargaining," 132-33.

43. Quoted in Edsforth, "Affluence, Anti-Communism, and the Transformation of Industrial Unionism," 122-23.

44. For fuller assessments of Reuther in this period see Nelson Lichtenstein, "Walter Reuther and the Rise of Labor Liberalism," in Melvyn Dubofsky and Warren Van Tine eds., *Labor Leaders in America* (Urbana and Chicago: University of Illinois Press, 1987); John Barnard, *Walter Reuther and the Rise of the Auto Workers* (Boston: Little, Brown, 1983); and Edsforth, "Affluence, Anti-Communism, and the Transformationm of Industrial Unionism," 118-25.

45. Wiener and Reuther carried on an extensive correspondence in 1949-1952 about this and other issues, especially atomic power and the peace movement. This correspondence is located in the Institute Archives and Special Collections, MC22, Boxes 2-3, MIT Libraries.

46. Transcript of "International Conference on Economic Objectives, February 19, 1949," 45-47; in Walter Reuther, Box 56, folder 1, WRL.

47. For example see "What Will Automation Do to Workers?". This same anecdote was spontaneously related to me by Irving Bluestone, a retired UAW Vice President and close associate of Reuther, when I interviewed him in October 1990. It is, in other words, now part of union folklore.

48. Specifically, the Reuther plan announced in 1953 called for 1) holding down profit margins; 2) increasing wages by directing a greater share of productivity gains to workers pay envelopes; 3) reducing personal income taxes in the lower brackets; 4) raising the minimum wage; and 5) increasing Social Security payments. See "Reuther Shocked By Automation."

49. The transcript of the full ninety minute broadcast dated June 9, 1957 is located in Walter Reuther Papers, Box 45, file 16, WRL.

50. "UAW-Ford Employment Figures," Kenneth Bannon Papers, Box 60, file 21, WRL.

51. "Automation - General, 1956-1957," Research Department Collection, Box 43, WRL.

52. "Preliminary Report of the UAW-CIO Committee on Automation," October 26, 1954, 7; in Ibid., Box 42, WRL.

53. "Proceedings of International Economic Conference, UAW-CIO," November 12-13, 1954, Masonic Temple, Detroit, 167; in UAW Region 6 Collection, Box 75, WRL [emphasis added].

54. Irving Bluestone, a key Reuther assistant who helped develop the UAW's work time policy in the early 1960s, very clearly recalled this consensus about the practical impossibility of beating GM or Ford in a strike for shorter hour when I interviewed him on October 11, 1990; notes in my possession.

55. Seth Mark Widgerson, "The UAW in the 1950s," PhD dissertation, Wayne State University 1989, 78-79. Widgerson recognizes the importance of the "30 for 40" movement but his account of the political struggle within the UAW is flawed by stereotyping and by the limited sources he uncovered. His claim that the union archives contain only one folder on the shorter work week is clearly erroneous.

56. Much of the material gathered by the committee is located in RDC, boxes 42-43; and Kenneth Bannon Papers, Box 59; WRL.

57. "Proceedings of a Special Session of the International Executive Board," Friday, April 12, 1957, Atlantic City, 6, UAW Region 6 Collection, Box 77, WRL.

58. "Partial Report No.1 - Resolutions," 27 in Research Department Collection, Box 42, WRL.

59. Widgerson, "UAW in the 1950s," 103-5.

60. Leo Fenster Papers, Box 6, WRL.

61. Minutes of local executive board, Local 45 Collection, Box 10, WRL.

62. The correspondence detailing the activities of the "30-40-60" movement is in the Fenster Papers, Box 6, WRL.

63. Interview with Irving Bluestone.

64. Both Harris' report, "The Mandate of the UAW Rank and File for Contract Negotiations in 1961," and interoffice correspondence regarding the report are located in the UAW Vice President's Office, Leonard Woodcock Papers, Box 58, WRL.

65. Chris Coulter, President Flint Local 581, to John DeVito, April 20, 1961 in Fenster Papers, Box 6, WRL.

66. Bluestone, "Automation, Collective Bargaining and Beyond;" and Irving Bluestone, "Impact of Automation and Technological Change," *Pacific Northwest Assembly*, February 1963; RDC, box 42; Nat Weinberg, "Automation and Collective Bargaining Policy in the United States," January 29, 1965; and "The Effects of Automation and Population Increase on Employment," Eighth Annual Clinic Day of Pala Alto, May 8, 1965; both RDC, box 43; also see correspondence in the Fenster Collection, box 6, file 16; and UAW Oral History Project Interview with Nat Weinberg, March 20 and April 30, 1963, 31-33: all WRL.

67. Transcript of this speech dated November 11, 1963 is in the Fenster Papers, Box 1, WRL.

68. Bluestone, "Automation, Collective Bargaining and Beyond," 10-16 is a very clear statement of this program.

69. Research Department Collection, Box 42, File "Automation— Bibliography," WRL.

70. Hartmut Seifert, "Employment Effects of Working Time Reductions in the former Federal Republic of Germany" and Elisabeth Neifer-Dichmann, " Working Time Reductions in the former Federal Republic of Germany: A Dead End for Employment Policy"; both esssays in *International Labour Review* 130, 4 (1991).

71. "Daily, weekly and yearly rest and weekly hours," *European Industrial Relations Review*, 210, July 1991, 24-29; also see Juliet Schor, *The Overworked American: The Unexpected Decline of Leisure* (New York: Basic Books, 1991), 81-82.

72. *Work Without End*, 312.

Chapter 7

1. For a broader discussion of "Labor-liberalism" see Nelson Lichtenstein, "Walter Reuther and the Rise of Labor-Liberalism," in Melvin Dubofsky and Warren Van Tine, eds., *Labor Leaders in America* (Urbana: University of Illinois Press, 1986). The Detroit portions of this chapter are in part a condensed version of certain chapters in the doctoral dissertation of the author. For a more detailed discussion of the impact of the second great migration on the politics of the UAW, the development of city of Detroit, and the evolution of post-War liberalism in Detroit see: Heather Ann Thompson, "The Politics of Labor, Race, and Liberalism: Detroit, 1940-1980," doctoral dissertation in progress, Princeton University.

2. For more on the UAW and its interaction with liberals in Washington as well as 1960s liberalism in general, see Kevin Boyle, "Politics and Principle: The UAW and American Liberalism, 1948-1968," doctoral dissertation, University of Michigan, 1990.

3. According to a survey of Detroit's Model Neighborhood Households, in 1968, 44 percent of all blacks were born in the South and, in 1972, half of all heads of households were born in the South. See "Cross-Section Sample Survey of the Model Neighborhood" for the Model Neighborhood Citizens Planning Conference, September 18-20, 1968, and "Detroit Model Neighborhood Housing Survey", April-June 1972, Box 14, Detroit City Planning Commission Collection, Burton Historical Collection, Detroit Public Library, Detroit.

4. Robert Sinclair and Bryan Thompson, *Metropolitan Detroit: An Anatomy of Social Change* (Cambridge: Ballinger Press, 1977), 10.

5. Ibid., 14-15.

6. Ibid., 14.

7. According to Dan Georgakas and Marvin Surkin, in their book *Detroit: I Do Mind Dying* (New York: St. Martins Press, 1975), in 1967 the Detroit Police Department served a Detroit population which was 32 percent black, while only 217/4740 officers, 9/250 sergeants, 3/220 lieutenants, and 1/65 inspectors (or higher) were black., 189.

8. "Percentage Distribution of Family Heads by Their Occupation and Race, Detroit 1969", The Research Division of the City Planning Commission, April 4, 1972, Box 15, Detroit City Planning Commission Collection.

9. Thompson, loc. cit.

10. For the most comprehensive and penetrating examination of the Detroit Race Riot, see Sidney Fine, *Violence in the Model City: The Cavanagh Administration, Race Relations, and the Detroit Riot of 1967*, (Ann Arbor: University of Michigan Press, 1989). For additional analytical and statistical information on all of the urban riots, including Detroit's, see *The Kerner Report: Report on the National Advisory Commission on Civil Disorders*, (New York: Pantheon Books, 1988).

11. In the Chrysler Jefferson Avenue plant, for example, over 90 percent of the workers in the hated metal shop were black. See Georgakas and Surkin, 227.

12. "Undated News Release" r.e. upcoming meeting between Eldon plant workers and the UAW President Leonard Woodcock, 2. Box 3, Ron Glotta Papers, Walter P. Reuther Library. (Hereafter WRL)

13. For more on the working conditions faced by auto workers during these years, and by black workers in particular, see Rachel Scott, *Muscle and Blood* (New York: Dutton, 1974), 119- 173 passim.

14. Steve Jefferys, *Management and Managed: Fifty Years of Crisis at Chrysler*, (Cambridge: Cambridge University Press, 1986), 179.

15. See Heather Ann Thompson, "The James Johnson Case: The Politics of Race in the Auto Plant and the Motor City," Unpublished paper, Princeton University.

16. *The United Justice Train*, "Life and Death at Jefferson" (January 1973). From the personal archives of auto worker Neil Chacker.

17. James A. Geschwender, *Class, Race, and Workers Insurgency: The League of Revolutionary Black Workers* (Cambridge: Cambridge University Press, 1977), 199.

18. *The United Justice Caucus* 5 (August 1973) as quoted in Geschwender, 202.

19. *The Detroit Free Press* (August 19, 1973).

20. Local 7 Rank and File, "Local #7 Sell-out." Leaflet. From the personal archives of auto worker Neil Chacker.

21. Geschwender, 84, 94. See Geschwender also for a comprehensive history of the League.

22. *Eldon Wildcat* (July 22, 1970). In the DRUM/Newspaper Collection. WRL.

23. For an overview of both the "hate strikes" and the birth of the TULC see August Meier and Elliot Rudwick, *Black Detroit and the Rise of the UAW* (New York: Oxford University Press, 1979). For a discussion of the "hate strikes and the TULC from the perspective of a dissident black auto worker, see Charles Denby, *Indignant Heart: A Black Worker's Journal* (Boston: South End Press, 1978).

24. Often the RUM groups had fewer actual members than supporters because they were very socially intimidating to mainstream black auto workers. Their youth, style, dress, and language tended to isolate them from workers, even while their emphasis on ridding the plant of racism was embraced. Author interview with the Thompson family—parents of slain auto worker Gary Thompson—April 11, 1991.

25. For a comprehensive discussion of DRUM at Dodge Main see Jefferys, passim.

26. For an example of this see, *ELRUM* (January 1970), 4, in the DRUM/Newspaper Collection.

27. Interview with John Taylor in Georgakas and Surkin, 108-121.

28. Jefferys, 181.

29. *ELRUM*, (January, 1970), 4.

30. Jefferys, 183.

31. Ibid, 183

32. Steve Babson, *Working Detroit: The Making of a Union Town* (New York: Adama Books, 1984), 174.

33. See the "dual-union" implications of DRUM in the DRUM platform and program reprinted in Jefferys, 176-77.

34. *The Detroit Free Press*, (July 24, 1973).

35. Jefferys, 152.

36. Author interview with C.H. Eschenbach, Labor Relations Supervisor at Chrysler, November 30, 1984.

37. Ibid.

38. Ibid.

39. Jefferys argues that the UNC was only "a small propaganda caucus by 1973", 262.

40. Eschenbach, loc. cit.

41. *The Detroit News* (July 24, 1973).

42. "Chrysler Beaten: How and Why. An Interview With Sitdown Leaders." *In Workers Power* (August 1973), Labadie Collections, Harlan Hatcher Library, University of Michigan.

43. *The Detroit Free Press* (August 30, 1973).

44. Frank Joyce and John Taylor, "Jefferson Shut-Down: Interview", *The Journey* (August, 1973) as quoted in Geschwender, 192-93

45. *The Detroit News* (August 8, 1973).

46. Jerome Scott, Thomas Stepanski, Karl Williams V., Chrysler Corporation, International Union, United Automobile Aerospace and Agricultural Implement Workers of America, UAW and its Local No. 47, Leon Klea, Dennis Baliki, Al Howe, T.J. Jackson, Elwood Black, Art Hughes, Anthony Canole, Doug Fraser, Wally Wallers, George Merrielle, Paul Rigillio, Don Scalu, J.W. Murphy, Paul Henn, Virgil Anderson, and Walter Ector, Jointly and Severally. Wayne County Circuit Court, Case # 75-066-303-CZ. Deposition of Jerome Scott, 1977, Box 4, Ronald Glotta Papers.

47. Jerome Scott, Thomas Stepanski, Karl Williams V., Chrysler Corporation, International Union, United Automobile Aerospace and Agricultural Implement Workers of America, UAW and its Local No. 47, Leon Klea, Dennis Baliki, Al Howe, T.J. Jackson, Elwood Black, Art Hughes, Anthony Canole, Doug Fraser, Wally Wallers, George Merrielle, Paul Rigillio, Don Scalu, J.W. Murphy, Paul Henn, Virgil Anderson, and Walter Ector, Jointly and Severally. Case # 75-066-303-CZ. Deposition of Leon Klea on September 19, 1977. Ibid., Box 4.

48. *The Detroit News* (August 8, 1973).

49. Ibid.

50. United Forge Workers Local #47, "Vote Strike on Friday." Leaflet. From the personal archives of auto worker Neil Chacker.

51. *The Detroit Free Press*, (August 11, 1973).

52. *The Detroit Free Press* (August 14, 1973).

53. The UAW's Pre-Hearing Brief before Arbitrator Gabriel Alexander, August 23, 1973.

54. This case is referenced in Note 46. For more information on the rising number of lawsuits filed by workers against their unions in this period see, R. Dinges, "Ruzicka Vs. GM: An Unlikely Hero of the Trade Union Movement—the Individual Employee in a Section 301 Case Who Has Been the Victim of Union Negligence," *Wayne Law Review*, Vol. 24, No. 5. (September, 1978).

55. Scott et al. vs. Chrysler et al. Deposition of Dennis Baliki on December 15, 1977, 75-77 and passim, Box 4, Ronald Glotta Papers. For full citation see n. 46.

56. Ibid. Also see, "The Truth Comes to Light in the Three Fired Workers Case," Leaflet by the Defense Committee for the Three Fired Workers," personal archives of autoworker Neil Chacker.

57. Ibid.

58. Ibid., 73.

59. Jack Weinberg, "Detroit Auto Uprising: 1973." 1974 pamphlet, author's possession.

60. *The Detroit News* (August 15, 1973).

61. *The Detroit News* (August 16, 1973).

62. "Mack Safety Protest", leaflet printed by the Concerned Mack Avenue Workers, personal archives of Neil Chacker.

63. *The UNC, 5* (August 1973), as quoted in Geschwender, 202.

64. Interview with a female auto worker from the Mack Plant on November 3, 1984 by the author.

65. *The Detroit News* (August 15, 1973).

66. *The Detroit News* (August 16, 1973).

67. *The Detroit Free Press* (August 17, 1973).

68. Ibid.

69. *The Fifth Estate* (September 1-14, 1973).

70. *The Detroit News* (August 18, 1973).

71. *Time* (February 2, 1972).

72. The average age in the plant was 23-24 years old. The plant was predominantly male because "no women were hired until 1970." Author interview with then-Lordstown Local 1112 President Gary Bryner, April 14, 1986.

73. Interview with Gary Bryner, January 16, 1991, by Robert Asher and the author.

74. Ibid.

75. Author interview with Gary Bryner, April 14, 1986.

76. "Report of the President, 1971-1972", WRL.

77. *The Cincinnati Enquirer* (January 7, 1972), Box 1, Robert Gutheridge Papers, WRL.

78. "Press Release" by Paul Cubellis, Box 8, Local 1112 Collection, WRL.

79. Interview with Gary Bryner, April 14, 1986.

80. Information on what the relief provisions were pre-GMAD is from author's interview with Gary Bryner, January 16, 1991.

81. A "DLO" is a disciplinary lay off given for certain infractions on the shopfloor, and it is for the duration of management's choosing.

82. Interview with Gary Bryner, April 14, 1986.

83. *Time* (February 2, 1972).

84. Local 1112, *See Here*, (September, 1971).

85. *See Here* (February, 1972).

86. Local 1112 General Meeting Minutes. January 9, 1972, Box 2, Charles White Papers, WRL.

87. Interview with Gary Bryner, April 14, 1986.

88. *See Here* (January 1972) and "Local #1112 to the Membership," February 4, 1972, Box 1, White Papers.

89. General Meeting Minutes Local 1112, March 12, 1972, Box 2, Charles White Papers.

90. J.D. Smith and Tony Zone to Leonard Woodcock, March 12, 1972, Box 8, Local #1112 Collection.

91. Irving Bluestone, "Boredom on the Assembly Line," *Harpers* (August, 1972).

92. "Letter from Irving Bluestone to Dave Poole" on January 17, 1972, Box 1, Local 1112 Collection.

93. *Business Week* (March 4, 1972).

94. *The New York Times* (April 16, 1972). A key reason for the union's success at Lordstown was that GM desperately wanted Chevy Vegas to keep coming off of the line to meet consumer demand. Another GMAD-provoked strike at nearby Norwood, Ohio ended in disaster for the union after 100 days. GM was able to wait the union out since it had no pressing need for the Norwood product.

95. *See Here* (February, 1972).

96. For a more detailed discussion of the Lordstown Strike and the Chrysler Wildcats, see Heather Ann Thompson "Lordstown Revisited," unpublished seminar paper, The University of Michigan, 1986, and Heather Thompson, "Detroit: Wildcat 1973", unpublished senior honors thesis, The University of Michigan, 1984.

97. *The Detroit News* (August 18, 1973).

98. Geschwender, 202.

99. Ibid., 199.

100. Jefferys, 179.

Chapter 8

1. J. Kuhn, *Bargaining in Grievance Settlement: The Power of Industrial Work Groups* (New York: Columbia University Press, 1961).

2. G. Brown, *Sabotage: A Study in Industrial Conflict* (Nottingham: Spokesmen Books, 1977), ix.

3. D. Georgakas, and M. Surkin, *Detroit: I Do Mind Dying* (New York: St. Martin's Press, 1975), 7.

4. M. Burawoy, *Manufacturing Consent: Changes in the Labor Process under Monopoly Capital* (Chicago: University of Chicago Press, 1979). This duality was also attributed to grievance bargaining by Sidney Lens, "The Meaning of the Grievance Procedure", *Harvard Business Review* Vol. 26, November 1948, 720-22.

5. M. Davis, "The Stop Watch and the Wooden Shoe: Scientific Management and the Industrial Workers of the World", *Radical America*, January/February 1975, 68-95.

6. David F. Noble, "Present Tense Technology, Part One", *Democracy*, Vol. 2, Spring 1983, 69-80; "Present tense Technology, Part Two", *Democracy*, Vol. 3, Summer 1983, 70-82; "Present Tense Technology, Part Three", *Democracy* Vol. 4, Fall 1983, 71-93; see also William Rodarmor, "Remark: The Luddite Legacy", *PC World*, Vol. 2, December 1984, 19-20 for a similar viewpoint.

7. J. R. Norsworthy, and C. A. Zabala, ""Effects of Worker Attitudes on Production Costs and the Value of Capital Input", *The Economic Journal*, Vol. 95, December 1985, 992-1002; D.F. Noble, "Present Tense Technology, Part Two", 72-74; T. O'Hanlon, "Anarchy Threatens the Kingdom of Coal", *Fortune*, January 1971.

8. This extends the notion of "voice" by R. B. Freeman, "The Exit-Voice Trade Off in the Labor Market: Unionism, Job Tenure, Quits and Separations," *Quarterly Journal of Economics*, Vol. 94, 198-0, 643-73 and R. B. Freeman, and J. Medoff, *What Do Unions Do?* (New York: Basic Books, 1984).

9. David F. Noble, "Present Tense Technology, Part Two."

10. Agreement between GM Assembly Division, General Motors Corporation Van Nuys Plant and Local 645, United Auto Workers, (January 18, 1977), 125-28.

11. This concept borrows partly from the work of J. A. Schumpeter, *Capitalism, Socialism and Democracy* (New York: Harper and Row, 1975), 81-86. Also see P. Adler, "Towards the Post Capitalist Firm? A Schumpeterian Research Agenda," Working Paper, Department of Industrial Engineering and Engineering Management, School of Engineering, Stanford University, 1987.

Chapter 9

1. Dearborn Assembly Plant, Agreements and Letters of Understanding: 1987 Local Negotiations, September, 1987, 14.

2. Agreements, 37-43. The contract actually specified 88 production classifications, but nearly two dozen of these were no longer filled. Skilled trades added another 20 or more classifications.

3. Agreements, 15, 53, 58-59.

4. "1989 Market Data Book," *Automotive News*, 3; Robert Sobel, *Car Wars: Why Japan is Building the All-American Car* (New York: 1984), 147.

5. *UAW Research Bulletin* (March 1992), 4, 14; Stephen Herzenberg, "Towards a Cooperative Commonwealth? Labor and Restructuring in the U.S. and Canadian Auto Industries," Ph.D. dissertation, Massachusetts Institute Technology, Economics Department (May 1991), 230.

6. "1990 Market Data Book," *Automotive News*, 3, 12; UAW Research Bulletin (March 1992) 1,17.

7. According to UAW workers and union officers at Dearborn Assembly in 1992, stampings came from Buffalo (floor pans), Mexico (rocker panels), and Woodhaven, Michigan (doors), as well as Cleveland and Maumee, Ohio, Indiana, and Pennsylvania. A small fraction of stampings came from the Dearborn stamping, frame, and engine plants. In addition to Nashville and Tulsa, Ford sourced a small portion of glass for the Mustang from the Dearborn glass plant. At one point in the 1980s, Nippon Kokkan, the Japanese steel maker, indicated an interest in buying the Rouge's steel making capacity.

8. UAW-Ford, "Modern Operating Concepts," training manual, 6-10 May, 1991, Dearborn Assembly, page 2 and Session 3, slides 13b and 16; James Risen, "Ford Official Brought Fresh Ideas to the UAW," *Detroit Free Press* (March 1, 1982), 1A.

9. Hillel Levin, "Labor's New Hope at Ford," *Midwest Business*, May 82, 110.

10. UAW-Ford National Joint Committee on Employee Involvement "Employee Involvement: What's it all About?," pamphlet (October 1980), 4.

11. For a list of representative EI projects, see UAW-Ford National Joint Committee on Employee Involvement, "EI: It Makes the Difference," /n.d.

12. Quote is from UAW-Ford, "Employee Involvement: What's it all About?," 4.

13. Richard Feldman and Michael Betzold, eds., *End of the Line: Auto Workers and the American Dream* (NewYork: Weidenfeld & Nicholson, 1988), 38, 44, 46, 105, 241.

14. James Risen, "Job Quality Plan Abused, UAW Says," *Detroit Free Press*, November 10, 1983, 1A; Ralph Orr, "Angry Rank and File Ousting Local Leaders," *Detroit Free Press*, June 7, 1984, 1A. For general critiques of EI/QWL in auto and other industrial settings, see Mike Parker, *Inside the Circle: A Union Guide to QWL* (Boston: South End Press, 1985), Part 1; Edward Lawler III and Susan Mohrman, "Quality Circles After the Fad," *Harvard Business Review* (January-February, 1985), 65-71; Jeremy Main, "The Trouble with Managing Japanese Style," *Fortune Magazine*, April 2, 1984, 50-56; Gregory Huszco, "The Long Term Prospects for Joint Union-Management Worker Participation Processes," in AFL-CIO Department of Economic Research, "Worker Participation," *Workplace Topics* vol. 2, No. 2, December 1991, 13-34.

15. John Hoerr, "The Payoff from Teamwork," *Business Week*, June 10, 1989, 58. For an evaluation of QWL's limited impact on measurable plant performance, see Harry Katz, *Shifting Gears: Changing Labor Relations in the U.S. Automobile Industry* (Cambridge: Cambridge University Press, 1985), 105-32.

16. James Womack, Daniel Jones, Daniel Ross, *The Machine that Changed the World* (New York: Rawson Associates, 1990), 13.

17. Ibid., 13-14, 99-102.

18. Toyota Motor Corporation, *The Toyota Production System* (Toyota City: Toyota Motor Corporation, 1992), 7.

19. Ibid., 7.

20. Womack et al, *The Machine that Changed the World*, 102-3.

21. Cited in Takeshi Inagami, "Japanese Workplace Industrial Relations," *Japanese Industrial Relations Series*, No. 14, (1988), 20-22. The survey was conducted in Japan among regular employees working for companies manufacturing steel, automobiles, and electrical machines; 65 percent were blue collar.

22. Ibid., 14-19; Nomura Musami, International Institute for Comparative Social Research and Labor Policy, "Model Japan? Characteristics of Industrial Relations in the Japanese Auto Industry," *Discussion Papers* (Berlin, July 1985); Kathy Jackson, "Transplant Wages Will Rise to Match Any Gains at Big 3," *Automotive News* (July 2, 1990), 60.

23. Beside the union and management, Japanese auto workers seeking assistance turned primarily to colleagues and family members. Hikari Nohara, "The Average Worker of a Large Japanese Company," paper delivered at the Conference on Labor Organization and the Future of Post-industrializing Societies, University of Milan, 11-13 (April 1988), Table 8; Tabata Hirokuni, "Changes in Plant-Level Trade Union Organizations: A Case Study of the Automobile Industry," University of Tokoyo, *Institute of Social Science Occasional Papers*, March, 1989.

24. Peter Wickens, *The Road to Nissan: Flexibility, Quality, Teamwork* (London: Macmillan, 1987), 168.

25. For a detailed account of work life at Toyota in the early 1970s, see Satoshi Kamata, *Japan in the Passing Lane: An Insider's Account of Life in a Japanese Auto Factory* (New York: Pantheon Books, 1982), 184.

26. Masaaki Imai, *Kaizen Communique* vol. 2, No. 3 (Winter 1988-1989. Published by the Kaizen Institute of North America, Camarillo, California.

27. Mike Parker and Jane Slaughter, *Choosing Sides: Unions and the Team Concept* (Boston, 1988), 16-30; Parker and Slaughter, "Managing by Stress: The Dark Side of Team Concept," *ILR Report* vol. XXVI, No. 1 (Fall, 1988), 19-23.

28. On the role of U.S. corporate welfare plans as a model for Japanese industry in the 1920s, see Sheldon Garon, *The State and Labor in Modern Japan* (Berkeley: University of California Press, 1987), 170-71.

29. Katz, 88-100; Parker and Slaughter, *Choosing Sides*, 151-53.

30. "A Task Comparison of NUMMI and BOC-Leeds Salary Finctions," typescript, addressed to "Douglas H. Tracy, Manufacturing Manager, J/N Platform, April 23, 1986," author's possession, 6.

31. See Sanford Jacoby, *Employing Bureaucracy: Managers, Unions, and the Transformation of Work in American Industry, 1900-1945* (New York: Columbia University Press, 1985); Nelson Lichtenstein, "The Man in the Middle: A Social History of Automobile Industry Foremen," in Lichtenstein and Stephen Meyer, eds., *On the Line: Essays in the History of Autowork* (Urbana: University of Illinois Press, 1989), 153-89.

32. Lowell Turner, *Democracy at Work: Changing World Markets and the Future of Labor Unions* (Ithaca: Cornell University Press, 1991), 53-62; Parker and Slaughter, *Choosing Sides*, 100-122.

33. Kathy Dahlstrom, "Scramble for Work Disassembles Union Solidarity," *Flint Journal*, December 27, 1988.

34. Joint press release, "UAW-GM National Negotiating Committee to include Japanese Plants on Pre-Bargaining Tour,": June 12, 1987.

35. Interviews with Frank Hammer, who was then Local 909 President and subsequently won election as Bargaining Chairman, and Al Benchich, Local Vice President. See Parker and Slaughter, *Choosing Sides*, 211-16.

36. Michelle Krebs, "Ephlin Explains Early Retirement from UAW Post," *Automotive News* (May 5, 1989), 6.

37. For varied perspectives on New Directions and the 1989 convention, see *Union Democracy Review*, No. 72 (October, 1989). For news accounts, see Louise Kertesz, "UAW Dissidents Lose Out; Bieber Programs Hailed," *Automotive News* (June 26, 1989), 1, 57; Krebs, "Ephlin Explains Early Retirement"; Helen Fogel, "Getting a Grip: UAW's Yokich Takes Hands-On Control of GM Department, *Detroit News* (August 14, 1989), 1D; John Lippert, "Cloud of Acrimony Hangs Over Auto Talks," *Detroit Free Press* (March 5, 1990).

38. "UAW Challenges GM," *UAW Solidarity* (March 1992), 14-16.

39. Between 1984 and 1988, Ford's passenger car sales rose 260,000 units, increasing market share from 18.9 percent to 20.6 percent; in 1988; its car assembly plants ran at 100 percent capacity. In the same period, GM's passenger car sales fell by over one million units, and market share dropped from 43.6 percent to 34.2 percent; ever after closing four factories, its remaining car assembly plants operated at only 87 percent capacity in 1988. See Harbour and Associates, *The Harbour Report: A Decade Later* (Rochester, Michigan, 1990), 62-68, 92-96.

40. Turner, *Democracy at Work*, 59-60.

41. Steve Babson, "Lean or Mean: The MIT Model and Lean Production at Mazda," *Labor Studies Journal* 18, no. 2 (Summer 1993), 3-24.

42. Local Agreement between Reatta Craft Centre and UAW Local 1618, effective January 4, 1989, 61-63; plant tour and interviews with local officers and team leaders, November 9, 1989.

43. Mike Oblak, UAW Local 900, Bargaining Chairman at Wayne Body and Stamping, panel presentation, "Union Power in the Workplace of the Future," Wayne State University Labor School and UAW Region 1A, November 23, 1991; interviews with team leaders and Bargaining Committee members; plant visit, December 15, 1993; Local Agreement between Local 900, UAW, and the Ford Motor Company, Wayne Body and Stamping, September 1990-September 1993, 12-36.

44. On the structure of UAW-Saturn representation, see Saul Rubenstein, Michael Bennett, and Thomas Kochan, "The Saturn Partnership: Co-Management and the Reinvention of the Local Union," in Bruce Kaufman and Morris Kleiner, eds., *Employee Representation: Alternatives and Future Directions* (Madison: Industrial Research Association, 1993), and Ben Hawk, "The Value of Knowing Your Union: Help for Inspiring WUMA's" *The Wheel: UAW Local 1853* (December 1992) 3-4. On the controversy surrounding this structure and the union's role, see David Woodruff, "Saturn: Labor's Love Lost?", *Business Week* (February 8, 1993), 122; John Lippert, "UAW Boss Says GM, His Union Fail Saturn's Star Rises, Dissent Divides Workers, *Detroit Free Press* (March 23, 1993), 7D. In a referendum vote in January 1993, 71 percent of the membership answered "yes" to the following question: "Shall the Local Union retain the current jointly selected Partnership structure and add one (1) additional elected Skilled Trades Representative to the existing elected structure?" The validity of

the vote is questionable given the wording and format of the referendum: 1) instead of an explicit alternative to the present system, the membership was only given a yes/no choice, meaning alternatives could only be imagined or rumored; 2) there were actually two questions included in the wording, but only a single yes/no answer; 3) these two questions implied opposite meanings, one emphasizing joint appointment, the other election. In the local union elections that followed in March 1993, the incumbent President who championed joint appointment won by a narrow margin, with 51 percent of the vote.

45. Rubenstein et. al., "The Saturn Partnership"; Jane Slaughter, "Workers Charge Saturn With Sacrificing Quality," *Labor Notes* (December 1991), 6.

CONTRIBUTORS

....

Robert Asher is Professor of History at the University of Connecticut and is General Editor of the SUNY Press series in American Labor History. He is the author of *Connecticut Workers and Technological Change* (1983) and has edited three previous anthologies. He is a co-editor of the forthcoming anthology, *The American Artisan: Explorations in Social Identity* (Johns Hopkins University Press). He is finishing a book on *Concepts in American History* (HarperCollins Publishers).

Steve Babson is a Labor Program Specialist at the Labor Studies Center, Wayne State University. He is the author of *Working Detroit: The Making of a Union Town* (Adama Books, 1984) and *Building the Union: Skilled Workers and Anglo-Gaelic Immigrants in the Rise of the UAW* (Rutgers University Press, 1991).

Lindy Biggs is Associate Professor of History at Auburn University, where she specializes in American industrialization. Her first book is *The Rational Factory* (forthcoming, Johns Hopkins University Press).

Raymond Boryczka is Chief of Research, Walter P. Reuther Library, and a Lecturer at the College of Urban, Labor, Metropolitan Affairs, Labor Studies Division, Wayne State University. He is the co-author of *No Strength Without Union: An Illustrated History of Ohio Workers, 1803-1980* (1980).

Kevin Boyle is Assistant Professor of History at the University of Massachusetts, Amherst. His book, *Politics and Principle: The United Automobile Workers and American Liberalism, 1945-1968*, is forthcoming from Cornell University Press.

Ronald Edsforth teaches American History at Dartmouth College. He is author of *Class Conflict and Cultural Consensus* (Rutgers University Press, 1987) and co-editor of *Popular Culture and Political Change in Modern America* (SUNY Press, 1991).

Stephen Merlino is a sociologist who has worked as a bicycle mechanic, a junior college sociology teacher, and a high school social studies teacher. He lives in Willimantic, Connecticut, and teaches at Lyman Memorial Senior High School, Lebanon, Connecticut.

Health Ann Thompson is a Ph.D. candidate in History at Princeton University. Her forthcoming dissertation examines the historical consequences of the second great migration of Southern African-Americans to Detroit and the politics of labor, race, and liberalism in that urban center between 1940 and 1980.

Craig A. Zabala, an economist and historian, lives in New York City. He is writing a book about wage-effort bargaining in the auto industry. The book will draw on original statistical analysis and his experiences as a worker at the GM plant at Van Nuys, California.

INDEX

....